David Stafford, a former diplomat, is the author of several books on Churchill, the Second World War, and intelligence history, including *Roosevelt and Churchill: Men of Secrets*, *Secret Agent: The True Story of the Special Operations Executive*, *Spies Beneath Berlin*, and *Churchill and Secret Service*.

With a first-class degree from Cambridge University and a doctorate from the University of London, he is currently Project Director at the Centre for Second World War Studies at the University of Edinburgh and has frequently served as a TV consultant and media commentator.

D0360809

TEN DAYS
TO D-DAY

Countdown to the
Liberation of Europe

DAVID STAFFORD

An *Abacus* Book

First published in Great Britain by Little, Brown in 2003
This edition published by Abacus in 2004

A CIP catalogue record for this book
is available from the British Library.

ISBN 0 349 11597 4

Typeset in Perpetua by M Rules
Printed and bound in Great Britain
by Clays Ltd, St Ives plc

Abacus
An imprint of
Time Warner Books UK
Brettenham House
Lancaster Place
London WC2E 7EN

www.TimeWarnerBooks.co.uk

*In loving memory of my parents,
and with gratitude to all those of the D-Day generation
whose sacrifices helped build
a better future for ours.*

CONTENTS

'Twas on a summer's day — the sixth of June: —
I like to be particular in dates,
Not only of the age, and year, but moon;
They are a sort of post-house where the Fates
Change horses, making history change its tune,
Then spur away o'er Empires and o'er States . . .
                         BYRON, *Don Juan*, Canto I

PREFACE

In peace there's nothing so becomes a man
As modest stillness and humility.
But when the blast of war blows in our ears,
Then imitate the action of the tiger.
Stiffen the sinews, conjure up the blood,
Disguise fair nature with hard-favoured rage.
WILLIAM SHAKESPEARE, *Henry V*

D-Day – 6 June 1944 – changed the course of a world war, and a century. As dawn cast its glow over the English Channel, the final great assault on Nazi Germany and the liberation of Western Europe began with the landing of more than one hundred and thirty thousand Allied troops on the beaches of Normandy.

These landings remain the largest seaborne assault ever attempted, a triumph of planning and brilliant execution whose scale, even sixty years on, remains breathtaking. 'The history of war has never witnessed such a grandiose operation,' remarked the Soviet dictator Josef Stalin, himself no stranger to ambitious projects. 'Napoleon himself never attempted it.'

Yet it could easily have failed. History is littered with disastrous efforts to beach troops on heavily defended shores. Hitler pinned his hopes on this perilous margin between victory and defeat. If the Allies were thrown back into the sea on D-Day, he promised, it would have consequences far beyond the Western Front. Field Marshal Erwin Rommel, his hand-picked choice to protect the Third Reich along the Atlantic Wall, famously predicted it would be 'the longest day' for the Axis powers and the Allies alike. Both were right. Had the Western Allies failed to find a foothold on the beaches of Normandy, 6 June 1944 would have been an appalling bloodbath and major catastrophe. Hitler would have been left to focus his energies on repelling the Red Army in the East. The captive peoples of Europe would have been sentenced to yet another year of Nazi rule and SS terror. The entire course and outcome of the war would have been radically, and unpredictably, different.

But the invasion *was* a success. Within weeks General Charles de Gaulle and his Free French Army were marching down the Champs-Élysées in Paris amid scenes of wild jubilation. Then it was the turn of Brussels and the Belgians to celebrate. Allied troops captured Aachen, the first German city to fall into their hands, in October 1944, and crossed the River Rhine on 1 March 1945. Less than a year after D-Day, Hitler was dead by his own hand. His monstrous 'thousand-year Reich' was over, its capital reduced to rubble, his people overwhelmed by famine and desolation.

Ever since D-Day, historians have pored over this epic event, telling and retelling a story that typically begins with the landing of the first parachute and glider divisions in the early-morning darkness, and ends with the final Allied breakthrough in Normandy in late July 1944. They have described the battles, recounted the exploits of individual divisions, corps, regiments, battalions and platoons, analysed the leadership of generals, debated Allied and German strategy, forensically examined the mistakes and the weaknesses of both sides, and re-fought the front with all the bountiful enthusiasm and benefit of hindsight.

This is not another such book. Nowadays, to anyone braving a cruel April wind whipping off the English Channel above Omaha Beach, it is clear that the military cemeteries of Normandy are not visited solely by campaign buffs, with their creased maps to hand for ready battlefield reference. Nor do the graves echo only with the grieving of veterans searching for fallen comrades or the sites of their own youthful exploits. Other generations of the young come too, to witness the scene of action, to pay their respects to those who guaranteed their current freedoms and to try to understand the magnitude of the task that confronted those who survived

D-Day, and those who did not. Along with British, American and Canadian visitors, and a sprinkling from Commonwealth countries such as Australia, New Zealand and South Africa, will be found those from nations liberated as a result of D-Day, not just France itself but also Belgium, the Netherlands, Denmark and Norway, as well as from occupied countries such as Poland or Czechoslovakia, nations that contributed so significantly to the Allied forces on D-Day. Germans come here, too, for their grief and pain remain as well. They too have their memories and their burial grounds, and the cemeteries of the defeated are perhaps even more poignant than those of the victors.

Some individual soldiers' stories appear here, but this is not just a book about the great invading armies or their generals and political leaders. It is also about the Wren working in England on her codes and signals, the resistance worker and his clandestine network, the secret agent cutting communications cables behind enemy lines, the political prisoner locked in a Gestapo cell, the intelligence officer feeding false information to the enemy, the Jew hiding from the Nazis in a Paris garret. The events of 6 June 1944 changed their lives as decisively as they did those on the front line. All, in their different ways, were caught up in what Eisenhower called 'the great crusade'. The D-Day story belongs to many nationalities, affected civilians and families as deeply as the men and women at arms – who themselves, let us not forget, were mostly civilians in peace – and forms a critical part of the European twentieth-century experience.

Everyone knew that invasion was coming. The newspapers and radio of the day, around the world, and especially in occupied Europe, speculated about it endlessly. Would the wait be over by early spring or perhaps a little later, in, say, July? Pundits debated it, Roosevelt and Churchill promised it, Hitler predicted it, people everywhere, on both sides, wanted it to begin, to bring an end to the nerve-racking tension. We know now, in fair detail, about the naval armada and Operation Neptune, about the airborne assault and the crawl up from the beaches into the hedgerows on that 'longest day'.

What was happening in the crucial few days *before* that fateful 6 June is much less clear. How did hope, expectation and dread affect ordinary men and women? The big unanswered question was not whether, but when and, more crucially, where would the Allies land?

This was the most carefully kept secret of the war, guarded even more preciously than 'Ultra', the Allies' great code-breaking and intelligence asset. And even the few who knew the date and place had no idea if the invasion would succeed. Hindsight can be a curse to understanding, because to those involved nothing was certain about the future. General Dwight D. Eisenhower, the Allied Supreme Commander, gave the final order to go and then scribbled a note in pencil on a scrap of paper. These were the words he would have to use to tell millions of people around the world if D-Day were to go horribly wrong and the invasion fail. He then jammed the note into the top pocket of his battledress and forgot about it.

To fully understand D-Day, we must imagine the people who made it work and the events which preceded it as they unfolded, people without benefit of post-war knowledge or our experience of the present. Many on the Allied side feared the worst, just as many Germans tried to imagine the best, and they often wrote as much in letters and diaries. Yet today the scale of the Allied victory often obscures both the dread and the optimism, and above all, the uncertainty. Memoirs written long after the battle can mislead as well as inform. Memory, after all, is not the same thing as experience, and certainly different from history, subject as memory is to constant re-editing, distortion and simple error.

The primary sources used here are letters and diaries written at the time in the ten days before D-Day by those who were involved, whether making the decisions as generals and statesmen or as a saboteur blowing up a railway line. Where those still living have contributed, their recollections have been checked wherever possible against contemporary documents. New material, particularly intelligence files and deception planning, is still being released from secret archives. This reveals much more about why the

Germans were taken by surprise when the invasion happened where it did, but also how they were deceived into thinking that the 'real' invasion was yet to come, further north in France. Old diaries are also emerging from their hiding places, now that their indiscretions may no longer hurt or compromise the living.

What follows is a tale of what went before, of the crucial days leading up to 6 June 1944, and of the hopes and fears about D-Day of a broad cast of participants and observers, including leaders on both sides of the English Channel, men and women in the Allied and German forces preparing for action, captive civilians inside Hitler's occupied Europe and operatives involved in the secret war of sabotage, intelligence and deception. Above all, it is a human story of people poised on the brink of an epic moment in history.

Map of Southern Britain and Northern France

Manchester

Nottingham

Norwich

Cottesmore

Birmingham

Tempsford
Cambridge

Bletchley

Woodbridge
Ipswich

Severn

Oxford
Thames

Brentwood

London

Cardiff

Bristol

Dover

Strait of Dover

Pas de Calais

Calais

Boulogne

Hiltingbury
Fareham

Southampton
Portsmouth

Brighton

The Solent

Isle of Wight

English Channel

Plymouth

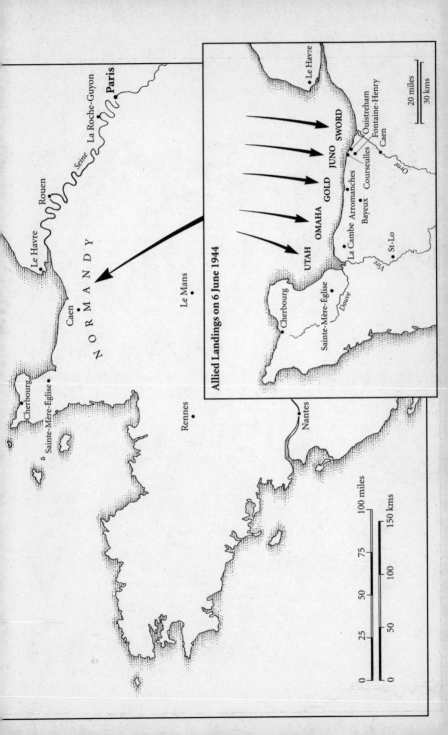

Allied Landings on 6 June 1944

1

WHAT VICTORY MEANS

Sunday 28 May

Sonia d'Artois jumped, and the slipstream caught her, pulling her sideways. Then the parachute snapped open and she was floating free in the moonlight. The roar of the aircraft's engines faded rapidly into the distance. The flannel skirt and heavy sweater she was wearing under her special overalls had kept her warm in the unheated plane, and her old hobnail ski boots would protect her during the landing. Suddenly the shapes of trees appeared out of the gloom, the land rushed forward to meet her and she flexed her knees just as she'd been trained. 'Don't look down,' they had warned her, 'or you'll get tangled in the cords.' But she couldn't help herself. She was still wrestling to free herself when she hit the ground hard and landed painfully in a ditch, wrenching her shoulder. Then she heard voices in French as the reception committee rushed out from behind the trees to help her. 'My God,' she heard one say, 'one of them's a woman.' But all Sonia felt was happiness and relief. She was back in France at last, behind enemy lines, and in time for D-Day.

Peter Moen stood on his narrow prison bed and furtively removed a small tack from the blackout curtain of the cell's only window. Then he took a sheet of the rough, greyish-brown toilet paper handed out grudgingly by his guards each day. One by one, with painstaking care, he pricked out the letters on to the paper until he had a word, then a sentence, then a page. It was slow and laborious work, but writing the diary kept him sane. Only in this way could he make sense of his suspended life. Prisoner number 5842 was now beginning his hundred and fifteenth day of incarceration. Early in the morning, when the guards were busy, he would peer through the window at the street outside and see the sun striking the local church, watch the cars swinging around the roundabout and glimpse the blue dot of a city tram jogging up the hill in the distance. The violent contrast with his own confinement inside was hard to bear. His head still hurt where he had been hit squarely across the face the day before for not responding quickly enough to a guard's command to stop playing cards. 'If that is an example of the Herrenvolk [master race],' he spelled out, 'I prefer to be a slave.'

When he had finished, he rolled the paper up tightly and pushed it through the cross-patterned grille of the ventilation shaft on the floor behind the cell's solitary table. There it would be safe. He had to be quick, though. Once, a guard had confiscated a page of the diary before he'd had time to conceal it. Fortunately, there had been no follow-up.

A hundred days before, Moen had written the following words: 'It is only those who are under the Gestapo's whip, with the death sentence as an ever-threatening danger, who completely understand what victory means.'

Glenn Dickin gazed out through the barbed-wire fence surrounding his holding camp in England, and thought of his family on the Canadian prairie thousands of miles away. He was cooped up inside a tent in a camp dotted with a myriad similar canvas roofs housing thousands of troops, one of the hundreds of makeshift bases that blanketed the British countryside. Fringed by a suburban scene of red-bricked semi-detached houses and rows of small shops, it lay only a few miles from the English Channel. His regiment had been here for almost two months and from here he had taken part in all the major landing exercises. The last one had been a full dress rehearsal that lasted six days. The sea had been rough, and he'd been forced to use his vomit bag. He'd returned exhausted but exhilarated. Since then he'd endured a constant round of briefings, distribution of new clothing and equipment, small-arms exercises and the assignment of waterproofed vehicles to spaces on the individual ships that would carry them across. Otherwise, life consisted of waiting for the big day they all knew was coming.

The camp had been sealed off from the outside world for three days. No one was allowed in or out. Beyond the barbed wire normal civilian life continued. He could see housewives shopping, children going to and from school and the occasional public bus. Dickin, a blue-eyed and fair-skinned lieutenant in the Regina Rifles, was twenty-two years old. Like most young men far from home, he kept up a façade of insouciance and constantly told his mother not to worry. Before the camp was sealed – and all correspondence to the outside world halted – he wrote to her that every day he watched fleets of heavy bombers pass overhead from their bases in England to pound the enemy. 'It is a beautiful sight to see,' he enthused. 'They are certainly making a nice job of softening up for the invasion troops.' And he finished off by promising that he'd do his best to be home by next spring to help with the house cleaning. But the next day he carefully asked his sister to let his girlfriend in Canada know if anything happened to him. She was not next of kin, and therefore not on the official list of those entitled to be told of the missing, the wounded or the dead.

Just a few miles to the west of the tented camp, blue-eyed, nineteen-year-old Veronica Owen sat in a garden in her sunglasses enjoying the glorious Sunday weather. It was still only nine o'clock, but, up early at dawn, she had already taken High Communion at the weathered old Saxon church just down the road. Like Glenn Dickin, she was mesmerised by the fleets of bombers passing overhead in the blue spring sky. 'Steel birds,' she called them. She, too, was writing home to her family. 'My Darling Mummy and Daddy' began her account of the weekend. Although she would have relished a game of cricket even more, the day before she'd played tennis with a girlfriend on a private grass court lent to them by a kindly neighbour. Despite being out of practice she had enjoyed it. The neighbour's wife had brought them welcome glasses of lemonade made out of ice and – a rare luxury – fresh lemons. In the evening another girlfriend had bicycled over for an hour's chat. By now, on the fourth page of her letter, the heat was curling the pages and her sweaty hands were beginning to smudge the ink, so she signed off with a 'God Bless'. Later that afternoon she read more of Lawrence of Arabia's letters, which she'd begun a few weeks before. Then she attended evensong and had a late supper.

It was a rare and very welcome day off work for her. Normally she spent most of the day and night deep underground. Veronica Owen was a Wren, a member of the Women's Royal Naval Service, one of more than seventy thousand women on land and sea working as dispatch riders, radio mechanics, teleprinter operators, radar detection finders, map plotters, cinema operators and typists. Her special task was to code and decode ships' messages. Every third night she was on watch from seven o'clock (1900 hours in the naval parlance she'd had to learn) to eight-thirty (0830) the next morning. Then she was free until 1300 hours the next day. Recently the work had become particularly heavy, and the issue of shifts like hers, lasting thirteen and a half hours, had even led to questions in Parliament. She also kept a small pocket diary. Here Veronica recorded the stresses of her work and the moments of relief that came all too rarely.

Lemonade also proved welcome to a thirsty young German soldier stationed in France, on its northern Atlantic coast. Walter Schwender, too, was enjoying the glorious Whitsun weather. Today he'd managed to get hold of a typewriter and, like the Wren, was writing home. Letters and small gifts brought his family closer. He'd sent them a package of cucumber seeds, and sometimes he sent back his ration of cigarettes. But he would have to gorge on the abundant strawberries himself. 'Dear All,' he began, and then stopped to have some wine. But the weather was too hot, so he poured himself a lemonade instead.

On duty he worked in an army repair shop, mending anything that needed fixing, from bicycles to typewriters, which is how he'd managed to get his hands on a machine today. Sometimes he just answered the telephone. The day before, he and his comrades had been given cigarettes again. But because these days he didn't trust the post very much, he might have to smoke them himself instead of sending them to his father. Frustrating news had come of yet another delay in the mail from Germany. He, too, found it too hot to write for long. After a page he signed off, explaining he wanted to go to the beach to swim. Like all soldiers at the front, he knew the mail he sent home was censored. But he did manage to convey one piece of significant news – all leave for the troops had been cancelled. 'Oh well,' Walter added optimistically, 'I hope that all this will be over soon.'

That same day, in a sweltering and occupied Paris, a middle-aged man, caged in a tiny room on the sixth floor of an apartment building on the rue des Écoles, worried frantically about his children. For Albert Grunberg, the Allied 'steel birds' were certainly welcome allies against the Germans. But they might also destroy his family. The man was a Jew, and he had been in hiding in this room, measuring just nine feet by seven, for a year and a half. The Germans had arrived to deport him in 1942 and a friendly concierge in a neighbouring building had smuggled him away. Since then he'd kept in touch with events by secretly listening to the BBC on a hidden radio. His wife, who was not Jewish and so relatively secure, brought him food. Their two sons, now grown up, were living and working on the edge of the French Alps, in Chambéry. But only this morning he had heard that Allied planes had bombed the city's strategically important railway marshalling yards.

Grunberg, too, was keeping a diary. As it did Peter Moen, it gave him comfort, providing more than just a record of daily events. To pour out his feelings, to relieve the pain of the bad times and to record the good moments, restored his balance. He'd found a hiding place for the diary on top of the toilet cistern in the corridor outside his room.

That afternoon his wife came to see him, trudging up the six flights of stairs. She found the heat stifling, despite her husband's best efforts to dampen the floor with cold water, and didn't stay long. Later that evening, he scribbled in his diary, they were still frantically trying to get news. Would the liberators free him, but in doing so kill their children?

The insides of the Allies' 'steel birds' were all too familiar to the bony-faced American paratrooper lying on his cot cooped up in a tent with eight other men at an American holding camp in the lush green fox-hunting countryside of England's Midlands. Unlike the Canadian rifleman Glenn Dickin, Bill Tucker was already a battle-hardened veteran. The year before, aged twenty, he'd made his first combat drop over Salerno in Italy. He'd volunteered after seeing newsreel movies of German and Russian paratroopers back home in Boston, and reckoned it was something he didn't need a college education for.

His canvas city lay within the perimeter of the old stone wall of a country house just twenty miles from Sherwood Forest. Outside lay a picture-postcard little town where the church bells rang in the evening and social life revolved around the friendly pubs. Molly, a blonde from Nottingham, was good fun for movies and dances and the occasional picnic. She was a test pilot for Stirling bombers, checking the instruments when they came out of the factory; but unfortunately she had a husband, a Royal Air Force fighter pilot serving in Malta. Still, Tucker enjoyed her friendship.

Bill Tucker, too, had just learned that from now on his camp was sealed off. No more sneaking off to the fish and chip shop. Training and waiting were now the order of the day. No more practice drops either. He was glad, given the tedious journey by truck to the nearest airfield and the frequent cancellations because of fog. An occasional game of football and endless rounds of cards relieved the tedium. Anything was better than crawling in his underwear through a pit of dead animals, as he'd done during basic training in Georgia, or shivering with the malaria he'd caught because he couldn't keep down the pills that were given him to fight it off, or squatting for hours over a stinking latrine wracked with dysentery, as he'd had to do at some fly-ridden base in the North African desert. The new boys fished out the flies from their food with a spoon before they ate it. The old sweats just squashed them into the gravy till they stopped struggling and swallowed them down with the food. At least, that was the joke.

Waiting was also the name of the game for André Heintz, a lithe young French schoolteacher, as he bicycled home that evening to Caen, the ancient capital of Normandy and favoured city of Duke William, the eleventh-century conqueror of England. Dominated by the huge citadel begun by the Duke in 1060, Caen lay just ten miles from the Channel, linked to its port of Ouistreham by the River Orne and a canal. He'd spent the day with his father helping plant beans on their small allotment on the outskirts of the city. It was one of the few small ways they could supplement their meagre weekly ration of food, and they bartered the vegetables for butter at a local dairy farm. His father had even given up smoking to save money.

André Heintz lived with his parents and sister in a large detached house in the centre of the city. Just a hundred yards away lay the heavily guarded military headquarters of the German 716th Division. To reach their house they had to pass through a barrier and show their identity documents. Every evening, after curfew, German troops rolled out a barbed-wire cordon. The previous night he'd heard heavy bombing along the Channel coast and there had been several air-raid warnings in the city itself.

Unknown to his parents or sister, André was actively working with the local Maquis, or Resistance. Mostly he helped forge identity cards for anyone in trouble, such as men evading obligatory labour in Germany, or members of the Maquis needing a new identity, or Jews on the run – although by now not many of them were left. More risky was his role in collecting intelligence about

German military installations. He bicycled around the city twice a week noting any changes in the composition of the German garrison or the arrival of new military equipment, and then passed on the information to his contact. This was an older man who lived on the coast and had clandestine ways of getting the material to London. Earlier that month another man had come from Paris and asked him to step up efforts to find more agents for such intelligence work, and to recruit as many young people as possible for an active Maquis group that would spring into action on D-Day. Since then he'd explored the countryside south of Caen, looking for possible hiding places. He'd also kept his eyes peeled for open fields with not too many trees, suitable for parachute drops.

Eighty miles to the south, near the city of Le Mans, ancestral home of the Plantagenet dynasty of medieval English kings, and already world-famous for its championship motor races, a fit-looking man in his mid-thirties sat on the veranda of an isolated château. Sydney Hudson was a British secret agent and was going over in his mind preparations for the coming night. The owner of the château was co-operative enough, and at nights the agent felt secure sleeping in his tent hidden in the wood at the back of the property. But Hudson had had a frustrating few weeks. The château was close enough to the Channel coast for the Gestapo to be dangerously active, and there had been a lot of arrests. The locals, mostly farmers, didn't seem too keen to get involved.

With two other agents he'd been dropped 'blind' – no reception committee to greet them – during the Easter weekend a couple of months before. Still, they'd made some headway. The wireless operator, an Englishman fluent in French like himself, had made contact with London, and they'd arranged a couple of successful drops of containers full of Sten guns and explosives. They'd begun to build up a small number of trusted contacts. What he really needed now was someone to act as a courier to keep him in regular touch with them and who could travel about the countryside relatively unnoticed. He'd worked with a woman once before and seen how much easier it was for her than him to move around without being challenged. With D-Day coming, this could prove vital. A few days before he'd sent a message to London, and they'd agreed to his request. The reply came in a punning coded radio message he'd heard one evening in his tent: 'La marguerite cueille les marguerites' ('Margaret collects daisies').

The drop was due tonight. Hudson wouldn't go himself. It was too risky, and anyway he had some recruiting to do. But he'd turn up the next morning when he knew the drop had succeeded and see what London had sent. Or rather whom. He was curious to meet her.

Inside 35 Crespigny Road, a small Victorian house in the northwest London suburb of Hendon, a man sat hunched over a radio transmitter tapping out a secret coded message. It was a German-made portable machine of 100 watts. The report was destined for Madrid, where it would be picked up by the Abwehr, German Military Intelligence. Here one of its most highly trained and efficient officers would pore over its contents. Over the past two years he had come to count on 'Arabel', the code-name of his agent in London, to send first-rate intelligence about forthcoming Allied military operations. Now that the tide of war had turned strongly against the Germans, Berlin was increasingly anxious to collect intelligence about them. The Abwehr had created a special Invasion Intelligence Department and was energetically attempting to infiltrate its agents into Britain via neutral countries such as Portugal, Spain and Sweden. Once there, they would report on troop movements, the identification of military units and the strength and location of American, British and other Allied forces. In short, any clues that would help identify where and when the Allied invasion would come.

Arabel had already been in place for two years. He'd done well during Operation Torch, the Anglo-American landings in North Africa in November 1942 – although in the end Berlin had not been able to make much use of the material. His control, an ambitious officer, did his best to supply Arabel with the very latest high-grade ciphers and secret inks, sending him plenty of money to cover his expenses as well as to pay the dozen or so sub-agents he'd succeeded in recruiting. After digesting and assessing Arabel's reports, the Abwehr man forwarded them by radio to headquarters in Berlin. Unfortunately, they hadn't always been valued or acted on by the German High Command. But recently he'd been gratified to hear that they considered Arabel a particularly valuable source. Field Marshal Gerd von Rundstedt himself, the Commander-in-Chief West, had evaluated a piece of intelligence sent by Arabel as 'especially important'. The head of the SS, Heinrich Himmler, who had recently taken over the service following Hitler's dismissal of its long-time chief, Admiral Wilhelm Canaris, had sent him a personal message of appreciation for the work of his network in Britain.

Things were looking up. He was now coming under heavy pressure to get his agents to provide intelligence about the coming invasion. As a former military attaché in Paris, he'd had plenty of experience in fitting bits and pieces of information together to build up a picture of an opponent's armed forces. What was the order of battle of the Allied troops? How many divisions, how many men? Where were they stationed? When would the attack come? Where? He was counting mostly on Arabel to find out and tell him. Recent reports from the agent were revealing an interesting build-up of troops in south-east England – suggestively close to the Dover Strait, the narrowest part of the Channel, and opposite Calais. Was this where the attack would come? In Madrid and Berlin, Arabel's controllers tried to fit the pieces of the jigsaw together.

No one but a handful of people knew the answer asked by the Abwehr, and certainly not the British secret agents, the French resister, the German soldier, the British Wren, the American paratrooper or the Canadian infantryman, all of whom had their various roles to play in the epic events about to unfold. Nor the fugitive Jew or the prisoner in his Gestapo cell, whose freedom, and probably lives, depended on the success of the liberating forces poised for action.

The D-Day secret was among the most momentous ever kept. Yet the build-up to it was one of the most public events of the Second World War. By the end of May 1944 over two million troops were stationed in Britain, five thousand ships had been gathered in ports and harbours around the coastline and thousands of bombers – the patriotic young Wren's graceful 'steel birds' and the possible harbingers of death to the sons of the Parisian Jew – were hitting targets round the clock in France. Only the day before, a thousand British-based Fortress and Liberator heavy bombers had also pounded targets inside Germany itself. Hundreds more medium bombers and fighters – including the deadly new rocket-firing Typhoons – had attacked railway bridges, airfields and aircraft, as well as ship-reporting stations vital to the Germans' invasion warning chain in northern France. Parachute flares and the flashes of exploding bombs over Boulogne and other towns fringing the Channel could be clearly seen from the English coast. From bases in Italy, American heavy bombers had severely mauled German-controlled oilfields and refineries at Ploesti, in Romania, and targeted railways and airfields along the Mediterranean coast of southern France. Newspaper reports talked of entire marshalling yards being pulverised to rubble. Transport chaos was causing severe power shortages. Electricity for domestic households was cut off from 7.30 a.m. to 8.30 p.m. In Paris, several Métro stations were closed and three lines completely shut down. Regularly, air-raid alerts over the French capital brought transport to a complete stop. The 'air invasion' of Europe, pronounced *The Times* of London, was already well under way. With liberation so clearly imminent, declared sources in the French Resistance, the fighters in the Maquis were impatient to play their part. But they wanted to fight as liberators, not be regarded as merely the passively liberated.

Across Europe, the Germans were in full retreat. In the east, Stalin's Red Army had capitalised on its great victories at Stalingrad and Kursk the year before and was now advancing steadily west towards the German heartland. It had just recaptured the Crimea and driven the Wehrmacht out of the Ukraine. In Italy, Allied armies had finally broken a bitter and bloody stalemate. Although their landings in Sicily in July 1943 had precipitated the overthrow of Hitler's loyal ally, Mussolini, subsequent fighting on the Italian mainland had gone badly wrong. Naples had been in Allied hands for months, but Rome remained occupied by the Germans. General Alexander's armies, bogged down on Hitler's strongly defended Gustav Line, had advanced only seventy miles in eight months. An attempted 'leapfrog' landing at Anzio, just south of Rome, had stalled. Since February, Allied forces had been held up at the great fortress monastery of Monte Cassino, blocking the main road north to the Italian capital.

Just two weeks before, however, the logjam had finally broken. Led by Free French and Polish troops, Allied forces finally took Monte Cassino on 18 May and a week later began their advance on Rome. Simultaneously, American forces finally broke out of the Anzio bridgehead thirty miles south of the Italian capital. Since then, advance units of the Allies had reached to within twelve miles of Rome. News from the Italian front now dominated the headlines. Every day brought news of a fresh German retreat in Italy as Hitler's exhausted troops fell back towards their staggered defences in the Alban Hills. Throughout the Balkans, in the mountains of Greece, Yugoslavia and Albania, armies of guerrillas were harassing the enemy and keeping thousands of German troops tied down. At last, after four long years, Hitler's forces were on the run.

Elsewhere the news was equally encouraging. In Asia, the Japanese Empire was rapidly shrinking. Here the tide of war had changed as early as mid-1942 with the great Battle of Midway, and the Americans, under the fire-eating General Douglas MacArthur, were continuing their hard-fought island-hopping towards the Philippines, Formosa and Japan itself. Recently the advance had quickened. The Solomon Islands had already fallen, and in April landings had begun in New Guinea. Just the day before, on 27 May, American troops had landed on the small island outpost of Biak, a key Japanese base off the northern New Guinea coast whose airfields offered yet another springboard for MacArthur's juggernaut. On the Indian subcontinent, the Japanese still held control of Burma. But at the towns of Kohima and Imphal, just inside the Indo-Burmese border, determined resistance by British-led forces under General William Slim was thwarting a Japanese effort to invade India itself, a desperate bid by Tokyo to throw the Allies off balance.

In Europe, everyone knew a massive Allied invasion of the continent from Britain was coming. The British Isles were now virtually sealed off from the outside world. Everyone going into or out of the country was subject to intensive scrutiny and control. Security measures to protect D-Day, Churchill had ordered, should be 'high, wide, and handsome'. Civilian travel between the British mainland and Ireland had been stopped altogether in February, to plug leaks of information through the German Embassy in Dublin. All mail coming into and leaving the British Isles was censored, and just over a month before, in spite of vigorous protests, the ban had been extended to all diplomatic communications by foreign governments, with the exception of the United States and the Soviet Union. Since April, most of the south coast of England had been sealed off to all visitors, as had a strip of the shore on either side of the Firth of Forth in Scotland. Lucky hotels outside the zone loudly advertised the fact, such as the Spread Eagle Hotel in Midhurst, Sussex – 'the Gateway to the South Downs' – which proudly proclaimed in *The Times* that it was 'Not Within Banned Area'.

Yet life went on elsewhere almost as if the war was already won. This was, after all, a bank holiday weekend. Massive queues formed at Paddington railway station in a stampede to leave London for resorts in the West Country, with hundreds of passengers waiting for up to six hours. The day before, people had started to queue at 7.45 in the morning for the afternoon train to south Wales. When it finally arrived the crowd rushed the barrier and police had trouble controlling them. Babies were handed over heads to women porters, who nursed them until their mothers got through. Several children got lost. That morning the newspapers announced yet further restrictions on rail travel. The number of concessionary fares taken by the wives of service personnel would be limited to two or three, depending on the service. They were to come into effect in three days time, on 1 June.

No wonder tempers got frayed. The heat was getting to everyone. Whit Sunday was the hottest day of the year so far, with fourteen hours of sunshine across the Dover Strait, the thermometer reading a record-busting 94 degrees Fahrenheit in the sun and 79 in the shade. It was not just the Wren Veronica Owen playing tennis, or Walter Schwender, the German soldier writing home, who needed a refreshing drink. The weekend also saw a crowd of thirty thousand happy spectators at Lord's cricket ground in London witness an Australian victory over the 'Rest of the World' – in reality a scratch team of mostly English players who, because of their age or for other reasons, were not in the armed forces – such as the legendary batsmen Wally Hammond and Len Hutton. In Nottingham, thousands of people watched a baseball match at the Notts County football ground between two teams from America's 82nd Airborne Division, with the Red Devils beating the Panthers 18–0.

Crowds flocked to cinemas in London's West End to see new releases such as *Tampico*, starring tough guy Edward G. Robinson as a torpedoed tanker captain who suspects his girlfriend of being the enemy agent who guided the U-boat to its prey. Also playing was *The Bridge of San Luis Rey*, based on Thornton Wilder's best-selling novel exploring the role of fate in the deaths of five people who perish during the collapse of a Peruvian rope bridge. 'For present day audiences up to their ears in war news,' remarked *Variety Review*, 'this picture will be a welcome divertissement.' On the London stage, John Gielgud was playing the lead in *Hamlet*, while the Playhouse Theatre bade a final farewell to the hugely popular *Our Town*, also by Thornton Wilder, a play about small-town American life featuring several American soldiers in the cast. If only its run could be extended, wrote the actress Dame Sybil Thorndike to *The Times*, it would prove invaluable in promoting understanding between Britain and the United States.

There was even a birthday to celebrate. Dr Eduard Benes, Prime Minister of Czechoslovakia at the time of the Munich Agreement, which in 1938 handed over much of his country to Hitler, and who was now the leader of the Czechoslovaks in exile, was one of the dozens of prominent European refugees living in London. The small Czech village of Lidice had become an international symbol of Nazi brutality in 1942 when its entire male population was murdered, its women and children deported to Germany and its houses razed to the ground in retaliation for the assassination by Czech resisters of Reinhard Heydrich, the deputy head of the SS and brutal ruler of the Czech 'protectorate'. Today Benes turned sixty. 'I am glad to think that at such [a momentous crisis in human affairs],' wrote Churchill, 'the Czechoslovak people, united and resolute under your leadership, despite their long, terrible suffering, are ready to play their part with us in close collaboration with our allies in the West and in the East in encompassing a final overthrow of the German tyranny . . .'

For Churchill, too, it was a holiday weekend. As usual, he and his wife, Clementine, left London for Chequers, in Buckinghamshire, the country retreat of British prime ministers about fifty miles north of the capital. A couple of days in the weathered half-timbered mansion gave him a short breather from the relentless pressures of London, as well as a chance to deal briefly with pressing family matters. Preying on his mind this weekend was the fate of his only son, Randolph.

Possessing his father's insatiable thirst for action and adventure, the thirty-three-year-old journalist and Member of Parliament had fought with the commandos in North Africa, taken part with the SAS in a daring behind-the-lines raid on Benghazi and landed at Salerno. Then he'd parachuted into Bosnia to work alongside the partisan leader, Marshal Tito, in his mountain retreat near the village of Drvar. 'His office is all lined with parachute silk and looks more like the *nid d'amour* [love nest] of a luxurious courtesan than the office of a guerrilla leader,' reported Randolph to his father, giving him an intriguing insight into the man whose forces were both fighting the Germans and waging a bitter civil war with their royalist Chetnik opponents for control of Yugoslavia.

But daily guerrilla life was tough, and Randolph shared in the hardships as an equal. 'He never fussed about the cold, hunger, thirst, sore feet or German bullets,' wrote one observer, 'and only raised hell when the Partisan barber wanted to give him a shave without hot water.'

Churchill worried constantly about his son. 'Give my love to Randolph should he come into your sphere,' he had telegraphed Tito just three days before. That very day his son narrowly survived a brush with death. German paratroops, backed up by Stuka bombers, attacked Tito's headquarters hoping to capture the Partisan leader and Randolph as well. After stiff fighting the Partisans and Randolph had evaded capture and disappeared into the mountains. Churchill had been informed, through British decrypts of German radio messages, about the attack almost as soon as it happened.

Today was Randolph's birthday and Churchill sat down and composed a letter to him. 'We are naturally following with some anxiety the news of the attack on Tito's headquarters,' he wrote. 'But today the report is that the airborne Huns have been liquidated.' After wishing his son good luck and telling him that he was in all their thoughts, the Prime Minister continued: 'We have a lovely day at where we live from time to time, and all is fair with the first glory of summer. The War is very fierce and terrible, but in these sunlit lawns and buttercup meadows, it is hard to conjure up its horrors.' He then passed on news about Randolph's three-year-old son, Winston junior, who had developed measles. 'I am ashamed to say I told him it was the fault of the Germans,' he joked, 'but I shall labour to remove this impression quite soon.'

Even as he wrote, Churchill was appalled by reports from France about the physical damage and human casualties being caused by the Allied bombing campaign designed to soften up the Germans before D-Day. For days he'd been having a furious argument about the raids with Air Marshal Arthur Tedder, deputy commander of the invasion forces. Were they really necessary? Churchill asked.

How many innocent civilians were being killed? Were they not likely to create a serious backlash against the Allies when they finally landed in France? He dictated a terse note to his Foreign Secretary, Anthony Eden, who shared his worries: 'We will talk about this tomorrow. Terrible things are being done.'

While weekends at Chequers got Churchill out of London, they were never just family affairs. Instead they provided an opportunity to entertain official guests from abroad, foreign politicians, Allied commanders temporarily on leave and other friends, cronies, and colleagues whom he wanted to have beside him. Among his guests this weekend was General Ira Eaker, commander of the Allied air forces in the Mediterranean, who agreed to carry the Prime Minister's letter to Randolph as far as Cairo.

So was Averell Harriman, a handsome American railroad tycoon turned diplomat. A close and trusted family friend, he was already involved in a passionate affair with the Prime Minister's daughter-in-law, Randolph's wife Pamela. Long a power behind the scenes in Washington, Harriman was now President Roosevelt's ambassador in Moscow and was *en route* to the US capital to brief him on recent conversations with the Soviet dictator Josef Stalin. What Harriman told Roosevelt now prompted Churchill to drop a line himself to Stalin. Ever since Hitler's attack on the Soviet Union in 1941, the Soviet leader had been pressing impatiently for an Anglo-American Second Front in France, and he had been briefed on its contours. But Churchill was anxious to reassure him. He told Stalin that all efforts in Britain were centred on Operation Overlord, the umbrella name for the West's planned invasion of the Continent from Britain, the first objective of which was to establish a lodgement area in France. Everything humanly possible would be done or risked to guarantee the success of the D-Day assault.

To his other major ally, Roosevelt, he also sent a message. Talk of a summit between the two of them in Bermuda had been in the air for some time, but Roosevelt had finally called it off for health reasons. Undaunted, Churchill urged him to come to London after D-Day. So far the President had not visited Britain at all during the war. In the jocular tone Churchill often adopted when faced with

Roosevelt's resistance, he added: 'Doctor Churchill informs you that a sea voyage in one of your great new battleships will do you no end of good.' But the appeal did Churchill no good, either. It was a presidential election year in the United States, and in a nation where anti-British sentiment still ran deep in certain quarters Roosevelt decided that his political health required he stay clear of London for the time being.

Of the risks to Overlord, Churchill was all too aware. From bitter personal experience he knew what could go wrong with amphibious landings on hostile shores. His early career had almost been wrecked by his part in the planning of the ill-fated First World War fiasco at the Dardanelles, when Allied forces had been slaughtered as they tried to land in Turkey. The raid on Dieppe in the summer of 1942 had sharply reminded him of the risks. Thousands of men, mostly Canadian, had been killed or captured in a bungled attempt to seize the French Channel port, a massacre that had shocked all those involved. To minimise the dangers now, and to anticipate every possible surprise, Churchill anxiously devoured every scrap of intelligence that crossed his desk.

His main source was Ultra, or 'Boniface' as he preferred to call it, a name conjured up early in the war to suggest a spy somewhere high up inside the German government. In reality it was the intelligence harvested by the code-breakers at Bletchley Park – the top-secret decrypting centre not far from Chequers – gleaned from the intercepts of high-level German radio messages that the enemy mistakenly, and disastrously for them, assumed were secure. Each day Churchill received a bundle of such reports, locked in a beige-coloured box to which only he and his intelligence chief had the key. This was Sir Stewart Menzies, otherwise known in Whitehall simply as 'C', after the initial of the first chief of the Secret Intelligence Service (SIS), Sir Mansfield Cumming. Today, even out at Chequers on a Sunday, C sent him twenty such 'Special Messages' – a euphemism that served to disguise the highly sensitive source. If the Germans ever got a whiff of how seriously their codes and ciphers had been penetrated, they would immediately change them and the Allies would be struck blind. As it was,

Churchill sometimes felt that he was peering straight through a window at German military moves.

Today he scanned the intercepts for any sign that the Germans had learned authentic details of the impending invasion. Or, alternatively, that they had swallowed elements of the careful deception plan designed to throw them off the scent. He was reassured by what he read. Two reports in particular were encouraging. One, sent to the German High Command by Field Marshal von Rundstedt, revealed that the pattern of Allied air attacks on targets in northern France was successfully masking the actual place where the invasion would take place. The bombing raids, reported von Rundstedt, were 'without recognisable point of main effort'; in other words, they were giving no definable clue as to where the landings might be. A second intercept, dated 27 May, just the day before, went even further. This concerned a German message stating that Allied bombing targeted at bridges across the River Seine highlighted probable enemy intentions against an area that was not within the invasion zone. Churchill ticked off the reports and returned them to his intelligence chief in their locked box the next morning.

As he read them, he also knew something else. Supply drops to the French Resistance in May had also been deliberately designed to throw the Germans off the scent. Just a few days before, Lord Selborne, the minister in charge of the Special Operations Executive (SOE), the top-secret agency Churchill had created in July 1940 to wage war behind enemy lines, had given him the figures. The supply ratio between the actual invasion area and its non-targeted neighbouring region had been deliberately set at 1:3, even though this meant sending aircraft over the most heavily defended areas of France. If the Germans were monitoring the flights, they might well draw the wrong conclusions about the intended invasion area.

So far, Churchill concluded, the D-Day secret seemed safe and the deception plan was working. But he couldn't be certain.

While Churchill basked in the sunshine at Chequers, Adolf Hitler was enjoying the clear mountain air of the Bavarian Alps at his own private retreat at the Berghof on the Obersalzberg, an area to which he'd regularly retreated since the 1920s either for rest and relaxation, or to compose his thoughts while planning major moves or preparing his speeches for the annual Nazi Party rally at Nuremberg.

It was at the Berghof, a few days before his attack on Poland that precipitated the Second World War, that he told the leaders of his Wehrmacht about his war aims. 'Our strength is our speed and brutality,' he had warned. 'Genghis Khan drove many women and children to death, deliberately and joyously. History sees him as a great founder of a state. What weak Western civilisation says about me doesn't matter. I have given the order — and I will have anyone shot who expresses even one word of criticism — that the aim of the war is not to reach definite limits but rather the physical destruction of the enemy. So, I have assembled my Death's Head formations . . .'

Enlarged from a previously modest country cottage, the Berghof boasted a huge picture window in the living room that could be raised and lowered, and enjoyed magnificent views over Berchtesgaden, Salzburg and the Untersberg mountain. Here, legend had it, the Emperor Charlemagne still slept but would one day awaken to restore the past glories of the German Empire. 'You see the Untersberg over there,' Hitler would say to his guests. 'It is no accident that I have my residence opposite it.'

He'd moved here temporarily that winter while his 'Wolf's Lair', the massive concrete command post hidden in the forests near Rastenburg in East Prussia, was being strengthened against air attack. Fleets of heavy Allied bombers were now regularly pounding Berlin and targets further east. The old Royal Palace in the heart of Berlin had just taken a direct hit that destroyed the famous Knight's Hall and Throne Room, as well as the chapel where Frederick the Great was baptised. But here, in the Bavarian Alps, Hitler was far removed from such dismal realities, as well as the relentless news from the Eastern Front about the advance of the Red Army.

In the rarefied air of the Berghof, life seemed reassuringly normal. Hitler rose late, dealt promptly with official matters and then retreated for an intimate afternoon lunch with guests and friends. They ate in the larchwood-panelled dining room with its bright-red morocco-covered chairs, plain white china, and silver bearing his personal monogram. Usually there were twenty or so people around the table. Invariably, to Hitler's left sat his long-time mistress, Eva Braun. Members of his personal SS bodyguard, wearing white waistcoats and black trousers, acted as waiters. Afterwards everyone strolled through the pine woods to the Tea House – one of Hitler's favourite spots, with its magnificent panoramic views over the valley – for coffee and cakes. Then, around the night fire in the richly tapestried salon, he would listen to recordings of Wagner's operas and talk until the early hours about subjects ranging from his early days of struggle in Munich to his plan to reshape the world. He slept in an ice-cold bedroom. His diet was vegetarian, and he drank no alcohol. Each day Dr Theodor Morell, his personal physician, would prescribe pills for the increasing number of ailments that troubled him. The Führer looked older than his fifty-four years. His face was heavily lined, his right eye often drooped, and he now walked with a stoop.

Despite, or perhaps because of this, he remained determined and defiant about his ultimate goals. Just two days before, he had met at the adjacent Platterhof Hotel with a group of senior military officers and generals. In a chilling speech that demonstrated that he had lost none of his fanaticism, he'd told them in no uncertain terms that their destiny was tied up with the fate of National Socialism and that this alone provided the basic principles that could now save Germany – leadership and intolerance, a refusal to compromise with the forces that threatened the nation's survival. He'd spoken frankly about the Final Solution, the elimination of the Jews. Could he have done it more humanely? 'Gentlemen,' he answered his own question, 'we are in a life or death struggle . . . don't expect anything else from me except the ruthless upholding of the national interest.' He reminded them that even as they met, the elimination of the Jews of Hungary was proceeding full steam ahead; a measure made possible, he emphasised, only because German forces had entered Hungary that spring.

As for invasion in the West, he veered erratically between welcoming it as an opportunity to smash the Allies and wondering if it would even happen that summer. Either way, he was confident of victory. If the Allies did invade, they would meet disaster and never dare try again. But if they did not, and their apparent preparations were no more than a gigantic bluff, he had secret weapons such as the flying bomb and new jet aircraft that would finish them off. London, he prophesied, would be transformed into 'a garden of ruins'. That is, if the Allies hadn't already fallen out between themselves, as history suggested that allies always did before five years; then the great East–West clash would break out, and Germany would be saved. Time, he was confident, was on Germany's side.

Yet occasionally reality broke through and Hitler was forced to think about the urgent issue being faced in the west by von Rundstedt, and above all by Field Marshal Erwin Rommel, commander of Army Group B, which contained the 15th and 7th Armies and stretched from the Netherlands in the north to the River Loire near France's Atlantic coast. If the Allied invasion were to happen, when and where was it most likely to come?

Hitler, like most of the German High Command, had long assumed it would be somewhere along the narrowest stretch of the English Channel north of the River Seine. Indeed, that hypothesis was built into the order, Directive 51, he had issued to the High Command in November 1943, which had underpinned the entire German defence effort since. Yet a few months later, in April 1944, he had suddenly started talking of Normandy and Brittany, in north-western France, as one of the possible targets that should also be kept in mind, and had asked for this part of the front to be reinforced. There was no obvious reason for his change of mind. Perhaps he deduced that, with their overwhelming naval strength, the Allies would not necessarily need to capture a major port in the early stages of an invasion – one among many factors which had encouraged the Germans to focus on the more easterly coastline containing ports such as Calais, Le Havre and Boulogne. Reports from agents who had penetrated the French Resistance and scored some major successes may also have played a part. No one ever quite knew what arcane sources fuelled Hitler's rich imagination.

He also held firm to an idea that had long obsessed him – that the Allies might additionally strike at Norway; not as the main invasion area, but perhaps in some significant diversionary landing or raid. Norway's countless fiords provided important shelter for German U-boats and the country as a whole was useful for guarding Germany's northern flank. For this reason, he insisted that a substantial army of occupation be kept stationed there. The slightest signs of resistance or espionage were to be fiercely suppressed.

In the end, however, what would matter most on D-Day itself was not Hitler's reaction, but that of his commander on the spot, Rommel.

The château of La Roche-Guyon lies on a bend high up over the River Seine about forty miles north-west of Paris and close to the gardens at Giverny made famous by Claude Monet's impressionist paintings of water lilies. Once a Norman stronghold – the ruins of the castle still dominated the hill – it had long been the ancestral home of the dukes of La Rochefoucauld. An eighteenth-century holder of the title had written a famous book of maxims, and his portrait hung prominently in the château's hall of arms.

Shortly after Hitler chose him in January 1944 as the man to defeat the invasion, Rommel had made the château his headquarters, but he permitted the duke and his family to stay in their private quarters and was on excellent terms with them. Tunnels were cut deep into the cliffs to provide accommodation for his officers and men. His personal rooms opened on to a rose garden, and his study was adorned with tapestries and an inlaid Renaissance desk. As well as acquiring a couple of dachshunds to keep him company, he had adopted a large sporting dog named Ajax to accompany him on hare-shooting expeditions into the countryside. After a hard day's work and supper, he would usually take an evening stroll around the park with his chief of staff, Lieutenant General Hans Speidel, and his naval adviser, Vice Admiral Friedrich von Ruge. His favourite spot was beneath two large cedar trees, from where he'd gaze out over the peaceful valley of the Seine and the western sky. Rommel liked France – its food, its wine, its people, its landscape. Yet it was an occupied land, and not even he could ignore the fact. 'What hatred there is against us,' he noted in his diary.

The fifty-one-year-old field marshal was Hitler's former commander in North Africa, where he had earned the title the 'Desert Fox'. An austere and hard-driven man, he had spent the previous five months frantically preparing the defences of the vast area of Western Europe under his command. 'The war will be won or lost on the beaches,' he declared one day while gazing out over a deserted beach. 'We'll have only one chance to stop the enemy and that's while he's in the water.'

As a result, the western coastline of France was now adorned both above and below the high-tide marks with a bewildering galaxy of anti-invasion obstacles. These included 'Belgian Gates', great twelve-foot-high iron and steel frames with legs bracing them against the tides, set in the water about three to four hundred yards from the high-tide mark; 'Czech Hedgehogs', four- or five-foot-high wooden or steel triangles primed with mines and shells, which were covered at high tide, so that any vessel hitting them would be holed; four-foot-high concrete cones; tetrahedrons draped with barbed wire; and sharpened wooden stakes festooned with mines. Behind the beaches were anti-tank walls, great barbed-wire entanglements and four million mines. And all along the coast, at regular intervals, were blockhouses, gun emplacements, elaborate trench systems, hidden machine-gun posts, fortified houses and huge, reinforced-concrete casemates for heavy artillery. Together these fortifications enjoyed the grandiose title of the Atlantic Wall.

In overseeing the enormous task of constructing these defences, and in battling with his superiors for reinforcements, Rommel had exhausted himself.

But today, even he took advantage of the sunshine to relax a little. He had himself driven in his Horch, his powerful staff car, to the nearby forest of Choisy, and then paid a visit to the Marquis of

Choisy, a frail old man and pro-German sympathiser whose son was fighting in the German army against the Bolsheviks on the Eastern Front. That evening, back at La Roche-Guyon, he stayed up late chatting with the Rochefoucaulds about the war. They, too, had gambled on a German victory and could only hope that their guest would repel any invasion. But the signs were not hopeful. Recently, for the first time, they'd been forced down into tunnels beneath the château as fleets of Allied aircraft on bombing missions flew overhead towards Paris.

Across the Channel, Rommel's opposite number was carefully guarding the D-Day secret. General Dwight D. Eisenhower had been appointed Supreme Commander of all the Allied invasion forces on the same day that Hitler had appointed Rommel – 15 January. Roosevelt himself had asked Eisenhower to take on the job at a meeting in Tunis, when the President was on his way back home after the first big wartime conference in Tehran with Churchill and Stalin. Because Roosevelt liked to talk about liberation rather than invasion, Eisenhower drafted his bulletins for public consumption accordingly. The media-savvy general knew that the battle for public opinion was vital in modern warfare. He spent most of this morning pre-recording the message he would release on the morning of D-Day.

Helping him was the media tycoon William S. Paley, chairman of America's most powerful radio network, the Columbia Broadcasting System (CBS), whose cast of stars included news reporters William L. Shirer, Eric Sevareid, Howard K. Smith and the legendary Ed Murrow, whose gravelly-voiced reports of the London Blitz in the dark days of the winter of 1940–1 had contributed so much to swaying neutral American opinion behind Britain. Eisenhower had first met Paley at the Dorchester Hotel in London, thanks to an introduction by his naval aide, Harry Butcher, himself a former CBS lobbyist. The two men had instantly hit it off and Eisenhower had given Paley a car, a driver and a generous supply of rationed petrol to enable him to travel freely around Britain. By June 1944 Paley, now in a colonel's uniform, was chief of psychological broadcasting at Eisenhower's headquarters. He was also occupying a luxurious suite at Claridge's – the hotel was known colloquially as 'Little America' because of its popularity with American officers – sporting Cartier gold ID tags and enjoying affairs with Pamela Churchill, Randolph's wife, and Edwina Mountbatten, wife of Britain's Supreme Commander in South-East Asia.

'Radio broadcasting is an arm of warfare just as are guns and bullets,' proclaimed Paley. This morning he nursed Eisenhower through his all-important D-Day broadcast. When they'd finished, the recording was carefully locked away in a vault.

After he'd finished his work for the day, the Supreme Commander relaxed in the garden of his temporary home in England. Telegraph Cottage was a modest, two-bedroomed house in Kingston, just outside London. Eisenhower had chosen it so as to be physically removed from the capital and the distractions of unwanted visitors. When he worked, he worked long and intensely. Like Rommel, he slept little, invariably rising early every day, well before his staff. He, too, had earned his spurs in the desert, as commander of Allied forces in North Africa. The two men were just a year apart in age, had strong and solid marriages, wrote regularly to their wives and had one son each. Rommel's was in the Luftwaffe as an anti-aircraft gunner; Eisenhower's was a cadet at America's West Point military academy.

The garden was ablaze with rhododendrons, poppies and both pink and white roses. Like Churchill, Eisenhower liked to dabble as an artist. Taking up a pencil, he tried sketching the large pine tree that stood in the garden, but was dissatisfied with the result and scribbled 'Baloney' on it. His desire to sketch, noted Harry Butcher, was further evidence of his boredom and impatience with the long period of waiting. The headlines in the Sunday papers didn't help – promises about the imminent liberation of Rome only highlighted the lack of action closer to home.

The longer the wait, Eisenhower knew, the greater the chance of the secret leaking out. With two and a half million men poised for action, it could hardly be otherwise. To ensure that everyone got the message, he stamped down hard on any leaks. One of the most spectacular involved Major General Henry Miller, chief supply officer of the US 9th Air Force. During a cocktail party at Claridge's, Miller had talked freely about his supply problems, but had added that these would be over after D-Day, which would come, he revealed, before 15 June. The instant Eisenhower was told, he had Miller reduced to the rank of colonel and sent him back to the United States. Miller's desperate plea to his old West Point classmate against the punishment proved useless: Eisenhower's broad smile masked a man of iron.

Shortly before nine o'clock that night, the young French school teacher in Caen, a city now shut down under its nightly curfew, had one final task to complete. André Heintz had no affection for the Germans. His grandparents had left their native Alsace in disgust after Germany annexed the province following the Franco-Prussian war of 1870–1, and his father had been driven from his home in Burgundy, eastern France, by German troops during the First World War. For his family to face occupation by the national enemy yet again was a humiliation too far for André, and he was determined to do anything he could to hasten its end.

Excusing himself to his parents, he disappeared into the cellar of the family home. From a shelf of tinned groceries he took down what the label announced was a tin of spinach. He removed the lid. Inside was hidden a small radio crystal set. Earlier he'd brought down a pair of earphones from a box concealed in the attic. He'd rigged up the set to the electrical circuit in the house, and the reception was good. At nine o'clock he heard the distinctive voice of the BBC. The good news it brought about the war itself, especially the imminent fall of Rome, was heart-warming.

But André was actually listening for something else. At the beginning of May a woman had come to his school while he was teaching a class. He'd hurried downstairs to meet her. She'd whispered six short messages into his ear and made him repeat them until he'd memorised them. They were the action messages that would be broadcast by the BBC after the news to announce the timing of D-Day. As soon as he received them, it would be his own special mission to alert the members of his group. This is what he was now listening for. Tonight, as on every night since the woman's visit, he heard many other messages destined for various agents behind enemy lines. But none had he memorised. For him, too, life had become a matter of patience and waiting.

Later that night Sonia d'Artois landed heavily in the French ditch that wrenched her shoulder so badly. The false identity card she carried bore the name Suzanne Bonvie and stated that she was a resident of Cannes. She was twenty years old, the second youngest female secret agent ever dispatched to France from Britain. Bruised and shaken, she joined up in the darkness with her two fellow agents, both men, who had jumped with her. Together they scoured the field for the containers dropped ahead of them. After a while they gave up, and local Resistance fighters took them to a nearby farm. Here she was more than glad to toss back a welcome glass of *calva*, the local apple brandy, and then, exhausted, fall heavily asleep in a comfortable bed.

Meanwhile Peter Moen lay uneasily asleep in his prison bunk. Glenn Dickin and Bill Tucker were bedded down in their canvas tents along with their comrades-in-arms. Veronica Owen was also asleep in the crowded room she shared with half a dozen others in a requisitioned villa outside Portsmouth. Albert Grunberg sweltered in his stuffy attic. Sydney Hudson caught a few hours' rest before bicycling out to the farmhouse to meet Sonia. Walter Schwender slept soundly after his day at the beach. And that night the Abwehr station in Madrid transmitted four messages to Berlin, numbered 862 to 865 and containing intelligence from agent Arabel about troop movements in Britain. Across the Dover Strait, thunderstorms and light showers helped clear the air.

2

IT CAN'T BE FAR OFF
Monday 29 May

There was no relief from the heat. By nine o'clock in the morning the thermometer had hit 96 degrees Fahrenheit in the Dover Strait and at five o'clock in the afternoon rose to 100. Across southern England it was the hottest Whit Monday for years, with the temperature in the shade registering 91 in London's Regent Street, the hottest recorded for over forty years. A freak storm swept across the north of the country, and three people drowned in a flash flood in Yorkshire.

In London the holiday mood continued. At Lord's, a mile-long queue formed to see England play cricket against Australia. When the gates finally closed just after midday hundreds of disappointed spectators found themselves on the wrong side of the turnstiles. England won the match with just ten minutes to spare. In Regent's Park the Bankside Players gave an open-air performance of Shakespeare's *The Winter's Tale* before a large audience. Thousands arriving by bicycle or horse and cart, or on foot, spent the day at Ascot for the horse racing. Chessington Zoo was packed. People dressed up. Men wore their well-preserved pre-war linen suits, women their brightest and lightest dresses. It was a day for children, the middle-aged, and the elderly. Young people in their twenties and thirties were noticeable by their absence – except for a small sprinkling of men and women in uniform enjoying a weekend's leave. It was a portent. London was emptying of troops. 'It's very quiet,' remarked a publican to one of the dozens of war correspondents gathering in the capital. 'It can't be far off now.'

Millions of uniformed men and women from the Allied navies, armies and air forces were waiting for action. On D-Day itself, one hundred and thirty-two thousand troops would storm ashore, to be followed over the rest of the month by several hundred thousand more. Most would cross to France by sea in purpose-built landing craft, escorted by hundreds of warships. This operation, the Normandy assault phase of Overlord and crucial to its entire success, was code-named 'Neptune' (and would in fact run until 30 June 1944). Its orders, printed on special presses in deepest secrecy, were three inches thick and a thousand pages long. In charge was Admiral Sir Bertram Ramsay, a sixty-one-year-old veteran who'd first gone to sea as a midshipman under Queen Victoria when Britannia and the Royal Navy ruled the waves. The mastermind of the heroic Dunkirk evacuation of the British Army from France in 1940, he had also commanded British naval forces during the invasion of Sicily in July 1943.

'Bertie' Ramsay carried considerably more punch than his slightly built frame suggested. Fighting for King and Country was in the family's blood. A Scot from the border county of Berwickshire, he was the youngest son of Brigadier General William Alexander Ramsay, who had commanded the Fourth Hussars when the young Winston Churchill was one of its subalterns. Both of Bertie's brothers were in the army, and his two sisters had married soldiers. He himself had chosen as his wife Helen Margaret Menzies, daughter of an army colonel. For Ramsay it had been a late marriage, and he and Helen had two small sons, David and Charles. Like most of those at war, he found solace in writing home, and his almost daily letters to his wife provided him with welcome therapy and relaxation.

In the First World War Ramsay had served aboard the Navy's greatest battleship, HMS *Dreadnought*, and then commanded a destroyer in the English Channel. The Dunkirk evacuation had earned him both plaudits and a knighthood. An impeccably dressed perfectionist, he expected the highest standards from his officers and crew. Sometimes, one of them remembered, 'he carried the aura of vinegar'. But he was fair and polite, and in a crisis always exuded confidence and calm. He never forgot a name and went out of his way to recognise the efforts of his hard-working staff, both senior and junior, who came to trust and respect him. 'He was a good man,' recalled one of the junior Wrens on his staff, 'and a very good boss, always cool, calm and collected. What was superb was the lead he gave to his staff, and his tolerance and kindness. I never met anyone like him.'

Ramsay was one of the three senior Allied commanders under Eisenhower's immediate command. Like them all, he was under tremendous pressure. At his Scottish home he would relax with the traditional Borders pastimes of horse riding, fox hunting, golfing and fishing, and he was a keen polo player. But at his headquarters outside Portsmouth his sporting options were limited. That afternoon he enthusiastically joined in a game of cricket against a team of Wrens. Despite the boiling heat, uncut grass and uneven wicket, he managed to contribute sixteen runs to his side's victory by five wickets. It provided a welcome distraction from the almost paralysing responsibility that lay on his shoulders. In addition it was a typical way of showing the Wrens how highly he regarded them as members of his team. The cricket-mad Wren, Veronica Owen, would have loved it.

But Veronica was standing watch at nearby Fort Southwick, Ramsay's communications headquarters. Cut deep into the chalk beneath Portsdown Hill, the great escarpment outside Portsmouth, the Combined Underground Operations Centre had first seen action during the Dieppe Raid in August 1942. Veronica had to descend 166 steps to reach the three parallel steel- and brick-lined tunnels a hundred feet beneath the surface, criss-crossed by numerous small passages into which were crammed the offices, galley facilities and dormitories used for the operations centre's round-the-clock vigils. It was an eerie experience, recorded one of her fellow

Wrens, 'to descend by endless flights of steps to the dark interior of the earth to find this huge organisation borne of the ingenuity of man, subtly lit by a brilliance vying with the sunshine above us, everything humming and buzzing with the urgency of the war effort. The climb up again at the end of the watch was the most trying part of all. Flight after flight of steps stretched ahead and when we were tired, they seemed insurmountable. Two or three times we would lean against the wall and pant, passed oftener than not by a grey-haired commander, taking the steps two at a time.'

On the hill above stood the remnants of the first Fort Southwick, which had also been built with invasion in mind. Only then, in the mid-nineteenth century, it had been fears of a French invasion that worried the nation. Palmerston, the Prime Minister, had ordered a string of forts to be built along the south coast of England. When this threat failed to materialise, they had become derisively known as 'the Palmerston Follies'.

Most of those in the bombproof tunnels were Wren ratings: wireless telegraphers, chart plotters, telephonists, coders and messengers. There was a handful of sailors and naval signals officers, as well as some more senior Wren cipher officers. During quiet watches they were allowed to catnap in the double-decker bunks and blankets provided for them. There was also a small galley serving hot soup and corned-beef sandwiches. Veronica didn't like the way their edges curled as they dried up in the dry and ventilated air. Sometimes, if things were busy, a couple of the Wrens would be summoned to work in the Plotting Office, along with all the gold braid from the Commander-in-Chief downwards.

Her day had begun at Heathfield, a large house outside Fareham requisitioned by the Royal Navy to house about a hundred Wrens. From here they were bussed back and forth to Fort Southwick. The owner, an old lady, still lived in the house. She would occasionally pass Veronica and give her a gentle and tolerant smile, but otherwise made herself so scarce that the Wrens regarded the place as their own. There was a large ground-floor sitting room, a dining room with long tables, and a kitchen. Most of the women slept crammed six to eight to a room equipped with bunk beds, although

Veronica was luckier than most. She was in one of four double rooms in the gardener's cottage, which had its own separate bathroom. Eventually, however, even in this little sanctuary, the numbers increased, bunk beds were installed and the lack of privacy often led to frayed tempers.

When off duty Veronica spent a lot of time darning holes in stockings and repairing clothes. On joining the Navy she had ceased to get ration coupons for civilian clothes, so she had to look after what she already owned. But she had plenty to eat, the eggs were real, not powdered, and there was no shortage of bread or cigarettes. Fareham had two cinemas and she went to them once or twice a week, and then on to the local tea shop before beginning her evening watch. She also regularly browsed in the local bookshop or sat and read in the local YWCA. Every month she queued for a packet of sanitary towels that were given to the Wrens, rumour had it, by the Queen.

That morning, after breakfast, Veronica got on her bike and made her way along the main road a mile and a half to the historic small town of Titchfield on the River Meon, which flowed into the Solent. She had been befriended by the town's vicar and his wife, the Reverend Frank and Mrs Spurway, and that spring had frequently bicycled over to spend any free evenings with them in the vicarage next to the ancient flint and limestone church, St Peter's.

With its Elizabethan half-timbered and Georgian red-brick houses, Titchfield provided a microcosm of English history, physically embodying the traditional England constantly evoked by Churchill in his wartime speeches. Here the Anglo-Saxons had first built a church, and here, in the Domesday Book of 1086, the Normans had noted the presence of a small settlement. In the thirteenth century an abbey, founded by the White Canons, had been erected, and King Charles I sheltered there before his arrest during the English Civil War. One of William Shakespeare's patrons, the third Earl of Southampton, had bought the abbey after its dissolution during the Reformation and the playwright, according to local legend, had stayed there. The chancel and south chapel of St Peter's church were lined with monuments to naval officers, colonial governors and soldiers who had served their country. Every visit to Titchfield provided Veronica with a lesson in English history and a record of its heroes and patriots who had fought, died and endured for the British Empire.

Most significantly of all, in the light of the epic drama in which she was now playing her part, King Henry V had stayed at Titchfield Abbey while he assembled his great armada of sixteen hundred ships in the Solent for the invasion of France and his historic victory at Agincourt in 1415. Victory for him, too, had depended on deceiving the enemy about where he would land on the coast. Fortune had favoured him and he had taken them by surprise and successfully stormed the great fortress of Harfleur, the most important port in Normandy. Every schoolchild knew by heart Henry's stirring address to his troops as he urged them on at the height of the siege, at least as Shakespeare had imagined it in his well-loved play. 'Once more unto the breach, dear friends, once more,' it memorably began, ending with his great peroration to the ordinary English soldiers on whom victory would depend:

> And you, good yeomen,
> Whose limbs were made in England, show us here
> The mettle of your pasture; let us swear
> That you are worth your breeding – which I doubt not,
> For there is none of you so mean and base
> That hath not noble lustre in your eyes.
> I see you stand like greyhounds in the slips,
> Straining upon the start. The game's afoot.
> Follow your spirit, and upon this charge
> Cry, 'God for Harry! England and Saint George!'

Even as the twentieth-century armada was assembling in the Solent, and its commanders were once again counting on surprise and the courage of the ordinary men who would wade ashore in the face of merciless enemy fire, the finishing touches were being frantically made at Denham Studios to the film version of the play starring and directed by the leading young actor of the day, Laurence Olivier. Its release a month after D-Day drew vast audiences across the country.

Veronica spent the morning helping cut sandwiches and prepare the food and tables for the local fête that afternoon, then left for her watch. The work was hectic, a sign of intensified naval activity in and around the Solent and the English Channel. Perhaps fired up by her visit to Titchfield, she delivered a short but eloquent speech to her fellow Wrens complaining that most of them didn't really understand the importance of their work. The service prided itself on convincing every single Wren, however humble their job might appear, that it was vital to winning the war. Veronica's youthful enthusiasm clearly carried her away, because before the watch was over a notice appeared on the board requesting silence during operations.

Unabashed, she returned home, where she found a parcel from her twin brother. Hugh was also in the Navy, serving in the Mediterranean as a midshipman on board the battle cruiser HMS *Aurora*. At various ports of call he would buy things for her that she couldn't find or afford in England. She particularly appreciated the silk stockings he sent from time to time. Now he was in Alexandria, waiting for his ship to be repaired after it had struck a mine. Having a brother at peril on the high seas, and a twin at that, spurred her on in her tasks.

Operation Neptune, and Veronica Owen with it, had entered the countdown phase. Glenn Dickin was one of the tens of thousands of infantrymen that the armada of ships would carry to the D-Day beaches.

Camp 7 in Southampton Marshalling Area C lay on Hiltingbury Common, close to the village of Chandler's Ford, just north of Southampton. Glenn's was just one of twenty-two such camps in the area, now bursting with a total of over fifty thousand troops and seven thousand vehicles. Each camp was divided into blocks of fifty pyramid-shaped canvas tents, which in turn were subdivided into 'villages' of ten. Each tent slept ten enlisted men. NCOs and officers had more comfortable arrangements. The camps were largely self-contained, with their own kitchens, latrines, showers, stores and entertainment areas. Camouflage netting strung over the trees helped disguise them from any prying German aircraft, although by now the Luftwaffe had long lost the battle for the skies over Britain and reconnaissance flights had virtually ceased.

Lady Diana Cooper, whose husband, Duff, was the British Ambassador in Algiers with General de Gaulle's Free French move- ment, spent her leave that summer motoring around southern England. 'Anyone who saw [one],' she noted of the camps, 'will always remember the dense concentration of steel, its whole bulk open to a sky miraculously clear of the enemy.' A barbed-wire security fence patrolled by American military police surrounded the camps. British Army units did housekeeping. On the streets outside, nailed to the telegraph poles, were signs warning: 'Do not loiter. Civilians must not talk to army personnel.'

Today Glenn decided not to write home. In April the troops had been ordered not to post letters in civilian mailboxes. Instead they went open to the army field post for censorship. Glenn regularly screened the mail of his own men in the first battalion of the Regina Rifles, one of the many distinguished regiments of the 3rd Canadian Infantry Division. The divisional commander, General Keller, had paid Hiltingbury a visit just a month before with King George VI and the commander of the Canadian forces in Britain, General Harry Crerar.

Just two weeks before, Eisenhower himself had arrived to give them a pep talk. Afterwards, breaking ranks, the men gathered around his jeep. 'How's the chow?' he had joked, an ice-breaker he'd used plenty of times before in visiting American troops. But he'd forgotten that the Canadians referred to their food, in the British style, as 'grub', and he'd been momentarily met with blank stares by his awe-struck audience until it was explained what he meant. The prairie boys were North Americans, but they defi- nitely weren't Yanks. Along with the Regina Rifles, Hiltingbury also held men from other Canadian regiments, such as the Camerons from Ottawa, the Winnipeg Rifles, the Canadian

Scottish from British Columbia and the French-Canadian De La Chaudière Regiment from Quebec.

Canada was Britain's single most important ally before America entered the war in December 1941, following the attack on Pearl Harbor, and over a hundred thousand of its troops had crossed the Atlantic before that. Until recently they had far outnumbered GIs. Canadians in their thousands were flying with Allied aircrews, and the 1st Canadian Infantry Division was slogging it out in Italy. In the North Atlantic, the Canadian Navy was playing a vital role in protecting convoys and sinking U-boats. Canadians were eager to play a role in liberating Europe. But they had a special reason also to dread the prospect of D-Day. In August 1942 the 2nd Canadian Infantry Division had spearheaded an Allied raid on the port of Dieppe, with terrible consequences. Of the almost five thousand men who took part, only two thousand returned, the rest being killed, wounded or captured within the first few hours. It was a loss proportionally comparable to the first day of the Battle of the Somme in 1916.

Dieppe was not just an operational fiasco. For Canada it was a national disaster whose shadow still hung heavily over the Canadian troops now preparing for D-Day. Would there be a repeat of the massacre on the beaches? Or would it finally be payback time? To avenge their comrades, some of the D-Day Canadian troops cut their hair Mohican style and carried hunting knives in their boots. At least one good thing came out of the debacle: the overwhelming conclusion that, for the landings to succeed, the enemy had to be obliterated or paralysed by overwhelming fire support from close naval bombardment, action from the air, and tanks on the beaches. That was now built into the plans. Altogether, troops from fourteen Canadian infantry and six artillery regiments would land on the beaches of France.

Briefings were already under way. Senior officers had been let into the top-secret D-Day plans four days before. Yesterday Dickin's platoon commander, Frank Peters, a twenty-eight-year-old married man from North Battleford, Saskatchewan, had learned all that he needed to know about the operation. But security – now more than ever – remained tight. Instead of being told the real names of their destination, they were given code-names. Only later, when Dickin set sail, would he learn the actual names of the landing beaches and the villages he would be liberating.

As the Allied bombing campaign against German targets in France intensified, not even the heavily controlled German press and radio could ignore the approaching sense of climax. Invasion was the topic of the hour. It was not just the heavy targeting of France. For the first time parts of the German North Sea coastline had been closed off to civilians, and the region around Bremen was designated an 'invasion danger' area. Never before had the Nazis declared the Fatherland itself in peril.

At the Berghof, Hitler spent another quiet day, taking his daily walk to the Tea House, enjoying the cool air and lunching with Eva Braun. After a recent visit to the Obersalzberg one of his senior field commanders had found the Führer calm and unworried. 'One can't help feeling,' noted Field Marshal von Richthofen visiting from the Italian front, 'this is a man blindly following his summons, walking unhesitatingly along the path prescribed to him without the slightest doubt as to its rightness and the final outcome'. In Berlin Hitler's propaganda chief, Dr Joseph Goebbels, was handing out a similar message to members of the media and military commentators. Across Germany, the newspapers were unanimous: Hitler and the High Command had foreseen every contingency, were in full control of events and Germans should not be afraid of the future. One correspondent even argued that the retreat in Italy was dictated solely by the need to economise on manpower. Far from being a setback, it had astutely foiled Allied hopes that the High Command would have to draw on its strategic reserve. Another paper boasted that German tanks would quickly take care of landings in France. The panzer divisions were being deliberately held back from the coast to counter airborne landings if they tried to squeeze the Germans from both sea and land. The great danger was Allied air power. But by contrast with the open plains of Russia, he argued, the French countryside was ripe for camouflage and concealed German air defences, and dug-in tanks would take care of the enemy.

The Nazi Press Service was openly scornful about Allied air power. The current British and American air offensives were mere 'fits of military rabies', it snorted, that had nothing to do with an impending invasion. Attacks on 'herds in Mecklenburg, on haystacks in Pomerania, on cyclists in Saxony and shepherds in Uckermark are unpleasant for those concerned', it commented scathingly, 'but have nothing to do with the struggle for decision in this war'. In fact, by not invading over the past weekend, Eisenhower had clearly 'missed the bus'. It would be another month before weather, moon and tide would be as favourable. Obviously he had not completed his plans. But whether he advanced or postponed them, he would always be caught in the German net.

All this bombastic comment reflected the Führer's own personal views. So did another recurrent theme. This was about the secret weapons being held in reserve. 'We know one thing,' asserted a Stuttgart newspaper darkly. 'We have certain things in store which, used at the right moment, will visibly change the fortune of war.' Over the coming days visitors to the Berghof were to hear a lot more threats like this.

'A tireless fighter in the cause of the Führer and the Reich' was how von Rundstedt summed up Rommel, a double-edged compliment noticeably devoid of praise for any actual results. On another occasion, speaking even more frankly, the German Commander-in-Chief West dismissed his subordinate as 'an unlicked cub – not a fox at all'. Relations between the two men were strained, a potentially disastrous prelude to the Allied invasion. Von Rundstedt resented the younger man's being put in charge of invasion defences and had little faith in Rommel's – and Hitler's – Atlantic Wall as a defensive shield. It was, he thought, purely imaginary.

The two men had also fallen out over the question of how best to deploy the panzer divisions. Rommel wanted the tanks to be stationed right behind the beaches where the Allies would land. It

was there, and within the first few hours, he believed, that the
battle would be decided. 'Believe me, Lang,' he had told his aide
in a much-quoted phrase while they stood gazing over a deserted
beach one day, 'the first twenty-four hours of the invasion will be
decisive . . . for the Allies, as well as Germany, it will be the
longest day.' Von Rundstedt, by contrast, believed the tanks
should be held well back from the coastline in reserve, so as to
strike hard and effectively when the exact location of the attack
became clear. The quarrel was solved only when Hitler imposed
a compromise. Rommel received three panzer divisions to station
where he wanted them, and he immediately placed the 21st,
which had been his favourite in Africa, close to Caen. The four
others in France would remain under the control of the High
Command, to be deployed by Hitler himself as he thought fit.
Rommel, in short, could not even dispose of all the forces in his
sector of responsibility.

Despite this, he retained his faith in Hitler, blaming instead the
Führer's advisers. The day before, during his Sunday drive out to
Choisy, he'd directed his anger about the Luftwaffe's abysmal failure to deal with Allied air attacks entirely on Reichsmarschall
Herman Goering, Hitler's designated successor. The people around
Hitler, he told Lang, simply failed to be frank with him; in other
words, if Hitler were properly informed, things would be different, and better. This was naive, but then Rommel was a soldier
tactician, not a politician. He also swallowed whole Hitler's views
on the great Crusade that had to be waged by France and Germany
against Bolshevism, not to mention Goebbels' propaganda about
Britain. Morale was low on the opposite side of the Channel,
Rommel had told his son Manfred just a month before, because
there was one strike after another. 'The screams of "Down with
Churchill and the Jews" and "We want Peace" are growing louder —
bad omens for such a risky offensive [invasion].'

But if and when it did come, Rommel was convinced, the invasion would be north of the Seine, on the coast closest to England.
Any suggestions that Normandy might be the target he greeted
with scepticism. His own intelligence officer, Colonel Anton

Staubwasser, supposedly an expert on Britain, had no independent sources of his own. To Günther Blumentritt, von Rundstedt's chief of staff, 'the English southern coast was an impenetrable sphinx'. Rommel's own chief of staff, Speidel, was actively plotting against Hitler. 'That asshole at the Berghof' is how he referred to Hitler behind Rommel's back.

It was no wonder that the exhausted and outmanoeuvred Rommel took solace in writing every day to his wife, Lucie, back at their home at Herrlingen, near Ulm in south-western Germany. His thoughts, like those of many others at the front this holiday Monday, were on his family – especially as he had just received news of heavy bombings of Stuttgart, the capital of Baden-Württemberg and rather too close to home for comfort. Today he wrote to her about the Allied bombings throughout France that had resulted in the deaths of three thousand French civilians. He was missing her. He'd even been thinking of surprising her with a visit on her birthday; his sleek black Horch could get him there in a few hours. He could pick up something nice for her in Paris. She would be fifty next week, on the Tuesday – 6 June.

There was no such chance for Walter Schwender to get home. Leave for all German troops under Rommel's command remained suspended, as it had been since April. He was based outside Nantes, an industrial port of nearly two hundred thousand inhabitants on the River Loire, its skyline punctuated by the cranes and derricks of its docks and shipbuilding yards. 'Nantes la grise', it was called – 'Grey Nantes' – as much for its hard-working ethic as for the low grey clouds that endlessly swept in from the Atlantic. This was, after all, the city in which King Henry IV had issued his famous Edict granting tolerance to Protestants in 1598, and a certain dour Presbyterian spirit hung in the air. With its large and unionised working class, the socialists and communists enjoyed a strong foothold in the city. The Germans had occupied it in June 1940 and the first signs of resistance had surfaced almost immediately with the blowing up of thirty-five trucks loaded with tyres. For that, the culprit had been shot.

But it was just over a year later, on 20 October 1941, that the Nazi occupiers really revealed their colours. The German commandant of the city, Colonel Karl Hötz, had just stepped out of the Café du Nord on his way to his office after his early-morning coffee when he was fatally shot in the street by two young communist resisters. Civilian hostages had already been taken, and now, on Hitler's orders, forty-eight of them were shot. The youngest was a boy of seventeen and a half. Then, beginning in 1942, the deportation of Jews from Nantes and the surrounding region had begun. Five hundred of them never came back. The following year, forty-two resisters in the city were shot after a trial that branded them 'bandits'. The gulf between the civil population and the occupiers, the latter aided by a small handful of fanatical French collaborators, was now clear. To add to the city's woes, in September 1943 devastating American air raids on the port killed some twelve hundred civilians. Thousands of survivors had fled to the safety of the countryside.

Not surprisingly, the Germans kept a large garrison in Nantes, which Rommel had recently visited twice to review its defences. Like everyone else, he knew that its downriver neighbour, the port of St Nazaire, had been the target of a daring and deadly raid by Allied commandos less than two years before. Here, sheltered by huge reinforced-concrete pens, lay dozens of the deadly U-boats that threatened Britain's transatlantic lifeline.

None of this grim background appeared to affect the carefree young Walter. Having typed his letter home the day before, he saw no need to write one today, and instead went off to swim at the beach. He'd always loved sport and the outdoors, especially cycling; it was one of the things he'd really enjoyed in the Hitler Youth. His brother Karl, who was two years older, had been a member, too. Walter also got interested in flying, and as soon as he left school at the then customary age of fourteen he become an apprentice as a building fitter with a company that constructed hangars for airships. Before moving to Nantes he had been stationed at La Rochelle, another port city, further down the French Atlantic coast. He liked being close to Nantes and the sea. Life was good, there was plenty of food and wine, lots of swimming, and the city wasn't always grey, as the long weekend of Pentecost had proved. Certainly not today, another scorcher. The war all seemed a long way away.

Churchill, unlike Hitler, was far from calm and relaxed. Daily headlines boasting of massive air attacks on targets in France intensified his worries. The bombing was killing and maiming too many civilians and he was afraid of losing the goodwill in France so necessary to the success of the invasion. He dictated another note to Air Marshal Tedder. 'You are piling up an awful load of hatred,' he declared. Others, however, and not just among the military, disagreed with the Prime Minister. Cardinals in France had issued a public appeal for the sparing of civilians. But in a broadcast reply over the BBC, the Roman Catholic leadership in Britain robustly insisted that the impending liberation of France required all possible disruption of German communications. The Catholic hierarchy in France, it was no secret, was uncomfortably close to the Vichy regime.

Once again the locked beige box with its Ultra intercepts demanded Churchill's attention. Today C sent him an initial batch of fifteen, following it up later with three more batches. Eight were military intercepts, one was a naval summary and four were diplomatic. As always, Churchill scrutinised them closely before scribbling his initials and date at the bottom to indicate that he had read them. The Bletchley Park experts had broken the diplomatic codes of several countries, which meant that Churchill could see what diplomats around the world were reporting.

Today's harvest was relatively modest. Recently he'd commented publicly and controversially on the neutral stance of both Turkey and Spain. He had long hoped to tempt Turkey into entering the war on the Allied side. But while criticising its policy of 'exaggerated caution', he also praised its recent decision to halt all export of chrome to Germany. As for the Spain of right-wing dictator General Francisco Franco, the victor over the Republicans in the country's recent bloody civil war, he had gone out of his way to commend its friendly and non-interventionist stance during the North African landings of 1942. Praise of any kind for Franco and his fascist regime was a red rag to democrats everywhere, and his remarks had provoked a storm of protest. Now he saw reports on his views offered by the Brazilian Minister in Ankara to his superiors in Rio de Janeiro, and from the Free French representative in Madrid to his office in Algiers. He also initialled the text of a telegram from a Free French diplomat who was briefing Algiers on behind-the-scenes manoeuvres involving the exiled King of Yugoslavia and his government. And, as if there had been any doubt about it, he read a report from the Japanese Ambassador in Berlin telling his masters in Tokyo that Allied air raids had inflicted heavy damage on parts of the government quarter of Berlin. Some of the military intercepts likewise confirmed heavy bombing damage elsewhere: in the Italian seaport of Genoa and in ports and cities along and behind the Mediterranean coast of France, such as Marseilles, Nîmes, Avignon and Montpellier. These provided useful confirmation of after-action reports by pilots and the careful monitoring of the local press.

But what Churchill really hoped to glimpse in the Ultra material were clues from the designated invasion area. What were the Germans thinking and doing there? One item in the box touched on the subject briefly. This was an order, somewhat garbled and incomplete in parts, from von Rundstedt to all fighting units under his command insisting that once fighting began they must keep their front-line troops ruthlessly up to strength. 'Experience has shown,' he declared, 'that battle strengths customarily decrease very rapidly in large scale fighting and reach a blatant disproportion to the undiminished or increasing strength of supply troops.'

Reading von Rundstedt's mind like this was helpful. But such direct reports from inside the German headquarters in France were rare. Today, as usual, most of the intercepts in Churchill's box brought intelligence from Italy or the Mediterranean. This was not surprising. Bletchley Park's work lay in deciphering radio messages. But in France the Germans were relying mostly on landlines for their communications. Not until battle began would they be forced to resort more fully to the dangerously insecure airwaves. This was happening in Italy because German military engineers hardly had time to install landlines before the positions were overrun in their headlong retreat. Hence the large number of intercepts from that battlefront. Landlines were far harder, indeed almost impossible, for the Allies to tap. Not surprisingly, therefore, and contrary to the widespread assumption that with Ultra the Allies enjoyed virtually unlimited intelligence about the Germans' every military move, Churchill's box threw partial and only fragmented light on what he was most anxious to know about. On the eve of the Allied invasion, the Prime Minister spent a lot of his time simply guessing, peering through the gloom, and hoping that the Germans would be surprised.

If Ultra's harvest of signals intelligence from France was thin, what else could be done to penetrate the curtain of secrecy about Rommel's preparations? One answer was human intelligence, or spies. The right people in key places might be able to provide crucial material.

In Caen, the heatwave continued. On this holiday Monday André Heintz once again bicycled out to help his father in the family allotment. This time they planted lettuce. One of the bikes broke down and his father patiently fixed it — it was practically the only way of getting around now, given the acute shortage of petrol. Then, as André always did, after dinner he disappeared down into the cellar to listen to the 8.30 BBC bulletin on his secret crystal set. His parents knew he listened to it, because he passed on the news. But they didn't know about his Resistance links and the hidden messages.

Or at least he didn't think they did. He hadn't told them, but he suspected that his mother might have guessed. Recently a courier had come to his house with a couple of blank identity cards for him to work on. But André wasn't in and the courier couldn't wait. It was getting dark and time for the night barrier that protected the German headquarters to come down. Only residents had a pass. So the courier stripped off his shoes and socks, handed the documents to André's mother and asked her to hide them. She had slipped the incriminating items behind the front of the upright piano in the living room and when André got home she gave them to him without a word. He doubted that she had told his father. Ignorance in such matters could mean the difference between life and death.

Tonight the young schoolteacher listened again in vain for the BBC action messages he had so carefully memorised.

Eisenhower was still at Telegraph Cottage, his treasured haven, where he focused single-mindedly on the immediate task ahead. His broad smile, easy manner and upbeat humour masked an iron will and immense self-control. Roosevelt had chosen him as Supreme Commander of Allied forces, and Churchill had agreed, because he'd brilliantly demonstrated his ability to lead the coalition of Anglo-American forces during the landings in North Africa, Sicily and Italy. He worked hard and conscientiously at becoming a leader. 'As the pressure mounts and strain increases,' he told his wife, Mamie, 'everyone begins to show weaknesses in his makeup. It is up to the Commander to conceal his: above all to conceal doubt, fear, and distrust.'

But the strain was beginning to tell. He was smoking forty Camel cigarettes a day, suffering from severe eye strain and had developed a ringing noise in his ears. He felt as if he were living on a network of high-tension wires, he told his wife. For him, too, letters home provided welcome therapy. He'd proposed to Mamie Doud on St Valentine's Day 1916 while stationed at Fort Sam Houston in Texas, and married her later that year. For the next twenty-five years she'd accompanied him dutifully to all his postings in the United States and overseas, including Paris, the Panama Canal Zone and the Philippines. But during the Second World War she stayed in Washington, at the Wardman Park Hotel, from where she contributed to the war effort by helping with various charities and even serving as a waitress at the Soldiers, Sailors, and Marines' Club.

Without his wife, to relax Eisenhower played bridge, hit a golf ball around or amused himself playing with his Scottish terrier

Telek – short for Telegraph Cottage. 'You can't talk war to a dog,' he said, 'and I'd like to have someone or something to talk to, occasionally, who doesn't know what the word means.' Here, too, he could fall back on his familiar comfort food: steak, fried chicken, pork chops, baked-bean casserole and hominy grits.

So long as he didn't need to move to his advance headquarters at Southwick House, a centuries-old mansion near Fort Southwick, he stayed put. He would go there only when he had to, closer to the invasion date. He'd personally fixed it back in mid-May, after careful calculations based on the most favourable configuration of tides and the moon. These calculations were complex and demanding. The landings would be at low tide, so as to expose Rommel's underwater obstacles and destroy them. But this low tide would have to follow at least an hour's daylight to permit the bombers and naval guns to weaken the Germans' defences, yet be early enough to permit a second low tide to occur before darkness fell, so that a second wave of troops could land. For the airborne offensive, timed to take place several hours before the seaborne landings, a late-rising full moon was required. The sea had to be reasonable for the landing craft and accompanying naval ships, and there had to be good visibility and ideally a fair wind blowing inshore to drive smoke into the eyes of the defenders. Two of these requirements, a low tide and a full moon, could be reliably predicted, and in early June they would coincide on the 4th, 5th, 6th and 7th. The ideal date, it had been agreed, was the 5th. But only fate could determine if the weather would oblige.

Only a tiny handful of trusted people knew the secret of the date and place of the landings. They alone received the documents circulating within SHAEF – the Supreme Headquarters Allied Expeditionary Force, which controlled Allied troops in action in north-west Europe – stamped with the special security classification that was even higher than Top Secret – 'Bigot'. Those who were 'Bigoted' were in on the D-Day secret. Those who were not could only guess.

It was an odd word to select, concocted by reversing the letters of 'To Gib', which was stamped on documents used by Allied officers sent to Gibraltar before the North African landings. 'Bigot' documents, including the meticulously prepared maps of the landing beaches, were created in utmost secrecy by workers cleared by special security screening, and were tightly guarded. 'Are you Bigoted?' was a question often encountered by those on the fringes of the D-Day secret. If they showed bemusement at the question, they were obviously not, and the curtain of secrecy abruptly descended.

Eisenhower –'Ike' to those around him – was acutely aware of how absolutely crucial secrecy – and hence surprise about the date and the place – was to the success of D-Day. So he had been alarmed the day before to receive a note from Churchill about lifting the ban on diplomatic communications by foreign powers in Britain. Its aim was to stop any leakage of information that might, deliberately or inadvertently, yield some damaging clue to the Germans about Allied plans. Embassies in London were pressing impatiently for the ban to be lifted as soon as possible after D-Day. Anthony Eden had asked Churchill to lean on Eisenhower and see if he would agree.

But the idea ran completely counter to the carefully worked-out deception plan for Overlord. 'Fortitude', as it was code-named, was not just designed to fool the Germans about when and where the blow would fall. It also had the all-important aim of leading them to believe that when the Allied landings did occur, they were merely a prelude to the real landings that would follow later and elsewhere. This meant that 'Fortitude' deception had to be maintained for several days *after* Allied troops hit the beaches on D-Day – to convince Hitler and his High Command that preparations were still under way for a second and more powerful assault in a different sector of their front. If the diplomatic ban were lifted too soon, thus permitting foreign embassies to send uncensored news out of the country, it could jeopardise the entire plan.

Eisenhower's chief of staff was the bulldog-faced General Walter Bedell Smith, who'd been with him since 1942. 'Beetle', as he was nicknamed, was Ike's crutch, trusty confidant and hatchet man. At his chief's request he'd drafted a reply to Churchill. Eisenhower carefully scanned it and gave it the OK. Politely but firmly he rejected the Prime Minister's request, including a compromise suggestion by Eden that they agree to D plus 7 (seven days after D-Day) for a lifting of the ban. 'It has been one of my main pre-occupations to persuade the enemy that our assault is to be made on a wider front than is in fact the case and that our first assault is merely the preliminary to the main battle' read his letter. 'I am extremely loath to surrender the advantage we have thus far gained . . .' He would prefer, he told Churchill, that no date at all be fixed for lifting the ban until he saw how events unfolded. Eisenhower with his heels dug in was an immovable force, even for Churchill. As events unfolded, the ban was not lifted until D plus 15.

Deceiving the enemy is a stratagem as old as warfare itself. 'You reap greater benefit from the skin of a fox,' wrote King Frederick the Great of Prussia in the eighteenth century, 'than from the hide of a lion.' But rarely before the Second World War was it deployed to such magical effect. The overall deception plan for Allied strategy in 1944 was known as 'Bodyguard', but the two main components relating to D-Day were code-named 'Fortitude North' and 'Fortitude South'.

Fortitude South was designed to fool the Germans about the real site of the landings in France, and specifically to suggest they would take place in the Pas de Calais, the area at the narrowest part of the English Channel, bordering the Dover Strait. This was a logical choice, and to most German commanders, most crucially to von Rundstedt, *the* logical choice. Not only did it involve the shortest sea crossing; it also provided the fastest land route to the Ruhr, Germany's industrial heartland, and offered the prospect of quickly capturing ports such as Boulogne, Dunkirk and Calais in order to bring in reinforcements. This meant that Allied planes could operate close to their airfields in southern England, and would lead the Allies quickly to the bases of Hitler's V1 missile-launching sites. For all these reasons the heaviest concentration of German troops in France lay in this area. Even after the attack on Normandy began, Fortitude South would work hard to convince Hitler that it was only a feint and that the Pas de Calais remained the real Allied target.

Fortitude North was aimed at persuading the Germans that Norway would be the target of significant diversionary attacks *after* the main invasion of Europe took place, and thus lead them to keep stationed there forces that they might otherwise deploy as reinforcements to France. This played on Hitler's known personal obsession with Norway. He had always described it as his 'Zone of Destiny', and permanently kept a huge army of some two hundred thousand men stationed there. At the beginning of May, thanks to Fortitude North, they were placed on a state of high alert, and in the middle of the month were reinforced by a first-class division. All resistance activities in Norway were brutally suppressed.

The Allies ingeniously deployed a multitude of techniques to implement deception. False army wireless messages, dummy aircraft, tanks, factories and oil tanks, active disinformation planted in newspapers, rumours deliberately spread overseas by British diplomats and intelligence agents were all skilfully deployed in a highly co-ordinated campaign to create in German minds a thoroughly misleading picture of Allied troop dispositions and intentions. In Scotland an entire fake army ostensibly headed for Norway was created out of decoys, false wireless messages and articles planted in newspapers. British agents in Sweden spread rumours of an impending attack on Norway, and even deliberately played the stock market to support the deception. In England Shepperton Film Studios built huge fake oil storage tanks close to Dover, replete with pipelines, jetties, truck bays and anti-aircraft defences. Designed by the up-and-coming architect Basil Spence, the dummy complex was officially visited by King George VI, General Montgomery and Eisenhower, and rumours were spread that it formed the terminal of a huge pipeline under the Channel to provide fuel to the armies landing close to Calais.

The troops supposedly threatening the Pas de Calais were those of the First United States Army Group, or FUSAG. Consisting of both real and notional formations, FUSAG was under the supposed command of General George S. Patton, 'Old Blood and

Guts', one of the most colourful and swashbuckling of American generals, famous for his exploits in Sicily. In reality Patton was commander of American troops destined to fight in Europe well after D-Day. His notional army was based in Essex and Suffolk, with its headquarters in Chelmsford. Patton wasn't shy about getting himself into the newspapers and his presence there would be amply noted by German intelligence. Many Germans thought he was the best Allied commander of the war, and might well assume that he had been given the toughest job for D-Day.

Everything by now indicated to Eisenhower that the deception plan was working. He felt strongly that any alteration, such as that just suggested by Churchill, threatened its success.

Crucial to D-Day deception was the work of double agents. These were spies in Britain or other Allied countries whom the Germans thought they controlled, but who in fact were working for the Allies. Provided with items of carefully selected intelligence to feed back to the Nazis – some of it true, most of it false – they helped fix the false invasion picture desired by the Allied planners. These agents were run by Section B.1A of the Security Service, or MI5, guided by an expert Whitehall committee known as the Double-Cross Committee. As the name could be written 'XX' and this denoted 'twenty' in Roman numerals, this body was also known as the Twenty Committee. It worked hand in glove with the deception experts at Eisenhower's headquarters, and both Eisenhower and Churchill were briefed on its work.

An agent code-named 'Garbo' was the Twenty Committee's single most important double agent. It was he who would plant the crucial disinformation that would convince the Germans that the initial invasion was merely a feint. For two years they had been building him up as a credible source. They had every reason to believe he was trusted by the Germans. If they played their hand well, Garbo would ensure that the Germans remained in the dark even after Allied troops hit the beaches.

In his sixth-floor hideout on the rue des Écoles, Albert Grunberg spent the day as he usually did, reading the newspapers, devouring a treatise on a philosopher such as Plato or enjoying a novel by a popular novelist like Jules Verne. He regularly tuned in to his small radio. By this time the occupants of the three neighbouring flats on his floor had been told of his presence by the concierge, Madame Oudard, and become silently complicit. Monsieur Bon, next door, had drilled a tiny hole through the wall from his kitchen and pushed through an electric lead to give Grunberg light to read by and power for his radio, which, for security, he listened to through earphones. He knew nothing about the upstairs neighbours, and on the fifth floor there were suspected collaborationists. Music and drama programmes kept him entertained during the long hours alone, while news bulletins kept him up to date. Yesterday he'd heard a national broadcast by Marshal Pétain, the aged Vichy leader. Dark days lay ahead, warned Pétain, but France should realise that the Germans were protecting Europe against Bolshevism. Calls to support the Resistance were not true French voices. If heeded, they would plunge the country into disorder.

Grunberg still remained in the dark about the fate of his children, Robert, aged twenty-five, and Roger, eighteen. But Pétain and all he stood for was anathema to him. For the victor of Verdun in the First World War who had signed the armistice with Hitler in the Second, he had nothing but contempt – 'the chief of traitors' he called him. He also suspected that the regime sometimes welcomed the civilian casualties of Allied bombing so as to denounce the barbarism of the 'Anglo-Americans' and to bolster its weakening support in the country.

Above all, he was a prime victim of the fervent anti-semitism of Vichy. It had been Pétain's police, after all, and not those of Hitler, who had come for him on that fateful September morning almost two years before, ringing his door bell at five minutes past eight in the morning just as he was finishing his breakfast cup of coffee, brusquely demanding to see his identity papers and asking him if he was a Jew. 'Yes,' he'd replied, 'but my wife and children are French.' It made not a jot of difference. 'Get a couple of blankets and two pairs of shoes and socks and follow us,' came the churlish reply, before courage had given him wings and he'd sprinted past them, leaped down the two floors of stairs to the outer door, run along the street to number 8 and then clambered breathlessly up to the little sanctuary where he'd been hiding ever since. The little chambermaid's room had been occupied by Madame Oudard's teenage daughter, Lucienne, known to everyone as Lulu, and had a comfortable large bed. Early on, before Robert had left to join his brother Roger in Chambéry, father and son had sometimes slept there together, rather than at home, in case the police came for them in the night.

At the time of the armistice, in June 1940, there were more than three hundred thousand Jews in France. Almost immediately the Vichy regime launched a campaign to marginalise and persecute them. First they had to register with the authorities, then they lost their businesses, were squeezed out of the professions or excluded from universities. Then they began to disappear, and in 1942 over forty thousand had been deported to the extermination camps of Auschwitz and elsewhere. By now, in the spring of 1944, the SS had virtually taken over the hunt for Jews in France from the Vichy authorities. They were helped in their efforts by zealots in the Milice, a French paramilitary force formed by the ardent pro-Nazi and First World War veteran Joseph Darnand. These were the most dangerous enemies of the Jews in France, because bluffing or fooling them was virtually impossible. Besides, they possessed the ferocity and fanaticism of true witch-hunters.

As D-Day approached, the SS was intensifying its efforts, and the first four months of the year had seen more arrests of Jews than during any comparable period the year before. Jews were now being rounded up from old people's homes, hospitals, prisons and children's homes, regardless of citizenship or passport. Previously distinctions had been drawn between Jews with French citizenship and other nationalities, or between Jews who had fought for France in the First World War and those who hadn't, or between converts and non-converts. Now, however, the SS was hunting every Jew.

Grunberg knew he would never be safe until the Allies liberated the city, the Germans were expelled and Vichy was overthrown. Just today he'd had yet another reminder of relentless anti-semitic persecution. Since his disappearance the French authorities had been trying to confiscate his business. Only the strenuous efforts of his wife, Marguerite, had prevented them. A friend with some legal expertise had been helping her. '*Un homme brave*,' he wrote in his diary. One day he would like to thank him. When he was free again.

Locked twenty-four hours a day in his cell in Oslo, Peter Moen had no way of knowing what was happening in the outside world, except for the occasional rumour seeping through the prison. He wasn't optimistic. 'I don't reckon with the war finishing this year,' he'd noted in March. 'The tempo is not good enough.' He was forty-three years old. In peacetime he had been an actuary with the Idun Life Insurance Company. For seventy-five days after his arrest he'd been held in solitary confinement. Several times he'd contemplated suicide. Then, in April, he'd been moved into cell D35 with two other men. One was a sailor, the other a gardener and stonemason. Both were men in their twenties. Afraid he couldn't trust them, he'd temporarily stopped writing his diary. Gradually he'd tested them out until he was satisfied they would keep his secret. He'd started up again with tack and toilet paper only ten days ago.

Today was the one hundred and sixteenth day of his incarceration. The cell was an improvement on the old one. It was on the third floor of the prison, so the sunshine penetrated and it was always fairly light. In solitary he'd been down on the ground floor, where the light never pierced the gloom and the walls were filthy. Still, everything was relative, and conditions remained harsh. He couldn't send or receive letters, have his clothes washed or repaired, or read and smoke. A bucket in the corner served as a toilet for the three of them, and with the warmer summer nights its stench, especially at night, could be overpowering.

Moen was still brooding over the iniquities of the prison system. The guard's brutal slap on the face the day before still rankled. So did the frequent small humiliations sadistically heaped on him by the prison guards' supervisor, a disagreeable man he'd nicknamed

'Donnerwetter' ('thunderstorm'). Knowing Moen's craving for tobacco, he liked nothing better than to blow smoke in his face every time they met. Even good-hearted guards felt they had to play tough. When one of the prisoners had asked one for some tobacco, the guard told him he would like to but didn't dare because – and here he made as if to tear off all his buttons from his uniform jacket – he'd be '*ganz nackt*', completely naked. Moen and his cellmates had then been accused, without reason today – unlike the day before – of playing cards. The guards, themselves at the bottom of the prison hierarchy, had to have someone to work out their fear and resentment on – the prisoners, the defenceless.

'Altogether despicable' pricked Moen into the coarse grey paper. Then he rolled it up and slipped it down the ventilation shaft. That night, as on every other night, he and his cellmates put up the blackout curtain with all its tacks in place. By 8 p.m., as regulations required, they were in bed.

Early that morning, several hundred miles further south behind enemy lines, SOE agent Sydney Hudson straddled his bike and made for the safe house where the agents who'd dropped the night before were being temporarily kept, near the town of La Flèche, just south-west of Le Mans. The leader of the reception committee told him that some of the containers and packages dropped at the same time had gone astray and been picked up by the Germans. Weapons and explosives, as well as one of the three agents, had made it safely to a nearby farm. The other two agents were in the room next door. Hudson opened the door. Instantly he recognised both of them.

Hudson was an SOE veteran on his second mission in France. On the first, also code-named 'Headmaster', he'd been quickly arrested by the Vichy police outside Clermont-Ferrand and sentenced to five years' hard labour. He'd spent fifteen months in prison, much of it in solitary, before managing to escape in a mass breakout and get himself back over the Pyrenees and through Spain via Gibraltar to Britain. Officially code-named 'Albin', he was leader of the Headmaster circuit, with the mission of building up a net of Resistance activists and obtaining weapons to equip them. When D-Day came, Hudson and his circuit were to target the telephone, cable, road and rail links that radiated outwards from Le Mans, a major communications centre for the Germans and headquarters of the 7th Army, commanded by General Friedrich Dollman. Headmaster was just one of dozens of SOE circuits tasked with causing maximum disruption behind enemy lines when the invasion troops landed. Just to the north of Headmaster but completely unknown to Hudson, the 'Scientist' circuit was operating in Normandy itself. Here, under the command of a Mauritian-born officer named Claude de Baissac, assisted by among others his sister, Lise, similar plans were being prepared to harass the Germans on and after D-Day. Elsewhere, throughout central and southern France, plans were afoot to cause maximum disruption in the critical early hours and days of the landings.

Hudson and his wireless operator, George Jones, had parachuted in just south of the area on Easter Sunday. Jones was also on his second mission to France. On his first, also with Hudson, he and the group's leader, Brian Rafferty, had initially escaped Hudson's fate and during the following five months Jones had kept in close contact with London by wireless telegraphy and laid the foundations of a major Resistance network in the Massif Central. This was despite a serious road accident in which he fractured his skull, broke a leg and lost the sight in his right eye. Then he and Rafferty had also fallen into Gestapo hands. Rafferty had been tortured and executed. Jones had been badly beaten up, but made a dramatic escape from prison in Vichy by jumping out of a window. Not surprisingly, he hadn't been too keen to return to France. But when Hudson asked if he'd be his operator again he'd said, 'Yes – provided you can get me plenty of cigarettes.' He smoked Gauloises heavily and liked to gamble on the horses. He also had a personal and family reason for returning to France. His father was detained in the notorious Drancy camp, outside Paris. Jones had in mind that, somehow, after the Allies landed, he might be able to rescue him.

Over the previous two weeks Hudson and Jones had established contacts, found a secure base and located safe houses, established wireless contact with Britain and taken delivery of air drops. The first drop, which brought enough Sten guns and explosives for a small army, had been heralded by a coded message broadcast over the BBC: '*L'oncle Bob mange la crème*' ('Uncle Bob eats cream'). It was more apt than London probably imagined. At his château base, Hudson enjoyed mounds of butter and cream cheese every morning for breakfast.

Of the two people now standing in front of him, he had last seen the man, a strongly built fellow in his early twenties, in Gibraltar, one of the group he'd escaped with. A natural risk-taker, and almost foolishly brave, he was called Raymond Glaesner, a native of Alsace. The SOE had given him the code-name 'Alcide'. But he was always known by his nickname, 'Kiki'. Not surprisingly for an Alsatian, he was completely bilingual in French and German. His wartime fate had been determined by one of those seemingly minor episodes that can so easily change a life. Eager for some sort of action, Glaesner had been undecided what to do. Walking along the street one day in his home town, he'd been roughly pushed off the pavement by a German. He'd lashed back, hitting the man in the face, and run off at top speed. After that he'd joined the Resistance, only to be caught up in the huge round-ups of 1943, which was when he'd first caught Hudson's eye.

With Glaesner was the woman Hudson had been promised by Baker Street. Straight away he recognised the twenty-year-old blonde with brown eyes and a trim figure. They'd met weeks before in London, at 32 Weymouth Street, the hostel used by the SOE's French section agents while waiting for their missions, and had been struck by her good looks. Then they'd gone their separate ways, but she'd lingered in his mind ever since.

Sonia d'Artois was fluent in French and English. Despite her British parentage – her father was an RAF group captain, her mother a Scot from Aberdeen – she had grown up in the South of France, in Cagnes-sur-Mer, and attended school in nearby St Paul-de-Vence. On the outbreak of war she'd returned to Britain and enrolled in the Women's Auxiliary Air Force, or WAAF. As soon as she was in uniform she applied for a job where she could use her language skills. Looking for adventure, she'd joined the SOE with enthusiasm. Her code-name was 'Blanche'.

Hudson had begun to feel that his progress in the Sarthe *département*, where he now found himself, was slow. For this he largely blamed the collapse of a large SOE circuit in France the year before, which had delivered hundreds of resisters into the hands of the Gestapo. The disaster had affected all areas of France, including Sarthe, and potential recruits were simply afraid. Also, life was comfortable and there was plenty of food. He needed all the help he could get. He was delighted to have Blanche to help him.

Private First Class Bill Tucker had been based at his training camp outside Quorn, in Leicestershire, since arriving on a snowy February day from a base outside Belfast. Yesterday he had been sealed off from the outside world. Now, as dawn was breaking, his regiment, the 505th Parachute Infantry of the 82nd Airborne Division, left the camp to be loaded on to trucks waiting outside the gate. It was goodbye to the White Horse Inn and the Bull's Head, the warm beer and games of darts, the boisterous weekends in Leicester or Loughborough, the friendly barmaids.

He was wearing full uniform and carried all his equipment. But the shoulder patch that identified his division, with its distinctive white letters 'AA' on the red and blue background and the single word 'Airborne' arcing above it, was covered. No one was supposed to know they were on the move. But word had got out and local people stood in front of their houses or peered through the windows to watch them leave, waving goodbye and wishing them well.

General Matthew Ridgway, commander of the 82nd, had given them a pep talk a few days before. The Hollywood-handsome Ridgway was a hero to Tucker, a soldier's soldier and a colonel's son who'd followed his father through West Point to a glittering career in the US Army. He demanded much but delivered more. In Sicily he led from the front, jumping with his men and showing almost reckless courage on the ground. 'There's a right way, a wrong way and a Ridgway' went the joke; one of his subordinates described him as hard as flint. His charisma quickly melted the youthful carapace of hard-boiled cynicism cultivated by the tough young soldiers under his command. To Tucker he was like a father who could do no wrong.

As he listened to Ridgway speak in his distinctive New York accent, he scribbled down notes. 'You men are to take part in a tremendous act in the history of mankind,' Ridgway told his men. 'You may not realise that at this time but you will realise it in time to come. You will be among the first few soldiers to land in the greatest invasion of history. Some of you will die but your missions will be remembered and cherished. Those who live will remember for the rest of your lives your part in this necessary, noble, and historical effort. You are assured by me that you will be on the winning side. All I can ask is that you do your best, and I will do mine. God be with each and every one of you.' Ridgway was a fan of Rudyard Kipling. Tucker felt his confidence rise several notches.

The 82nd was known as 'the All-American', because when it was formed it contained men from every state of the Union. Its great rival, the 101st Airborne, was nicknamed 'the Screaming Eagles'. Together they formed the elite of the US armed forces, with their calf-length jump boots and the coveted silver parachute badge on their breast. But the 82nd had the honour of being the elder of the two, the first airborne division in the history of the US Army. Within it, the fiercely independent 505th Parachute Infantry regiment stood out as the toughest and best-trained of the lot.

Colonel James ('Slim Jim') Gavin, its commander, was every bit as brave and resolute as Ridgway. Not only that, but at thirty-seven Gavin was to become youngest general in the American army since the Civil War. Like Tucker, this Brooklyn-born son of impoverished Irish immigrants had supplemented the family income with hours of paper rounds before signing on for the army at eighteen. All his men were volunteers, glad to get the $50 a month extra jump pay and three square meals a day. Most of them came from the wrong side of the tracks'. Many were farm boys from the South, 'barefooted shit-kickers', for whom getting up at 5.30 a.m. meant an extra hour's sleep in the morning. Their average age was twenty-four. Every one, it was said, was a replica of Gavin. The macho spirit was shared by officers and men alike. To show how tough they were, usually after a few drinks in a bar or dance hall, they'd jump off the balcony or exit out of a second-floor bathroom window.

Morale was high when they left in the convoy of covered trucks. Tucker had spent a lot of his time since enlisting back in 1942 being shunted around. He'd crossed the Atlantic crammed with twelve thousand others into the hold of a decrepit liner grandly named the *George Washington*, as part of a seventy-ship convoy. It was so crowded that they had to sleep in shifts, one night on deck and the next in a bunk. To get any of the inadequate meals he had to queue for two hours. After a couple of days the hold stank so much of food and stale sweat that he'd taken to spending most of his nights on deck gazing at the phosphorescent fish as they skimmed the waves alongside. The ship was a former German liner, the SS *Bismarck*, which had been seized for reparations at the end of the First World War. Now it was carrying Americans who believed they would deliver a knockout blow to Germany. Later, after landing at Casablanca, Turner had endured a four-hundred-mile rail journey through the searing Moroccan heat in a 'forty and eight' freight wagon, so called because they were designed to hold either forty men or eight horses. There was no proper room to sleep, move or do anything else. Toilet facilities were wherever they stopped in the desert.

After that, the move from Quorn was almost luxurious. Now Tucker arrived at what was to be his final destination in England before D-Day: a large hangar at the huge US air base at Cottesmore in Rutland, England's smallest county. A company of men occupied each quarter of the hangar. There were comfortable cots, and the food was good and plentiful, as it was for all the men destined for the invasion. Security was watertight. Barbed wire and military police sealed their world. No other base personnel were allowed to come close to them, and they were forbidden to talk to the cooks. Tucker wondered why. He felt like a prisoner. Neither he nor any of his fellow paratroopers had yet been told where they were going. They speculated endlessly among themselves. The Netherlands? France? Yugoslavia? Tucker always liked to take a long shot. Besides, ever since being a kid he'd always liked the idea of one place in particular. So he opted for Norway.

In Madrid, the Abwehr officer Karl Kühlenthal was feeling pleased. His agent Arabel in Britain had recently been given a job at the Ministry of Information in London. It was here that propaganda for European countries under occupation was being prepared. Arabel was now studying British and American propaganda directives prepared earlier for the North African landings and the Italian campaign. It was quite obvious, claimed Arabel, that these had been drafted in order to trick the Germans, and there was a lesson to be learned from this. If an Allied landing in Europe was followed by a Ministry directive forbidding any speculation about a second landing, it could be safely assumed that one would take place.

Five days before, Arabel told Kühlenthal, he had signed the Official Secrets Act, a sure sign he'd have access to precious information. Now, on Whit Monday, he sent a signal telling Kühlenthal all about his study of the previous directives, and adding a lengthy description of the Political Warfare Executive, the agency charged with all foreign propaganda based on directives from the War Cabinet, the Foreign Office and SHAEF. Kühlenthal had every reason to feel pleased. At last they'd got a man on the inside.

Arabel had recently revealed a second ace up his sleeve. Back in 1942 he had reported his successful recruiting of a man he referred to as 'Agent Four'. This was a Gibraltarian who had taken a dislike to the British after being forcibly evacuated, along with the rest of the civilian population, from his home on the Rock. He was now in Britain, working as a waiter for the NAAFI in a secret underground base in the famous underground caves at Chislehurst, in Kent. At the beginning of May he'd contacted Arabel asking to meet him at

Winchester railway station. There he'd revealed that he had just been posted to a new military camp in Hampshire. It housed the 3rd Canadian Infantry Division, and the troops had just been issued cold rations for two days, and also lifebelts. It was obvious, Agent Four commented, that the invasion was imminent.

A small but convincing detail he provided was that the troops had also been given vomit bags. So impressed were Kühlenthal's masters in Berlin that they made sure that the report went all the way to the top, to none other than Hitler himself. It was yet another pleasing sign that the Abwehr's sources were trusted at the highest level in the German High Command.

What was the name of the camp in Hampshire? Arabel asked Agent Four. To this query, he received the answer: Hiltingbury. It was the very same camp where Glenn Dickin and the Regina Rifles were now waiting for their invasion orders.

3

HIT THE BEACH HARD
Tuesday 30 May

'In Italy the Allied advance is continuing at full speed and they're only thirty kilometres from Rome. Still no news of the children.' In his stuffy chambermaid's room Albert Grunberg was seriously worried. Not a letter, not a phone call, not even a telegram had reached his wife from Chambéry since the bombing, and he was imagining the worst. The kindly Madame Oudard hadn't helped by bursting into tears when she'd heard the news. It would be ironic if his two sons were killed in what they thought was a safe haven – and at the hands of the Allies, not the hated Boche.

Not that the twentieth-century world offered many sanctuaries. He had thought that France was safe when he'd arrived in Paris as a fourteen-year-old orphan from Romania on the eve of the First World War, happy to leave behind him the waves of anti-semitism that periodically swept through this unstable Balkan country. He'd settled down, married a Frenchwoman, built up a successful hair-dressing business and had two sons, Robert and Roger. Then, abruptly, his new world had imploded in 1940 with the arrival of the Germans and the compliant Vichy regime. Where was safe these days?

The paralysing lack of news about his sons came as a terrible blow. Psychologically he'd recently started readying himself for the day when once again he could walk with them openly in the sunshine down the rue des Écoles, taking the air, politely raising his hat, and saying hello to his neighbours. Madame Oudard had noticed the change in April when he'd started wearing a tie again. Sometimes he would even greet her on one of her clandestine short visits, wearing his hat as well, just as though he was about to pop outside and buy a newspaper, a portly figure with carefully combed black hair, a neatly trimmed moustache and little round spectacles perched on the end of his nose. Was it all going to come to nothing? Would his personal liberation prove empty after all? Would he be walking down the sunlit street only to be wearing a black armband of mourning? That is, of course, if someone didn't actually betray him first. Just in case, Madame Oudard had located a second emergency hideaway in a tiny cupboard on the first floor of the building. In the meantime he could only wait, hope and be patient.

On the other side of the Channel, Veronica Owen enjoyed a slack morning. She lay out in the afternoon sun reading Lawrence of Arabia's letters, mostly about the writing of his classic memoir *The Seven Pillars of Wisdom* and the period he worked with the then Secretary of War and Air, Winston Churchill, immediately after the First World War. 'More and more fascinating,' she scribbled in her diary. In the early evening the bus came to Heathfield and shuttled her off to Fort Southwick for a night's watch. It lasted till four in the morning; a long night, but she found it pleasantly quiet. Admiral Ramsay noted a similar temporary lull in the tempo of naval activity, and at last found time to thank the sixty or so Wrens at Southwick House for all their hard work. 'Only a few days to go and thankful for that,' he jotted in his diary.

Veronica's choice of reading revealed an adventurous and restless spirit. The war had already changed her. At the time of Dunkirk and the collapse of France she'd been fifteen years old and attending Sherborne, a typically regimented girls' boarding school in Dorset. Soon after, like thousands of other British schoolchildren, she had been evacuated to the safety of Canada and Toronto. 'It's like running away,' she'd protested furiously at first, until her father pointed out that she'd be one less mouth for the transatlantic convoys to feed. Along with thirty other girls from Sherborne she'd joined Branksome Hall, a girls' school in the city.

She'd loved the Atlantic crossing. She'd always wanted to go to sea, and even when it was rough she enjoyed the excitement of being totally surrounded by the vast expanse of the Atlantic waves. In Canada she was overwhelmed by the welcome: milk and biscuits in Montreal, the sleeping car that delivered her to Toronto, the kindness of the family that took her in, the novelty of it all, the Mounties with their red uniforms, the strangeness of little things like saying 'gas' instead of petrol, cars driving on the right, cereals, oranges and buns with honey for breakfast. There was less routine and discipline, more freedom and open hospitality, more frankness of speech. Relaxation in England consisted of country walks and reading. In Toronto it was movies, meals in restaurants, shopping and late nights out. Her hosts even had a Chinese cook, and she found the meals delicious. But she felt a constant need to be doing something concrete to help the war effort, so in her free time she occasionally worked for the Red Cross. The young woman who returned to Britain two years later at seventeen and a half – the earliest age at which she could join the Wrens – was far more grown up than her parents expected.

In Canada she'd consciously played at being more English than the English, adopting little stratagems such as saying 'actually', 'jolly good' and 'awfully', symbolic small ways of showing patriotic solidarity with war-battered Britain. Being far from home had heightened her patriotism. 'England is the most splendid, fine and most loveable country in the whole world,' she enthused to her parents shortly after getting back. By then she was taking her course on naval coding at HMS *Cabbala*, the Navy's aptly named shore-based training establishment for Communications at Lowton St Mary's, near Warrington, in Lancashire: the Cabbalists were a medieval sect who attached great significance to numbers and spent their lives decoding what they believed were symbolic passages in the Bible. On top of her training, Veronica's transatlantic crossings had given her a picture of what naval signals involved.

No doubt, too, they explained her outburst to her fellow Wrens the day before about the vital role of coding. At Branksome Hall she'd been head girl of the Sherborne contingent, and never quite lost the habit of being in charge. 'Try again,' she'd urge, frowning, when one of her watch couldn't quickly complete a decode, or 'Have you played with it? Just coax it along a little.' When they weren't simply calling her Vron, her friends would sometimes tease her that she was their 'nagger number one'.

Sonia d'Artois was barely a year older than Veronica. But her dare-devil spirit was already poised more precariously on the dangerous edge of things. She was still at the safe house, resting after her para-chute drop into France. She'd gone through the regular SOE training for agents. At the five-day introductory course at the requi-sitioned English country house where instructors weeded out the unsuitable and subjected the others to a battery of psychological and personality tests, she'd been awakened roughly at night to see if she spontaneously spoke English or French, preparation for some sudden nocturnal swoop by the Gestapo or the Milice. They'd tested her observation powers by suddenly asking how many pic-tures hung on the wall by the stairs and what they depicted. A psychologist had shown her ink blots and observed how she made sense of them. She'd described it as 'the Madhouse'. Then she'd gone to the remote highlands of Scotland for six weeks to toughen up physically. They taught her how to map-read, how to kill a sentry silently using a double-edged knife or with the edge of her open hand, and how to assemble and dismantle Sten guns and weapons of all kinds and nationalities, including German ones, because the French Resistance often had to rely on captured weapons.

What she'd enjoyed most was learning about explosives. How to make them, what sort of ingredients she might easily find in France, how much to use to blow up a railway line or bridge; where best to place a charge so as to get the biggest bang for the buck; what sort of detonator to use and how to set the timer to give her enough time to get away; all the exact and demanding detail that meant the difference between success and failure. This, with all the risk it involved, she had loved. So much so that she'd decided to make it her speciality. After that, at the SOE's 'finishing school' on the sprawling Beaulieu estate in the New Forest, she'd been briefed carefully on personal security: how to detect if she was being followed, tricks for throwing off a tail, how to stand up to questioning and interrogation, what to try to do if tortured (hold out for forty-eight hours to let the others get away). Then she'd done some practice parachute drops.

It had all finished with an exercise in Manchester in which she had to rent a room pretending to be a young widow with a small son. To authenticate her cover, she carried a photograph of a child; in reality it was of her younger brother, Michael. Returning one night, she'd discovered her room had been ripped apart and the mattress slashed open by someone searching for incriminating documents or secret codes. She'd been arrested and interrogated by men posing as Germans who threatened her with torture. It was tough and realistic, but she hadn't cracked, and finally she'd been given her mission.

Now she was facing her first real-life test. It was already off to a poor start. The container full of authentic French clothes she'd planned on wearing had landed on a road and been picked up by a German convoy. So the Germans already knew they were looking for a woman. She tried not to dwell on the methods of torture she'd been told about at Beaulieu and reminded herself what she'd been instructed: that the best security was to know as little about the work of other agents or Resistance groups as possible. That way she couldn't betray what she didn't know. Meanwhile she had to get out of the clothes she was wearing. For one thing they were too damned hot. For another they were a giveaway to any suspicious German or collaborator – and there were plenty around.

Sydney Hudson had an idea. He'd met a couple of businessmen in Le Mans and one of them ran a small clothing store. He'd ask them for help. In the meantime they decided to lie low for another day or so until the Germans gave up looking for them. Then they'd head out to Hudson's château hideaway and start work on their D-Day plans.

Bill Tucker was spending his first day quarantined behind barbed wire at Cottesmore airfield. Half his regiment had been sent to Spanhoe, a temporary wartime airfield ten miles away. Contact between the two camps was strictly forbidden except for the two chaplains, one Protestant, one Catholic. As the big day approached, the two clergymen were busier than usual. Parked on the runways stood seventy C-47s, the twin-engined wartime Douglas DC3s that would carry the men to their destination. Painted in camouflage khaki, the planes wore three broad white stripes on each wing, the Allied recognition signal for D-Day. Each carried a 'stick' of eighteen men. At the two airfields a total of some two thousand men of the 82nd Airborne were getting ready to go.

Most of the day Tucker spent going over his equipment, checking it was all there and in good shape, and helping make up bundles of supplies that would be dropped along with him. His special job was to work an LMG 42, a light machine gun, which came with its separate tripod. After the drop, he'd be one of a two-man team required to operate the weapon, one man carrying the tripod and ammunition in a bandolier around his neck, the other the barrel. When they got tired, they'd swap. Altogether it weighed about thirty pounds, and for the drop itself was packed in a special equipment bundle slung under the C-47's fuselage.

Parachutes came in a multitude of colours. Tucker's main parachute was khaki, while his reserve parachute, worn in front, was white. A red parachute meant ammunition. Blue indicated medical supplies. Food was yellow. The different colours made identification quick and easy at the drop site. They made the landing sites resemble colourful fields of flowers. Speed of recognition was of the essence in the first confused moments of battle.

The list of Tucker's own personal equipment for the drop was formidable. First there was his jump suit, olive-green uniform, camouflaged helmet, main parachute, reserve parachute, boots, gloves and Mae West life jacket. Then came his Browning automatic rifle, a Colt 45 pistol, knives for cutting himself free from his harness on landing as well as close combat, several rounds of ammunition, an aluminium water bottle in a canvas cover, a first-aid kit that included a couple of morphine needles, a gas mask, three days' supplies of rations, several hand grenades tucked into the two slanted pockets on his chest and the reinforced pockets on his hips, a blanket, a change of socks and underwear, and a couple of cartons of cigarettes. The load almost doubled his weight. But it guaranteed that in the first few hours after landing he would be essentially self-sufficient. Unlike the regular infantry, paratroopers lacked any immediate back-up of supplies and had to take everything with them they could. There lay the real risk, because the enemy would be well entrenched and supplied with heavy artillery. Paratroopers were men who were up against the odds, and knew it.

Finished with his checking for the day, Tucker spent a quiet evening while other members of I Company played volleyball or indulged in high-stakes craps or poker. Rummaging around in a Red Cross box at the back of a hangar he'd picked up a book entitled *A Tree Grows in Brooklyn*, by the American writer Betty Smith. He decided he'd while away his wait at Cottesmore by reading it. Back home it was a best-seller. The fictionalised story of an impoverished German-Irish girl growing up in the ethnic melting pot of Brooklyn during the First World War, it was a book about courage and survival and never giving up. Tucker thought it terrific. It occupied the rest of his spare time until he left. He still had no idea where he was headed, or even when he would go.

Yet, even as he was checking his gear, the cancellation of the 82nd Airborne Division's D-Day mission was under active discussion.

Dwight Eisenhower spent the morning at SHAEF headquarters at Bushy Park, just outside Kingston. Code-named 'Widewing', it was a hurriedly thrown together complex of Nissen huts, tents and improvised brick buildings. Ike's own office had a tin roof, cracked linoleum, peeling paint, concrete floors and flickering fluorescent lights. Tucked away in a corner of the site, it highlighted the loneliness of his position as Allied Supreme Commander. Sometimes visitors found him putting an imaginary golf ball across the floor of his office to relieve the stress.

Today was one of the worst so far for lonely decisions. For the last few days one of his chief deputies had been challenging a key part of the D-Day plan. Air Vice Marshal Trafford Leigh-Mallory, his British tactical air commander, had become alarmed by intelligence reports about German troop movements into the invasion area. Rommel had moved his 91st Infantry Division uncomfortably close to where the 82nd Airborne was scheduled to drop. Ike had already agreed that the drop site should be shifted further west. But Leigh-Mallory remained unhappy. The day before, at a stormy meeting at Widewing which Eisenhower had left to his deputy commander to handle, Leigh-Mallory had warned of disaster. Afterwards he'd telephoned Ike personally to emphasise his worries. 'Put it in writing', Ike replied.

At midday Leigh-Mallory's letter was hand delivered to Bushy Park. The D-Day air drops of both the 82nd and 101st Airborne Divisions should be cancelled, it repeated. If they weren't, Leigh-Mallory feared savagely high losses to the paratroopers, a 'futile slaughter' that would contribute nothing to the battle. The C-47s, he reminded Eisenhower, were unarmed and would be flying in full moonlight over German-controlled territory bristling with ack-ack guns. Fifty per cent of the paratroopers would be dead even before the landings began. After reading it, Eisenhower spent the afternoon secluded in Telegraph Cottage to think it all over.

'It would be difficult to conceive a more soul-racking problem,' he confessed later. If Leigh-Mallory was right, he would carry for ever on his conscience the 'stupid, blind' sacrifice of thousands of America's young men. Yet if he cancelled the air drops he would throw the entire carefully plotted D-Day plans in jeopardy. They'd been designed to seize the western end of the beachhead, securing the flank while the infantry fought its way ashore and throwing up a barrier to German reinforcements. Cancel the air drop and you could forget the entire landings. The risks simply had to be accepted. Besides, he suspected that Leigh-Mallory's protests were partly designed to cover himself against American losses. It was the last thing Eisenhower needed at this late hour, a team member going 'wobbly'. That evening he telephoned Leigh-Mallory and told him that the air drops were on. Then he dictated a formal letter confirming the decision. It was short and brusque, reminding his subordinate of the need to maintain morale among the troops and not depress them with pessimistic forecasts. They had a tough job to do but had to remain fired up. Sergeant Bill Tucker would be boarding his C-47 after all.

'I think at times I get a bit homesick,' Ike had written forlornly to George C. Marshall, the US Army's Chief of Staff in Washington earlier that month, 'and the ordinary diversions of the theater and other public places are denied me.' Playing solitary golf in his office was not enough to relieve the stress. He needed family close at hand. So Marshall had immediately agreed to his request to let his son and only child, John, join him at his headquarters. Eisenhower was looking forward to it. John was about to graduate from West Point and Ike had agreed to send a personal message to be read out to the graduating class on the big day itself – Tuesday 6 June.

Before retiring for the night he wrote a couple of personal letters to friends who had been in touch from the States. He also sent a letter to the Combined Chiefs of Staff in Washington emphasising the vital role of security in the days ahead. The Germans must continue to overestimate the number of men at his disposal so that they would mistakenly hold back troops to take care of the additional landings they thought would follow. And no suspicion should reach them of Allied plans to use artificial harbours instead of existing ports to get supplies ashore. Otherwise they might guess where the landings would take place. As D-Day approached, deception and security remained at the top of the agenda.

By now the whole of the United Kingdom itself was an armed camp almost as tightly controlled as those imprisoning Glenn Dickin and Bill Tucker. No news was to escape to the outside world that might give away the smallest clue about the nature and timing of Allied plans. It wasn't just foreign diplomats who suffered. Travel in and out of the country had virtually ceased and the few people who were permitted to do so had to pass intensive scrutiny. Overseas mail was heavily censored and international telephone calls and telegrams carefully monitored. The armed forces' security units stamped down hard on servicemen escaping or attempting to leave their camps, whether simply desperate for fish and chips and a beer, to meet up with a girlfriend or to desert.

MI5, Britain's security service, was especially vigilant. 'Loose Lips Sink Ships' proclaimed one common poster stuck up in factories around the country. When a trade unionist innocently gave a clue to a special D-Day-related shipping device he was working on, MI5 rapidly swooped down and interrogated him. It was precisely the kind of case that Eisenhower had in mind in alerting Washington. No damage was done and the man was cleared of any treacherous intent. But the case was potentially so serious that it was included in the regular monthly report MI5 sent directly to Churchill. These had begun the year before, initiated by Duff Cooper, who was then in overall charge of security. A close friend of Churchill, he'd been spending the weekend at Chequers, where he'd aroused the Prime Minister's curiosity with details of the double-cross game being played by MI5 against the Germans. Would he like a monthly report? wondered Cooper. Churchill said yes, and Cooper had spoken to the head of MI5, Sir David Petrie. Pointing out that such reports would not just keep Churchill informed but would also provide MI5 officers with morale-boosting evidence that their work was appreciated at the highest level, Cooper stressed that they should be kept short and 'confined to incidents of exceptional interest'. Since then Churchill had devoured the monthly reports. Now he was scanning them more closely than ever for any signs that D-Day might be at risk.

By this time the Prime Minister had returned to London from Chequers. The capital was back at work after the long weekend, and life outwardly appeared reassuringly normal. *The Times* reported an outbreak of foot and mouth disease among cattle in Yorkshire, an increase in the number of divorce cases, the sale of books from a country house under the hammer, and carried the usual quota of personal advertisements for nannies, used cars and colonic irrigation. It also featured an article discussing the relative merits of using rabbits, geese, tethered goats and hens for keeping grass short in the absence of petrol for lawnmowers. A nature piece on woodland birds anxiously wondered, 'Are Chiff-chaffs scarce this year?'

Churchill had weightier matters on his mind. To the outside world his address in the capital was 10 Downing Street. But in reality he spent much of his time immured in the vast underground bunker known as 'the Annexe', hidden just a hundred yards away beneath the Treasury building in Great George Street. Protected from bombs by five feet of reinforced concrete, the six-acre maze of rooms and corridors included sleeping accommodation for Churchill and his wife, as well as offices and bunks for his key military advisers. Here, too, were meeting rooms for pivotal committees such as the Joint Intelligence Committee, the Chiefs of Staff and the War Cabinet itself.

At 6.30 that evening Churchill sat down to chair a regular meeting of the War Cabinet, the select inner circle of his government. His military advisers had already been hard at work. The Chiefs of Staff and Joint Intelligence Committee held long discussions in the morning and the Cabinet Secretariat finalised a lengthy report on the measures put in place to protect the security of Overlord – most of them related to the restrictions on travel and communications initiated two months before.

As D-Day approached, the Prime Minister was in a tetchy and impatient mood. The first package of Ultra intercepts from C today had consisted mostly of frantic Wehrmacht messages from the Italian front reporting on the relentless advance towards Rome of Anglo-American forces and the increasingly desperate problems facing German troops as road and rail links were steadily cut by bombing. Instead of calming him, however, the reports only fired him up. Field-Marshal Sir Alan Brooke, Chief of the Imperial General Staff – Britain's top soldier – kicked off the War Cabinet's agenda by reporting on the splendid progress of General Sir Harold

Alexander's forces in Italy. Churchill responded, not with praise but with a demand for 'a scoop', meaning the instant capture of Rome. For Brooke, who was equally keyed up by the tension of impending events and suffered from an intense love-hate relationship with Churchill, it was simply too much, and he lost his temper.

Nor was Churchill's mood improved when they turned to the still simmering issue of the bombing of targets in France. Here, too, his daily intercepts had stirred him up, one of them being a report from von Rundstedt's headquarters outside Paris to the High Command in Berlin giving details of an Allied thousand-bomber raid on France just five days before. He and Tedder were still arguing about the policy. Although he found equally worried allies among his political colleagues, they were forced to accept that they would have to wait until they'd received an official report from SHAEF.

And that was Churchill's problem, the explanation for his worse than usual petulance. The simple fact of the matter was that military events were now out of his hands. He was a distant spectator of the battlefront in Italy and had little more than a front seat in the stalls for the Overlord drama now unfolding. Ike was directing, and the overture had already begun. It was noticeable, for example, that the Joint Intelligence Committee that morning in the Annexe hadn't even included D-Day-related intelligence on its agenda because that was now in the hands of the experts at Bushy Park.

Being in the audience rather than on stage for great historic events had never suited Churchill. Now that the stakes were so high he could hardly bear it, and sudden bursts of temper were common. Just two weeks before, at the final great five-hour briefing on Overlord held at St Paul's School, in Kensington, in front of King George VI and all the Allied top brass, Churchill had turned up, cigar in hand, but as one of the audience, not as a member of the cast. Eisenhower had opened the meeting and General Bernard Montgomery — the legendary 'Monty' of El Alamein, who had sent Rommel's men packing in the North African desert towards the end of 1942 and would command the Allied land armies in

France – had talked them through the strategy he'd mapped out to begin once the men hit the beaches. Churchill had merely asked one or two questions, and at the end grudgingly told Eisenhower that he was 'warming' to the project. Eisenhower was glad to have him on board. But it was obvious that Churchill was not in charge.

Yet at least there were political strings he could still pull. Here things were threatening to spin out of control; stormy weather lay ahead on more than the military front. And he knew that potentially it could wreck the entire enterprise.

It was exactly a year to the day since the tall, ungainly figure of General Charles de Gaulle had stepped from the aircraft that had taken him from exile in London to a dingy military airstrip outside Algiers. Since then he'd made the capital of French Algeria – still considered an integral part of metropolitan France – the headquarters of the *de facto* provisional government of France. His was a government-in-waiting which, when liberation came, would once again raise the tricolour above Paris. He'd outmanoeuvred his rivals, created a fighting force of some four hundred thousand Free Frenchmen overseas, and won the loyalty of resistance groups inside France itself. The desperate days of June 1940, when his lonely appeal from London through the BBC for his compatriots to continue the fight against Hitler had largely fallen on deaf ears, had faded into a distant memory. Now he stood poised to return in triumph as the undisputed leader of his country.

In Algiers, installed comfortably in Les Oliviers, a spacious three-storey villa overlooking the sun-drenched Mediterranean city, he had his immediate family around him: his wife, Yvonne, whose beloved home town of Calais, a mere twenty miles across the water from Dover, was regularly being hammered by Allied bombing; Anna, their sixteen-year-old younger daughter, afflicted with Down's syndrome, on whom they both doted; and Élizabeth, a lively young woman with an Oxford degree busy monitoring the foreign press for her father's government. Only their son, Philippe, was absent, on service with the Free French navy. Although the villa possessed a comfortable study, de Gaulle rarely worked at home. Instead he had his office in Les Glycines, a smaller villa closer to town, where he worked in cramped, stuffy conditions among a jumble of typewriters and camp beds.

This was where, just three days before in the afternoon, he'd received the British Ambassador on official business. Duff Cooper, Churchill's urbane former Minister of Information and the man who'd inaugurated the monthly MI5 reports for him, was a keen Francophile and friend of Free France. For weeks a troublesome question of major significance had been hanging unresolved between Algiers and London. What role would de Gaulle play in the D-Day enterprise? The Free French leader had not been involved in any of the invasion planning and remained ignorant of its date and location. Would he be told in advance, and if so, when? And what would happen when Allied forces began to liberate French soil? Would de Gaulle's provisional government simply take over, or would the Allies rule through a military government with its own temporary laws and currency? To most people the answers appeared simple. As the obvious national leader of France, de Gaulle should be told about D-Day and allowed to run the country as it was gradually freed from German rule. 'There is ourselves or chaos,' as Algiers put it.

Yet to Churchill and Roosevelt the issue was far from simple. The American President in particular was deeply hostile to de Gaulle and adamant that military government should be applied to liberated France. His view sprang partly from a legalistic doubt about de Gaulle's legitimacy, partly from advice by White House counsellors with past close connections to Vichy. But mostly it came from personal antagonism. De Gaulle was haughty, arrogant, demanding, difficult. To be a leader, he believed, was to be aloof. 'My own nature warned me and experience had taught me,' he wrote, 'that, at the summit, one can preserve time and strength only by remaining on the remotest heights.' It was also a matter of pride. France, a Great Power, had been humiliated by its collapse in 1940. In restoring its greatness, de Gaulle vowed that he would never stoop or beg, even when – indeed, especially because – he was so dependent on American and British assistance. Roosevelt, a cheery, 'slap-on-the-back' sort of politician, found this both incomprehensible and offensive.

Churchill had been driven almost mad by de Gaulle's obstinacy and intransigence, and at times came close to breaking completely with him. Yet deep in his heart he respected his courage in continuing the fight in 1940 and couldn't simply cast him aside. Churchill was now caught between Roosevelt and de Gaulle. For weeks he'd been prevaricating. But finally he'd agreed to invite de Gaulle to London and instructed Duff Cooper to give the French leader the news. But the British Ambassador had found de Gaulle in one of his volcanic bad moods. 'I had hoped he would be pleased,' he noted, 'but he . . . was as grumpy and sulky as usual, complaining bitterly about the intention of the American government to issue their own francs when they entered France.'

De Gaulle was still simmering in Algiers when the War Cabinet met. Churchill had not yet mentioned a date for the invitation, but he now told his colleagues that he was thinking of setting it for dawn on D-Day itself. As de Gaulle would need forty-eight hours' notice before leaving and would require twenty-four hours to reach Britain, he would arrive in London on D plus 3, when, Churchill promised, he would be taken 'fully into confidence'. This would prevent any risk of compromising the D-Day secret by the Free French, whose security had always worried the Allies.

But the idea got a sharp thumbs down from both the Foreign Secretary, Sir Anthony Eden, and Clement Attlee, the Labour Party leader and Deputy Prime Minister. Public and parliamentary opinion was heavily in favour of de Gaulle. Just that morning *The Times* had reported that the first French heavy bomber squadron to be formed in Britain was helping Bomber Command in its attacks on French targets, published a photograph showing de Gaulle shaking hands with pilots during a recent visit to a French squadron based in Italy, and referred disparagingly to the 'cobwebs of uncertainty and misunderstanding' disfiguring relations with Algiers. Both Eden and Attlee feared that Churchill's proposal would further inflame French resentment and make de Gaulle even more difficult to handle than ever. He should be in London before D-Day, Eden suggested, so that he would not fly off the handle when he heard of the landings and issue some inflammatory statement from Algiers. After a heated discussion Churchill backed down, although not before winning agreement that the Chiefs of Staff should comment on the security risks involved. The issue was merely postponed, not resolved. In Algiers, de Gaulle remained volatile and impatient, his arrival in London a potential bombshell under D-Day plans.

Later that evening, down in his bunker, Churchill turned to his second and third batches of Ultra intercepts from C. While they revealed satisfying chaos among Wehrmacht forces in Italy, including a severe shortage of fuel, a diplomatic intercept revealed some serious rifts inside the Yugoslav government-in-exile over Churchill's efforts to broker a compromise deal between King Peter and the communist leader, Marshal Tito. Yugoslavia was perilously close to open civil war, an ominous harbinger of the political tumult shortly to sweep the Balkans. But de Gaulle remained by far the more serious problem.

André Heintz had backed General de Gaulle from the beginning. The decision sprang from personal loyalties and the visceral patriotism that ran strong in his family. As a fifteen-year-old he'd spent five months learning English with a family in Bristol, an arrangement set up by his father, a classics master, with his counterpart at Bristol Grammar School. There they'd teased him about his name, nicknaming him '57' after the famous brand of tinned goods. Now, he secretly called his little crystal set '58'. He'd kept in touch with his Bristol friends, and felt ashamed that, with Pétain's 1940 armistice, France had abandoned its British allies. Living near the Normandy coast, he'd also watched the Germans preparing for their invasion of Britain over the summer of 1940, and was unimpressed. Many of the units were Austrian, men who had never even seen the sea and were terrified of it. He intuitively felt then that they'd never succeed, and that Britain would hold out. Memories of the stirring sound of the fife and drums of the Bristol school's Officer Training Corps would often flood back, strengthening his resolve to be worthy of his English friends.

He'd been initiated into resistance work in the autumn of 1940. A Canadian teaching at Caen University had introduced him to a fellow countryman, a Mademoiselle Arnaud, who was helping Allied airmen who'd escaped or evaded capture. She was also collaborating with a Polish chaplain, Father Makulec, who was busy with pastoral work among immigrant Polish workers in Normandy. That, and contacts with Polish refugee students at the university, had led André into working with the underground Franco-Polish network initiated by the priest. Makulec loathed the Germans. Once, in front of André's mother, he'd said: 'André, you know, if we don't want to have another war with the Germans before another twenty years, we must each kill three Germans before the war is over.' His mother, appalled, had told André never to see the priest again, but he'd disobeyed. Makulec had been contacted by Polish intelligence agents in France working with the British, and during the Blitz on London in 1940 had been asked to provide intelligence about the aerodromes being used by the Luftwaffe and the places they were hiding their bombers. One of André's first resistance missions took him to a farm close to Carpiquet aerodrome, just outside Caen. The farmer employed a Polish maid, and from German airmen coming for eggs and milk she and André had managed to glean some useful information about the planes and their targets.

He'd also learned to be agile. Makulec's network had been broken up in 1941, and soon afterwards André had joined the Organisation Civile et Militaire (OCM). This in turn was decimated by arrests in 1943, so he'd linked up with yet another, Libération Nord, adopting the pseudonym 'Théophile'. At the lycée where he taught he'd also organised a small group of teachers and assistants known as the Saint-Jo group, to circulate clandestine newspapers.

Today it was again very hot. The morning newspapers were full of stories of French cities being bombed. There was a thunderstorm, followed by some rain in the evening. Throughout the day air-raid warnings kept the city on edge.

André knew his family was more vulnerable than most. The military headquarters at the end of their street was home to General Richter, the commander responsible for defending the nearby coast. André had handed the exact map co-ordinates of the building over to his contact, the man he met every week or so at the station where the commuter train from Ouistreham arrived in Caen. Then they'd been sent on to London. One day, he guessed, the Allies would attack the headquarters. He could only hope their aim would be good. He kept the secret of what he'd done to himself; he didn't dare tell his parents or his sister.

He knew at first hand the risks he was running in working for the Resistance. Until the month before he'd been meeting inside the church of Saint-Sauveur with his principal contact, a fellow school-teacher named Alexis Lelièvre, who used the cover name 'Yvon'. They'd chosen the church because it was approached by three different streets so that each could use a different entrance. The 6.30 morning Mass was the best time, before they both went to work and before the Gestapo was up and active. Kneeling together, they'd discreetly exchanged messages. Yvon posed the questions, André provided the answers – mostly concerning what he'd noticed about German troops and vehicles while bicycling about the city.

Recently, during a family dinner, his father had asked about the day's news. Before André could answer, his sister chimed in that her classes had been cancelled. Why? asked her father. 'Because the Gestapo arrested our teacher,' she replied. André had felt himself go as white as the tablecloth and his throat constrict. He knew that her teacher was Yvon, his contact. And just that very morning, Yvon had failed to turn up for the usual morning meeting. They'd agreed that if one of them failed to arrive the other would wait for no more than fifteen minutes. André, however, had done what he shouldn't – he'd walked all around the church looking for his contact for longer than that. Then he'd returned home.

Trying desperately to behave normally, he'd carried on eating his dinner. That night he slept on the floor beside his bed fully dressed in case he needed to make a rapid escape. He never saw Yvon again. Since then he'd dealt with the man who came on the train from Ouistreham.

Rommel was frustrated. At 6.20 that morning he left his château at La Roche-Guyon at the head of a convoy of staff cars on yet another tour of inspection of his Atlantic Wall defences. Today he was going to watch a demonstration of multiple rocket launchers and smoke projectors at Riva-Bella, a beachside resort of small villas and houses on the Normandy coast next to Ouistreham. Situated at the mouth of the Orne canal linking Caen to the sea, it was an important strongpoint. Its casino had been fortified, obstacles and mines covered the beach down to the low water mark and every one hundred yards there was a bunker armed with cannon flanking minefields and trenches. A five-storey concrete bunker, nearly fifty feet high, dominated the skyline, its powerful rangefinder constantly scanning the sea approaches to the Bay of the Seine some twenty-five miles to the east.

His outing to the coast provided an all too graphic view of the catastrophic damage being inflicted by Allied bombers. Accompanying him were the principal officers under his command: General Dollman, commander of the 7th Army, whose area included the coast from Normandy to the mouth of the Loire; General Hans von Salmuth, in charge of the 15th Army protecting the Channel coast east and north of Normandy and up to the Netherlands, which, in Rommel's view, was most likely to be the invasion target; Admiral Theodor Krancke, the head of Navy Group West, headquartered at Paris; Vice Admiral Friedrich von Ruge, Rommel's own naval adviser; and General Erich Marcks, commander of the 88th Infantry Corps in Normandy. In the morning they drove through Mantes and the still smoking wreckage inflicted by overnight attacks on the small island in the middle of the Seine that linked the town's two bridges. The journey back after lunch – a typically spartan Rommel affair from a field kitchen – was constantly interrupted by air-raid warnings. The crossing at Mantes was knocked out only an hour after they passed over the river.

By the end of the day every bridge on the Seine between Elbeuf and Paris had been smashed into ruins. Two thousand American planes, including Typhoons, Thunderbolts and Mustangs, struck across northern France and Belgium, hitting not just the Seine bridges but also railway lines, aircraft factories, radio installations and aerodromes, and encountering little resistance from the Luftwaffe. All day the sun had shone once again from a clear blue sky with visibility perfect for Allied bombers. The wings and fuse-lage of these deadly aircraft heated up to unbearable temperatures. Pilots stripped off their clothes, flying almost naked, but the insides of their cockpits burned their bare skin, and when the planes landed back in England ground crews had to cool them down with buckets of water before handling them. Long-distance strategic bombers were also hammering cities and factories deep inside Germany and central Europe. 'At a cost that is not to be taken lightly,' wrote one war correspondent in *The Times* that day, 'the Allied Air forces are marking upon the map of Europe the lines that will frame the picture of the great campaign of liberation . . . The invasion of Europe, though not its occupation, is already in full process. The enemy at least has no illusions about the share of the air forces in this great plan.'

Certainly Rommel could see the results for himself. The demon-stration of rocket launchers at Riva-Bella had been a great success, making a powerful impression on its audience. But the deadly impact of Allied bombs and the obvious inability of the Luftwaffe to stop them was even stronger. When he finally returned that night to La Roche-Guyon, Rommel, humiliatingly, had to cross the Seine by boat.

Up at the Berghof, Hitler greeted his now regular midday visitor, his personal physician, Dr Theodor Morell. The chubby doctor had run a fashionable clinic for skin and venereal diseases in Berlin, and after receiving treatment from him for eczema Hitler had taken a shine to Morell's unorthodox treatments and patent medicines. The doctor could have lived in one of the surrounding chalets if he'd wanted to, like many of Hitler's acolytes. But he preferred to remain fifteen hundred feet lower down, ensconced in a comfortable hotel in Berchtesgaden, well beneath the mists that frequently eddied around the forested paths of the Berghof, and away from the smokescreens now regularly being produced to mask the landscape from Allied bombers.

Hitler was still suffering from insomnia, a lack of energy and tremors in his left leg. Since March Morell had been injecting him with his own patented multi-vitamin treatment, Vitamultinforte, as well as with intravenous shots of glucose and iodine and intramuscular shots of the male sex hormone Testoviran, concocted from bulls' testicles. The cumulative effect of all this medication was, according to medical experts, that Hitler's personality was liable to sudden changes: his eyes would flash dangerously, his language would become wild and his mood swings more violent than usual. Hitler also regularly provided Morell with samples of his faeces for analysis. A week before, the doctor had taken a cardiogram reading from his patient which appeared satisfactory.

Morell kept a diary in which he referred to Hitler simply as 'Patient A'. He also maintained index cards for each of his patients on which he kept a record of what he'd administered. Today he wrote down two simple words for Patient A: 'double glucose'. This was what he gave Hitler for extra calories and to strengthen his heart. Obviously the Führer was feeling more than usually tired.

He had plenty on his mind to exhaust him. Quite apart from the impending Allied invasion and the imminent collapse of Rome, he was still absorbing the latest humiliation at the hands of the Red Army on the Eastern Front, the collapse of Sevastopol. After a two-day onslaught by Stalin's forces Hitler had reluctantly ordered the evacuation of the fortress. But in the five-week battle for the Crimea, thousands of German troops had been taken prisoner and over seventy thousand killed.

Furious at his army leaders about the Crimean fiasco, he'd then had a major row with Goering and the air staff over the new Messerschmitt ME-262 jet fighter. Along with the V-1 flying bomb, this was one of the 'secret weapons' that he repeatedly talked of as war winners that he would unleash on the Allies. A revolutionary two-engined jet aircraft flying at speeds of over five hundred miles per hour, it far outstripped any existing Allied planes. It had been designed as a fighter, but Hitler, ever the obstinate autodidact, dreamed of turning it into a high-speed bomber that would bring the Allied invasion forces to a standstill. He'd ordered as much, but, in the labyrinthine murk of Third Reich bureaucracy and political power play, his wishes had been ignored. Exactly a week ago, standing in front of his picture window gazing out over the mountains, he'd flown into a rage and ordered bluntly that his orders be followed straight away. The next morning Goering had crept back to the Berghof with the news that this would involve a total redesign of the plane that would take at least five months. If Hitler had been counting on the ME-262 to stop the invasion in its tracks, then the Allies would have to oblige him by holding off on their assault for quite a while yet.

Combined with the Luftwaffe's woeful failure to fend off raids on German cities, Goering's abject confession about the ME-262 immediately prompted adoption of a desperate expedient. 'Terror from the air' would be met with 'people's justice', meaning that downed Allied aircrews could be killed without the perpetrators being punished. This, Hitler hoped, would kill two birds with one stone. It would both provide an outlet for popular anger about the air raids and seriously damage Allied aircrew morale. Goebbels had endorsed such a policy on the radio the previous month. But so far the German people had shown little inclination to follow it.

So today Hitler's secretary, Martin Bormann, sent to all Gauleiters, or district governors, throughout the Reich a secret letter headed 'Justice Exercised by the People against Anglo-American Murderers'. Bormann claimed that in recent weeks low-flying Allied planes had repeatedly strafed children in the street, women and children in the fields, farmers ploughing and civilian vehicles on the roads. Furthermore, he alleged, there had been several cases where the aircrew had had to make forced

landings or had baled out, and had then been lynched by the out-
raged public. 'No police or criminal proceedings,' concluded
Bormann, 'were lodged against the citizens involved.' It was a
clear instigation to murder. The message was passed down, by
word of mouth only, to local Nazi leaders.

Outside Nantes, Walter Schwender was still in a good mood,
enjoying the warm weather and swimming whenever he could.
He hadn't heard recently from his family and felt behind with the
news; letters were taking a couple of weeks to get through. When
they did, he knew they'd been censored, because they'd been specially stamped. All correspondence between the soldiers and their
families was scrutinised, and sometimes Walter took a small,
almost childlike delight in seeing how much he could get away
with. Back in 1942, when he'd first been sent to France, he'd
underlined certain letters in one of his messages home to spell out
the word 'Isoudun', meaning Issoudun, the small town in central
France where he'd been stationed before going on to the Atlantic
coast.

His mother also took risks. Just a week ago he'd received a letter
from her which prompted him to make the comment: 'They will
have had a surprise when they saw what kind of thing you wrote
about the SS. But you were absolutely right.'

Criticism of the SS across Germany was now seriously worrying
the Nazi security police as it scanned the private mails. Letters
home from front-line soldiers speaking of horrifying conditions
and heavy casualties, especially on the Eastern Front, were leading
families actively to discourage their sons from volunteering for
Himmler's Waffen (armed) SS. Originally intended as the Nazis'
internal shock troops, the SS had evolved into a powerful fighting
force with fully equipped divisions rivalling those of the army. To
their rugged fighting qualities they also brought the sleek fanaticism
of ideological conviction and they were inextricably implicated in
the criminal savageries inflicted on Jews and other civilians alike. In
the cruel and remorseless world of the Eastern Front, writes one
historian, 'the SS formations stormed through the steppes,

marshes, and forests of Russia, both heroes and victims of a ghastly chapter of human error and hallucinations'.

Walter's family was one of those all too aware of the price to be paid. His elder brother, Karl, had volunteered for the SS. Perhaps he'd been impressed by the propaganda the two of them had constantly heard during their time in the Hitler Youth. Hitler declared he wanted a youth before which the world would tremble. 'I want a violent, domineering, undismayed cruel youth. Youth must be all that. It must bear pain . . . The free, splendid beast of prey must once more flash from its eyes. I want my youth strong and beautiful. In this way I can create the new.' The Hitler Youth would provide a staging post into the party. 'Think German, act German,' he cajoled them.

But Karl was also strongly attracted by the career possibilities offered by Himmler's Blackshirts. After working in a pharmacy and learning about photography, he had decided he wanted to become a cameraman and signed up hoping to join a propaganda unit. Instead he soon found himself a front-line soldier in the Leibstandarte SS Adolf Hitler, the most memorable force in Nazi military history. Originally formed as Hitler's personal bodyguard, it had become an elite division of the Waffen SS and by 1943 had been re-equipped as a panzer unit.

'God is struggle and struggle is our blood, and that is why we were born,' ran one of the songs of the Hitler Youth. And that is why they died, too. By early 1943 Karl had been conscripted into a tank crew fighting off the Red Army encirclement of Kharkhov, in the Ukraine. General Paul Hausser, in command of the 2nd SS Panzer Corps, desperately sought Hitler's permission to withdraw his troops before they were slaughtered. Although Hitler, as he almost always did in such cases, refused, Hausser disobeyed and escaped the Soviet trap on 15 February. But it was too late for Karl. The day before, he was killed by a shell that hit his tank, and he joined the millions of other young Germans who died in the service of Hitler's manic vision. He was twenty years old. No wonder that in letters to Walter he had been urging him not to join the SS. 'My beloved Karl, killed in action 14 February 1943,' Walter scribbled on the back of the photograph he now carried around with him. But secure behind the Atlantic Wall, and still naively trusting in Nazi promises, he felt far removed from the dangers that had taken his brother.

By 6.30 that morning, as Rommel and his convoy were setting off for the Normandy coast, Peter Moen and his fellow prisoners of the Gestapo were awake and dressed in cell D35 ready for their inspection by the guards. He had suffered another bad night's sleep. The prison was at 19 Mollergaten, the former chief police station of Oslo, which had been taken over by the Germans. But the police still used the garages at the back, coming and going all night in their noisy, wood-fuelled cars, their drivers shouting and laughing and revving the engines. The only thing that helped was to stuff his ears with cotton wool. But even that didn't work too well.

Hitler's obsession with Norway had turned the country into an armed camp. The Fortitude North deception campaign only heightened German vigilance. In addition, Allied planes found rich pickings off Norway's coast. Just that morning *The Times* in London had described it as one of RAF Coastal Command's 'happy hunting grounds'. Germany desperately needed Swedish iron ore and Finnish nickel, which had to be carried by sea, while the huge German garrison needed constant supplies and ammunition. This seaborne traffic was giving the RAF many welcome opportunities to strike with torpedoes, bombs and rockets.

Nazi troops had invaded Norway and swept into Oslo in April 1940, a month before the Wehrmacht's full-scale assault on the Low Countries and France. The small Scandinavian nation had only gained full independence from Sweden in 1905, and was fiercely patriotic. Yet, ironically, it had also nourished the figure whose name became the byword for treason and collaboration in the Second World War, Vidkun Quisling. An embittered ex-army officer and founder of the Norwegian Nazi Party, Quisling was in league with Hitler and demanded his country surrender to the Germans. King Haakon VII and his government answered with a resounding no, then sailed to exile in Britain, as did thousands of other Norwegians. Hitler appointed a Reichskommissar to rule the country, sent in over two hundred thousand troops, tried to turn the coastline into an impregnable fortress, and let loose the Gestapo.

Resistance steadily grew. With no free press and all private radios declared illegal, clandestine newspapers soon became the only source of news and information. At first they were single-sheet cyclostyled or stencilled bulletins. Their aims were to disseminate news heard secretly over the BBC and pass on instructions from the government-in-exile in London about how to carry on the struggle at home. Gradually they became larger and more sophisticated, run off in their thousands on illegal presses and distributed round the country by a network of couriers. Soon the most important became *London Nyatt*, or *London News*, but there many hundreds of others. After October 1942 anyone involved with the illegal press could face the death penalty.

For two and a half years Peter Moen had been one of the chief editors of *London Nyatt*. Then, earlier that year, he had taken on the task of running all illegal newspapers in the country. Barely had he taken over when the Gestapo suddenly rounded up him and hundreds of others working with the underground press. It was a sure sign of Hitler's determination to keep Norway under his thumb. Yet the nation still had its role to play in Allied plans. In April the SOE had issued a directive for Denmark and Norway in connection with Fortitude North. Resistance groups would not be asked to act exclusively for deception purposes in case this caused reprisals or further Gestapo repression. Instead wireless traffic to resistance cells would be increased and decoy stores dropped by parachute to suggest preparations for an impending assault on the southern part of Norway. This campaign of deception was to last for as long as possible after D-Day.

For Peter Moen and the others incarcerated at 19 Mollergaten, it meant no early liberation – and the ominous possibility that the Germans would use them as hostages in the future against impending ill fortune. 'I am afraid of mass executions,' Moen had confided to his diary a few weeks before. 'We are dangerous witnesses.'

At about the same time as Moen was being inspected by the guards in Oslo, Glenn Dickin and the rest of his platoon at Hiltingbury Camp were being let into the secret of D-Day.

After breakfast Glenn was ushered into the special briefing centre, a large Nissen hut with heavily curtained windows surrounded by barbed wire and constantly patrolling armed guards. Inside, lit up by bright electric lights, was a large model, about ten feet square, surrounded by wooden plank seats that reached almost to the ceiling. A massive map on the wall revealed a coastline and towns and rivers. Even now, however, the final secrets remained tightly guarded. All the map's features were identified with code-names.

Glenn took his seat on one of the planks. Now, at last, he discovered that his destination was France, and that his platoon would be among the first to land, at just five minutes after 'H-Hour', the precise minute at dawn on D-Day when every single movement in the heavy and detailed briefing books was to begin. He heard about the beach, the firmness of the sand, the underwater obstacles, the distance he would have to run to solid ground through enemy fire, the location of minefields and marshy ground. He learned about the little coastal town with its fixed-gun emplacements and machine-gun posts, its pillboxes, the roads and narrow streets that led from the beach into and through the town, its fortified houses and garrisons, and the size of its population. It was code-named 'Alba'. The small sector of beach itself was identified as 'Nan Green'. They all heard more than they wanted to know about the waiting German forces, the firepower they could unleash, the way their machine guns could fire down and along as well as across the sands. Glenn found out about how he would be transported across the Channel and what the rest of his battalion would be doing alongside him. He gazed intently at enlarged black and white aerial reconnaissance photographs no more than a few days old, and tried hard to visualise and fix every detail in his mind. And he heard, time and time again, the words, 'Hit the beach – hit it hard and go like blazes!'

When the briefing was over, the commanding officer of the Regiment, Colonel Foster Matheson, spoke to the regiment as a whole. As he listened, Glenn knew once again that he was in good hands. In peacetime the tall and handsome forty-year-old Matheson was a company accountant from Prince Albert, Saskatchewan, a solid family man with three children, and a stalwart of the local militia. Soft-spoken but firm, he had been in command of the men almost from the start. He knew them all, and they had confidence in him. Now, deliberately and methodically, as though he were reading a company ledger, he went over their mission and wished them all good luck.

A wave of relief swept over the men. At last they could grasp something concrete and knew what lay ahead. They'd found the waiting oppressive, and it got more and more unbearable each day. Apathy and depression set in. Life was curiously suspended. Outside the barbed wire, normal life went on. But for the men in the camp it had lost any meaning and nothing existed to replace it except the knowledge that fate had singled out every one of them. But for what, was unclear. One war correspondent sealed in another holding camp, close to Glenn's, caught the mood well. 'It made you reluctant to walk, to talk, to eat, to sleep . . . Just waiting, waiting, until your number came up,' he wrote. 'You had no method of assessing the black space ahead . . . It was not fear that oppressed you, but loneliness. A sense of implacable helplessness. You were without identity, a number projected in unrelated space among a million other numbers.'

But now, let in on the secret, the men of the Regina Rifles could see how deeply and detailed the invasion had been planned. It was profoundly reassuring to hear about the massive aerial bombings and naval shelling that would soften up the German defences even before they hit the beach. On either side of them other units would be landing to lend support. There would be airborne landings by parachute and glider to help clear the way. They were no longer in the dark or alone, and that felt good.

So did the companionship between the platoon and the regiment. They all hailed from Saskatchewan, and had places and friends in common. One of Glenn's oldest friends, Gordon Brown, was also in Hiltingbury. They'd lived across the street from each other in Manor, gone to the same school, signed up together and attended the officers' training course together in Victoria. When Gordon married Jean in 1941, Glenn was an usher at the wedding. Then, in June 1942, they'd crossed the Atlantic, sharing the same wardroom on a troopship that was part of a fast convoy able to give U-boats the slip. It was the worst month of the war for sinkings by U-boats. In mid-Atlantic they'd passed a much slower convoy of about a hundred merchant ships and later they'd learned that a disturbingly large number had failed to make it to Britain. In England, the two friends had then endured two years of waiting and the endless landing exercises together.

Hiltingbury wasn't home. But in the circumstances, it was perhaps the next best thing.

In London's Park Lane Hotel another war correspondent, a Canadian, was awaiting his orders to join Glenn Dickin and the others when they crossed the Channel. At 9 a.m., the telephone rang. The voice at the other end said: 'Please report with all your field kit at 4.30 this afternoon.' As his jeep sped towards Southampton, he felt elated and relieved, glad to be on the move at last. Yet as he gazed at the green and luxurious countryside hurtling by, it suddenly felt as though he was leaving home. England had been good to the Canadians, he thought.

That same evening, in Madrid, the hard-working Abwehr officer Karl Kühlenthal transmitted to Berlin more tantalising intelligence items gleaned from Arabel, his agent in Britain, about the build-up of Allied forces in southern England. Kühlenthal's driving desire to succeed sprang partly from a need to prove himself to his superiors, who had once regarded him with deep suspicion. This was because he was part-Jewish, an awkward fact that had been overcome only because he was a protégé of Admiral Canaris, who had arranged for a special dispensation declaring him to be an Aryan. Since then he'd nursed Arabel along in Britain, demonstrating a remarkable capacity to cope with his agent's quixotic and temperamental personality.

Kühlenthal had no reason to doubt that Arabel was delivering prime material. Tonight, for example, he was forwarding Arabel's report on two large new American aerodromes near Ipswich with up to seventy Liberator bombers visible on the runways and considerable evidence, by way of tanks, armoured vehicles and troop movements, of a large build-up in the same general area of East Anglia, all of which pointed to the arrival of the US 28th Infantry Division. This evidence came from one of Arabel's sub-agents, a Welshman code-named 'Dagobert', whom Arabel had recruited in 1942 and who in turn ran several sub-agents of his own. One of these had also reported a large number of tented camps concealed in the woods in Kent housing troops of the US 59th Infantry Division. 'Saw hundreds of vehicles in this area marked with the American . . .' read this sub-agent's report before it became garbled in transmission and then lost in the ether. All this was of tremendous value. Gradually, Berlin was piecing together the jigsaw that would reveal the picture of Eisenhower's invasion plan.

Yet of potentially even more exciting promise was another item passed on by Kühlenthal that night. Arabel had now begun his new job in London and was providing inside intelligence on the Political Warfare Executive (PWE) and its propaganda work for Eisenhower and SHAEF. 'At present,' reported Arabel, 'no directive has been issued in respect of future operations . . . I hope that the competent German agencies will be enabled, on the basis of the information now procured by me via this link, to recognise the real intentions of the Allies concealed behind the official British propaganda.' Kühlenthal's prize agent added: 'I confidently believe that thereby and with the reports of my agents it will be possible to ascertain major Allied operations in good time.' Arabel clearly had the potential to blow wide open the Allies' D-Day secret.

Or so thought Kühlenthal and his masters in Berlin. For while Arabel was dazzling them with his intelligence from Britain, he was also blinding them to the fact that he was working under the control of not one but two intelligence officers. To the Germans, Kühlenthal appeared to be in control. In truth, however, the person really pulling Arabel's strings was a British intelligence officer. Arabel's true loyalty was to his British control, not to the Abwehr man in Madrid.

For Arabel was none other than the British double agent code-named 'Garbo'. And he was the key figure in the Fortitude South deception campaign that Eisenhower on this same day was telling Washington he was so anxious to protect. In the countdown to D-Day, Garbo was to deliver a prize beyond measure.

The Garbo story had begun three years before, when a woman approached the British Consulate in Madrid saying she knew some-one who was keen to work for the British by going to Germany or Italy to carry out espionage. 'Walk-ins' like this are deeply sus-pect – they are often engineered by hostile intelligence services – and her offer was peremptorily rejected. Several months later the US Embassy in Lisbon received a similar approach from the same woman. Eventually she admitted that the would-be volunteer was her husband. In March 1942 he was finally interviewed by a British intelligence officer in Lisbon. Soon afterwards he was smuggled on to a ship in Lisbon and taken to Gibraltar, from where a flying boat took him to Plymouth, in Devon, for even more interrogation.

England made an immense impression on him. 'I arrived,' he recalled, 'when the country was just about to appear at its best, the days were getting longer and the sun, the little sun there is at this time of year, came peeping through the cloudy skies, welcoming us with its warmth and friendliness.' When he landed he was met by two men. One introduced himself as Mr Grey, but knew no Spanish. The other spoke his language like a native. Since then, the two of them had forged an unlikely but remarkable partnership and the Spaniard had become an outstanding double agent. It had taken a lot of time and effort to make him credible to the Germans. But the fruits of their labour were now ready to be harvested.

In the meantime the great invasion armada was poised to begin its epic journey. Two weeks before, Eisenhower had fixed Monday 5

June as D-Day. 'H-Hour' was fixed at just before dawn. There were now just six days to go. Once again, it was a warm day in the Dover Strait with the thermometer registering 92 degrees in the early afternoon. There was a fresh breeze and a slight drop in the barometer, but nothing to indicate a break in the pattern of excellent weather and smooth seas. Overnight, an attack by ninety-five heavy RAF bombers had virtually destroyed a German radar and wireless control base outside Cherbourg. The destruction of the most important headquarters of the German Signal Intelligence Service in North-West Europe completed an offensive started three weeks before to eliminate the German early-warning system against invasion. Coupled with the devastation wreaked on Luftwaffe airfields close to the Normandy beaches, it delivered a crippling blow to German defences.

4

RUMOURS GET AROUND

Wednesday 31 May

The blockships began their slow move out from Scottish ports and headed for the English Channel. They would be sunk off the French coast to provide protective breakwaters around the beaches. The first loading of troops on to the vast armada now began along the west coast of Britain. They would have the longest journey to the invasion. Operation Neptune was under way.

Deep in the tunnels beneath Portsdown Hill, Veronica Owen was on night watch. It was 1.35 a.m. Two and a half hours to go. To fight off her overwhelming desire to sleep she reached for her fountain pen. 'My Darlingest Darlings,' she began, updating her parents on her reading of Lawrence of Arabia and her plans to see *Madame Curie* at the cinema in Fareham later that day, and filling them in about a tiff with a room-mate that had resulted in their not speaking to each other for the past two weeks. They'd finally made up, only for hostilities to break out again that very night while on shift together over who was to sleep in which bunk. 'All very complicated and stupid,' she confessed.

Stress was rising in the Wrens' packed dormitories. So was some indefinable tension at Fort Southwick that heralded momentous events. Veronica had already picked it up. 'If you don't get any letter from me for a long time,' she wrote, 'then don't worry or think I've gone abroad or gone to sea or am ill . . . rumours get around in this place and I don't for a moment think it will ever happen – but now you know, you know!' Veronica had been well drilled in security during her training. Professional actors serving in the Navy performed scenes to show how easily secrets could be carelessly given away. Since the beginning of the month letters written by the Wrens had been subject to censorship and stamped 'Maritime Mail'. Inspection was random, and most of Veronica's letters went through untouched. But this one was opened and stamped to indicate it had been read. The censor obviously found it harmless. But it gave an unmistakable hint to her parents that something big was going on.

Veronica was a rating, not an officer. Her job was to code and decode the signals sent between ships at sea, or between ship and shore. Any signal involving secrecy was marked in one of five ascending categories, from the least serious, 'Restricted', through 'Confidential', 'Secret' and 'Top Secret', to 'Hush Top Secret'. Work on Restricted messages was done by ratings. All the rest, encoded in higher-grade ciphers, was carried out by officers and involved the use of decoding machines. But for her work on the Restricted material, all that Veronica required were code sheets and a pencil – and an agile mind. She was skilled at her work. Her service record described her as 'very good' in character and 'above average' in her work.

Veronica and her family knew better than most the need for discretion and vigilance. It wasn't just that her twin brother was also in uniform. Both her parents were actively engaged on battle fronts of their own. Commander J.H. Owen was a retired First World War submariner who was now writing up battle reports in the Admiralty, and Veronica had opted for Coding and Signals because of her father's contacts. Her mother was running the Red Cross section in London looking after Royal Navy and Merchant Navy prisoners of war. Before that she'd worked for MI5. She'd done the same during the First World War, and only left when the spy-catchers moved out of London to Blenheim Palace, in Oxfordshire, in 1940 to escape the Blitz. Veronica's parents were now living in a cramped hotel in London's Bayswater after giving up their family house in Hertfordshire. In reality it provided little more than an off-duty sleeping billet. The Owens were at war.

So were the Schwenders. It was still sweltering in Nantes, and Walter Schwender was back in his swimming trunks. He was delighted to read in a letter from his mother, posted eight days before, that two of the three parcels he'd sent from France with cigarettes and other items he didn't need had finally arrived. He hastily scribbled a dozen lines of reply on a sheet of graph paper he grabbed from office supplies. 'We don't know what to do any more,' he complained, 'because it's so hot.' Not so for his mother, however. She was complaining about the cold back home.

Home. That was Altstadt, close to the border with France, a village of a few hundred people about twenty miles from Saarbrücken, capital of the Saar. Its coalfields and blast furnaces had been given to France in 1919 under the Treaty of Versailles as reparations for war damages, while political control was turned over to the League of Nations. Although Altstadt was rural and many people owned farmland or kept chickens and pigs, most of them worked in a nearby mine or smelting plant. Walter's home, where he was born in March 1924, was typical, with a stable and a pig's trough in the yard outside. When he was eleven years old a plebiscite was held over the return of the Saar to Germany. The streets were hung with German flags, and from the big chestnut tree in the Schwenders' front garden flew the Nazi swastika flag. Ninety per cent of the population voted for a return to Germany, and the decision was met with a frenzy of nationalist rejoicing throughout the Third Reich. It all formed a potent backdrop to young Walter's political education.

There were other things he remembered about his home town. The water, for example, so good and fresh, unlike the brackish liquid delivered by the taps in Nantes.

Altstadt's water also tasted better than the rusty fluid that gurgled from the taps where his parents were living now. They'd temporarily moved to the east when his father, Wilhelm, had got a job transfer. Schwender senior was a salesman specialising in building supplies. As a small businessman in the years before Hitler's rise to power he'd stood out in Altstadt, where most of the workers voted for the Communists – the strongest political party in the village. He was an early member of the Nazi Party, long before it became useful in getting a job. Now he worked for I.G. Farben, the largest chemical company in the world. Its production of synthetic fuels and rubber fitted nicely with Hitler's vision of economic autonomy for Germany. In 1933, the year he seized power, the company was the single largest donor to Nazi Party coffers.

In 1940, anticipating war with the Soviet Union, I.G. Farben, assisted by the SS, began secretly building an additional factory to produce synthetic rubber and methanol. Lured by generous tax exemptions, plenty of raw materials and the prospect of cheap labour, the company chose a site next to a concentration camp for political prisoners. It was eventually to become I.G. Farben's largest single project, with an investment capital of almost a million Reichsmarks. Wilhelm Schwender had been sent there, and later brought his wife, Ella, and the family out to join him. They were living in a small house outside the factory perimeter, close by the railway tracks. Walter knew it well, because on his few official leaves that was where he went. That's how he knew the water tasted rusty.

The place his parents now called home was in Upper Silesia, the former German area of Poland annexed by Hitler. The Poles called the town Oswiecim. But Walter knew it by its German name: Auschwitz.

'One way or another you'll get a cross' ran the joke in the French Resistance – either a medal or a gravestone. André Heintz had already survived a close shave with the arrest of his contact in Caen. Fortunately, their security was good and Yvon hadn't cracked under Gestapo torture. But you never knew, and were never certain whom to trust. The shadow world revolved on an axis of betrayal as well as comradeship.

Today André was at the lycée, teaching English, while his father cycled out to their allotment to plant tomatoes. Thousands of able-bodied Frenchmen who could have been working the fields and factories were in Germany as conscript labourers. André could have been one of them. In June 1943 he'd been ordered to report for work building a dam outside Frankfurt an der Oder. Instead he'd fled home and gone to stay on a farm near his grandmother's house in the Cherbourg peninsula, where he'd helped out with haymaking and the cider harvest. Six months later, after a friend in the labour office in Caen surreptitiously switched his file to the 'unfit for labour' category, he'd returned home, collected a valid ration card and taken up his teaching job.

Spring was bringing ever greater hardship to Normandy, and to Caen in particular. The region was rich in dairy products, and the export of milk and cheese, especially to Paris, was an economic mainstay. But the recent Allied bombing of the railways had cut off the capital as a marketplace and thousands of cows were going unmilked. All available meat and milk was commandeered by the Germans, mostly to feed their two hundred thousand troops now stationed in Normandy. There was a thriving black market and prices had risen sky high. Across France, rationing was getting worse. People's clothes were looking shabbier, their shoes were wearing out, queues for food were growing longer and black marketeers were becoming wealthier. The streets were virtually empty of cars but packed with bicycles, and horse-drawn transport was enjoying a revival. Trains were few and crowded, and increasingly in the Paris region and across northern France they ran late or not at all. People improvised, got by, survived. Tuberculosis and polio were on the rise. Normal life now embraced the anomalous and the perverse. Resistance had grown steadily, and by 1944 was harnessed to the Allies in London. De Gaulle had created the French Forces of the Interior (FFI) under General Henri Koenig, the heroic commander of the first Free French troops to fight alongside the British in North Africa. Based in London, Koenig was now co-ordinating action behind enemy lines with Eisenhower's headquarters. France was divided into resistance areas. Normandy was designated area 'M'.

Normandy's most effective intelligence network was code-named 'Century'. Financed and supported by Britain's Secret Intelligence Service, or SIS, also known as MI6, but reporting to a Free French officer in London code-named 'Colonel Rémy', or simply 'Rémy', it was run by a cement salesman in Caen. Assisted brilliantly by the local chief engineer for roads and bridges, Century eventually numbered more than fifteen hundred agents. Many had legitimate access to government offices and official passes for travel, and they collected a huge amount of invaluable information about conditions in Normandy. The network's most spectacular coup came through the bravery and quick-wittedness of a forty-year-old painter and decorator. While decorating the inside of a German office in Caen, he spotted lying on a desk a pile of top-secret blueprints of the Atlantic Wall. Quickly hiding the material behind a mirror, he managed to return later and smuggle it out. Eventually it found its way to London, hidden inside a biscuit box of *crêpes dentelles*, a Breton delicacy, aboard a leaky old lobster boat going from Pont-Aven to the fishing banks off Lorient, where it rendezvoused with a British special operations trawler – one of the secret flotilla of small boats run by MI6 across the Channel. Since then, London had sent in a stream of requests for specific items of intelligence. Closely associated with Century was the OCM, which drew its members mostly from the professions and the civil service. But, relentlessly, the Abwehr and Gestapo had been rounding up OCM activists until, by May 1944, most of its leaders were under arrest, dead, or in hiding.

Creation of the FFI heightened the tempo of resistance and intensified German efforts to destroy it. Working with the Nazis was a handful of deadly French collaborators who often penetrated covert networks. Arrests, executions and deportations inevitably followed. German measures could be brutally harsh. In 1942, along the model already experienced in Nantes, eighty hostages from Normandy had been deported to Auschwitz in reprisal for the sabotage of a German troop train. The work of an Abwehr penetration agent known as 'Raoul de Normandie' had later led to the discovery and destruction of most of the hiding places where guerrillas had stored their weapons.

To cap it all, on this very day, just six days before D-Day, the Gestapo arrested General Koenig's chief military delegate in Normandy. The head of resistance in the region immediately went into hiding. A new wave of fear, insecurity and suspicion swept through the movement. To all intents and purposes, the underground in Normandy on the eve of D-Day had been decapitated.

André Heintz caught wind of all this, but was fortunately isolated from its results. He was not even aware that the men for whom he worked were members of the OCM. The least he knew about that, the safer both he and they were. And he was careful never to ask. It was enough to know that he was working for de Gaulle to liberate France.

Nor did André know that only that day Eisenhower had changed his mind about how to use the French Resistance on D-Day. So far, planning had envisaged calling out resistance groups unit by unit and region by region. But today it was decided to throw all this out of the window and to send out the crucial BBC action signals to all groups at once. One reason lay in the well-founded fear that so many Frenchmen were eager for action that a gradual call-out simply wouldn't work and resistance would flare up spontaneously the moment the Allies landed. Another was the desire to stretch the Germans to the full from the very start, and thus delay reinforcements being rushed to the bridgehead. But the most decisive reason was that only a general uprising would keep the Germans guessing about the real site of the main landings. In other words, the call for a general rising by the French Resistance was essential to support the deception plan, now seen by Eisenhower as crucial to the entire enterprise.

After a couple of nights in the safe house, Sonia d'Artois spent most of the day bicycling with Sydney Hudson along quiet side roads to his base at the Château des Bordeaux about twelve miles away. It was flat and easy countryside but she was still wearing the clothes she'd dropped in and found them uncomfortably hot. Her shoulder, wrenched when she landed, was still hurting a lot. They took frequent rests in the shade. It was hard going, but she'd been toughened up by several gruelling training marches through the rugged mountains and glens of Scotland.

This was not the only legacy of her SOE course. On the first day at Wanborough Manor, the stately home in England where the initial weeding out of recruits took place, she'd been ushered into the drawing room with about thirty other recruits. Each was wearing a number around his or her neck. 'Who would you pick to go on a forty-eight-hour leave with in London?' asked the instructor. Sonya had already spotted a dark-haired and smartly uniformed man in the group and wrote down his number. The attraction was mutual, for it turned out that he had written down her number. Later, in Scotland, he was the leader of her team.

Guy d'Artois was a French Canadian from Quebec, and seven years older than Sonia. He'd had preliminary training at Camp X, the SOE training school in Canada where potential agents from North, Central and South America were screened for suitability. They shared a fascination with explosives. After rising early in the morning they'd regularly been dispatched with a map reference and told to blow up a bridge a few miles away, over the mountains. Sonia was hopeless at map-reading. But Guy was an expert, and soon they became a special little team. Guy started giving her private navigation lessons in a snug room with a nice big fireplace. Back in London, they'd got married. It caused quite a row inside the SOE. Colonel Maurice Buckmaster, the head of the French section, tried to talk her out of it but took one look at her determined face and threw in the towel.

After a lively wedding reception at the Royal Air Force Club in Piccadilly, Buckmaster had dropped a bombshell. Sonia and Guy had been briefed to go on a mission together, but now they were married, ruled Buckmaster, that was not allowed. If they were captured and the Gestapo learned they were married, one of them might be tortured in front of the other. 'Well then, I'm not going at all,' Sonia had stormed. But she soon changed her mind. Accompanying Guy to the plane that was to fly him on his mission as explosives instructor for an SOE circuit near Mâcon, in eastern

France, she encountered Buckmaster standing on the airstrip. 'I'm sorry, Toni,' he said, using her pet name, 'but let me know if there's anything I can do.' She'd instantly pleaded. 'Yes, there is. Get me a mission as soon as possible.'

That was how she now found herself trailing across country with Hudson in her shabby old ski boots. She wondered what Guy was doing.

She was also in turmoil. The first time she'd met Sydney Hudson in London she'd been immensely attracted to him, only to learn that he was married. Then she'd got married to Guy. But her feelings about Hudson hadn't changed. No one had told her she was being sent to join him in France. All she'd known before the drop was his code-name, 'Albin'. She'd been flabbergasted when he'd appeared at the farmhouse. My God, how am I going to handle this? she'd thought. The answer wasn't getting any easier to find.

In Oslo, a dangerous new phase in resistance to Nazi rule began. Ten days before, the Germans had ordered all Norwegian men between the ages of twenty-one and twenty-three to register for forced labour. So many refused that the deadline for registration was extended. The time limit had expired just the day before. That night saboteurs blew up a large factory in the city making transformers, generators and other electrical equipment. Smaller attacks took place across the country, with labour offices a popular target. Widespread rumours were circulating that the Nazis would soon force every Norwegian to reply in writing to the question: 'Are you in favour of delivering Norway to Bolshevism?' This was a theme increasingly being stressed in the Nazi-controlled press across Europe. In Norway leading quislings were giving speeches on the subject across the country.

Denied access to the radio and newspapers, Peter Moen knew none of this. Outside his cell the Norwegian midsummer days were lengthening perceptibly as the sun's parabola flattened and it hung over the horizon almost until midnight. In two or three hours its glow would gently strengthen again, pushing aside the darkness to cast its pale northern light across the landscape and animate the city beyond his window. Yet, in the stringent blackout, Moen and his cell were clothed in a dispiriting half-light. His routine was now reduced to talking with his cellmates or trying to carve out a small niche of personal space and shut himself off from them, coming to terms with his fate and keeping his diary.

Today he simply pricked out the contours of his daily life, complained about the noisiness of the cell and noted that the only time he even felt fresh air on his face was the fifteen minutes once a week he was allowed to stretch his limbs in a little 'air cell', a narrow, fenced-in enclosure at the back of the prison. Once every two or three weeks he was permitted a bath, and he had his head shaved weekly by the prison barber. The man was a fellow Norwegian who worked in other prisons as well, and Moen regularly pumped him for news from the outside world. But, afraid of losing his privileged job, the man remained obstinately tight-lipped. Sometimes he promised to pass on an extra piece of bread or some tobacco, but he never delivered on that either. By now Moen considered him almost as bad as any active collaborator.

His real life, it often seemed, lay firmly in the past. Now, he woke every day at 6.30 a.m., ate dinner at 12, had supper at 5.30 and was in bed at 8. No other world existed.

By contrast, in London eyes were fixed firmly on the future. It wasn't just the inexorable Allied advance towards Rome, nor the rising expectations about the coming invasion, that dominated the headlines. Horizons stretched further than that, and peace itself had become a constant topic of speculation. Advertisements in *The Times* reflected hopes of the future. One today promised that when wartime controls were removed British omnibus companies would once again demonstrate the unrivalled value to the community of road passenger transport owned and operated by private enterprise. Roche Vitamins claimed that wartime production of vitamins by the ton was paving the way to improved health in the future for everyone. The personal ads optimistically featured Hornby model railways for sale for a new generation of children. President Roosevelt's recent public musings on the shape of the post-war United Nations were reported at length, and new vistas in India were heralded with details of the Bombay Plan of National Development.

Even the texture of daily life was normal enough to imagine a future without war. Gunby Hall in Leicestershire was given to the National Trust. Sadler's Wells Ballet was performing *Swan Lake*. The Amalgamated Engineering Union celebrated its Silver Jubilee, hopeful that nine more unions would soon join forces with it. Prisoners of war had recently returned home from Germany in exchanges organised by the Red Cross. Southern Rhodesia was heralding development plans promising 'a great future for immigration'. The Stock Market was doing well, with industrials performing strongly, especially textile firms and car makers, which were already unveiling plans for post-war expansion; the same was true in New York, where active trading saw the market close firm. British Portland Cement increased its dividend, and the City of London gave a positive response to a government White Paper on post-war employment policy. The antics of two monkeys, named Jack and Jill, also seemed to herald a return to more carefree times. They'd escaped from a Wild West show on Hampstead Heath over Whitsun and taken refuge twenty feet up a large beech tree. Since then their handlers had been sitting patiently below with a large cage and dwindling hopes. The night before, in the blackout, the monkeys had descended from their leafy refuge, picked up the cakes and milk, and scampered back up to safety. In the meantime the show left town. A crowd gathered to cheer on Jack and Jill.

The Churchills were also a family at war. In addition to Randolph, Churchill's other children were all involved in the war effort, and so was his wife. 'My most brilliant achievement,' wrote Churchill, 'was to persuade my wife to marry me.' His thirty-five-year marriage to Clementine Hozier had given him a strong emotional anchor during his often tempestuous political career, and produced four adult children including Randolph.

Their eldest child, Diana, was married to Duncan Sandys, an MP and chairman of the War Cabinet's Committee for defence against Hitler's V weapons. She herself was an air-raid warden. Sarah, their third child, was a twenty-nine-year-old actress who had made her first film, *He Found a Star*, in 1940. For the last three years she'd been working as a photo-reconnaissance analyst for the Royal Air Force, helping build up the intelligence picture so vital for D-Day. Mary, their youngest child at twenty-one, was an ATS officer at a heavy anti-aircraft battery in Hyde Park. 'I thoroughly enjoyed watching her give the orders as the girls operated the instruments and the men manning the great gun turned the wheels furiously with their hands to swivel the gun and train its barrel up to the sky,' recorded her nephew, Winston Churchill junior.

As for the family matriarch, Clementine was a formidable personality unafraid of speaking her mind to her husband and occasionally calling him to order when stress and impatience made his behaviour intolerable. Quite apart from her heavy load of official entertainment, she was deeply involved with the Red Cross, the YWCA and the British War Relief Society of America, which had helped organise the 'Bundles for Britain' charity programme earlier in the war. She also founded the Churchill Club, next to Westminster Abbey, where professional men and women in the US and Canadian armed forces could meet their British counterparts for meals, drinks and concerts. She shared all Churchill's secrets, including that of D-Day.

Churchill's political agenda today was dominated by post-war affairs, although he began the day by instructing General Alexander to exploit the impending fall of Rome to the utmost. It was a 'vast, world-wide event,' declared the Prime Minister, 'and should not be minimised. I hope that British as well as Americans will enter the city simultaneously.' This matter out of the way, he turned his attention to a number of troublesome international issues.

The most intractable was Poland. Britain had gone to war with Hitler over his invasion of the country in 1939, thousands of Poles were fighting alongside Allied forces and the underground Home Army was poised for a national uprising. But Britain also had another, and more powerful, ally – the Soviet Union, Poland's eastern neighbour. Polish-Soviet relations were soured by centuries of hatred and suspicion. Poland's very existence as an independent nation had been won after the First World War largely at the Russians' expense, and after the Nazi-Soviet Pact of 1939 Stalin had seized back most of eastern Poland. Determined to destroy the backbone of Polish national resistance, the KGB, the Soviet Union's secret police, had then murdered thousands of Polish Army officers, burying them in a hidden mass grave at Katyn. Against stubborn Polish opposition, Stalin was now demanding a new post-war Soviet-Polish frontier and a government more friendly to Moscow. Increasingly hostile to the exiles in London, he'd recently created a shadow pro-communist government in the liberated areas of Poland. The future of the country for which Britain had gone to war five years before was now emerging as one of the most troublesome issues between the wartime allies.

Churchill was caught in the middle. He admired and respected the Poles for their bravery and resistance, but he needed the Red Army even more to defeat Hitler. Especially now, with D-Day looming, he had no desire to offend Moscow. Today he lunched with Stanislas Mikolajczyk, the Prime Minister of Poland, and afterwards they were joined by Count Edward Raczynski, the Polish Ambassador in London. 'This was the first of our meetings at which I began to wonder whether Churchill was overtired,' recorded Raczynski, as Britain's leader urged the Poles to drop their anti-Soviet attitude and told them that they could not expect British and American soldiers to risk their lives for them if the Poles insisted on driving a wedge between the West and Moscow. It would be better, Churchill insisted, to win the war first and then defend Polish interests through the United Nations.

The future of the Balkans was also causing headaches. Here, too, the Red Army's advance was raising anxiety. Would Bulgaria, Romania and Greece all fall under the hammer and sickle? Churchill hoped not. How about proposing to Stalin a sphere-of-influence agreement by which the Russians could take Romania in exchange for Greece remaining in the Western camp? He dressed the deal up as a temporary wartime expedient, but no one could be fooled into thinking that it wouldn't herald a peacetime settlement. He spelled his idea out in a telegram marked 'Personal and Top Secret' and sent it off that morning to Roosevelt in Washington.

As if that weren't enough about the post-war world, at six o'clock that evening he chaired a War Cabinet meeting plagued with a similar vexing agenda. After a lengthy and tetchy discussion about a post-war oil deal with the United States he finally had to agree that the United Kingdom should take a tougher line with Washington to protect its interests. This was followed by an item dealing with the control of post-war shipping, and after that came a report on the constitutional arrangements for the colonies of Malaya and Borneo after their liberation from the Japanese.

Only at the very end of the meeting did Churchill turn to D-Day. One item dealt with Eisenhower's request for continuing the censorship of diplomatic communications until well after the landings. The other was what to do about de Gaulle. Discussion was mercifully brief. Churchill had already conceded Eisenhower's point about deception, and diplomatic communications would be suspended until D plus 7, subject to further review. And he had also decided to invite de Gaulle to London immediately. The Chiefs of Staff were still fiercely opposed to this idea. But Eden was a powerful advocate, and Churchill now backed him. As soon as the War Cabinet meeting was over, he sent a telegram of invitation to Algiers.

Churchill always played his hand with an ace up his sleeve, because most members of his War Cabinet didn't receive Ultra intercepts or even know about their existence. Today he held an even more interesting hand than usual. One item in particular helped explain why he had finally come to a decision on Eisenhower's request.

As usual, the intercepts were full of encouraging reports from the Italian front. General Eberhard von Mackensen, commander of the German 14th Army in Italy, was complaining that his troops had received a 'severe mauling', and warned his superiors in Berlin about rapidly deteriorating morale, particularly among NCOs. This made Churchill hope that Rome might fall even sooner than expected.

However, Churchill's ace was not this. It was another item in C's locked box, and was not a military intercept at all but a 'blue jacket', meaning a diplomatic intercept, yet another revealing product of the outstandingly successful breaking of Japanese codes. This one was pure gold.

Baron Hiroshi Oshima was the Japanese Ambassador to Berlin. Four days before, he had visited the Berghof, where he spent two hours listening to Hitler's latest views on the military scene. Oshima then returned to Berlin and from there sent a seven-part telegram to Tokyo reporting what he'd heard. Allied code-breakers had recovered parts of the long message, although some of it was lost. No matter. What Churchill read that night in his Whitehall bunker reassured him on a point that had recently been causing him and his Chiefs of Staff extreme anxiety.

According to Oshima, Hitler believed that there were eighty divisions in England now poised for invasion. This was a 50 per cent overestimate – good news for Churchill. It meant the Germans were certainly anticipating more offensives than the Allies were actually planning. Indeed, Hitler had gone on to paint a scenario that bore a remarkably pleasing resemblance to the picture being etched by the deception campaign. 'After having carried out diversionary operations in Norway, Denmark, the southern part of the west coast of France and the French Mediterranean coast,' Oshima reported the Führer as telling him, 'they would establish a bridgehead in Normandy or Brittany and, after seeing how things went, would then embark upon the establishment of a real second front in the Channel.'

Hitler's reference to an Allied bridgehead in Normandy was only the latest in a series of alarming reports that the D-Day secret might have been leaked. Early in May, Churchill had been deeply alarmed when the Bletchley Park code-breakers decrypted a Luftwaffe message predicting, on the basis of RAF bombing attacks in France, that the main Allied landing would take place between

Le Havre and Cherbourg, which basically meant Normandy. It had given him the jitters, and he'd pestered both C and the Chiefs of Staff for more reports and for reassurance. All they could do was point out that no evidence existed to indicate that the German High Command, or even von Rundstedt in Paris, shared the Luftwaffe's view. Still, he'd insisted that everything should be done to confuse the enemy.

Churchill's anxiety, and that of his Chiefs of Staff, had deepened over the previous two weeks as intelligence revealed that the Germans were reinforcing the Normandy front with the transfer of the 21st Panzer Division to Caen and the strengthening of ground troops in the Cotentin Peninsula. And just two days before, on Monday 29 May, the Joint Intelligence Committee itself had concluded that the Germans now regarded the Le Havre-Cherbourg area as 'a likely, and perhaps the main, point of assault'.

On the face of it, therefore, Oshima's report, with Hitler's reference to a bridgehead in Normandy or Brittany, provided grounds for alarm, and as a result it was sent with maximum priority to the D-Day commanders as well as to Churchill. On reflection and closer analysis, however, it offered some considerable reassurance. It showed that Hitler was merely *guessing* between Normandy and Brittany, and then plumping firmly for the Pas de Calais as the focal point of the *real* invasion. This placed even greater importance on Fortitude South, and explained why Churchill had acceded to Eisenhower's request. A continuing ban on communications after D-Day would encourage Hitler to believe that a second attack was coming and so refuse to divert his troops to the real bridgehead in Normandy. Fortitude South, Churchill now knew for certain, was working its magic even in the Berghof itself.

Eisenhower also knew about Hitler's remarks at the Berghof. The Allied Supreme Commander was spending his final day at Bushy Park before moving to his advance base near Portsmouth. He wired to Washington emphasising yet again the vital need to keep under wraps the construction of 'Mulberries'. These were huge, hollow concrete structures (some measuring up to 200 feet long) that would be towed across the Channel and sunk off the shallow beaches of Normandy to create 'harbours' at which the Allied ships could dock. Floating or pontoon roads would link the Mulberries to the beaches. If the slightest whiff of these brilliant inventions reached the Germans they would realise that the first invasion wave was the only one coming.

Ike always stamped down hard on security breaches, especially in his own operations. Back in April, he'd shown no mercy at all when Major General Henry Miller almost revealed the date of D-Day. There had been a similar episode early in May when an inebriated US Navy officer had talked too freely. Ike sent both of them home. Security also involved physical threats. Today Ike learned that Allied intelligence had detected German efforts to locate his headquarters. Just in case German paratroopers arrived, his staff had their sidearms ready.

Yet even now Eisenhower found time to contemplate the post-war world. An old business friend from the States had recently written to him about his plans for post-war building construction. 'I think you're quite right,' Ike replied, 'in giving some thought to the great problems that we are going to have to face after the military one has been completely settled.' He also wrote to his brother, Milton, about a proposal to make a movie about his life. The producers were offering a minimum of $150,000. He wouldn't personally touch the money, he wrote, but if Milton could strike a deal so that the money benefited some educational institute, he'd be interested. Eisenhower had strong ideas of his own about what such a movie should highlight. It should stress, he told his brother, the 'initiative, effort, and persistence' of the average American family. Individualism, not collectivism and regimentation, should be picked out for praise. In recognition of Britain's role in making him Allied Supreme Commander, and to promote post-war recovery and co-operation, the revenue from the movie should be used to fund grants to American students to attend postgraduate courses in British universities.

On the eve of D-Day, Eisenhower's eyes were already fixed firmly on the peace and the Anglo-American alliance that lay ahead.

'Come please now with your colleagues at the earliest possible moment and in the deepest secrecy. I give you my personal assurance that it is in the interests of France. I am sending you my own York [aircraft] . . .' As Churchill's message winged its way to Algiers, Charles de Gaulle was still far from happy. Deep down, he feared a trap. Roosevelt and Churchill still had not recognised his French Committee for National Liberation (FCNL) as the legitimate, albeit provisional, government of France. If he flew to London, he feared, he might be pressured into making a speech in support of Overlord without winning the concession he wanted. Then Eisenhower would be free to impose military rule, sidelining de Gaulle's own organisation. To this, the General remained fiercely opposed.

After all, France was not an enemy country. True, Pétain's Vichy government was now little more than a puppet of the Nazis. But the French people had increasingly demonstrated their hostility to the occupiers and were paying an extravagant price. By now the official ration was down to one thousand calories a day. A million and a half French prisoners of war still languished in German camps. Tens of thousands of French workers had been deported to the Reich for forced labour. Yet, despite repression, torture, deportation and death, France was demonstrably eager to join the armies of liberation.

For de Gaulle, resistance was not some abstract concept. He and his family were suffering personally from Nazi oppression, like millions of others. His eldest brother, Xavier, was on the run from the Gestapo, and Xavier's daughter, Geneviève, was in a concentration camp. A student when the Germans entered Paris, she'd abandoned her studies to join the Resistance, working as a courier and newspaper editor. She'd been betrayed to the Gestapo and spent six month in prison in Fresnes, south of Paris, before being sent to Ravensbrück in January 1944. De Gaulle's sister, Marie-Agnès, had also been arrested, spending a year in Fresnes before being transferred to Germany. Her husband was now languishing in Buchenwald, another of Hitler's concentration camps. De Gaulle's brother, Pierre, also had been arrested, and was now imprisoned in Schloss Eisenberg, an internment camp near Brux in the Sudetenland; his wife and five children had fled by foot over the Pyrenees into Spain and reached the safety of Morocco. And his youngest brother, Jacques, a paralysed victim of polio, had been smuggled into Switzerland. Here was another family at war. When de Gaulle spoke of the bravery of the French Resistance and national liberation, he spoke from experience and the heart. He wasn't going to throw everything away just to please Churchill. So he sat in Algiers and pondered his next move.

At 8.35 that night, the secret transmitter in Crespigny Road, Hendon, began sending its nightly message to the Abwehr in Madrid. 'One mile south-west of Butley on both sides road to Woodbridge is large engineers' camp and park of six [6th] US Division. Many tents pitched out in open are plainly visible from the air . . .' it began. Over the next three hours many similar items were sent.

Most of the information was false. The 6th US Division was nowhere near the East Anglian town of Woodbridge. Garbo was painting a deceptive map of the Allies' order of battle in Britain. By suggesting a large build-up of forces in south-east England he was confirming Hitler's conviction that the Allies would launch their invasion across the Channel at its narrowest point, in the Dover-Calais area. At Zossen, the German High Command's bunkered headquarters hidden in the pine forests outside Berlin, analysts had already pieced together a map showing the estimated position of every known Allied unit. In showing a dense concentration of forces in south-east England the map revealed how wrong they were. Much of this was thanks to Garbo.

Garbo's real name was Juan Pujol. Born in Barcelona in 1912, he was the son of a prosperous businessman and his elegant Andalusian wife, Mercedes García. When the Spanish Civil War broke out Pujol was twenty-four and managing a poultry farm just north of the city. Caught up in the maelstrom, he was a reluctant participant determined to survive. He was conscripted into the Republican army but later deserted to General Franco's Nationalists, and by dint of subterfuge and native cunning had not fired a single bullet by the time the war ended three years later. Spain lay in ruins, and the outbreak of the Second World War a few months later only darkened its prospects. 'I could see another catastrophe looming over the horizon,' said Pujol, 'and thought more than once about leaving Spain, where hatred and a thirst for vengeance between victor and vanquished was rife.'

Now married, Pujol turned his energies to finding an escape route to freedom. Offering his services as a secret agent to Britain seemed to provide a way out of Spain. The decision led him along a tortuous path that was marked, one observer noted, by 'a miasma of lies and deception'.

After his wife's initial approach to the British was turned down, Pujol contacted the Abwehr in Madrid and offered his services to the Germans. This was a deliberate ploy. If they accepted him, he would then return to the British with convincing credentials as a man who could fool the opposition. It worked. By employing lies and half truths, a skill that had helped him survive the Civil War and was now second nature, Pujol convinced Karl Kühlenthal that he enjoyed useful contacts with the Spanish secret service that could get him to Britain. Here, he promised, he would work for the Germans. Kühlenthal gave him a crash course in secret inks, provided him with questionnaires and furnished him with cash and cover addresses to which he should send his reports. He also gave him the code-name 'Arabel'.

Armed with all this, Pujol and his wife proceeded to Lisbon, from where he sent a message to Kühlenthal claiming that he was in Britain. Over the next few months he concocted several reports purporting to be personal eyewitness observations of British life. Most of the information he gleaned from reference books in Lisbon's public library, supplementing it with material from newsreels, newspapers and magazines, and enriching it with his vivid imagination. Sometimes the task carried him away, especially when it concerned matters of social custom in a country that he had never visited and whose language he did not speak. Once, supposedly reporting from Glasgow, he noted that 'there are men here who do anything for a litre of red wine', a claim that would have startled the average Glaswegian. He also began to invent an army of fictional sub-agents.

After he had built up a sizeable portfolio of such reports, including congratulatory replies from Kühlenthal, his wife then made her second approach to the British through the American Embassy.

By this time British intelligence officials were becoming concerned about Arabel. They were intercepting Kühlenthal's messages to Berlin and had become intrigued by his supposed agent in Britain. Some of the agent's reports seemed substantial and plausible, especially when he correctly reported the sailing of a convoy from Liverpool. Despite all MI5's best efforts, was there, after all, a German agent loose in the country?

Finally, in early 1942, the penny dropped. Arabel and the man offering his services in Lisbon were one and the same person. It was then that British intelligence had brought him out on the flying boat to Plymouth and decided to exploit his uncanny skills as a double agent. Later they brought out his wife and set the two of them up in the house in Hendon.

Pujol's track record of deception was already so brilliant they had little trouble choosing his code-name − that of the greatest living actor in the world, the enigmatic Hollywood screen star Greta Garbo.

At Hiltingbury Camp, Glenn Dickin was now in the hands of the gigantic military machine charged with getting every man and vehicle of the invasion armada out of the holding camps and down to the English coast, on to the ship that would carry them across the Channel, and then into the right landing craft that would deliver them to the precise map reference point on the beaches of

France. It was like a gigantic travel agency, with every single move meticulously plotted and timed to deliver the passenger to his correct destination.

Glenn's buddy Gordon Brown was now in the thick of it. The first priority at Hiltingbury was to get the regiment's vehicles, now all carefully waterproofed, under way. For the past twelve months Gordon had been the Transport Officer in charge of some seventy drivers and crew of Bren gun carriers, anti-tank guns, jeeps, trucks and mortar carriers, as well as the Norton motorbike assigned to him for his personal duties. He and Glenn had volunteered together back in 1940 and for Glenn, who was four years younger, he was like an older brother.

Home to them both was Manor, a small community of three hundred people in south-east Saskatchewan, gently rolling farming country on the great North American plain that stretched from Texas in the south to Alberta in the north. 'Here,' rhapsodised a local guide for travellers on Highway 13 leading from the Manitoba border, 'our motorist feels that he is entering God's Country. Stretching before him to the north-west he sees a vast expanse of prairie farmland . . . ascending gradually to the tree-covered summits of the Moose Mountains which line the horizon twenty five miles away.' Manor had a climate of extremes. In winter the temperature could drop to –40 degrees Fahrenheit. The snow, piled high by the blizzards that swept unhindered across the treeless prairie, would often blanket the ground until early May. Then, in a matter of weeks, the thermometer would soar to 104 degrees, propelling the shoots of wheat, rye and barley skywards until, as far as the eye could see, the fields were an unbounded sea of rippling yellow broken only by the occasional solitary grain elevator.

Manor's first permanent settlers had arrived in the 1880s, followed by the Canadian Pacific Railway just twenty years before Glenn was born. With its tree-lined streets, four-roomed brick-built school, handful of hardware and grocery stores, bank, drugstore, post office and blacksmith, it was a typical self-contained prairie town. Its lifeline was the railway. The twice-daily passenger train – heading eastwards to Manitoba and Ontario and the big cities of Winnipeg, Toronto and Montreal, and westwards over the Rockies to British Columbia and Vancouver – also brought mail, milk, poultry and other small supplies. Electric power was still only sporadic, supplied by a local privately owned generator and switched off at midnight except for dance nights, when it continued until two in the morning. Drinking water came from wells, the most important being on Main Street, and there was no piped sewage system. Every home had its outhouse, generously supplied with out-of-date copies of Eaton's or Simpson's mail-order catalogue.

Most soldiers in the Regina Rifles hailed from small farming communities like Manor, hardy young men handy with a gun or knife, used to hunting and outdoor life, and accustomed to physically demanding labour and difficult living conditions. That was how the regiment had earned its nickname 'the Johns' – from 'Farmer John', the mocking city-slicker term they'd proudly adopted as their own. Few of them had had much education, having left school in their early teens. Their average age was twenty-three. A fair sprinkling of them were Métis of mixed European and indigenous descent.

The annual cycle of planting and harvesting governed the human calendar. Glenn's family owned dairy cows, and every morning he delivered milk to customers before going to school. At close to six feet tall and strong, he was a good athlete and excellent hockey player. Along with another friend, 'Dutchy' Doerr, he ran the local skating rink for a year when he was sixteen, and when he wasn't playing hockey he liked to curl or play pool. Glenn was an even-tempered soul, quiet and good-humoured, liked by everyone. He was usually top of the class as well.

In Manor, as in most other prairie communities, conservative family values held sway. Every Sunday pulpits, especially those of the United Church of Canada (formed by an amalgamation of the Presbyterians, Methodists and Congregationalists), resounded with denunciations of the evil of drink. As a teenager Glenn had seen three local referenda on whether the local hotel should be permitted to open a beer parlour. The hotel won, but on condition that drinkers should not be visible from the street, and on no account were they to stand or walk while carrying beer mugs. Thus were rowdyism and disorder to be held at bay. Glenn was too young to drink anyway, but his father had been a bit too fond of the bottle, and Glenn had his own opinions about booze. He'd been surprised to find that the officers' mess served alcohol. Even more shocking, when he and Gordon travelled through the Rockies to the officers' training centre at Gordon Head, outside Victoria in British Columbia, they'd discovered that some of their companions on the train were carrying flasks of whisky.

Since then, though, he'd loosened up a bit. After a hard day's square-bashing he and Gordon had come to appreciate a beer or two. The real eye-opener came when they discovered British pubs, which served all kinds of liquor, and where men and women could stand and drink at almost any hour of the day. Gradually Glenn had learned that an evening in the pub could ease the ache of boredom or homesickness. Which now made it all the harder to get through the next few days imprisoned in the clutches of Movement Control. All pubs were off limits.

In Paris, Albert Grunberg spent an agonising day. The lack of news about Robert and Roger was becoming ever more ominous. No mail at all was getting through to Paris from the provinces and the telephone service was virtually non-existent. But Madame Oudard had tapped lightly on the door, bringing her morning newspaper. And there it was, below the headlines – detailed news about the bombing of Chambéry. It was worse than Albert had even imagined. Three hundred people were dead and more than six hundred wounded, out of a population of twenty thousand. 'I'm in despair,' he wrote. 'On reading this I went pale and felt all reason desert me.' Desperately, he tried to distract himself by finding small tasks in the tiny room. But it was no good. His mind just swirled round and round until he felt he was going mad.

All this was bad enough. What made it worse was his brother, Sami.

The two boys had left Romania together, settled in Paris and made their new lives side by side. Sami was ten years older, the guardian angel, the father figure who'd guided him intellectually, seen that he'd got a good professional training, helped him out financially and even taught him to play the banjo, because every life needs a bit of music. Whether he wanted it or not, Sami was always there.

Except that by now, in middle age, it should really have been the other way around. Sami had never really grown up, and led a pretty wild and unconventional life. Recently he'd been living with a girl-friend and her parents. At least that's where he'd been officially registered in August 1941 when the police came knocking at 5.30 a.m. to drag him out of bed, along with three thousand other Parisian Jews, to take them to Drancy, the notorious detention camp on the outskirts of the city where they were kept before being deported to camps in the East.

Sami had been luckier than most. After eight months in deten-tion he'd been released, and for the past ten months had been holed up with his brother in Lulu's little room. What had helped save him was his status as a veteran of the 1914–18 war, when he'd worn a French uniform – a small concession by Vichy towards Jews who'd served France. But he'd been scarred badly both psy-chologically and physically, lost almost eighty pounds in weight and almost died.

Now Albert's brother was driving him mad. Two of them in a small room sharing a bed was bad enough, especially as Sami was a heavy snorer so that Albert rarely got a good night's sleep. But they were really getting on each other's nerves. Temperamentally incompatible, they now spoke to each only when they had to, which avoided a lot of rows. 'We love each other,' recorded Albert, 'but we can hardly stand each other.' Today was even worse than usual. Desperate to voice his anxiety about his sons, Albert told Sami the news as soon as his brother got out of bed – earlier than usual – at 9.30. But Sami responded as he often did, trying to pro-tect his younger brother by talking of something completely different. Exasperated, Albert had sulked in silence until the early afternoon. 'Never for a second do my darkest thoughts go away,' he wrote in despair that night. 'It's appalling.'

Early that morning Erwin Rommel swept out of the château at La Roche-Guyon in his Horch to inspect the destruction along the Seine. What met his gaze was a dismal scene of broken girders, twisted rails and smashed arches. So far in May, Allied planes flying night and day had made some sixty-five thousand sorties, pulverising bridges not just over the Seine but also across the Meuse and Scheldt further north. It all convinced Rommel that he was right about air power. If the enemy could do that to the bridges, what havoc would they wreak on the panzers when they advanced to confront the Allies as they left the beaches? That was why he'd argued so strongly to have the tanks placed close to the coast from the start, dug in firmly to turn their firepower on the invaders in the first few critical hours. He'd had to compromise, but at least he'd been able to position one of the three divisions he'd wrung out of Hitler, the 21st Panzer, close to Caen. This heavy targeting of the Seine just reinforced his opinion that the Allies would land along the shores of the 15th Army sector from Le Havre north up to Calais and even beyond.

Highlighting the mechanised panzers, however, gave a misleading view of German forces in Normandy. Rommel commanded an army that was remarkably old-fashioned, especially when contrasted with Allied forces. Battle-tested men were scarce and most officers, commissioned or non-commissioned, were over-age and second-rate. Horse and foot power held sway. Horses still pulled heavy artillery, the troops either walked or used bicycles and the bulk of supplies arrived by train, not road. Even then, there was a shortage of horses. As for the panzers and other motorised elements, they depended on ample fuel supplies and the Allies were taking care of that by targeting oilfields and refineries in Romania. Shortages were already becoming apparent. Rommel, famous for his lightning and aggressive strikes in the desert, was now in charge of a largely static force and committed to a fixed defence on the beaches. His own constant and restless inspection tours contrasted tellingly with the heavy immobility of the men he commanded.

Even as he was inspecting the previous day's damage, Marauder bombers of the 9th American Air Force struck at three more bridges. By the time they'd finished, the railway bridge at Rouen was half under water.

At Cottesmore airfield, paratrooper Bill Tucker continued the tedious work of checking his equipment. As one of the three million American servicemen and women who passed through Britain in the Second World War he was part of an enormous force that had virtually transformed the island into an occupied country.

'Oversexed, overpaid, overfed, and over here' was the legendary complaint levelled against GIs in Britain. Occasionally the friction resulted in a fistfight. As a result, considerable official effort was expended on explaining Americans to the British, and vice versa. The renowned American anthropologist Margaret Mead, famous for her best-selling book on female adolescence and sexual behaviour, *Coming of Age in Samoa*, tried her hand at improving Anglo-American relations between the sexes. 'Americans,' she explained in the magazine *Army Talk*, 'have to adjust to the different pace of personal relations in Britain, not to go fast at first, and British girls . . . need to learn that while the Americans move very fast at first . . . afterwards they go more slowly than the British, enjoying each step in getting acquainted . . .' Eisenhower's press officer extolled the merits of British pubs in breaking down cultural barriers. 'The so-called British reserve breaks down completely inside of a pub,' he noted. 'A lot of real friendships and a lot of real understanding is developed over a glass of beer.' Bill Tucker knew this from experience, and had personally found nothing but goodwill and friendliness. He'd been invited into people's homes, regularly spent evenings over a beer in the pub 'shooting the breeze' with a British paratrooper he'd befriended, and he admired the British. 'There was a spirit there you could feel,' he said, 'a warmth, they made me feel at home.' As he left the small town he even thought it felt more like home than Boston.

Ike, as Allied Supreme Commander, was determined to emphasise the solidarity of all the forces under his control. D-Day wasn't just a combined operation between land, sea and air forces, as forcefully exemplified in Tucker's own role as a paratrooper, dependent on the air force for transport direct to the battlefield yet fighting on land. It was also a multinational enterprise. Most of all, it was an Anglo-American joint venture. *The Times* that day carried a statement issued by SHAEF. Under the headline 'The Invasion Star' it reported that all service vehicles belonging to the invasion forces, whatever their nationality, were to carry a large white, five-pointed star, prominently displayed, a symbol and example of the integration of national forces. 'All troops and equipment, no matter of what origin,' it reported, 'have no nationality in General Eisenhower's command.'

Another item that day also highlighted the theme of Anglo-American unity. The day before had been Memorial Day, the American equivalent of Armistice or Remembrance Day, an occasion to honour the fallen of past wars. Ceremonies had been held across Britain. One event in particular stood out. At Madingley, a village on the outskirts of Cambridge, a large military cemetery had recently been opened for the thousands of Americans, mostly airmen, who were dying in the massive air offensive over Europe. By now two huge American air forces were based in Britain: the US 9th, the tactical air force striking at targets directly related to the impending D-Day operations, whose weapon of choice was the B26, the Marauder, a two-engined cigar-shaped bomber with short wings known as 'the flying prostitute' because, went the joke, it had no visible means of support; and the US 8th Air Force, flying B17 Flying Fortresses and B24 Liberators, both great four-engined beasts used for the heavy bombing of strategic targets such as factories and oil refineries deep inside the Reich. The majority of their bases lay in central or eastern England, and Cambridge was the principal town in the east of the region. From the cemetery, eventually to house almost four thousand American dead, the tower of Ely Cathedral could be seen sixteen miles away across the level fenland – a welcome landmark to many an exhausted aircrew returning from a mission across Europe.

The American contribution to liberation was also celebrated in more upbeat ways. *The Times* carried items about baseball games around the country, reported on American baseball results, both National and American League, and made much of a forthcoming baseball game to be held at Wembley, the sacrosanct home of English football. The American Red Cross had established 'dough-nut dugouts', which its customers preferred to the British snack bars serving sandwiches and cakes. An exhibition in Wigan of Americana sparked a lively debate about the supposed British heirs of Pocahontas, the legendary daughter of the Native American chief Powhatan, who'd saved the life of Captain John Smith, mar-ried the Virginian settler John Rolfe and died at Gravesend after accompanying him to England with their son in 1616. And Alistair Cooke's *American Commentary* was already a firmly established fea-ture on BBC radio.

At 7.30 that morning in Plymouth, two Americans stepped off the night sleeper from London and a naval launch sped them out to the heavy cruiser USS *Augusta* for breakfast with Admiral Kirk, commander of the D-Day Western Naval Task Force. After a tour of the harbour, now bursting with D-Day vessels of every kind, they boarded the destroyer USS *Davis* and headed out into the open sea.

The elder of the two Americans, a fit-looking, silver-maned sixty-year-old, was Colonel William Donovan, head of the Office of Strategic Services (OSS). Appointed head of the new agency in 1942 by President Roosevelt, Donovan had lived up to his sobri-quet of 'Wild Bill' – earned for his buccaneering exploits in the First World War – by breaking all the rules, offending just about every vested interest in Washington and poaching the best talent available to make the OSS the equal, and rival, of Britain's Secret Intelligence Service, Political Warfare Executive and Special Operations Executive all rolled into one. Top of his agenda was get-ting agents into France to help with D-Day.

In 1942 Donovan had reached an agreement with the SOE over supplying and supporting resistance movements in Europe, and some of his early agents were trained at the British-run Camp X in Canada. But with their well-established networks already in place, British secret intelligence chiefs had resisted Donovan's plans for independent American networks. The burgeoning wartime Anglo-American special relationship had its limits, and where secret intelligence was concerned the experienced and battle-hardened British assigned the Americans a distinctly junior role. 'It has become increasingly and painfully clear that British SIS is exerting its power and influence to prevent the establishment of [OSS intelligence] as an equal, independent, and co-ordinate secret service,' noted one exasperated OSS London officer. SIS chief Sir Stewart Menzies had insisted that Americans should only be part of joint operations, and Donovan had been forced to agree. But privately he envisaged OSS as the foundation stone of an independent post-war American central intelligence agency.

The man accompanying Donovan was David Bruce, director of OSS European operations. Born into the Virginia gentry, the forty-four-year-old Bruce was tall, suave and married to Ailsa, daughter of the multimillionaire Andrew Mellon. For the previous two years he'd been working out of 70 Grosvenor Street, in London, a heavily guarded and nondescript office block halfway down the street leading from the American Embassy. The building was now filled with keen if, in many cases, inexperienced intelligence operatives, and one of those youthful officers was William J. Casey, who was later to become a prominent Director of Central Intelligence. 'The London in which we lived and worked,' he recalled, 'had the feeling of a city under siege. The beleaguered atmosphere enveloping the city came from the buildings drab and unpainted, the preponderance of uniforms of all sorts and varieties, the scarcity of motor vehicles, and the strangely mingled sense of shabbiness, devastation, and commitment.'

A confirmed anglophile, Bruce had also been a member of 'The Room', a pre-war quasi-intelligence group founded by wealthy New Yorkers consulted frequently by Roosevelt. Bruce's smooth patrician skills had been tested to the full in fighting turf wars with the US military, negotiating with intelligence chiefs of the European governments-in-exile and liaising with the cautious British. Finally he and Menzies had hammered out a joint Anglo-American project code-named 'Sussex'. Two-man teams of French agents, one an observer, the other a wireless telegrapher, would be parachuted into France to provide operational intelligence – especially from rear areas rather than the battlefield area itself – of direct interest and value to Eisenhower's headquarters. SHAEF experts had duly provided a priority list: German communications centres for movement in and out of the coastal belt; railway centres within France and from Belgium into France; major motor transport parks; main crossings over the Seine and Loire; major German military headquarters; and principal German Air Force airfields and repair centres. Unlike Sydney Hudson's Headmaster and other SOE teams, their task was not to initiate sabotage or other direct action. Instead they were to lie low, stay out of view and report.

The Sussex project was another sign of the top priority being given to D-Day by Allied intelligence. Networks of SIS agents already existed in France, and many of these had already provided excellent information relevant to D-Day. But it was feared that tightening German security measures might render them immobile, cut them off from their communications or lead to their being penetrated and broken up at the very moment they were most needed. Superimposing the Sussex agents over the existing system was a form of reinsurance. To be doubly sure, it was also decided to keep them completely sealed off from existing groups in France, as well as from the French Resistance, just in case these were penetrated or compromised. Given recent Abwehr successes, the strategy was paying off. Half the Sussex groups would be under SIS control, covering areas to be liberated by the British. The remainder would be under OSS.

For the previous few weeks Bruce's men had been frantically training the Sussex agents in fieldcraft and getting them into place. By now thirteen were at work in various locations requested by

SHAEF, the last three having been dropped just two days earlier. That same day radio messages had been sent to those in place requesting them to begin sending in their intelligence reports. Certain specific questions, SHAEF insisted, should be answered by Saturday 3 June.

The first American Sussex agent, a twenty-three-year-old Frenchman code-named 'Plainchant A', had been dropped to the location heading the OSS Sussex list as its top priority: Le Mans, close to where Sydney Hudson and Sonia d'Artois were hard at work on their sabotage plans. He arrived equipped with a .45 automatic and three ammunition clips, grenades, maps, signalling equipment, suicide tablets and a Klaxon set, a ground-to-plane voice wireless communications system. Just ten days before, his wireless operator had finally made his first radio contact with Britain.

At this critical moment for D-Day, Bruce might have been expected to stay in London. True to character, however, 'Wild Bill' Donovan wanted to be in on the D-Day action himself, and just a few days before had flown into London. Even more typically, he'd defied specific orders against doing so. More typically yet, he'd ordered Bruce to accompany him – and to keep a diary. This was also against the rules. Being on the front row for the D-Day show was why they had come to Plymouth, to accompany the Western Naval Task Force to Utah Beach – the most westerly of the five Allied landing sites on the Normandy coast – and watch the landings from offshore. Bruce had already started his diary. One of the first things he noted was that the captain of the *Davis* had still not received his D-Day briefing or communications codes, having arrived just four days before with a convoy he'd escorted across the Atlantic. To Bruce, it all seemed a bit late in the day.

In Portsmouth, Admiral Ramsay kept his diary up to date. The report from his Admiralty meteorological adviser for the next few days was not so satisfactory, he noted, 'the cloud being our chief anxiety rather than the state of the sea'. But it wasn't serious enough to merit more than a sentence. Early that afternoon a thunderstorm over Boulogne moved out into the Channel and caused the temperature to drop. Later a second storm, far more severe, lasted into the evening and there was heavy rain. By five o'clock the temperature in the Dover Strait had fallen to 56 degrees and that night the weather was fine but cool. The heatwave that had stifled Western Europe for the past five days was finally over. But there was no let-up in the bombing. That night, along the south-east coast of England, buildings shook from explosions across the Channel as RAF heavy bombers again delivered their deadly loads against German coastal defences.

5

THE HOUR OF COMBAT
IS COMING

Thursday 1 June

In London, *The Times* offered a reminder of why liberating Europe remained a battle to be fought. News of the 'War behind the Wall' was invariably a tale of suffering and savagery. 'In Norway,' wrote an unnamed correspondent, 'the firing squads are busy . . . Norwegians are offering massive resistance – which is not always passive – to the latest mobilization of labour.' The Nazis understood that this struggle was only a foretaste of what would come when patriots across Europe linked up with the invasion, and if they could crush resistance now, they would. So it was vital that the underground should pick its moment with care. The Germans had already been putting out false reports of landings in order to trick resisters into showing their hand. But only the Allied Supreme Commander would give the authentic word when the moment for action came. In the meantime the shadow warriors would continue to wreck railways, destroy power plants, disrupt war production in factories and sabotage shipyards. 'Such exploits call for the highest courage,' enthused the correspondent, 'and the men and women who carry them out have the homage of the free world. They readily and fearlessly pay the last penalty. Such savagery does not deter; it incites to further resistance.'

News from Greece graphically confirmed the message. After rounding up suspects in a village close to Mount Olympus, German soldiers had stopped to sunbathe and swim by a mountain stream when they were savagely attacked by guerrillas using guns and knives. When they'd finished, 150 German bodies littered the ground and their guns and ammunition had vanished, along with the guerrillas, back into the mountains. Similar episodes were now commonplace across the occupied Balkans, tying down German troops in a savage and relentless war of attrition, amply aided by agents, weapons and gold supplied by the SOE and other Allied agencies.

In Caen, André Heintz put on the earphones of his crystal set. The local newspaper that morning was full of articles about farmers complaining about a drought but there had, in fact, been a welcome spot of rain. Ouistreham was bombed, but nothing very serious, not like Rouen, where reports were filtering in of over a thousand civilians killed by the Allied raids.

It was just before 9.15 p.m. André tuned into the BBC, wondering if the warning message would come that night. He'd been doing this for long enough now for the task to have become almost boring. But he knew that when he heard the critical words, all that would vanish and the rush of adrenalin would be as great as the excitement he'd experienced just a few months before on another resistance mission.

On the Normandy coast, just to the east of the fishing harbour of Port-en-Bessin, close to Bayeux, the Germans had built a huge battery on the cliffs at Longues equipped with four enormous guns with a range of twelve miles. All were hidden under camouflage netting so that they couldn't be spotted from the air. The farmer who owned the land carefully paced off the distance between the casemates, the edge of the cliff and the command and observation post. He then repeated the measurements to his blind nine-year-old nephew until he had memorised them perfectly. Later the boy hitched a ride into Caen, armed with a pass claiming he was visiting an uncle, and gave the figures to a Resistance friend of André's named Jean Guérin, an expert at map-reading and coding messages. After composing his message he signed it 'Alain Chartier', the name of the Norman fifteenth-century poet who'd written 'La Belle Dame sans Merci', a title which John Keats was to borrow nearly four centuries later for a memorable poem of his own. Then it was sent by radio transmitter to Britain. Guérin asked André to listen out for any sign that the message had been received. A few days later, on his crystal set, he heard the words 'Alain Chartier poète bas-normand est né à Bayeux' ('the Norman poet Alain Chartier was born at Bayeux'). It was a thrilling moment to know that London had received and appreciated their work. It was also good news for the radio operator, because it meant that he wouldn't have to repeat the message. With the Germans ruthlessly hunting down illegal radio transmitters, many an operator had been caught while re-sending a message that had somehow got lost in the air waves. The Germans had actually intercepted this message, and half a dozen direction-finding trucks had been spotted in the area, forcing the Resistance to shut down all communications for nearly three weeks.

André now adjusted the earphones and listened intently to the faint litany of personal messages he could hear riding in on the airwaves: 'Messieurs, faites vos jeux' ('Gentlemen, place your bets'); 'La sirène a les cheveux décolorés' ('the siren has bleached hair'); 'L'électricité date du vingtième siècle' ('electricity dates from the twentieth century'). Nothing to do with him. Then more: 'L'espoir brûle toujours' ('hope springs eternal'); 'Le chameau est poilu' ('the camel is hairy'); 'La lune est pleine d'éléphants verts' ('the moon is full of green elephants').

And then, suddenly, there it was. The few words he'd drilled urgently into his mind during a furtive meeting at the school just days before.

He'd been teaching a class of boys when a caretaker came in and told him that a Madame Bergeot urgently needed to speak to him. He was immediately suspicious. Bergeot was the real name of the man who'd replaced the ill-fated Yvon as his main intelligence contact, but for security's sake he was always known as Courtois. Was this a Gestapo trap? Was the woman some sort of agent provocateur? Leaving the class to amuse itself, he hurried downstairs to the main entrance. Playing the innocent, he took the woman by the arm and led her into the street as if he didn't want to be seen with her in the school. In reality, he wanted to find out if there was a Gestapo car lurking outside.

Glancing around, he saw nothing suspicious and led her back inside. She hurriedly whispered some phrases in his ear and ordered him to memorise them carefully. She told him the words that would indicate the invasion was getting close, the individual message giving him twenty-four hours' notice, the lines instructing different kinds of sabotage to begin: against railway or telephone lines, or for guerrilla action.

The final phrase he memorised was a code for postponement of the invasion: 'Les enfants s'ennuyent dans le jardin' ('the children are getting bored in the garden'). Just at that moment he heard a commotion upstairs and remembered his students back in the classroom – by now exhibiting boredom of their own. Hastily thanking Madame Bergeot, he leaped up the stairs and back to his duties. Too late. Alerted by the noise, his headmaster was already on the scene. Only with the greatest ingenuity had André been able to invent an excuse for his absence, and fortunately the headmaster chose not to pry too deeply. But he'd never forgotten the phrase. Afterwards, as instructed, he sent postcards of the Bayeux Tapestry to all the members of his group with the two simple words, 'Bons baisers' ('love and kisses'), written on it, notice to get ready for action.

He had no problem now in recognising the words 'L'Heure du Combat viendra' ('the Hour of Combat is coming'). It was the general warning message for Section M1 of the French Resistance – his sector, Normandy – to be ready for all kinds of action. He could expect the invasion any time that month. His job now was to alert all his contacts to stand by and be ready

André Heintz was not the only person listening in to the BBC that night. In addition to André's fellow resisters and British agents across France, a slight, dark-haired Abwehr officer named Oskar Reile was similarly engaged.

A former police inspector from Danzig, Reile had cut his counter-intelligence teeth in the Rhineland, preparing the way for Hitler's reoccupation of the region in 1936. Now he was head of Abwehr III, counter-espionage, in Paris. His headquarters in the Hôtel Lutetia, on the Left Bank, was not far from Albert Grunberg's hideout. He had spent months targeting Resistance cells and SOE networks, and recruiting informers. In October 1943 he had enjoyed a lucky break. After successfully penetrating an SOE circuit, he'd learned not just about the BBC open-code system in general, but about one warning message in particular. This was a slightly modified version of the first stanza of a famous sonnet by the nineteenth-century symbolist poet Paul Verlaine, 'Chanson d'Automne':

> Les sanglots lourds
> Des violons
> De l'automne
> Bercent mon coeur
> D'une langueur
> Monotone.

('The heavy sobs of autumn's violins lull my heart with a monotonous languor.') The first part of this verse, including the word 'autumn', meant invasion within the next month. The second part would alert circuits to landings within the following forty-eight hours.

In reality, the code poem was destined to go to just one SOE circuit, code-named 'Ventriloquist', operating south of the Loire and run by Philippe de Vomécourt, an agent to whom Sydney Hudson had first been parachuted before making his way north to the *département* of Sarthe. Moreover, it related specifically to railway sabotage and not to other targets such as telecommunications or roads. It was not, as has often since been claimed, *the* general warning to *all* SOE circuits in France. But Reile was right in thinking it gave a crucial clue to the imminence of D-Day. Ever since, his radio monitors had been on the alert for the message.

Tonight, along with André Heintz, Reile's men, hunched over their radio receivers, heard the crucial opening words of Verlaine's sonnet: they now knew that the long-awaited Allied invasion would take place within the month.

Rommel spent the morning of 1 June at La Roche-Guyon discussing with an official from Goebbels' propaganda ministry in Berlin what line to use against the Allies when the invasion took place. Then, in the afternoon, he set off for yet another inspection tour of the Atlantic Wall defences. Significantly, in light of his belief about the likely site of the invasion, he chose the stretch of coastline around Dieppe, north of the Seine. Again, as on his recent tour to Riva-Bella, his visit proved a sobering experience. Twice during the day the mobile coastal gun battery at Ault was bombed by the Allies, forcing him to order its withdrawal until its concrete emplacements were completed. Overwhelming Allied air power and German lack of preparation remained all too obvious.

While Rommel toured Dieppe, General Erich Marcks, the commander of his 84th Corps, visited the small seaside resort of Arromanches-les-Bains, part of the sixty-mile front along the Normandy coast defended by only two of Marcks's divisions and which he regarded as the weakest sector of his whole command. Two weeks earlier Marcks had told his wife that he had the feeling that the Allies would be ready to attack on his birthday – 6 June. Today, gazing out over the sea from a hill outside the town, he turned to an aide at his side and virtually repeated his prediction. 'If I know the British,' he said, 'they'll go to church next Sunday for one last time, and sail on Monday. Army Group B says they're not going to come yet, and when they do it'll be at Calais. So I think we'll be welcoming them on Monday, right *here*.'

The first day of the new month found Adolf Hitler at the Berghof, continuing the placid routine he had been following throughout the spring. He would rise late, spend the morning at meetings, in conference or making telephone calls and then, after lunch, would take his afternoon stroll to the Tea House for pastries and chat.

After dinner in the evening he would entertain his guests with films, music and conversation that would last until the early hours of the morning. Often he would launch into a rambling monologue on some long familiar subject such as the fight against the Jews and communists, or the rise of the Party. At other times he would lapse into a lengthy silence, his eyes fixed on some distant point invisible to his audience, scarcely listening to the others. Captive visitors found it intolerable. 'He can be Führer all he likes,' said Goebbels's wife, Magda, of such evenings with Hitler, 'but he always repeats himself and bores his guests.' Nicolaus von Below, Hitler's Luftwaffe adjutant, who was by now a constant companion in this domestic routine, remarked how much this period resembled the pattern that had prevailed before the war. But now, as the tide of war was poised decisively to change, high up in his mountain retreat Hitler seemed oblivious to the powerful currents swirling menacingly below.

Indeed, as things worsened by the day, he retreated more and more into a private and isolated world of memory and illusion. 'It was disturbing,' noted von Below, 'to observe how his contact with reality was tending to slip away.' By now Hitler had been at the Berghof for almost five months. In Berlin, his ministers and cronies squabbled between themselves, ran and enlarged their bloated personal fiefdoms and fought for his attention. Occasionally one of them would appear at the Berghof, summoned by the Führer, and there would be a mad flurry of activity. Then the guest would leave and everything would seem normal and placid again to Hitler, the clear mountain air refreshing his spirits, the dark green woods blanketing the hillsides with their unchanging foliage, the small mountain streams splashing in the distance and the evening sun following its reassuring and eternal ritual of transforming the snow-covered Alpine peaks into gold and pink. High above, the eagles soared endlessly on the thermals.

Peter Moen, immured in his cheerless Oslo cell, was facing his one hundred and nineteenth day of imprisonment. Around him, as *The Times* of that morning reported, the tempo of Norwegian resistance was visibly, and audibly, increasing. His arrest, and those of the other workers in the clandestine press, had caused the closure of thirteen underground newspapers. Yet by now national sentiment was so thoroughly aroused, and hatred for the occupiers ran so deep, that the arrests in February 1944 proved little more than a temporary setback. Quisling's zealously repeated appeals for collaboration with Hitler's forces had fallen on mostly deaf ears. But his National Socialist Party and its armed wing, known as the Hird – modelled on Himmler's SS – attracted just enough fanatics to pose a serious risk to Norway's resisters. Quisling himself now carried little credibility with Reichskommissar Josef Terboven, the Nazi-appointed governor of the country.

The King and his government remained defiant in London. This day, indeed, King Haakon and Crown Prince Olaf paid a highly public visit to an exhibition about prisoners of war being held in Pall Mall. The Norwegian merchant fleet, the fourth largest in the world, was voluntarily in Allied hands. An increasing number of Norwegians were being taken in small boats and fishing vessels back home across the North Sea and infiltrated into the country on sabotage and intelligence missions. Milorg, the nationwide military resistance, was working closely with the government in London and had organised Norway into fourteen districts, each subdivided into sections and areas with its own small army of resisters. In Oslo, the underground Central Committee of the Resistance, operated like an alternative government. Known as the 'Home Forces', it enjoyed the loyalty of nearly all Norwegians. For all that Norway might appear a sideshow, at no point could they forget the war around them. That night new long-range fighter and torpedo bombers of the Royal Navy's Fleet Air Arm launched a heavy attack on a German supply convoy off the Norwegian coast, shooting down several Messerschmitts and other fighter planes that attempted to intercept them.

As soon as they heard about Nazi plans for labour conscription, the exiled government issued an order through the BBC: no one should obey Nazi demands. The punchcard machines to be used for labour registration now became a prime target for sabotage. Young men fled their homes, creating the phenomena of the 'boys in the forest', a force akin to the Maquis in France. When the Nazis responded by refusing to issue ration cards to those who failed to collect them in person, the resisters simply organised a raid and stole eighty thousand cards being transported from a printer's. In total, only about three hundred young men across the country actually registered for labour service.

All this was the fruit of earlier resistance by such patriots as Moen. Today his mind was focused on rations. What he and his cellmates received was 'incredibly good', he confessed in his diary: sausage, jam, cheese, liver sausage, sardines. The problem was not the quality but the quantity, which was very little, so that hunger was a constant companion. The situation was getting worse, too. Until recently prisoners who'd won the right to receive parcels from home could also receive one kilogram of food every fortnight, and they usually shared it around. But in retaliation for the increased resistance outside, the privilege had been revoked. Soon Moen would be recording that breakfast consisted of nothing more than two small pieces of bread, half a small crust and a cup of ersatz coffee; the midday meal was a small piece of fish, five small potatoes of which one was rotten, and a cup of fish soup; and the evening consisted of bread and a cup of thin and mealy soup.

What he found even harder to bear, however, was the complete absence of tobacco. Deprived of the most elementary tools of mental stimulation, such as books and newspapers, he found denial of this most basic of drugs almost intolerable.

His only consolation was knowing that he was not much worse off than many civilians in the country. Rations had sunk to new lows, food queues were commonplace and getting longer, ersatz soap and coffee had long since replaced the real items and people were reduced to wearing paper shoes with wooden soles, sleeping under paper blankets and carrying handbags manufactured of fish scales. When he could forget he was in a Gestapo cell, Moen could even feel himself lucky.

In the war behind the Atlantic Wall, resistance had become a river in spate fed by a myriad streams. The underground press run by people like Moen informed and mobilised millions of people. André Heintz and countless thousands like him fed titbits of intelligence to the Allies. Hundreds of SOE agents such as Sonia d'Artois and Sydney Hudson laid elaborate plans for sabotage when D-Day came.

Across France, now the main focus of Allied efforts, the groups of armed young men of the Maquis, hiding in the hills and forests, were being armed with air drops of weapons by the Allies. Most of them began as draft dodgers, refusing to register for the Nazis' compulsory labour conscription programme for work in Germany's factories. This first act of refusal led inevitably to others. Without valid ration or identity cards, they became hunted outlaws. Inevitably, they melded eventually into the wider underground world of armed resistance.

Albert Grunberg's path resembled theirs, except that simply for being a Jew he was declared an enemy of the Reich. But when they had come for him, he also had run away. His escape took courage, and transformed him overnight into a resister. Those who helped him in his circle of silent complicity were also resisters, because, in the eyes of the Nazi occupiers and of the Vichy government, to help a Jew was a crime against the state. Likewise, to denounce a Jew earned a reward. Only that April the SS, in its relentless drive to hunt down the remaining Jews in France, had introduced a new system. 'The bonuses should not be too high' read the order. 'Nevertheless they should be high enough to give encouragement . . . the bonus will be generally larger in the cities than in the country.' As a result, the menace from informers had become even greater than before.

Most at risk among Albert's helpers was Madame Oudard, for giving him shelter and taking him food. She was also imperilling her family. Her mother, Mémé, and her children, Lulu and Michel, helped prepare Albert's meals. Despite her age, Mémé would even climb the six flights of stairs from time to time and chat with Albert about politics. So would Michel, while Lulu sometimes gave him a small demonstration of the physical exercises she was learning at school. Then there were Monsieur and

Madame Bon, his neighbours on the sixth floor, who allowed him to use their kitchen when they left town, a specially welcome blessing when things got too difficult between him and his brother Sami. It became his bolt hole. The Ouvrards, another couple on the same floor, were both employees of the Métro. They gave him food, as did his other next-door neighbours, the Maillards. The Fuseys helped by simply being discreet enough not to enquire who was living in the maid's little room. Downstairs, Professor Chabanaud, who worked at the Museum of Natural History, indulged Albert's desire for discussing philosophical and scientific issues. Any one of them could have betrayed him. All were risking their lives.

Today, at last, Albert received the news he'd been desperately waiting for. The papers had carried reports on the bombing of Chambéry, and in the hairdresser's shop his wife, Marguerite, busy at work, was imagining their son Roger, who lived in the town centre, which had taken the brunt of the attack, buried deep under the ruins. She'd found time to write both sons a frantic little note. But her efforts to reach them by telephone or send a telegram had failed.

Then, at five o'clock in the afternoon, came a familiar small tap on his door and there, unexpectedly early, stood Madame Oudard. In her hand was a letter. She thrust it at the startled Albert and disappeared down the stairs as quickly as she'd come. He just had time to notice her hair. She'd been waiting her turn for Marguerite to give her a perm when the letter came. Marguerite had read it before passing it on to her, and she had dashed along the street without giving a thought to what she looked like.

The letter was a short little nothing, just a few scribbled lines. But it meant everything. 'We're fine,' he read. 'The town's been bombed but the shelters here are built into the rocks and there's nothing to fear . . .' There, at the bottom, he saw the unmistakable signatures of his sons. Overjoyed, he still found time to make his usual daily entry in his diary. Madame Oudard's hastily presented small gift, he wrote, was 'la chère lettre salvatrice' – 'the dear letter of salvation'. His sons were safe. But it was salvation for himself, his peace of mind, and an end to the agony and the fears, that he meant.

Sonia d'Artois was finally relaxing. After their hot and wearying travels from the safe house, she had reached the Château des Bordeaux near the small village of Amné, the night before. She'd had a good night's sleep in a tent hidden in the trees behind the property, and thankfully at last had been able to change into the lighter summer clothes provided by Sydney Hudson's contacts in Le Mans. The only thing spoiling it all was her shoulder, still causing her a lot of pain.

That morning she sat on the terrace of the château at the end of a long table with a big steaming bowl of coffee in front of her for breakfast. There was bread, luscious mounds of soft white cheese, and butter. Luxury, she thought – even though the coffee was the ersatz kind now universal in occupied Europe, made of ground-up chicory and bitter to the taste. She felt at home. At last she was back in France.

Watching her, Hudson wondered how she'd turn out. He'd asked for a woman but she was very young, only just twenty, and this was her first mission. The SOE had begun to send female agents into France in 1942, but only slowly had prejudices against using women on front-line missions been overcome. The head of French section intelligence in the Baker Street headquarters was a remarkable and formidable woman, Vera Atkins. But using women at the sharp end of war went against the grain of tradition, especially when the enemy was the Gestapo. No other British units even contemplated exposing them to such danger. But the SOE was unconventional and ready to break all the rules.

It was need as much as anything that changed things. As networks rapidly expanded in France, agents needed couriers to travel around the countryside or between towns and cities keeping them in touch with one another. They must be invisible people who wouldn't draw the attention of the Germans, who could travel unnoticed in trains and on buses, who could pass through search barriers, who appeared innocent and harmless. Women.

Inside the SOE the issue was hotly debated. Finally it went to the very top – to Churchill himself. 'You're using women in this?' asked the Prime Minister. 'Yes,' came the reply, 'but we think this is a very sensible thing to do, don't you?' Churchill grunted. 'Yes,' he said. 'Good luck to you.'

In increasing numbers they were now turning up in France, most of them women like Sonia who'd lived in France or with Anglo-French backgrounds. Experience showed they could be just as effective as men. Bravery came into it, but also subtlety, imagination and adaptability. Initially they were 'invisible' to the Germans, but by now the Gestapo was waking up to the fact that being female didn't automatically mean 'harmless'.

Hudson noticed how Sonia seemed at home and watched appreciatively as she sipped her bowl of coffee like a local. Her accent was perfect, too. Teasingly, he called her 'Marguerite', the codeword used in the SOE message to announce her arrival. She laughed, and he sensed immediately that they'd get on.

They sat on the terrace, enjoying the food and mapping out their plans for D-Day.

It was none too soon. That evening at 9.15, George Jones, hiding with his radio set in the woods behind them, tuned into the BBC. He listened to the stream of personal messages broadcast over the next fifteen minutes, most of them mysterious and meaningless to him. Then he heard the words he'd been primed for. Three separate messages specifically designed for Hudson's Headmaster circuit, each one geared to a particular target: 'Les gigolos portent des bracelets'; 'Les visites font toujours plaisir'; and 'Les fleurs sont des mots d'amour'. The gigolos wearing bracelets indicated railways, the pleasurable visits guerrilla activity and roads; and the floral words of love, telecommunications.

Twenty-four hours before D-Day, each code would be confirmed with another short phrase.

Transmission of the BBC messages meant the D-Day machinery was shifting into high gear. No attempt was made to disguise the fact. 'From time to time the Navy fades out of public view,' declared Admiral Sir William James, Chief of Naval Information at the Admiralty, while opening an exhibition of photographs about the Royal Navy in London, 'but now it is about to appear again. Before long we will reach that stage when we begin to launch a big amphibious expedition.' Churchill's Minister of Production gave a similar hint in a lunchtime speech to the Clockmakers' Company of London. No army would ever go into battle so well equipped, claimed Oliver Lyttleton, as the one Britain would be launching on the Continent. In Washington the Secretary of War, Henry Stimson, also hinted strongly at momentous events. Over 3.6 million American soldiers were serving overseas, he announced, and 'the period of decisive action is now at hand'. This was the day that Admiral Ramsay formally assumed control of Operation Neptune. Eisenhower spent his last day at Bushy Park before moving his advanced headquarters to Portsmouth.

Ike had been holding meetings for several days now with his chief meteorological officer, Group Captain James Stagg of the RAF. From now on, Ike would convene a daily conference for all his commanders to receive an official briefing from Stagg. 'We're all extremely weather conscious now,' noted Harry Butcher. Forty-three years old, Stagg was a Lowland Scot, tall and redheaded, 'a scientist to the bones,' one chronicler has written, 'with all the scientist's refined capacity to pass unimpassioned judgement on the evidence, a man of sharp mind and soft speed, detached, resolute, courageous'.

D-Day was still fixed for Monday 5 June. Today was overcast with light rain, the hot spell finally broken. Later the sun came out briefly, but by mid-afternoon it was covered by low cloud. The sun was now rising before 6 a.m. and setting after 10 p.m. In London the official blackout stretched from 10.52 p.m. to 5.03 a.m. The days were still getting longer. A full moon was due on 6 June.

Eisenhower was feeling confident. 'Weather forecasts while still indefinite are generally favourable,' he cabled George C. Marshall, the US Army Chief of Staff, in a personal and top-secret Bigot message that day. 'Everyone is in good heart and barring unsuitable meteorological conditions we will do the trick as scheduled.' One reason for his optimism was the powerful sense that the disparate parts of the vast Allied machinery he commanded were finally striving harmoniously together towards a single goal. The night before he'd gone to Stanmore, the RAF headquarters on the north-west edge of London, to discuss the destruction of high-powered German radio stations along the French coast used for jamming Allied radar. Present was Air Marshal Sir Arthur Harris, the single-minded head of RAF Bomber Command, who'd put up a powerful fight against having his bombers placed under Ike's control for D-Day, and who was openly sceptical about tactical bombing. But Ike had been delighted to overhear the belligerent 'Bomber' Harris say to an associate, 'Why can't we take on one of these radio stations tonight?' For Harris to volunteer his planes for such a difficult and risky task was an unusual and welcome sign. That night, recorded Harry Butcher, Ike 'told the air people to give hell to the areas of the landing'. By this time focusing on the landing areas would give nothing away to the Germans, given the poundings being delivered everywhere else.

Far less welcome were noises emanating offstage from Churchill. Late in the afternoon Ike received an urgent message from Admiral Ramsay. Churchill had concocted an apparently madcap scheme for D-Day.

That morning the Neptune commander travelled up to London for a meeting at 3 p.m. with the Prime Minister in his under-ground Map Room. To his surprise Ramsay also found King George VI present with his private secretary. To his even greater astonishment Churchill revealed that both he and the King intended to accompany the troops across the Channel on D-Day. Appalled by the idea, Ramsay pointed out the risks, and as soon as he could decently escape he got on the phone to Eisenhower and urged him to intervene. But Ike had already told Churchill that this was a crazy idea. Imagine, he'd said, 'that the ship on which you're sailing is hit. We'd have to divert four or five ships to rescue you and you'd be a burden to the entire battle' – not to mention the catastrophic consequences if the Prime Minister were killed.

To add to Ike's worries, he also learned that, with the action moving to Portsmouth, Churchill was intent on descending on the city for the weekend. General Montgomery, who also heard the news, was apoplectic. 'If Winnie comes, he'll not only be a great bore, but may well also attract undue attention here,' he exploded. 'Why in the hell doesn't he go and smoke his cigar at Dover Castle and be seen with the Lord Mayor? It would fix the Germans' attention to Calais.'

Remarkably, Ike shrugged it all off. Churchill determined was not a man to be stopped. Besides, so far as the Prime Minister sailing with the D-Day armada was concerned, he was confident it wouldn't happen. For one thing, he was sure the War Cabinet would forbid it. He also knew that Churchill in reality was deeply opposed to the King's going, so in the end could hardly demand passage for himself. Ike, in fact, had been skilfully outmanoeuvring Churchill. As soon as he'd heard of the Prime Minister's scheme, he had contacted Buckingham Palace and mobilised the King to oppose it. As for Churchill descending on Portsmouth, it was better to have him close by, where he could be controlled, than in London concocting more crazy plans. Having Churchill publicly wave a cigar to the world's press in Dover, moreover, as the exasperated Montgomery had blurted out, would be too obvious a ploy and was likely to backfire. As it was, Ike felt sure the existing plans were working. Even as he schemed to contain Churchill's enthusiasm, his deception staff were discussing the measures to support operations after D-Day. Assuming the landings succeeded, they agreed to maintain the threat to southern Norway and the Pas de Calais; if the Normandy bridgehead got bogged down, these threats would be supplemented by increasing those to Norway, and targeting Bordeaux.

Nonetheless, Ike's personal diplomacy was being sorely stretched, and Churchill was testing the limits of everyone's patience. He was still on the rampage about civilians being bombed in France, and the rapid approach of D-Day was whipping him into a frenzy of excitement. 'My God,' confided an exasperated Sir Alan Brooke to his diary that evening, 'how difficult it is to run a war and to keep military considerations clear of all the vested interests and political foolery attached to it.'

But war and politics march hand in hand, and everyday life went on, including commerce and business. The London Stock Market was buoyant, with heavy demands for industrial shares, and widespread gains. Wall Street also showed strong and active trading. Advertisers were catching the mood. 'The Dawn Must Break' ran a headline in *The Times* that day. 'Through the shadows of Night we have laboured to hasten the victorious morn. Now with advancing day our thoughts turn to the safe necessities of a peaceful life.' The makers of Chubb locks, with an illustration to match, were keen to cash in on the impending invasion.

There was no liberation, however, for Jill, one of the escaped monkeys whose antics had been amusing Londoners over the previous few days. Repeated attempts to lure the two down from their Hampstead tree had failed. Jack was eventually recaptured, but Jill was shot dead. Another sobering item for wildlife lovers was news of a diminishing number of nesting sites for swallows. Crowds flocked to West End cinemas to see films such as *For Whom the Bell Tolls*, starring Gary Cooper and Ingrid Bergman at the Carlton, or Cary Grant and John Garfield in *Destination Tokyo* at the Warner. Noël Coward's *Blithe Spirit* was enjoying its third successful year at the Duchess Theatre, and at the Aldwych Lynne Fontanne and Alfred Lunt were featuring in *There Shall Be No Night*. The British Archaeological Association held its annual meeting that afternoon at 4.30 p.m., and at the Guildhall School of Music Austrian refugees in Britain presented a bronze head of Beethoven to the City of London. At 9.40 p.m. the BBC Home Service broadcast Emilie Hooke, soprano, and Peter Pears, tenor, singing a song cycle by the Czechoslovak composer Janacek. Its title, *Diary of a Young Man Who Vanished*, aptly caught the sinister uncertainty hovering over the fate of so many of his countrymen under Nazi rule.

In his concrete-lined Whitehall bunker, Churchill again devoured his daily diet of Ultra messages. They were gratifyingly full of intercepts of German military communications from Italy revealing the exhaustion of all available reserves, and were spattered with words and phrases such as 'hard costly struggles', 'enemy penetrations', 'withdrawal' and 'increasing Allied pressure'. They also included a complaint by von Rundstedt about continuing transport shortages in France that were hindering the construction of Atlantic Wall defences.

At midday he sat down to chair a meeting of his War Cabinet. They discussed Yugoslavia, where it was now clear that efforts to build bridges between the royalist Serbs and Tito's communist partisans were doomed to failure. They also rejected, as a patent effort to embarrass the Allies, a Gestapo scheme to exchange a million Jews for ten thousand trucks and supplies of coffee, tea, cocoa and soap. But the trickiest issue by far remained de Gaulle.

Roosevelt was still refusing to discuss the post-liberation government of France with him, and no arrangements were in place for the French leader to make a broadcast to France on D-Day. All other exiled leaders, such as King Haakon of Norway and Queen Wilhelmina of the Netherlands, were scheduled to address their countries. Churchill, now obviously impatient with his White House ally, was adamant that de Gaulle should be included. Only that morning Lord Selborne sent him a strongly worded letter. 'From the point of view of the French Resistance groups in Operation OVERLORD,' wrote the minister in charge of the SOE, 'a personal broadcast by de Gaulle to the resistance movements in France would have an *immense* psychological effect on D-Day . . . there is no getting away from the fact that his personal influence with the fighting elements among the French is of the highest importance.'

In Algiers, however, the diplomatic tango continued. Duff Cooper received Churchill's telegram inviting de Gaulle to London. But when he noticed that it failed to make any promise about discussing the post-liberation government of France, he decided not to pass it on to de Gaulle, who he was certain would explode with anger. Instead he consulted René Massigli, de Gaulle's foreign policy expert. The two men hatched a plan. De Gaulle should be urged to go to London, but if the Americans still refused to discuss civil affairs he should return promptly to Algiers, thereby publicly embarrassing Roosevelt and the Americans into making concessions. Massigli knew he would still face problems in getting de Gaulle to travel to London. So he asked that Churchill be told of the plan and tell de Gaulle he agreed with it. Cooper returned to the British Embassy to send the telegram.

In the meantime de Gaulle spent the day at his overheated office in Les Glycines brooding over his treatment by the Allies. Roosevelt, deeply suspicious of what he termed de Gaulle's 'messianic complex', was badly out of touch with pro-Gaullist feeling in France. As recently as February his personal chief of staff, Admiral William Leahy, had absurdly advised him that the most reliable person to rally the French after D-Day remained Marshal Pétain. Hundreds of American were being trained in the USA to go to France to administer the country after its liberation, and printing presses were producing thousands of special occupation banknotes. De Gaulle was well informed about all this and deeply and angrily humiliated by it. As for Britain, there had once been an appalling screaming match in London, with Churchill shouting at him across the table, 'You are not France. I do not recognise you as France!'

Yet de Gaulle's own insensitive behaviour frequently invited such responses. Only six months before he'd met with Churchill at Marrakesh, where the Prime Minister was recuperating from pneumonia after his exertions at the Tehran Conference. De Gaulle's visit came after several months of political quarrelling with the Prime Minister, and he arrived in a tetchy mood. Clementine Churchill, who spoke excellent French, invited him to walk in the garden before lunch. At a certain moment the conversation had become awkward. 'General,' said Mrs Churchill in the same forthright way she sometimes had to adopt with her husband, 'you should be very careful not to hate your friends more than your enemies.' He had taken the advice to heart, and out of the Morocco encounter had flowed increased

British support for the French Resistance and a pact on Free French participation in D-Day.

All that now seemed at risk.

Taut relations with de Gaulle in Algiers were echoed in dealings over the resistance with Free French leaders in London.

From 10 Duke Street, a house tucked away behind Selfridge's department store on Oxford Street, the Free French had built up a formidable espionage and sabotage organisation. Known as the Bureau Centrale de Renseignements et d'Action (BCRA), it was run by Colonel 'Passy', the pseudonym of André Dewavrin, an energetic and loyal follower of de Gaulle. With his ready co-operation, the Allies had developed an elaborate plan for action by the French Resistance to help with D-Day. Its forces would be supplied with weapons and ammunition, yet carefully harnessed, to be unleashed only when and where they could directly benefit Allied forces – hence the elaborate system of coded messages for people such as André Heintz. But the overriding need to keep the D-Day secret as tightly controlled as possible meant that Free French officers could not be told about the time or place of the landings. Toiling hard alongside their American and British allies, Free French officers increasingly resented their exclusion from invasion planning.

OSS officer William Casey witnessed one such scene just before D-Day in the Operation Sussex planning room at 70 Grosvenor Street. The Free French were deeply involved, helping, among other things, to choose safe and suitable drop sites. One of the most helpful Frenchman was Colonel 'Rémy', the pseudonym of Gilbert Renault-Rouilier, a pre-war Breton insurance executive who'd built up an impressive intelligence network in France known as the Confrérie de Notre Dame (CND). It was Normandy-based members of Rémy's intelligence network, Century, who had successfully smuggled the plans of the Atlantic Wall to London.

Rémy was standing in front of a large map pointing at a spot where he recommended that the next Sussex team be dropped. But as the site was located right behind one of the Normandy landing beaches, it was immediately rejected as unsuitable. Yet no one could tell him why. Suspicious, Rémy asked if he had accidentally hit on an invasion secret. If so, he asked, couldn't they please tell him, so that he could do his job properly? An embarrassing few moments followed, until he was told politely but firmly that even at this last-minute date OSS could not tell him when and where D-Day would happen. Never fully involved in, nor fully excluded from, D-Day planning, Free French officers like Rémy and Passy had to rein in their frustration.

For the second night running, planes of RAF Bomber Command hit the railway yards at Saumur, on the River Loire. After twenty minutes the pall of smoke grew so heavy that another set of pathfinder markers had to be dropped for the second wave of incoming planes. The railway linked Tours with Nantes, Walter Schwender's temporary home on the Loire.

His second home, Auschwitz, lay hundreds of miles to the east on the River Vistula, close to the historic city of Cracow. After Poland's defeat in 1939, the Nazis opened a concentration camp there for political prisoners as part of a broader and more ambitious plan to transform the town and its surroundings into a model of German settlement in the East. The local Polish population was deported and their houses made available for Germans. The camp's first inmates were mostly Poles. By 1944 it had become the largest, the most international and the most notorious of all Hitler's concentration camps.

Early in 1942 the SS inaugurated a second camp, some two miles away, known as Auschwitz II, or Auschwitz-Birkenau, after the German name for the adjacent village, Brzezinska. A great deal of careful thought went into its construction, and its first architectural plans were drawn up by a graduate of the famous Bauhaus school of art and design.

By now the organised mass murder of European Jews was well under way. Birkenau functioned as one of its principal extermination camps, equipped with gas chambers and crematoria, and it was linked to the European railway network by a specially constructed branch line. Heinrich Himmler, the head of the SS, visited it in July 1942 and personally witnessed the gassing of a group of Dutch Jews. He was so pleased with what he saw that he authorised an expansion of the facilities and a speed-up in its work. Afterwards he inspected the I.G. Farben plant, finishing the day with a grand reception attended by SS and Auschwitz dignitaries. Now, in mid-1944, Birkenau's gas chambers were functioning overtime to dispose of the Jews of Hungary, who were arriving daily by the trainload.

Located about three miles to the east of the two main Auschwitz camps, adjacent to the small village of Dory, the I.G. Farben Buna plant drew its labour force from a camp known as Auschwitz-Monowitz, or Auschwitz III. Monowitz was one of about forty satellite camps spread out over a wide area around Auschwitz. Varying in size, these were built near mines, foundries and factories working directly or indirectly for the armaments industry, and I.G. Farben was only one among several German corporations involved. Monowitz was the largest of the satellites, and acted as headquarters for the others.

About six hundred yards square, and surrounded by two barbed-wire fences, the inner of which was electrified, Monowitz contained about sixty wooden huts, each housing 250 men crammed two together to a bunk. Over the main entrance gate were inscribed the words grotesquely familiar to concentration-camp inmates across Nazi-occupied Europe: 'Arbeit Macht Frei' – 'Work Makes You Free'. In the middle was a large roll-call square, and facing it a bed of grass, where a gallows would sometimes be erected for a hanging. There was a hospital run by SS doctors, and even a brothel, although it was strictly out of bounds to Jews. The camp's inhabitants included prisoners of many different categories, nationalities and languages. In 1944 90 per cent of its inmates were Jews. All were deemed young and fit enough to escape the gas chambers, so long as they remained able to work.

Walter Schwender's father, Wilhelm, worked in the Buna plant, travelling every day from his house in the small village of Babitz.

This was situated close to Auschwitz at the confluence of the Vistula and Sola rivers, and, like most of the other nearby villages, its Polish population had been expelled, their property confiscated, and their houses given to Germans. Babitz lay right by the railway tracks and adjacent to the Birkenau camp, and even had a small auxiliary camp of its own for raising livestock. Only the wilfully blind could not see what was happening around them, and even temporary visitors to the I.G. Farben plant could see the chimneys of Auschwitz and note the awful smell. But racial superiority and anti-semitism lay at the heart of Nazi ideology, and the SS relentlessly portrayed the Jews and political prisoners as enemies of the German people. Walter and his parents questioned none of it or, if they did, kept their thoughts to themselves. The Buna prisoners worked in striped concentration-camp uniforms with coloured triangles indicating their status: green for criminal, red for political and a yellow star for Jews. 'You could see,' said Walter's father, 'there were lots of criminals.'

By this time also, the Buna plant had become the focus of intense Allied interest. This was not because of the prisoners, but because its potential manufacture of synthetic rubber and fuel made it an important strategic target. Regular flights over the Auschwitz complex had begun in April, when bombers of the US 15th Air Force based in Italy made their first photo-reconnaissance sortie. The day before, yet another flight had taken photographs of the plant with a view to a major bombing raid.

That day, too, the SS administration in the main Auschwitz camp tallied up some grotesque statistics. The deportation of Jews from Hungary to Auschwitz, eventually involving over four hundred and thirty thousand souls, had begun in mid-May. Since then nearly ninety pounds of gold had been taken from the teeth of those sent to the gas chambers. The day before, two trains out of the one hundred and forty-seven that would eventually make this particular journey of death, had arrived from Hungary, their sealed cattle trucks crammed with a human cargo of eight thousand Jews. The journey had taken three and a half days. Without food or water, fifty-five died *en route*, and another two hundred simply went mad.

When the trains finally arrived on the railway siding at Birkenau, and the doors were pulled open by SS guards, six thousand men, women and children were immediately marched to the gas chambers. Two thousand – a thousand each of the fitter and younger men and women – were sent to the barracks for forced labour.

'Units in the clutches of Movement Control' read the War Diary of the Regina Rifles for Thursday 1 June. 'All movements taking place by craft load.' Glenn Dickin was about to say farewell to Hiltingbury Camp and to Britain.

Since his transatlantic crossing two summers before, he'd seen a lot and changed his views on a number of things. A rural boy closely attuned to the landscape, he'd responded warmly to the British countryside. Riding his motorcycle along the Sussex Downs, he'd thrilled at the views and marvelled at the peace and tranquillity of it all. 'There's no doubt about it,' he told his mother, 'the English landscape is very pretty. I like the old village we're in. It is certainly quiet and restful.' Trees and flowers abounded, and the roses, 'lovely big ones', were abundant. Being closer to the action also lifted his spirits. Every day he could see history unfolding in the skies. 'Scads of big and little screaming fast and powerful planes,' he enthused.

Yet the contrast with Canada was often painful. Prices were high, he disliked the Limey officers he encountered, English cigarettes he considered unsmokable and pleaded for packs from home, and he didn't much warm to the English girls he met in his first few mess dances. British newspaper articles about life across the Atlantic even made him angry. They claimed that the dollar was only worth half the English pound, yet daily experience showed him that a pound went only half as far as it did at home. 'I am sure not very pleased with the initial outlook I have obtained on the Mother Country,' he confessed.

His early training in Britain had also been tough. Within a month of his arrival he was at battle school, being woken at 5 a.m. for a three-mile run before breakfast, a four-mile march to the training site, a whole day running around in full battle gear and a four-mile march back to base. All too often this was endured in pouring rain, and there never seemed to be enough food. Like a kid at summer camp, he peppered his letters home with want lists: tinned meat, grapefruit and apple juice, cheese, home-made jam and his mother's canned chicken drumsticks. 'Sure hope we can get this bloody war over and get back to Canada where I can eat big steaks and drink lots of milk' ran a typical lament. Fed up, at one point he'd even tried to get into the paratroopers, guys 'always whipping about with big planes towing gliders and so on having a hell of a time'. Failing that, he hoped for the Royal Canadian Air Force. But neither happened.

Now, two long years on, he'd thawed to new experiences and was enjoying life. Along with going to pubs, he'd seen a huge number of movies, including such wartime classics as *Mrs Miniver* and *Tortilla Flat*, and had even found a nice English girl to date for a few months, a brunette whom he took to dances on the back of his motorbike and whose parents welcomed him warmly into their home. When he'd moved on to a second camp in another part of the country he'd found a replacement, a blonde this time, of Dutch ancestry. 'I have met some pretty nice people and have had some pretty good times,' he wrote home for his first Christmas. He also liked his first officers' mess, the library of a seventeenth-century stately home with a gold-painted ceiling, thousands of books and an enormous fireplace and mantelpiece sporting two carved figures, 'one a babe with a sheaf of arrows, the other a man with a laurel wreath around his head'. Outside, in the grounds, grazed a herd of deer.

He and Gordon Brown were now playing hockey for their regimental team and spending their leaves together in London at the exclusive Savoy Hotel in the Strand, a popular wartime venue for officers from Canada and the United States. They'd go to a supper dance, see a West End show or two and rubberneck celebrities flitting through the lobby. One stay coincided with a visit by two Hollywood stars, the comedienne Martha Raye and the glamorous Kay Francis, who'd played Florence Nightingale in the biopic *The White Angel*. The women were starring together that year in *Four*

Jills in a Jeep, in which a quartet of glamour girls entertained the troops, a case of art imitating life because both were renowned for their morale-boosting tours to the forces. Glenn even spotted Raye wandering around the lobby in a mink coat. He also spied the stage and screen star Burgess Meredith, who, the previous year, had directed the Office of War Information introductory film for GIs, *Welcome to Britain*. 'You will probably remember him in *Winterset* and *Tom, Dick and Harry*,' he informed his family. 'He looks exactly the same as he does on the screen.' Another encounter that left a strong impression was with a Czechoslovak girl who'd fled her country when the Nazis took over. 'A very cosmopolitan bunch of people,' the new sophisticate wrote home to Manor.

He'd travelled a lot, too. He'd got to know Brighton, Bournemouth and the Isle of Wight, he'd seen Stonehenge, and he'd ridden on his motorbike through Wales and Gloucestershire, where his prairie eye marvelled at the ubiquitous stone walls of the Cotswolds – 'old stone fences', he called them, with 'no cement holding them together and hundreds of years old'. He'd been to Scotland, where he'd taken a commando training course at Inverary on Loch Fyne, and he'd been taken up in a four-engined Stirling bomber by Gordon's cousin, Reg, who was in the air force, and they'd flown out over the North Sea close to the Dutch coast for a bit of bombing practice. He was even getting a bit blasé about it all, and scarcely now noticed the heavy bombers or the squadrons of fighters skimming the hedgerows on their way to France that had once so entranced him. Glenn was definitely maturing. He'd even taken to listening to Winston Churchill's speeches on the radio. 'He is always good,' he told his mother.

A few miles away, another young Churchill fan seized the chance to lie in until ten that morning before 'mucking about' in her room getting ready for her afternoon watch at Fort Southwick. Veronica Owen's schooling had left her steeped in English history, one of her favourite subjects, and Churchill's carefully crafted speeches evoking the great moments of the nation's past always moved her deeply. So did the films she devoured two or three times a week at the local cinema, epics of struggle and victory, such as the life of Madame Curie, or *Song to Remember*, about the Polish composer and patriot Chopin.

Yet there was more, a family connection that uniquely linked Veronica with Britain's wartime leader. Churchill had spent the 1930s out of office, a pariah within the Conservative Party led by Stanley Baldwin and Neville Chamberlain, and a maverick on major issues such as Home Rule for India, the abdication of Edward VIII and the appeasement of Hitler. To occupy himself, but also to preach the lessons he gleaned from history, he spent much of the decade toiling over a massive four-volume biography of his illustrious ancestor John Churchill, the first Duke of Marlborough, victor of the great battle with the French at Blenheim in 1704.

To help him, Churchill assembled a team of historians and researchers, and for the naval background he had selected Veronica's father. By then retired from the Navy, and already a keen naval historian active in the Navy Records Society, Commander Owen spent four years working with Churchill on the Marlborough biography, and eventually even produced his own monograph on the subject, *The War at Sea under Queen Anne 1702–1708*. As a result, as Veronica's twin brother Hugh later said, 'we were brought up to admire WSC even during his years in the wilderness'. A linear descendant of the great duke born in the palace that carried the name of his greatest victory, Churchill, as Veronica needed no telling, was now leading the nation's fight against the latest, and by far the worst, of a litany of tyrants who had conquered Europe.

After her watch, she returned home, changed quickly out of her uniform, and bicycled into Titchfield for supper with the Spurways. When she'd first arrived at Fort Southwick, she'd been able to spend happy and welcome breaks with her parents in London. But since April and the restriction of leaves to within a twenty-mile radius, she'd not had a chance to see them, and the Spurways had become surrogate parents. She was still a bit awkward with them, but tonight proved an ice-breaker. Conversation just flowed and her shyness suddenly fell away. 'It's so lovely to get away and talk about real things,' she told her parents, 'not only clothes, lipsticks, other Wrens, and men!' There was another plus, too. Frank Spurway had once played cricket for Somerset, so they had an enthusiasm in common. 'Just talked and talked until five to 11.0!' she scribbled in her diary, after frantically racing back to Heathfield and missing the eleven o'clock deadline by a couple of minutes.

Packing his gear at Cottesmore and waiting for the big day reminded Bill Tucker of his training at parachute school. Its staff were like expert torturers, he thought. 'Flash Gordon', the lieutenant in charge, had been a man with a curse for everything and everyone. His cronies spied on the recruits, punishing them with push-ups. Once Tucker was caught moving an eyeball and made to do fifty. On his first training jump he sat white-faced with his buddies in a huge hangar. He'd never been on a plane before and 'Geronimo', the paratroopers' war cry, was played endlessly to hype them up. A plane taxied up outside and he was ordered in as number three on the jump. After it circled the field once, the jumpmaster ordered them to stand up. Tucker still thought it was just a dry run. Then, suddenly, the jumpmaster barked 'Jump!' and number one got a kick up the backside to help him out of the door. Before he knew it, Tucker felt a slap on the back of his legs, and he was suddenly tumbling out of the aircraft head first. He was still doing the count they'd all been taught, 'one thousand, two thousand', when he felt a terrific shock as his parachute opened and he came to a standstill in mid-air. It was a wonderful feeling. 'I jumped!' he shouted exuberantly as he touched ground.

Since then he'd done dozens of drops, but the only combat one was at Salerno. He'd been supposed to drop into battle earlier, on a mission to capture German-controlled airfields outside Rome at the time of Italy's surrender. The date had been 8 September, his birthday. They'd been in the air for an hour after take-off from their base in Sicily when the mission was cancelled. The next day the battalion had been summoned together by its commander, Major Edward Krause. Nicknamed 'Cannonball', Krause was always on the warpath. The operation had been cancelled because the Germans had got wind of the mission. 'Men,' said the commander with his usual profanity, 'last night we had history by the balls, but Fate lifted up his leg and farted on us.'

Then, at Salerno, Fate had behaved itself. That night Tucker felt no fear. 'I figured I was a lucky man with the ability to forget the past and not think a hell of a lot about the future.' He just worried about throwing up, because he was still struggling with the stomach problems, dizziness and weight loss from his North African exploits. It was a bright, moonlit night. Down below he could see ships burning in Salerno Bay as the Allies struggled to get a foothold in Italy. The green light had gone on, out he'd jumped head first and suddenly realised he was moving through the air far too fast. Something had gone wrong, so he pulled his reserve chute and managed to land safely. But he'd landed separated from the others. Then it dawned on him that he was on European soil 'loaded with Germans'. Grabbing his rifle with lightning speed, he felt ready to die. From then on, Italy had been nothing more than endless hills, sickness and – when he felt better – great beauty.

What, he wondered, would Norway be like?

'. . . saw fifty big field guns packed without guard on road side. Convoy sixty vehicles going towards Southend. Along both sides of bypass parking places are marked out for thousands of vehicles but not yet occupied. Huge camp east of Brentwood-Tilbury road and south of Grays . . .'

In his semi-detached house in Hendon, Garbo's radio operator tapped out his message to the Abwehr in Madrid, confirming the huge Allied build-up in south-east England and focusing German attention once again on an impending attack in the Pas de Calais. Karl Kühlenthal had reason to be pleased with his agent Arabel.

Since the scare over Normandy two weeks before, Allied deception planners had been urgently beefing up Garbo's role. They didn't dream of persuading the Germans to remove any of their forces from Normandy; that was too much to expect. Their main hope now was to keep Hitler's troops in the Pas de Calais pinned down in expectation of a landing there, meaning that one of the two armies under Rommel's command, the 15th, could not intervene in Normandy. Sustaining Garbo's credibility in Berlin was now absolutely critical. If the deception plan was really to work, his messages would have to continue *after* D-Day. The longer the Germans believed his story, the better for the battle over the Normandy beachhead. Final approval of the beefed-up deception campaign had been granted just two weeks before. So far, everything suggested that the big fish in Berlin were swallowing Garbo's bait.

Yet everyone remained on tenterhooks. Earlier that day there had been a chilling reminder of how fragile Garbo's existence as a double agent really was. The elaborate picture he was creating for the Germans possessed as little reality as the movies that had transformed his Hollywood namesake into a worldwide celebrity. At any moment the celluloid could snap, the projector break down or the house lights suddenly go up.

The Double-Cross Committee, which ran Garbo and his fellow agents, were terribly aware that the entire illusion could be brought to an abrupt and unwelcome halt. That afternoon they met at 2.30 at their offices in St James's Street, in the heart of London's West End. One item on the agenda bore directly, and urgently, on Garbo's continued credibility.

Ironically, the greatest threat both to him and the entire double-cross scheme came from the Allies' own success. As German defeat loomed, a number of Abwehr officers began to desert the sinking ship and ensure their survival by offering to help the Allies. One of them was an officer named Johan Jebsen, from Lisbon. He appeared to have some genuine anti-Nazi sentiments, and passed on some useful items of intelligence. Then, in January 1944, he placed a bombshell under the entire double-cross scheme. In a report to London he named some of the German agents being run against the British out of Lisbon. Number one on the list was Arabel – Juan Pujol.

This apparent 'gift' posed an appalling dilemma in London. If Arabel continued to operate as normal, it would suggest strongly that he was working under British, not German, control. Once Jebsen himself realised this, argued the double-cross experts, who could tell what might happen? He might be pro-British now, but could his loyalties at some point shift back to Berlin – in which case he would obviously expose the agent? Or would the Gestapo sniff him out as a traitor and arrest him? Could he withstand torture, or would he give the game away to save his own skin? 'In short,' noted the chairman of the Double-Cross Committee, Sir John Masterman, 'the German turncoat, trying to assist us, would in fact destroy the entire system.'

The Committee debated the choices. They could pull Jebsen out of Portugal, but that would cause the Germans to suspect the double agents with whom he'd been in contact. The Secret Intelligence Service could assassinate him, but that would spark a major German investigation. In the end they chose to do nothing except monitor his activities intensively. For a while nothing alarming had emerged.

Then, just four weeks before, disaster had struck. The Bletchley Park code-breakers picked up an Abwehr signal revealing that Jebsen had been kidnapped from his house in Lisbon. Driven across the Franco-Spanish border in a car with Diplomatic Corps immunity, he was on his way to Berlin for interrogation by the Gestapo.

The worst-case scenario had come to pass. Since then Garbo's very life as a double agent had teetered on the brink. Had Jebsen, known by the code-name 'ARTIST' in London, given the game away? Was there even a scintilla of evidence that the Germans had got wind of the double-cross system and seen through Garbo? In other words, was the entire D-Day deception plan about to collapse in ruins? Only the code-breakers could provide the answer. They had feverishly been poring over intercepted Abwehr messages to uncover why ARTIST had been arrested. If they could discover that, then they could calculate whether Garbo was really in danger.

The news revealed at 58 St James's Street shortly before three o'clock brought a sigh of relief. ARTIST's trouble with the Germans, reported the experts, almost certainly sprang from his efforts to fiddle expenses rather than from doubts about his political loyalty. They also thought it was unlikely that any suspicions he may have had about the double-cross system would be revealed in questioning by the Gestapo. There was no need, they concluded, to assume that Garbo was fatally compromised. The double game could go on. The D-Day deception scheme remained securely in place.

At 10.30 a.m. David Bruce and 'Wild Bill' Donovan arrived on board the destroyer USS *Davis* at Belfast and boarded the *Tuscaloosa*, the American heavy cruiser that would take them to the Utah beachhead. After lunch with Admiral Deyo, during which they all agreed that Pearl Harbor had been a blessing in disguise by forcing the United States out of its lethargy, the two OSS men visited British officials onshore. Later, back on board ship, they watched a film starring Errol Flynn as 'Gentleman Jim Corbett', the legendary nineteenth-century prizefighter whose polished and well-spoken manners belied his toughness in the ring.

So far Bruce was worried about both what he'd seen and what he'd heard. More American naval support had been required for Neptune than originally envisaged, and the competing demands for shipping from the Pacific had delayed the arrival of reinforcements. 'Even tonight,' he noted in his diary, 'officers of some vessels are being briefed for the first time on their intricate tasks in the great operation; and certain of the ships recently arrived from America are lacking necessary equipment, including such items as crystals, smoke floats and their igniters, and sufficient supplies of ammunition to continue their duties, unless the landing is quickly successful.'

On land, however, things were going better for Allied intelligence agents in Operation Sussex. That night, three more successfully landed in France.

This was the day that Canadian war correspondents, shut up on the Isle of Wight, were let in on the D-Day secret. In a room at the Fountain Inn in Cowes, a British officer unrolled a map of the

French coast. 'This is the plot,' he whispered. 'We are landing in the general area here between Cherbourg and Le Havre.' One of the group felt an immediate surge of relief. Now he knew. They would be landing on broad, sandy beaches extending for miles, with barely a cliff to be scaled. Not a heavily defended port to attack, either. It would not be another Dieppe.

As more and more people were briefed on the landings, anxiety rose about a possible leak. What if one of the tens of thousands of soldiers sealed in their camps (like Glenn Dickin or Bill Tucker), or one of the war correspondents, revealed what he knew, either deliberately or accidentally? Would this blow the entire D-Day secret? Or could the danger be contained? The Allies were about to find out.

Late that evening the scrambler phone rang urgently on the desk of a major at the Counter-Intelligence office at Western Command headquarters in south Wales. The area housed thousands of American troops destined for the follow-up landings after D-Day. It was already sealed off, with all entry and exit points controlled, roadblocks in place and hundreds of Military Police and soldiers checking identity cards and traffic. There was already a security scare under way. The night before, a United States Army Air Force sergeant had got drunk in a bar in Redditch, flashed the special French currency notes he'd been issued and boasted he was leaving for France 'on the 4th or the 5th'. Intelligence officers were now busy trying to smother the story.

The call was from a colonel in Security Intelligence at Montgomery's London headquarters at St Paul's School. 'You've got to help,' he said. 'It's very serious. Drop everything else.' The previous night a British NCO from one of the assault units due to land early on D-Day had escaped from his camp in Hampshire, carrying with him sufficient detailed knowledge about the beach and tides to identify its location. He'd since vanished into thin air. But there was a chance he was heading to Wales, where both his girlfriend and parents lived.

Immediately, the Military Police and Field Security were alerted, and round-the-clock surveillance placed on the NCO's home. 'He must be caught before the damage is done,' insisted the Colonel. 'The danger is that he knows near as dammit *where and when*.'

When midnight came, the NCO was still on the run.

That night the weather was unsettled in the Channel. The day was marked by a mix of light showers and short bright intervals, and the temperature hovered in the low sixties. But by evening a fresh south-westerly wind had begun to blow and the sky turned overcast, with low banks of thundery cloud. The sea was running strong and there was a worrying drop in the barometer.

6

SOLDIERS IN VERY GOOD HEART

Friday 2 June

No one could miss it. Spread over several columns in *The Times*, and fringed with a thick black border, the warning was explicit: 'THE PUBLIC IS ADVISED TO AVOID TRAVELLING.' In view of the 'increasing pressure' on the railway system it would be necessary to withdraw, without notice, many more trains this summer. The notice drew the eye as forcibly as the headline announcing the imminent fall of Rome and pleas from the Vatican for respectful treatment of the Eternal City. Whoever raised a hand against Rome, declared the Pope, would be guilty of 'matricide to the whole civilised world and in the eternal judgement of God'. After hearing Gigli in Verdi's opera *Un Ballo in Maschera*, Field Marshal Kesselring, the commander of Hitler's forces in Italy, ordered the evacuation of the city. Its hotels emptied of German officers, staff cars were loaded up, and the infantry began marching north.

In London, the day was bright, warm and sunny. The invasion forces were on the move. Thousands were already loaded on to their transports, stuck in convoys or waiting in ports. Others had already reached the 'hards', hundreds of temporary concrete embarkation platforms constructed along rivers, beaches and estuaries to load the vast armada and its heavy equipment of tanks, guns, trucks and supplies. Dozens of ships were sailing towards the assembly area south of the Isle of Wight in the English Channel. HMS *Nelson*, from which Churchill still hoped to see the action, left its base at Scapa Flow, in the Orkney Islands, heading towards Milford Haven, on the south-west coast of Wales. Admiral Ramsay spent the afternoon observing troops loading at Southampton and nearby Gosport. 'All soldiers in very good heart,' he noted in his diary.

At 6.30 p.m. two midget submarines were towed by trawler from Portsmouth into the English Channel. The tow ropes were made of nylon that would have made twenty thousand pairs of stockings, worth a fortune on the black market. Just fifty feet long and only five feet wide, each of the submarines sported a single bunk shared in shifts by its four-man crew, a diesel engine identical to that which drove a London bus and batteries leaking hydrogen gas that caused headaches and vomiting. Their mission was to surface off the Normandy coast immediately before the D-Day landings to act as navigational markers for the British and Canadian forces. Until then, they would remain submerged just offshore. Rather than the traditional grey and black, they were painted yellow and green, to camouflage them from the air as they lay waiting in the shallow water.

As soon as he could get away from his day's teaching at the lycée, André Heintz hopped on his bike and headed for the university. Here the concierge handed him a letter addressed to a 'Monsieur Conto'. This was the name she knew him by, one of the several *noms de guerre* he used, with false identity papers to back it up. He didn't want any incriminating evidence coming to his home address.

The letter was postmarked Hermanville-sur-Mer, a small village on the coast outside Ouistreham. It had been posted at 5 p.m. the previous afternoon. 'I'll meet you at 8.45 Gare St Pierre Saturday 3 June. Cordially yours, Courtois,' read Heintz. 'Courtois' was the code-name of his intelligence contact, the husband of the woman who'd passed on the warning messages that unforgettable day at the lycée. In reality the Resistance chief for the whole of the Calvados *département*, his real name was Jacques Bergeot. The Gare St Pierre was the small station near the docks in Caen, linked to Ouistreham by means of a narrow-gauge railway. It was their usual rendezvous place.

That evening André followed his nightly ritual of listening to the BBC for any warning messages, but there were none. Outside, the evening was hot and overcast. Overhead he heard hundreds of Allied bombers heading up the Seine towards Paris. Earlier in the day the BBC French-language broadcast had talked of the coming 'national insurrection' called for by de Gaulle, which the Free French leader had linked with the impending national liberation. This was not to be confused with some spectacular and sponta-neous mass uprising, insisted André Gillois, the movement's spokesman. Rather, it would be a meticulously planned and care-fully modulated series of moves that would vary in type from region to region and involve different people in different ways. Everyone, therefore, should strictly obey the instructions that would reach them, either via the organisations to which they belonged or on the radio. 'Listen in for our orders,' he concluded, 'they will be your guide.'

How much longer would André have to wait? Whenever he felt impatient or downhearted, he would remember his friends in Bristol. So far they had suffered almost worse than he had, their city the target of some devastating German bombing and – although he didn't yet know it – one of his best friends from the school there had been killed during a raid. For a while André had even been able to keep in touch with them. One day he'd received a letter postmarked in neutral Lisbon and giving a post-office box number there. It was from the family in Bristol, and he'd replied to it via the box number. He'd stuck to strictly personal news, because he was certain the letter would be censored by the Vichy authori-ties. But he'd assured his friends that although life in Nazi-occupied France was difficult, he and his family shared the same feelings as them and were holding on. He'd even told them that to keep up their morale they tried hard to follow Kipling's advice in his famous poem 'If': 'If you want to be a man, my son . . . If you can force

your heart and nerve and sinew . . .' In another letter he'd also told
his friends he was trying to read as many English books as he could,
and he'd quoted a verse from a poem by Alfred de Vigny that he felt
hid a great deal behind the lines:

> Gémir, pleurer, prier est également lâche
> Fais énergiquement ta longue et lourde tâche
> Dans la vie où la sort a voulu t'appeler
> Puis, après comme moi, souffre et meurs sans parler.

> (To groan, to weep, to pray are equally cowardly
> Carry out with vigour your long and heavy task
> In the life that fate has called you to
> Then afterwards, like me, suffer and die without a word.)

Today Glenn Dickin finally left Hiltingbury for his jumping-off
point at Southampton. His convoy's route had been meticulously
planned. It had to arrive at its exact embarkation point at the correct time to board the right ship. Progress was slow. Stretching
inland for many miles, hundreds of other convoys were waiting to
load. In suburban streets children played games between the tanks
and housewives brought out cups of tea and home-baked cakes to
the men. The war correspondent Alan Moorehead, tracing an
almost identical route, recorded his own journey this way: 'Five
miles an hour. Down Acacia Avenue. Round the park into High
Street; a mile-long column of ducks [amphibious vehicles] and
three-ton lorries, of jeeps and tanks and bulldozers. On the side-
walk one or two people waved vaguely. An old man stopped and
mumbled, "Good luck." But for the most part people stared silently
and made no sign. They knew we were going. There had been
rehearsals before but they were not deceived. There was something
in the way the soldiers carried themselves that said all too clearly,
"This is it. This is the invasion." And yet they were cheerful still. It
was a relief to be out of the camp and moving freely in the streets
again. Every now and again the column halted. Then we crept on
slowly again towards the hards.'

It took Glenn Dickin, too, most of the day to reach Southampton. He was carrying emergency rations to see him through the first few hours on the other side. Packed in a waterproof box were slabs of raisin chocolate and cubes of oatmeal and meat extract. These would be instantly transformed by the addition of hot water produced by the miniature folding cooker and fuel tablets that nestled in his pocket. Even faster was his can of self-heating soup. All he had to do was light the wick at the end of the can and very soon the soup would be ready.

He was also wearing his new D-Day helmet. Up until then Canadian troops had been equipped with the same uniform, berets, boots and weapons as the British. Only his shoulder patches, buttons and badges distinguished him as a member of the Regina Rifles. But, for D-Day, a decision had been made to issue special helmets. It would mark Glenn clearly as a member of the 3rd Canadian Infantry Division, one of the 'D-Day Canadians'. From the front it resembled the American helmet, but at the back it sloped and provided more protection for the sides of the head. 'It's amazing,' wrote Glenn's buddy Gordon Brown, 'what a special identification can do for a unit from a morale point of view. We were very proud of the fact that the 3rd Division was the only Canadian Division taking part in the D-Day invasion.'

Glenn also had his admission ticket to the 'big show', his special embarkation tag, issued to him at Hiltingbury. It came in two portions. Each was marked with his name, number, rank and position as second-in-command of B (Baker) Company and the serial number of his ship. As instructed, he carried the tag in his paybook. As he boarded the ship an officer would remove one half of the tag as a record of exactly when, where and how he'd embarked.

Finally his convoy arrived at the docks. Heavily burdened with equipment, Glenn slowly climbed up the gangplank of the ship that would take him across the Channel. A pre-war Union-Castle passenger liner named the *Llangibby Castle* from the Britain–South Africa run, she was still staffed by her civilian crew under charter to the Admiralty. Glenn handed in his tag, following procedures. Three miles off the coast of France, he would clamber down into the small landing craft that would take him on the final run up to Juno Beach.

Just before landing, Glenn would give the other portion of the tag to another officer, who would collect all the other tags from Glenn's unit in a special bag marked with the ship's number and the date, place and exact time of disembarkation. The bag would then be sealed. 'It is imperative,' read the Top Secret order setting out the procedure, 'that units exercise particular care in this regard as the second portion of the embarkation tag may prevent inaccurate information being sent to the individual's Next of Kin.' This care and thoroughness were reassuring evidence that everything about D-Day had been thought out to the last detail. But it also offered Glenn a sharp reminder that within a matter of hours the tag might be the only way of recording when and where his body had come ashore.

Algiers was clothed all day in a heavy sea mist that matched the obscurity still hanging over de Gaulle's D-Day plans. He had still not made up his mind whether he should fly to England. Brooding in his office at Les Glycines, he remained angry and resentful at his treatment by the Allies.

Around mid-morning Duff Cooper called to see him carrying yet another urgent appeal from Churchill begging him to come to London as soon as possible. The Prime Minister was under intense parliamentary pressure to sort out the mess. Throughout Britain and the United States there was a growing sense of impending political disaster that could seriously threaten military events. 'Now, as the invasion hour approaches,' wrote a correspondent in *The Times* that morning, 'the need for a solid agreement on civil administration [in France] becomes daily more urgent.' In New York the *Herald Tribune* was even blunter, blaming the problem on the pure caprice of President Roosevelt. The stand-off could only be explained by the President's personal dislike of de Gaulle, and put down to 'offended pride and mere prejudice'. He should be aware, it concluded, that the blood of American soldiers should not be expended for such petty reasons.

For nearly an hour de Gaulle argued that there was no point in going to London if the Americans refused to join in talks about civil affairs. He simply wasn't going to do what Churchill asked just because it was convenient for the Allies. It did not suit *him*.

Cooper left Les Glycines empty-handed and reported de Gaulle's comments to René Massigli, who said again that he was prepared to resign if de Gaulle refused Churchill's invitation. Massigli was not alone. By now de Gaulle was coming under pressure from his own side to find a way out of the impasse. Meeting that afternoon, the French Committee for National Liberation urged him, with only a few dissenting voices, the communists' included, to fly to London.

At 10.30 p.m. Cooper again called on Massigli. By now the British Ambassador was in a jaunty mood, for today was his Silver Wedding anniversary. Besides having enjoyed a magnificent lunch provided by two old friends, Princess Marie de Ligne and Princess Galitzin, who inhabited a splendid old Moorish house on the outskirts of Algiers, he and his wife Diana had hosted a dinner at the embassy for which his staff had unearthed some bottles of real champagne, and they'd enjoyed 'quite a feast'. He found Massigli, as usual, friendly and keen to repeat his promise to resign if de Gaulle continued to refuse the invitation to London.

Buoyed up by this encounter and the day's events, Cooper returned to de Gaulle's office just before midnight. Later he wrote in his diary: 'We had a very animated discussion and I spoke to him very frankly and at times rather rudely, but he took it all in very good part.' De Gaulle in fact deeply respected Cooper as the only British government minister – he was at the time First Lord of the Admiralty – to have resigned over Munich. In addition, Cooper spoke his mind frankly, as did de Gaulle. He was, the General recorded, 'a superior man upon whom fate had showered many gifts . . . as a humanist, he loved France; as a politician, he dealt with affairs with noble serenity . . . Placed between Churchill and myself, he made it his duty to absorb the shocks.' At this crucial moment for D-Day, when mobilising resistance in France fully behind the invasion was vital, the personal trust and respect between these two men in Algiers helped open a door.

After letting off steam, they reached the kernel of the matter. If he went to London as Churchill requested, asked de Gaulle, would he be allowed to communicate freely with his government in Algiers using his own ciphers? Cooper reminded him that Churchill had already promised that. 'Repeat it on your own responsibility,' said de Gaulle. He would, replied Cooper, but he was not a member of the British government. If Churchill reneged, however, he would promise there and then to resign.

That was good enough for de Gaulle. Promising that he would give a definitive answer by ten o'clock next morning, he escorted Cooper out into the balmy night air. 'How many passengers does Mr Churchill's plane take?' he asked as they shook hands.

It was an encouraging sign.

At their hideaway in the château outside Le Mans, Sonia d'Artois was beginning to get the measure of Sydney Hudson. He was older than her by quite a bit, thirty-five, with the clear blue eyes she remembered from London and a calm, detached manner that straight away put her at ease. She instinctively felt she could trust him.

Hudson came with plenty of first-hand experience behind the lines. He, too, felt at home in France, because in a way it *was* home – or almost. He'd grown up in Switzerland, close to Lausanne, a French-speaking city on the north side of Lake Geneva, facing the spa town of Évian-les-Bains and the French Alps. His father had been in business there, and Sydney, an only child, enjoyed a pampered life of skiing, tennis and socialising with the local élite. But his family never ceased feeling British. When war broke out he left for London and enlisted in the Royal Fusiliers. Most of 1940 found him guarding England from the expected invasion and working with the Auxiliary Units, the top-secret underground force being trained for clandestine war in case the Germans succeeded.

Soon he was finding the Army's rigid hierarchy and stuffy protocol intolerable, and was impatient for action. Eventually he wangled his way into the SOE, where his fluent French – albeit with its unmistakable Swiss twang – was seized on as a valuable asset. Like Sonia, he'd gone through the full training syllabus in England and Scotland. His own dummy mission had involved a sabotage attack on the Manchester Ship Canal.

He'd been parachuted first into unoccupied Vichy France, dropping 'blind' with Rafferty and Jones in September 1942, and finding a hideout in a small village nearby. His almost immediate arrest had come as the result of a tip-off to the police from a neighbour; at least, that's what he guessed. After escaping fifteen months later, he'd made his way by foot in thick snow over the Pyrenees to the safety of Spain and then Gibraltar, and arrived back in London in March 1944. Like all agents who'd fallen into enemy hands, he was thoroughly interrogated before being cleared for another mission.

After a short bout of training, Hudson, with two other agents – one of them George Jones and his wireless telegraphy set – was dropped on Easter Monday near Issoudun, in central France. From there he and Jones made their way north, as instructed by the SOE, and eventually found the Château des Bordeaux and its sympathetic young owner, Edmond Cohin. Soon after, Hudson had been shocked to learn that the third person with whom he'd parachuted, a young Anglo-French Jewish agent named Muriel Byck, part of another network, had died of sudden heart failure. What made it worse was that he heard later, among the BBC's open-code messages, the words 'Michelle pense à son frère Simon' ('Michelle is thinking of her brother Simon'), a greeting from Muriel to Sydney using her code-name. She'd passed it on just before her death and the BBC had innocently transmitted it along with all the others.

Made wary by his previous capture, Hudson took nothing for granted. As soon as he could find an alternative hideout, he hid Jones and his radio set some distance away from the château and lined up a couple of alternative safe houses. He kept all the embryo

Resistance groups under his control strictly separate from one another. 'I was well aware of the danger of gossip,' he noted. '"Do you know what happened last night? There was a parachute drop in the field next door! Don't tell anybody, will you?" and so on until it got to the ears of a Gestapo informer.'

Disposing of parachutes proved a major headache. French women, deprived of dress fabric for so long, were tempted to make blouses out of the nylon. This exposed them to immediate suspicion and arrest, and could give away an agent's location to the Gestapo. Hudson had been told during training that the parachutes could be burned. But when he tried to do it in a fireplace in the château, his efforts resulted in a thick black liquid spreading all over the floor, to the horrified dismay of the housekeeper. After that he packed up all parachutes tightly and sank them under a bridge over the moat. Another security precaution was that when any of the agents was away from the château, a duster would be prominently displayed at a window of the main building. If anything was wrong, it would be taken in by the housekeeper. Hudson had got into the habit of always checking to see if the duster was there before going in for breakfast.

At 11.30 p.m. Churchill finally abandoned his fantasy of accompanying the troops to the beaches. It had been a long and exhausting day for all concerned.

That morning, his special train pulled into station just outside the tiny village of Droxford, a few miles west of Southwick House. It could have stopped closer, but there was a tunnel nearby which offered shelter in case of a Luftwaffe air raid. The Prime Minister was accompanied by his bosom friend Field Marshal Smuts of South Africa, his personal chief of staff, General Sir Hastings Ismay, and a retinue of his personal staff.

Before leaving London he had sent Roosevelt the text of the speech that King George VI planned to deliver on D-Day. Highly religious in tone, it asked the nation to pray for success. It also contained a few words from the Queen: 'She well understands the anxieties and cares of our womenfolk at this time . . . she feels that many women will be glad in this way [through prayer] to keep vigil with their menfolk as they man the ships, storm the beaches, and fill the skies.' Churchill also told the President that once Overlord was successfully launched he wanted to reopen the Arctic convoys to Stalin's Russia.

Just as he was leaving London, he received a letter from the King. 'My dear Winston,' it began, 'I want to make one more appeal to you not to go to sea on D-Day.' Reminding his Prime Minister that he had now dropped his own plans to watch events unfurl at sea, the monarch pointed out that Churchill would be inaccessible to the War Cabinet at a critical time. 'Please,' he urged, 'put aside your personal wishes and do not depart from your own high standard of duty to the State.'

Churchill did nothing about the letter all day. He was still itching to sail with the troops. Once a soldier himself, he had always craved action. 'A man who has to play an effective part in taking . . . grave and terrible decisions of war,' he once argued, 'may need the refreshment of adventure.' As well as providing a personal tonic, however, his experience of the First World War, when high commanders and politicians had loftily issued orders from afar, had convinced him that a personal visit to the front made for better tactical and strategic decisions. 'I had seen many grievous errors,' he wrote, 'made through the silly theory that valuable lives should not be endangered.'

In the afternoon, to discuss last-minute details of the operation and see for himself the vast armada of ships now gathering in the Solent, he visited Eisenhower at his advance headquarters in Southwick House.

Augustinian monks had established a priory at Southwick centuries before and it was here, local legend had it, that Edward the Black Prince left for his foray across the Channel in 1346 before the victorious battle of Crécy. The dissolution of the monasteries during the Reformation delivered Southwick's eight thousand acres into the hands of the grateful local squire. One of his descendants, the bewhiskered and autocratic Colonel Evelyn Thistlethwaite, still held sway over the mansion and its adjacent village. The houses, most of them red-brick and half-timbered, many with thatched roofs, were still owned by the squire, who could be spotted riding around his vast estate in a horse-drawn coach or seated in the back of his chauffeur-driven vintage Rolls-Royce. Social life, such as it was, centred on the two village pubs, the Golden Lion and the Red Lion, where Monty sometimes sipped an orange juice and Ike enjoyed a local beer.

The modern world had abruptly intruded into this feudal time warp in 1941, when the Royal Navy requisitioned the mansion, a large Georgian-style house built on Jacobean foundations, as a Navigation School. Two years later its proximity to Fort Southwick's underground control centre made it the natural choice as Eisenhower's advance headquarters. Its tree-covered grounds and small lodges provided excellent accommodation and cover for the small city of Nissen huts that quickly mushroomed to house its staff and the D-Day commanders.

Spurning personal quarters in the mansion, Eisenhower opted for a more spartan caravan, which lay concealed beneath trees surrounded by the tents of his personal staff. He had a living room, kitchen, study and bedroom, scattered with piles of cheap novels and photographs of his wife, Mamie, and his son John, in his West Point uniform. 'My circus wagon,' Ike called the caravan, which was equipped with three telephones, each a different colour. The red one linked him directly to Washington. The black one went to Southwick House. And the green one gave him access to Churchill in the underground Map Room in Whitehall.

He spent his first hours at Southwick House writing out his Order of the Day for 5 June for distribution to the invasion troops. 'Soldiers, Sailors and Airmen of the Allied Expeditionary Force,' he began, 'you are about to embark upon the Great Crusade, towards which we have striven these many months. The eyes of the world are upon you. The hopes and prayers of liberty-loving people everywhere march with you. In company with our brave Allies and brothers-in-arms on other Fronts you will bring about the destruction of the German war machine, the elimination of Nazi tyranny over oppressed peoples of Europe, and security for ourselves in a free world.' He ended by saying: 'I have full confidence in your courage, devotion to duty, and skill in battle. We will accept nothing less than full victory!

'Good Luck! And let us all beseech the blessing of Almighty God upon this great and noble undertaking.'

Liberation and freedom were his message for D-Day, words that echoed those prepared for the King. Ike repeated them in a special top-secret order he simultaneously issued to his air commanders. It was essential to remember, he told them, that much of the air fighting would take place over the heads of friendly people who had endured the savagery of the Germans for years. Aircrew must strive their utmost to avoid all but military targets. The Allied air forces were the spearhead of the liberation forces and 'the herald to the oppressed peoples of Europe of our approach'. He counselled them: 'Be careful that nothing is done to betray this trust or to prejudice our good name in the eyes of our friends still dominated by the Nazi tyranny.'

Behind the text lingered the controversy prompted by Churchill's worries about civilian casualties. Only the day before there had been a row between Ike's subordinate commanders about whether or not to bomb French villages and towns on D-Day and after the invasion, to delay German troops movements in the battle area. Churchill's view, articulated by Air Marshal Tedder, Eisenhower's Deputy Supreme Commander, was that such attacks risked high civilian casualties and the destruction of historic monuments for possibly very little gain. Air Marshal Trafford Leigh-Mallory, the air commander-in-chief for Overlord, held that strategic considerations should be paramount. Whatever the non-military costs, he argued, they must be prepared to stop the Allies being pushed back into the sea.

The row simmered overnight. At ten o'clock that morning Ike settled the argument at his new headquarters. He came down firmly on the side of bombing, and implicitly against Churchill, by deprecating any suggestion that they should hold off because of a fear of civilian casualties, although he felt it vital to keep the

Sonia Butt and Guy d'Artois on their wedding day, April 1944. SOE did not like to send married agents into the field together, believing them particularly vulnerable to Gestapo interrogation tactics if caught. *(Sonia d'Artois)*

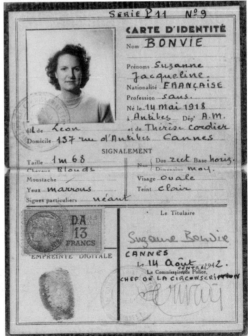

The forged identity papers that Sonia d'Artois used in France and saw her safely through many a German roadblock.
(Imperial War Museum)

Sydney Hudson, leader of the SOE 'Headmaster' circuit, and who worked with Sonia d'Artois, feared that D-Day had arrived before his network was fully prepared. *(Special Forces Club)*

SOE and the French resistance assisted the D-Day landings by sabotaging rail and telecommunications links. *(The National Archives, Kew)*

A peacetime actuary, Peter Moen – seen here with fellow resisters – became an editor of *London Nyatt* ('London News'), one of Norway's most important underground newspapers.
(Norges Hjemmes-frontmuseum, Oslo)

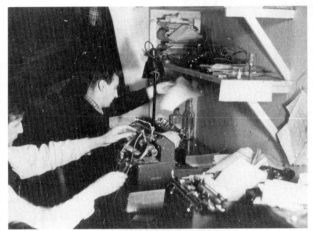

Here Moen is seen (extreme left) working the clandestine presses.
(Norges Hjemmes-frontmuseum, Oslo)

In the Gestapo cell he shared with two other prisoners, Peter Moen pricked daily entries into his secret diary.
(Norges Hjemmes-frontmuseum, Oslo)

Rifleman Glenn Dickin had never left Canada. Homesick for the prairie while training for D-Day, he sought out his English relatives.
(Family of Glenn Dickin)

An all-American boy from Boston, Bill Tucker trained in Georgia with the 82nd Airborne Division for his D-Day drop into France.
(Bill Tucker)

Despite her youthful looks, Veronica Owen carried out serious and responsible work at Fort Southwick. *(Family of Veronica Owen)*

Deep in the Fort Southwick complex, the Wrens were integral to the flow of communications that underpinned Operation Neptune. *(Imperial War Museum)*

Walter Schwender (left) enjoys a carefree moment with his comrades in France.
(Family of Walter Schwender)

Both Walter Schwender and his brother Karl were twenty years old when they were killed. This is the death notice issued, 'in deepest grief', by the family: 'For Führer, the German people and the fatherland both our beloved, noble boys sacrificed themselves and lost their lives.'
(Family of Walter Schwender)

Für Führer, Volk und Vaterland, haben sich unsere beiden lieben, braven Jungens geopfert und ihr Leben gelassen. Unser ältester Sohn und Bruder

ϟϟ-Grenadier

Karl Schwender

gefallen am 15. 2. 1943 im Alter von 20 Jahren ,im Osten und sein Bruder, unser zweiter Sohn

Gefreiter

Walter Schwender

gestorben am 15. 9. 1944 an einer schweren Verwundung in einem Kriegslazarett im Westen im Alter von 20 Jahren.

In tiefstem Schmerz:
Familie Wilhelm Schwender.
Altstadt-Saar, z. Z. Auschwitz/OS, den 17. Oktober 1944.

Schoolteacher André Heintz longed for action but was assigned to the quiet secrecy of intelligence gathering.
(Collection André Heintz)

One of the results of his mission: a German pillbox secretly photographed by Heintz in Caen.
(Collection André Heintz)

Heintz listened in on a crystal set concealed in a tin of spinach to coded instructions broadcast from London.
(Collection André Heintz)

Hidden in his tiny Paris room, Albert Grunberg heard news of the D-Day landings on his radio set. *(Collection R. Grimberg)*

The master deception agent Juan Pujol, known to the Allies as 'Garbo' and to the Germans as 'Arabel'. *(The National Archives, Kew)*

Three days before D-Day, Hitler played paterfamilias at the Berghof following the wedding of Eva Braun's sister, Gretl, to one of his adjutants. He and his personal secretary Martin Bormann helped to choose the gifts.
(Bayerische Staatsbibliothek)

In the isolation of the Berghof, Hitler felt confident that his forces could easily repel an Allied landing.
(Bayerische Staatsbibliothek)

Supreme Commander of Allied forces Dwight D. Eisenhower directs manoeuvres in Britain shortly before D-Day. *(Popperfoto)*

Eisenhower's diplomatic skills were often strongly tested in keeping his invasion team together. Here, seated centre, he is talking to General Sir Bernard Montgomery; to his right is Air Chief Marshal Sir Arthur Tedder. Standing, left to right, are Lieutenant-General Omar Bradley, Admiral Sir Bertram Ramsay, Air Chief Marshal Sir Trafford Leigh-Mallory and Lieutenant-General Walter Bedell Smith. *(Pictorial Press)*

Churchill had to abandon his romantic idea of accompanying the invasion forces on D-Day. Only later, as seen here, did he hit the Normandy beaches. *(Camera Press)*

General Charles de Gaulle, leader of the Free French, learned the details of D-Day just hours before the invasion. *(Camera Press)*

Appointed by Hitler to repel any invasion of France, Field-Marshal Erwin Rommel
– seen here inspecting the 21st Panzer Division in May 1944 – was at home in
Germany when the Allies landed. *(Popperfoto)*

YOUR TALK
MAY KILL YOUR COMRADES

One of the reasons why Rommel
and Hitler were left to guess the
location of the invasion was that
Allied personnel (servicemen and
civilians) were careful to keep it
a secret. Although there were
occasional breaches.
(Imperial War Museum)

It was in a holding camp like this one outside Southampton – the build-up of troops and materiel hidden so far as possible – that Glenn Dickin waited for D-Day. *(The National Archives, Kew)*

The day before D-Day and an Englishwoman hangs out her laundry while invasion equipment and troops fill the street behind her. *(Imperial War Museum)*

Burdened down with equipment to keep him self-sufficient for the first forty-eight hours of combat, an American paratrooper at last boards his transport plane for the early-morning D-Day drop that Bill Tucker would also make. *(Imperial War Museum)*

Flying above the seaborne armada, B24s of the United States 8th Army Air Force return to England after a bombing raid early on D-Day. *(Imperial War Museum)*

Canadian troops land on Juno Beach in an assault craft, as did Glenn Dickin early on D-Day. *(Imperial War Museum)*

Canadian soldiers take cover from snipers shortly after landing in Normandy. *(Imperial War Museum)*

Piccadilly Circus: Londoners devour news of the landings on the evening of D-Day. *(Popperfoto)*

And at around the same time, dusk on D-Day, Glenn Dickin was killed. He was buried next to his comrades in the churchyard at Fontaine-Henry. *(Family of Glenn Dickin)*

numbers down to an absolute minimum. The written warning to his air staff was both an effort to draw a line under the controversy and a peace offering to Churchill.

With the seventy-two-hour countdown to D-Day under way, Ike also began holding twice-daily conferences for weather briefings in the library of Southwick House, a large room lined with dark-oak bookcases and furnished with a scattering of easy chairs and sofas. The morning briefing, held just before he resolved the bombing controversy, was disturbingly inconclusive, setting everyone's already tightened nerves further on edge. Group Captain Stagg had the difficult task of not just briefing the Allied Supreme Commander about the likely weather on D-Day, but also of establishing consensus among the various meteorological services, who in turn advised him. The day before he'd picked up the changing weather pattern developing out in the Atlantic and noted in his diary that it heralded 'a very marginal and difficult situation'. He'd suggested to a senior American officer on Ike's staff that the Supreme Commander be told that not all the experts agreed on what it meant for D-Day. 'For heaven's sake, Stagg,' came the brusque reply, 'get it sorted out . . . General Eisenhower is a very worried man.'

Yet this morning consensus remained elusive. The Americans at Widewing were predicting clear weather. But the British Admiralty and Air Ministry ominously noted incoming depressions over the North Atlantic whose development was hard to predict. Playing safe, Stagg told Ike that for 5 June he could rule out neither gale-force winds nor a low cloud ceiling of nine hundred feet, either of which would make airborne operations and air-to-ground support impossible.

Twelve hours later, after he had bid goodbye to Churchill, Ike again assembled with his team in the library, the heavy blackout curtains now drawn tightly shut. 'Untrustworthy' was Stagg's forecast for D-Day weather, although he admitted that the experts' views were far from unanimous. 'Finely balanced' was another phrase he deployed to convey their doubt. After listening patiently, the Supreme Commander asked his chief meteorological adviser, 'Well, what do you think?' Stagg looked him in the eye. 'If I were to answer that, sir, it would make me a guesser, not a meteorologist.'

With that Eisenhower had to be satisfied. But he was edgy all the time now. Returning to his caravan earlier in the evening, he found a GI taking down a movie projector and screen. As Ike was running late the show would have to be abandoned so that GIs at Southwick could see the film too. He had always insisted that the troops should come first, often missing a showing himself because all available copies were in use. But tonight he rounded on his naval aide, Harry Butcher, and gave him 'a good cussing out' for arranging the showing at a time that would keep the GIs up too late, like a bunch of tired children. 'I knew then that he really had the pre-D-Day jitters,' noted Butcher.

Admiral Ramsay wrote in his diary that night that the coming deterioration of the weather was 'very much on one's mind'. Ironically, the day outside had been fine, with long, sunny periods, and when night fell, the sea in the Dover Strait became calm after a breeze died down. But then broken banks of cloud began to build up, obscuring the moon.

To add to the burden at Southwick House, there was worrying news about Ultra and Fortitude. 'The white lilacs have flowered,' the announcer had read two nights before in the BBC's coded messages to France. It was a signal to a man named Gustave Bertrand, telling him to make for a secret landing ground where an RAF Lysander would make a night landing and pick him up to take him back across the Channel to England.

Few people carried so many secrets about Ultra in their head as Bertrand. As the head of the French Secret Service's codebreaking bureau in the 1930s, he had worked closely with the brilliant team of Polish code-breakers who had first cracked the secret of the German Enigma machine. When Hitler's armies defeated France in 1940, Bertrand and his team retreated to the relative safety of the Unoccupied Zone in the south. There they had continued their work until the Nazis entered southern

France after the Allied invasion of North Africa in November 1942. Bertrand had gone underground, and joined the Resistance. But in January 1944 he was captured while on his way to a rendezvous in Paris with a British agent to pick up some radio equipment. Terrified that under torture he would reveal the Enigma secret, Bertrand agreed to collaborate with the Germans. But this was only a trick to gain time, and a week later he escaped from their clutches and disappeared. Since then the Secret Intelligence Service had been desperately trying to get him out of France and back to England. By interrogating him they would be able to discover if he had revealed anything to the enemy to save his skin.

Despite the BBC message, Bertrand had not yet arrived. Now, only three days before the launch of Operation Overlord, no one knew if he had given away the Enigma secret and with it that of Fortitude. For if the Germans knew that Enigma was betrayed, they could be using it to outwit the Allies. The Lysander was due to fly out to France tonight to pick up Bertrand. Then the Allies would know.

Anxiety was also running high about the British soldier on the run from his holding camp, and the phones were ringing frantically in the headquarters of both Montgomery and Eisenhower. News that he'd been captured that morning close to his parents' home in Wales did little to calm things down. The most urgent question now was: what, if anything, had he told anyone? And how had he got from Hampshire to Wales? What contacts had he made *en route*? 'We need to know within the hour,' Montgomery's headquarters insisted to the harassed major at Western Command. 'Don't hesitate to arrest and isolate anyone in possession of information from him. We've got to know how bad it is, and whether it can be sealed off. We don't care how you get the story out of him, or how you plug the holes. But, for God's sake, be quick.'

It proved easier said than done. Despite the major's skilful and practised interrogation, the NCO refused to talk. He even resisted the silent treatment, periods stretching into minutes when the major simply stared at him without saying a word. Most people found this intolerable, and eventually spoke just to break the tension. But not this one. In the room next door the telephone rang. It was the colonel in Security Intelligence in London, demanding news. 'For God's sake, hurry,' he pleaded.

The staring match continued. Then the interrogator resorted to another old trick, that of making an offensive and false accusation. Often it provoked an indignant denial, breaking the ice, and the first step to more. 'I've just sent for your mother,' he said. 'How do you think she'll feel when I tell her that, when the moment came, you funked it and betrayed your comrades?' This time the trick worked. The soldier flushed red. 'I have not betrayed them,' he said. 'I know what's going to happen. I'm going to be shot. Well, go ahead. But I didn't shop my mates.'

Then his story came tumbling out. After he'd heard his unit's briefing he'd realised there was a good chance he'd never come back from D-Day alive, and he decided he wanted to see his parents and girlfriend one last time. He'd managed to give the sentries the slip and hitchhiked home, spending the night in a nearby US Army camp after talking his way inside. Along the way, he confessed, he'd given some of his French currency away as souvenirs. Over several drinks, he'd also told some of the GIs what he knew about the invasion.

Drastic measures were called for. The American camp was instantly sealed off, its inhabitants questioned and several GIs identified who'd heard the invasion secret. They hadn't yet been briefed on D-Day themselves, and their camp was still unsealed. Immediately, its perimeter was cordoned off, guards were brought in from other units and all outside telephone calls were prohibited or monitored. Yet this was only half the story. Descriptions of the lorries and their drivers who'd given the NCO his lifts were circulated to police forces all along his route, and they were eventually traced. Voluntarily, the drivers all agreed to remain confined to their homes for several days. So did the soldier's parents and girlfriend. The NCO himself was court-martialled and given a sentence of ten years.

This was not the only serious security scare during the ten days before D-Day. Some British soldiers escaped from a camp near London and went on a drinking binge. There was also the strange case of the *Daily Telegraph* crossword puzzle. Over several days in May and early June, the answers to certain clues consisted of words such as 'Utah', 'Mulberry' and 'Omaha' – all related to some secret aspect of D-Day. Finally MI5 interrogated the man, a school-master, who'd devised the puzzles. It all appeared to be an innocent, if strange and even incredible, coincidence. Only many years later did it emerge that the schoolteacher had turned for suggested clues to his pupils. One of them had hung around vari-ous holding camps, occasionally picking up unfamiliar or exotic words that he'd then passed on to the teacher.

Innocent or not, serious or otherwise, such incidents heightened anxiety as D-Day approached. Its secret was tottering precariously on the edge of a precipice.

Despite the reassuring news the day before about the kidnapped German Abwehr officer Johan Jebsen, those closest to Garbo remained highly nervous. Only they knew how complex, vulner-able and dangerous the game really was. Back in February, after Jebsen had produced Arabel's name as an Abwehr agent, one case officer had become so concerned about the thin ice underlying the entire operation that he had called for the immediate abandon-ment of Garbo. He had been overruled by the Double-Cross Committee. But he remained ready to pull the plug at any time.

This Doubting Thomas was none other than Garbo's own British controller, the Spanish-speaking officer who had greeted him when he'd stepped out of the flying boat at Plymouth two years before. His name was, appropriately, Tomas Harris.

An extraordinary and enigmatic figure, he was just four years older than Pujol and had been working for MI5 since 1940 as its principal expert on Spain. Through his mother, Enriqueta, who was Spanish, he spoke the language and understood the country's cul-ture and mentality as if he'd grown up there. His father, Lionel, was a wealthy Mayfair art dealer specialising in works by the Spanish masters El Greco, Velázquez and Goya. Tomas followed his father into the business and travelled widely in Spain to buy paintings for the gallery. During the Spanish Civil War he made several trips to the north of the country, snapping up *objets d'art* from fleeing Spanish refugees.

Harris himself was also an artist and sculptor. At fifteen he had won a scholarship to the prestigious Slade School of Art and subsequently moved to the Courtauld Institute to do postgraduate research on art of the Spanish Baroque.

On the outbreak of war he was an exotic fixture on London's social scene, with his raffish good looks, neatly trimmed beard, hand-rolled yellow cigarettes of black tobacco that stained his fingers chestnut brown, and his cultivated air of mystery. By now running a gallery of his own, he was also very wealthy. Gregarious and generous, he and his wife, Hilda, enjoyed throwing lavish parties in their Mayfair home. Among his friends he counted man-about-town and BBC talks producer Guy Burgess, Kim Philby, who had been a war correspondent in Spain during the Civil War, and the up-and-coming young art historian Anthony Blunt. Decades later the three were exposed as some of Britain's most notorious Cold War spies. But for now they were inveterate party-goers with a fondness for good living. Harris, claimed Philby once, tongue in cheek, 'maintained that no really good table could be spoiled by wine stains'. It was Burgess who first introduced Harris to British intelligence, when he recruited him and his wife to help out as 'housekeepers' at the training school for secret agents run by the SOE's predecessor, Section D of the Secret Intelligence Service. When that work came to an end, Blunt, who'd by now joined MI5, introduced him to the security service.

Harris quickly proved an adept and talented operator, impressing everyone with his energy and imagination. 'His soft, soulful eyes would suddenly take on a wild look when he had a bright idea,' noted one British intelligence officer who came to know him well, 'and would retain a certain wild, glazed look when he was painting or sculpting.' He was also a strong and persuasive personality. 'If you looked at a picture with him,' declared one of his

West End art-dealer contacts, 'you found at the end of twenty minutes you were thinking the same as him.'

Harris's skill lay now in convincing the Germans that the picture he was painting through Garbo was nothing less than authentic.

Accompanying Churchill to Portsmouth in his special train was his box of secret intercepts. Most came from the Italian front, where the Germans were in full retreat. One was a message from Kesselring to the High Command in Berlin reporting on the 'excessively strained' situation. Another was the German commander's plea to Heinrich Himmler to make available the SS Panzer Lehr division for coastal defence. Churchill also scanned the naval summary: U-178 had arrived in Bordeaux carrying a cargo of rubber, tin and wolfram, this last used for making aluminium, from the Far East; and four U-boats were moving south from the protected fiords of Norway towards western France for refitting with *Schnorchels*.

This was worrying news. A *Schnorchel* was a tube rather like a periscope which sucked in surface air and allowed submarines to run their noisy diesel engines and recharge their batteries while still submerged. In theory, a U-boat equipped with a *Schnorchel* would never have to surface, and was thus far less vulnerable. Although the Americans had invented the device as far back as 1897 and the Dutch Navy was using it before the war, only the Germans were now exploiting it. In practice the device was temperamental and unreliable. But in theory it heightened the U-boat menace to the Allied D-Day invasion fleet.

From another of the intercepts Churchill also learned that the German Foreign Ministry was denouncing Allied bombing raids as 'terror attacks', which meant that downed Allied aircrews were no longer entitled to protection from the German military or police authorities, a sinister harbinger of things to come, for RAF crew were later executed in concentration camps. In another intercept he read a message sent from Berlin to Lisbon by the Portuguese chargé d'affaires reporting that a German war communiqué had, for the first, time referred to an Allied 'invasion'.

This suggested, said the chargé, that the High Command had received some hard information to confirm it. Widespread rumours were also circulating of landings by sea in the Netherlands, by air inside France and inside Germany itself, around Hamburg and in Schleswig-Holstein. Yet the official line in Berlin remained optimistic. 'German officers,' the chargé told Lisbon, 'particularly those who have returned from the Eastern Front, are still convinced that the Germans could easily wipe out the Russian Army once the threat to the West was over.' This intercept suggested to Churchill that complacency and confusion reigned supreme in the enemy camp.

After visiting Eisenhower, Churchill returned to his train. At 11.30 p.m. he picked up his scrambler telephone and told the King's private secretary, Sir Alan Lascelles, that he had cancelled his D-Day plans. Then, after midnight, he began a handwritten personal letter to the King. It opened with a defiant bang but ended with an obedient whimper. 'As Prime Minister and Minister of Defence,' he began boldly, 'I ought to be allowed to go where I consider it necessary to the discharge of my duty, and I do not admit that the Cabinet have any right to put restrictions on my freedom of movement . . .' After going on to repudiate any comparison between his own constitutional position and that of the monarch, he abruptly finished by telling the King that he would obey his wishes, 'indeed commands', motivated as they were by concerns for his safety. 'It is a great comfort,' wrote Churchill in a barely veiled hint that he could have made it a resigning issue, 'that they arise from Your Majesty's desire to continue me in your service.'

Churchill's disappointment at being thwarted leaped off the page. The letter signed, it was handed to a dispatch rider, who hurtled off into the darkness to deliver it to the Palace. It wasn't just Eisenhower who was suffering from pre-invasion jitters.

At La Roche-Guyon, Rommel was showing remarkable calm. He had long convinced himself that the Allies would land their troops at high tide to give their men the shortest distance possible to cross the exposed beaches under fire. This was what they had done elsewhere, and he saw no reason why they should do it differently now. Consulting his moon and tide tables, he saw that no high tide would coincide with a suitable moon before 20 June. Paperwork took up his morning, but after lunch he went out shooting with his friend the Marquis de Choisy. Von Ruge went with them. 'I had a lovely view of the Seine Valley,' recorded the naval adviser in his diary. 'As for game, I only saw a tiny squirrel, but [there were] continuous air attacks on the Seine bridges.'

In his Paris headquarters Field Marshal von Rundstedt was also looking closely at the sky. The Allied invasion would need four consecutive days of good weather, he wired the Supreme Command in Berlin, but no such period was foreseen. He too was certain that the coming week would be quiet.

Even as von Rundstedt made his prediction, Abwehr officer Oskar Reile was passing on to the Field Marshal's staff and the Gestapo what he had learned the day before from his intercept service about the BBC warning messages and the Verlaine sonnet. The Gestapo forwarded the news to the High Command in Berlin and to the General Staff's experts in Foreign Armies West.

Hitler's most astounding technical achievement on the Obersalzberg was an elevator rising to the top of the Eagle's Nest, a pinnacle of rock reaching some two thousand feet above the Berghof. At enormous cost, estimated at thirty million Reichsmarks, and taking three years' labour, a tunnel had been blasted out of solid rock and a lift with a gold-plated door and cushioned seats installed. To reach it required a terrifying drive of four and a half miles up a steep and twisting road marked by hairpin bends and sheer rock walls. At the top, in a vast circular room with panoramic views, telephones linked the Führer with virtually every capital city in the world. There was also a sunbathing terrace, dining room and private quarters.

Yet Hitler rarely visited the place, afraid that lightning might strike it when he was using the lift, or that a sniper would shoot him on the slow and winding road leading up to the tunnel. For most of the time the whole project remained a plaything, an asset that he conspicuously failed to exploit. It aptly symbolised the sterile world in which he now moved.

Hitler was warned that invasion might be close. High Command staff had checked their tide tables and concluded – contrary to Rommel's view – that any day between 5 and 13 June would be a likely time for the Allies to move. Hitler was also told about the BBC messages and Reile's intelligence. The warnings appeared to make no impact. On the contrary, to the fury of Walter Warlimont, Deputy Chief of Operations at the German High Command, Hitler that very morning ordered the 19th Luftwaffe Division from France to Italy. This was doing nothing more than 'dancing to the enemy's tune' thought Warlimont.

Intelligence, even if accurate, is wasted on a closed mind. By now, in his own growing social isolation, Hitler was immune to any challenge to his strongly held convictions. Surrounded by yes-men and sycophants, he was free to indulge his fantasies unchecked. Jodl, Keitel and the rest of the High Command served mainly to implement his will.

Busy in his Wehrmacht repair shop outside Nantes, Walter Schwender wrote no letter home to his family in Auschwitz. There, at the Buna plant, another young man was at work among the pipes, rails and boilers that were scattered about the factory complex like fragments in some hellish junkyard.

For him, writing home was not an option. He was a prisoner, one of the Jews in the Monowitz camp kept alive for their labour. The worse the war went for the Germans, the more they squeezed their captive workforce. In April, as the result of pressure from SS chief Heinrich Himmler, an order had been issued to all concentration camps in the Third Reich that 'work must be, in the true sense of the word, exhausting in order to obtain maximum output'.

The prisoner was dressed in the thin striped concentration-camp uniform with a yellow Star of David sewn on the jacket. He had been there since his arrival in a transport train from Italy five months before. On his left arm was a tattoo with his number: 174517.

Primo Levi had been stripped of his name and personal identity the day he arrived. By now, emaciated with hunger, he had seen dozens of fellow inmates fall sick and disappear, unexplained, into the void. In all, some forty thousand slave labourers worked at Buna, which, despite the strenuous efforts of the Nazis, had yet to produce a single ounce of synthetic rubber. As Walter's brother Karl had noticed, some of the prisoners were indeed criminals, marked out by a green triangle. Many of them were also 'Kapos', deliberately put in charge of the other prisoners by the SS. They were, Himmler explained that month to a gathering of his generals, the *Unteroffizier* corps for the whole concentration-camp community. The Kapo had to see that his prisoners worked and kept their barracks clean. If not, he would be instantly demoted. He would return to his bunk in the barracks, where he would be killed on the first night by his fellow prisoners. 'That he knows,' explained Himmler grimly. 'The Kapo is given certain privileges. I have not – I may say this in all plainness – to devise a welfare system here, but I have to bring in the *Untermenschen* from the streets and set them to work for Germany – for victory.' In this hierarchy of brutality, the Jews were at the bottom of the pile, the slaves of the slaves.

Buna was as large as a small city. In the middle of this nightmare metropolis stood the Carbide Tower, an edifice constructed by the inmates. The bricks, noted Levi, were cemented by 'hate and discord, like the Tower of Babel . . . and in it we hate the insane dream of grandeur of our masters, their contempt for God and men, us men'.

Their youth linked Levi and Walter Schwender. Otherwise a chasm of cruelty, contempt, ignorance, prejudice and indifference separated their two worlds.

Only one small thing did the two young men share. 'The water is tepid and sweetish, with the smell of a swamp,' noted Levi, echoing Walter's complaint. Even after four days without a drink in the transport train, he'd had to spit it out. The SS was forbidden to drink it. His thirst gave Levi the first real taste of the madness of Buna. Desperate for a drink, he had spotted an icicle hanging outside the window of his hut, and reached out to grab it. A guard outside had brutally snatched it away. 'Why?' asked Levi. 'Here,' answered the guard, 'there is no why.'

In Washington DC, Franklin D. Roosevelt held a press conference. Pressure to help the Jews of Europe had been mounting for months. Earlier in the year he had set up the War Refugee Board to rescue Nazi victims. One suggested solution was the creation of 'free ports', or temporary havens, but so far bureaucratic foot-dragging had produced no visible results. 'The hope that all is not black in the world for his children can be strong sustenance for a man starving in a camp or entering a gas chamber,' wrote one anguished American commentator. 'But to feel that your friends and allies are wishy-washy folk who mean what they say but haven't got the gumption to live up to it must brew a poisonous despair.' Roosevelt now announced at his press conference that he was considering the conversion of an army camp in the United States into just such a haven.

In his chambermaid's room in Paris, Albert Grunberg was recovering from another exhausting encounter with his brother. The day before, Sami had launched into a litany of self-pitying complaints about how his dreams of prosperity had evaporated for ever, as he would now never be able to live off the rents from his property. Albert was in no mood to listen. How would his brother react, he angrily asked, if he went on and on in the same way about his children all the time? It simply wasn't dignified, he chided Sami, to wail endlessly about his misfortune. To cap it all, Sami declared he was feeling ill, took himself off to bed and then kept Albert awake all night by snoring.

On this day one thousand Jewish men, women and children arrived at Auschwitz from Drancy, the seventy-fifth deportation train from France to arrive at the death camp. After the usual SS selection on the platform, 239 of the men and 134 of the women were given numbers and admitted to the camp. The remaining 627 were herded to the gas chambers. The previous shipment from Drancy, ten days before, had delivered twelve hundred Jews, of whom 732 had immediately been gassed.

Among them was Albert Grunberg's cousin, Jacques Cling, along with his wife, Simone, and their two teenage sons, Maurice and Willy. Arrested by French police at their home on the rue Monge in Paris, they'd been held at Drancy for two weeks before the three-day journey to Auschwitz. They died as a family. Simone, tragically unaware of their fate, had insisted that Maurice, who had been inexplicably left off the arrest list, be fetched from his school to accompany them. 'Nous sommes en pleine terreur blanche,' wrote Grunberg in his diary when he heard news of their arrest.

Veronica Owen had the day off. She lay in bed until 9.30, and after breakfast bicycled back to the Spurways to pick up a bunch of roses she'd left behind in her frantic rush home the night before. At least she'd been on her bike, which enabled her to get home quickly in the dark. Sometimes she'd had to walk. Before April and the travel restrictions, when she'd been able to spend her three-day leaves with her parents in London, she'd had to return to Fareham by train after sunset. This meant a scary fifteen-minute walk to Heathfield alone along an unlit, tree-lined road. To keep up her spirits she'd memorised poetry, and walked down the middle of the road declaiming aloud 'This royal throne of kings, this sceptred isle' and other patriotic verses from Shakespeare, Wordsworth, and Browning until she was safely past the trees and back in her cottage.

After a cup of tea she returned to Heathfield and lay around for most of the rest of the day reading more of Lawrence of Arabia's letters. 'Can hardly put him down,' she wrote to her parents. Then she added a curious note. Everyone had been sure that the invasion would be in May, but now all eyes were fixed on Rome. Had talk of the Second Front been all a bluff? 'I wonder,' she wrote before the bus arrived to take her to Fort Southwick for her evening watch, 'if we ever will go into the north of France?'

At 19 Mollergaten, Peter Moen pricked out '120th Day' in his toilet-paper diary. Today, like some scientist recording the discovery of a hitherto unknown species, he made notes on his cellmates. Both, he noted, were 'ordinary or common or garden men'.

All the prisoners were classified as 'political'. But this merely meant that in one way or another they had fallen foul of the occupying authorities. Some of them were black marketeers, others had brawled with German soldiers and some, like Moen, were genuine resisters. The sailor – prisoner number 5984 – was behind bars for striking a German soldier during a drunken fracas, and, so far as Moen could guess, had enjoyed several peacetime brushes with the law as well. He'd been involved in gang warfare, talked knowingly about robbery with violence and occasionally reminisced about a gang leader known as 'Harry the Foot' because of his mastery at kicking opponents during fights. He and the gardener-stonemason, a quiet man numbered 6025, were polar opposites in character and quarrelled constantly. Moen found acting as intermediary tedious, and was irritated by the gardener-stonemason's sanctimonious tone towards the sailor. He himself was intrigued by him, finding him an exotic figure remote from his own experience. Any attempt at intellectual discussion was a waste of time, but the sailor had a magnificent sense of humour that helped pass the time. 'A heavy-hearted prisoner is really a burden,' wrote Moen, '– positively an extra punishment.'

There was no risk of that with the sailor. They taught each other a few foreign words and phrases, the sailor instructing Moen in Finnish and the peacetime accountant responding with some words of French on the theme of women. Sex, in fact, consumed much of their talk. Women and drunken brawls formed the bulk of the sailor's repertoire, and his vocabulary was rich in profanities. As he recounted his exploits, his brown eyes glinted and he'd interrupt himself frequently with raucous laughter. 'Erotically he is a wild animal, he says and does anything to attain his end – physical possession,' noted Moen. His affairs lasted only so long as they interested him, and then he was off without warning or farewell. 'He says he has no illegitimate offspring – or so he says,' Moen concluded, tallying up the moral balance sheet.

Bill Tucker had grown up as a Methodist, although he was not a regular churchgoer. But he wasn't an agnostic either, and considered himself deeply religious. Waiting at Cottesmore, wondering about his fate, he was drawn to the services conducted by the Protestant chaplain, the Reverend George 'Chappie' Woods.

A dark-haired man in his thirties, the Reverend Woods had signed up with the 82nd Airborne two years before at Fort Benning and gone on to earn the coveted silver wings and jump boots after the required five drops. He'd jumped at Salerno with the rest of them, to become the first chaplain in United States history ever to make a combat drop. Before the war he'd been the rector of an Episcopal church in Indiana. He was a popular figure at the base, and Tucker liked him: 'Whenever there was a service I went. I always said my prayers.'

Unlike Glenn Dickin, who was surrounded by familar faces from his own province and even his boyhood home and school, Tucker carried little from his past to comfort or reassure him. He'd left his family firmly behind him. 'I had a difficult upbringing,' he said, 'and I just forgot about home. Occasionally I'd send a one-pager off, and I had a girlfriend there but she ditched me for a B-17 pilot. It was all in the past.' Instead he drew strength from his buddies, men from different backgrounds and states across America.

His best friend was Larry Leonard, from Missouri. The two of them had hit it off straight away. Stationed together at Cookstown in Northern Ireland, they chased girls, got drunk and frequented the movies. Afterwards they'd fuel up on French fries and steak. 'A lot of our guys hung around the milk bar,' recalled Tucker, 'and some of them had girlfriends. But girls in Cookstown were few and far between because they had been warned by the priests to stay away from the United States Army.'

Things had looked up since he and Larry had arrived in England, though, and they spent most of their passes in the market town of Loughborough, going to pubs and dances. When Tucker was dating Molly, the test pilot, Larry and his girlfriend would join them in a foursome for nights out on the town. Now, cooped up together at Cottesmore, the two men were inseparable. Tucker had got himself transferred to Larry's machine-gun squad almost as soon as they'd arrived at Quorn; they passed the time in Larry's tent, yacking about this and that and going endlessly over their combat routine. When they landed on solid ground on D-Day, wherever that was, they would be handling the machine gun together, a two-man combat team, each man trusting the other with his life.

At one o'clock that afternoon, three heavy bombers, flying in a 'V' formation, came out of an overcast sky and circled over the Soviet air base at Poltava, in the Ukraine. Soon another seventy planes were circling at one thousand feet. Then, in an impressive display of air power, they landed with clockwork precision at one-minute intervals on the runway. Four-engined Flying Fortresses of the US 15th Air Force, they had just flown the first air-shuttle operation mounted by the Soviet Union and its allies.

The joint Russian-American effort at Poltava was given the code-name 'Frantic', and it was an enterprise loaded with important tactical, strategic and – as a symbol of East–West cooperation – political potential. The bombers were based in Italy but their targets lay in Central and Eastern Europe. By landing behind Soviet lines after completing their missions, instead of having to fly back to Italy, they could carry less fuel and bigger payloads. They also avoided the heavy anti-aircraft defences along the Italian route, while bad weather over the Alps no longer ruled out raids. Beyond these day-to-day tactical advantages lay the prospect of opening up many more targets which the Germans would have to defend with their already badly depleted anti-aircraft defences and fighter aircraft. The effect on the morale of the German satellite states of Hungary, Bulgaria and Romania could also be significant as they witnessed punishing examples of Soviet-American military co-operation.

Efforts to set up bombing bases for Allied aircraft in Russia had begun as soon as the Red Army began its inexorable advance west in 1943, and Roosevelt had raised the issue with Stalin at the Tehran Conference in November of that year. The Soviet leader had confirmed to Averell Harriman early in February 1944 that he approved the idea. 'Uncle Joe' had exhibited keen interest in everything from the necessary runway length to the octane content of the aviation fuel. But such interest didn't extend to the practicalities, which proved almost insurmountable in the face of suspicious and torpid Soviet bureaucrats. Frantic, it transpired, was no misnomer. How, insisted wary officials, were hundreds of American personnel to be vetted before being allowed into the Soviet Union? Eventually, after weeks of haggling, group visas were provided, only for the wrangling to begin all over again when individual American technicians had to fly back to Italy for temporary consultations and the issue of entry and exit visas arose again. American requests for complete control over communications were also heavily resisted, not by the Soviet Air Force, but by the Foreign Ministry. The compromise, honoured mostly in the breach, was to have Soviet representatives present in all communications installations, with the right of access to everything from weather forecasts to operational reports.

Poltava, the designated headquarters for Operation Frantic, was the historic site of a decisive battle in 1709 immortalised by Pushkin in an epic poem. Here Peter the Great's forces had inflicted a heavy defeat on the Swedish Army under Charles XII in their epic struggle for control of the Baltic. Guards, mechanics and housekeepers were to be provided by the Soviets, and in theory American and Russian staff were to eat, sleep and work in exactly the same conditions. Moscow also supplied the women who, in record time, laid the heavy steel mats that formed the mile-long runway.

The base was ready by the end of May. 'It was strange to see there,' wrote one eye-witness, 'in the heart of the Gogol country, hundreds of GIs eating vast quantities of American canned spam, and baked beans and apple sauce, drinking gallons of good coffee, making passes at the giggly Ukrainian canteen waitresses, and commenting flatteringly on the Ukrainian landscape, which was just like back home in Indiana or Kentucky.' Many of the Americans were of Polish or Russian extraction. 'My grandma is in Kiev and I've got aunts and uncles all the way from Smolensk to Bessarabia,' said one GI. On Sundays there was creamed chicken and apple pie. Every night there was a movie, alternating between American and Soviet. American airmen danced with the female clerks and mechanics, and smoked thousands of American cigarettes.

The Americans had three targets in mind for the first mission, planned for 1 June, one of them being Galatz, in Romania, Albert Grunberg's home town. As a courtesy, they sought Soviet approval, but were infuriated when all three targets were rejected by the Red Army General Staff with no explanation or alternatives offered. Unintentionally, it transpired, the Americans had chosen targets whose bombing would attract dangerous German attention to sites important in the forthcoming spring offensive to be launched by the Red Army. Still under wraps and in the final planning stage, it was due to be launched soon after D-Day.

The Americans chose another target and a later date, but this time without seeking Soviet approval: the Luftwaffe base at Debrecin, in Hungary. 'The Russians pay off on results,' General Ira Eaker, commander of the Allied forces in the Mediterranean, told his men, 'and by God I want results.' After carrying out the raid, the Flying Fortresses had turned east, and escorted by long-range American Mustang fighters and Soviet Air Force Yaks, had reached Poltava dead on time. The brigade of Russian women breathed a collective sigh of relief as they watched their precious steel runway stand up to the weight of the gigantic bombers and the first ever Soviet-American air operation against their common enemy landed safely. The first man on the ground was Eaker. Perhaps inspired by his recent weekend with Churchill at Chequers, he lit up a cigar. Then he pinned a couple of decorations on the Soviet generals who had helped prepare the base. Late that night Moscow Radio triumphantly broadcast news of the operation. It had all been made possible, it stressed, by the westward advance of the Red Army.

Still on board the *Tuscaloosa* at Belfast, David Bruce and America's intelligence chief spent the crisp and clear day paying official visits to the Governor of Northern Ireland, the Duke of Abercorn – 'a charming man of 75,' noted Bruce in his diary, 'with a purple nose and a fondness for port' – and Sir Basil Brooke, the Northern Ireland Prime Minister, who was a cousin of Sir Alan Brooke, Chief of the Imperial General Staff. Back on board, they resumed their study of the Neptune and Overlord plans. The ships' captains, recorded Bruce anxiously, were 'struggling to keep abreast of the forest of literature in the invasion plans that daily pour across their desks'.

7

THE NADIR OF STRAIN
Saturday 3 June

In Caen, André Heintz cycled down to the railway station near the docks for his 8.45 a.m. rendezvous with his intelligence contact Courtois, who was travelling from Ouistreham. The train arrived on time, although by now very few did. The Cherbourg to Paris train, due in Caen at nine that morning, was delayed by sabotage on the line and didn't arrive until nine in the evening. Allied bombers were also doing their best to wreck railway lines and bridges, and no trains at all arrived from Paris. Over the course of the day André saw dozens of planes overhead. Several alerts in the city sent people hurrying for shelter. His father, trying to buy wood for the stove, finally gave up because of the frequent interruptions. The weather was dry and warm.

Usually the two resisters would stroll innocently together from the station back into the city while André surreptitiously handed over some newly made false ID card, brought Courtois up to date with his recruiting efforts or passed on anything of military significance he'd observed around town. Recently Courtois had told him to focus his efforts on spotting anti-aircraft batteries. 'We only had bicycles,' recalled André, 'but we each had an area we covered twice a week to see what was new. Also we knew farmers and other people in the country who told us stuff and so we quickly learned if a new anti-aircraft gun arrived or an existing one was moved.'

Today André had an especially interesting intelligence tip to pass on. One of his neighbours, a judge, had a German staff officer billetted with him. The judge had come across a document in his 'lodger's' room revealing that the Germans were deeply pessimistic about their defences. He had tried to memorise the text. It went something like this: 'Possibility to hold out on the beach for three hours. Second line of defence around Caen, one day. Rear line of defence along the Falaise hills.' There had also been a map, but the judge had sensibly left it where he found it, reckoning that its absence would be immediately noticed.

For André, and ultimately the D-Day planners, such an item was important. 'It gave us hope,' he said, and it confirmed what the Allies had long suspected about the 716th Infantry Division, which was headquartered in the city and had the main job of defending the nearby beaches. Consisting of two regiments, it contained a high proportion of 'Ostroops', soldiers forcibly conscripted from ethnic groups such as Poles, Czechs, Ukrainians and Russians and now under the command of German NCOs and officers. Few of them were fanatically inclined to die for Hitler. The average age of the Division's men was also higher than that of the toughest German fighting divisions. It was unlikely to put up much of a fight.

André and Courtois parted, agreeing to meet up again on Tuesday morning, 6 June. Neither yet had the slightest idea where or when D-Day would take place. 'I don't know why,' recalled André, 'but we imagined the landings might take place on a Sunday. We were all by now impatient.'

This was the day Bill Tucker finally learned where and when he'd make his D-Day drop. Ushered into a tent at Cottesmore airfield, he saw a large table with a military model and aerial photographs. The first thing that caught his eye was the word 'Normandy'. So it wasn't going to be Yugoslavia, as some of the guys had guessed, or Norway, which had been his own best bet, but France. He had a few words of high-school French, about the only one in I Company who did, and he was surprised and excited by the news. He knew who William the Conqueror was and thought Normandy a beautiful name.

He was even more entranced when the briefing officer revealed the name of their target: Sainte-Mère-Église, a small town on the Cotentin Peninsula, at the western extremity of the invasion area. Another lovely name, he thought. Staring at the photographs, he could see, in the middle of the town, a square bordered by trees, with a church and a nearby cemetery.

The drop would take place several hours before the seaborne forces landed on the beaches. The 82nd, along with the 'Screaming Eagles' of the 101st, would seize the entire area to prevent the Germans rushing through reinforcements to attack American troops as they struggled ashore on Utah and Omaha Beaches. British airborne troops would do the same to the east. With each end of the beachhead secured, the troops would have a chance to obtain their foothold. The fate of the entire D-Day enterprise hung on the success of the airborne troops.

Tucker's job and that of his battalion was to seize and hold Sainte-Mère-Église itself. Its capture was critical since it lay directly on Route Nationale 13, the main road from Cherbourg to Bayeux, running north and south down the peninsula, and the only first-class route the Germans could use for reinforcements. Tucker's 2nd platoon would spearhead I Company's attack. They were to hold the town until infantry advancing from Utah Beach arrived.

As he looked at the mock-up and photographs, Tucker thought it all looked pretty clear. He could even identify the headquarters house being used by the German commander, one of several locations they'd been ordered to seize. There weren't many questions. 'Everything seemed pretty clear-cut and everyone had a sense of confidence that the people higher up knew what they were doing,' he remembered. When the briefing was finished they were told to get a good night's sleep because the next day, Sunday the 4th, would be a long one. Their C-47s, lifting off on Sunday night, could expect to reach France at about 1 a.m. on Monday. It felt good to know, at last, his D-Day mission.

Over most of England the weekend started fair and dry, with temperatures reaching the low seventies. At Wembley Stadium in London the highlight was a baseball game featuring several professional players between teams from the US 9th Air Force and American ground forces. The pitchers used a portable artificial mound to stand on and speed their throw, a first for Britain. The crowd was warmed up by a softball game – similar to baseball but played on a smaller pitch and with the ball delivered underhand – when Canadian Military Headquarters took on the United States Army. Twenty thousand tickets at a shilling apiece were sold. Clement Attlee, Churchill's deputy prime minister in the coalition government and leader of the Labour Party, introduced the teams. The Canadians won 4–1. The American ground forces easily outmatched their Air Force compatriots at 9–0.

It was a strictly North American day in the hallowed ground of English soccer, completely overshadowing a cricket match at Lord's featuring the National Police Team. It was a visible reminder that the United States and Canada had kept Britain afloat during the war and were now poised to free Europe. In three years of Lend-Lease almost five million tons of food had crossed the Atlantic to Britain, including more than half a million tons of tinned meat and fish and similar quantities of tinned milk, lard, bacon, cheese and dried fruit.

Still, as the weekend newspapers warned readers, digging for victory remained an important war cry. 'Plant your sprouts out *now*,' exhorted the Ministry of Agriculture. A Cambridgeshire company appealed to the nation's gardeners with 'a broccoli completely different for gourmets'. Its advert in *The Times* claimed that 'Curtis's Nine-Star Perennial Broccoli once planted lasts years and produces many heads of fine quality when green vegetables are so dear and scarce'. Chez-Vous cleaning service, in a spurt of optimism about the end of Luftwaffe bombing, offered to 'save you time and trouble . . . Bombed upholstery and carpets cleaned. Costs recoverable.'

London theatres remained busy. The ever-popular J.B. Priestley's *How Are They At Home?* was playing at the Apollo and Ivor Novello's *The Dancing Years* continued to entertain crowds at the Adelphi. At the cinema, Ginger Rogers and Ray Milland were appearing in *Lady in the Dark* and Olivia de Haviland was starring in the title role in *Princess O'Rourke*.

Yet even the capital's liveliest night owls couldn't help notice a distinct if subtle change of mood and pace. The crowds were a bit thinner, taxis were now easier to find and the streets felt quieter, even subdued. Above all, the swirling masses of uniforms that for weeks had been clogging the pavements and packing the restaurants and nightclubs were noticeable by their absence. It was obvious to everyone that the long-awaited invasion of Europe was about to begin.

Over France, in the biggest daytime blitz yet, Allied bombers continued their pre-invasion smashing of enemy defences and communications. One group of Spitfire fighters concentrated on the Caen and Cherbourg areas. Flying at tree-top height they gunned German convoys, staff cars, and even single dispatch riders. As one pilot put it, when they'd finished the countryside 'looked absolutely dead, apart from the bonfires which marked the attack'.

Veronica Owen took advantage of the good weather. After a morning's lie-in she bicycled into Fareham for lunch at the YWCA, then went to stay overnight with friends nearby. She sat out in the sun most of the afternoon and arranged flowers in the local church. That evening she went with her friends to see a play, *The Last of Summer*, at the local King's Theatre before enjoying an early night and, she thankfully recorded, 'a lovely comfortable bed'.

By now Fareham also was falling oddly quiet, reverting to the slow-paced rhythm of life the little market town had enjoyed before the war. For the last few days it had been at the epicentre of a massive trek by thousands of Allied forces heading for the coast. For weeks before that, the surrounding countryside had been packed with holding camps. In the town itself troops slept alongside the pavements and in gardens, endlessly tinkering with their vehicles, their hands smeared with oil. Many were Canadians. 'Some had been there for a month and others were in and out within a few days,' remembered one resident. 'They used to come in and ask if they could cook an egg . . . The women in the road would make tea for them when they could and if there were plenty of apples about they would make them apple tarts. They were a friendly, smashing bunch of blokes. Girls could walk about through those troops and there would never be any problem at all.'

Veronica had happily and safely explored the area on her bicycle. 'Patriotism was all around us,' she wrote. 'As we biked, we talked of the war to defend the villages and countryside.' Because of her father's naval background, she had grown up first in Devonport, in the West Country, then outside Chatham, close to the royal dock-yards on the Thames. This was new terrain to her, the discovery of a more rural England visibly steeped in the past.

But the intrusion of the present had been starkly apparent. She'd first noticed the troop build-up in late April during one of her exploratory rides, when she'd passed tanks and army vehicles moving south or stationary by the road. 'Tons of "traffic",' she recorded. 'They were huddled to the side of the road, using hedges and trees for camouflage and the soldiers lying in the road sleeping, silent, reading . . .'

Now, almost overnight, the streets were deserted. 'We knew it was D-Day,' one local said, 'because when we woke up in the morning they were all gone.'

Ships of the Western Naval Task Force were already under way from Scapa Flow, Belfast and the Clyde, and landing craft for Omaha and Utah Beaches began to leave their moorings in Devon and Cornwall. It was bright and clear, but on board the *Tuscaloosa* David Bruce was picking up forebodings about D-Day. He heard more complaints about the heavy demands being put on the US Navy and the constant last-minute changes of plan. The latest involved the airborne drops. The C-47s transporting Bill Tucker and his fellow paratroopers of the 82nd and 101st Divisions had been rerouted to pass directly over American naval vessels. The ships had been ordered to fire at no planes, unless clearly identified as enemy, at a range greater than one thousand feet. The plan, feared Bruce, offered a perfect opportunity for German bombers 'to slip in'. As for 'Wild Bill' Donovan, Bruce recorded that he felt 'too easy an optimism over the success of the assault prevails'.

That morning Eisenhower noted despairingly that the weather in England was verging on unpredictable. Outside it remained calm and sunny. Yet Stagg was still forecasting a serious deterioration in the Channel weather for D-Day. Worse, he couldn't tell Eisenhower exactly how bad things would be. The experts remained divided, and at the morning's weather conference no clear picture emerged. It seemed possible that while sea conditions would be tolerable, low cloud could seriously jeopardise the carefully planned air support. Should the Allied Supreme Commander risk those anyway, or post-pone the whole operation hoping for better weather later? If so, he would have to order back ships already under way. This could only increase the chances of a major security breach.

He faced an agonising decision. Most of the morning he spent composing a long memorandum outlining the problems he faced. The document both explained his thinking and, in military parl-ance, 'covered his ass' if things went wrong. D-Day casualties were already expected to be high even if the landings succeeded. If they failed, things could be horrendous. Top of his list of problems was the continuing crisis over de Gaulle, which was important for operations because the General obviously commanded the loyalty of the only French troops taking part in D-Day, and of the whole of the French Resistance. It was all, Eisenhower wrote, 'a sorry mess'. Reading between the lines, it was clear he blamed Roosevelt for badly misjudging the widespread support in France for the General.

Then came the weather, capricious and unpredictable, an issue made even worse because the weathermen could not agree. 'Probably no one that does not have to bear the specific and direct responsibility of making the final decision as to what to do,' he wrote, 'can understand the intensity of these burdens.'

As Allied Supreme Commander he had also to confront political issues not faced by his subordinate commanders. He was always being reminded of one in particular. If he delayed the invasion, how would the Russians react?

Ever since Hitler's attack on the Soviet Union, Stalin had been demanding an Allied Second Front in Europe. It had not come in 1942, and although the Allies had invaded and knocked out Mussolini's Italy the following year, Stalin still expected, and kept on demanding, a major Western offensive aimed at the Nazi heartland. At the Tehran Conference in November 1943, Roosevelt and Churchill had finally delivered, guaranteeing the launch of Overlord for the spring of 1944. The promise set the seal on the Big Three alliance. To renege on it now was out of the question. In April the two Western leaders had jointly sent a 'personal and most secret' message to their Soviet ally confirming the deal. 'The general crossing of the sea,' they told him, 'will take place around "R" date . . . we shall be acting at our fullest strength.' 'R' date, passed on directly to the Soviet General Staff in Moscow by the Allied military missions in Moscow, was 31 May, give or take a few days to allow for tide and weather.

It had also been agreed that the Soviets would launch a massive summer offensive of their own to coincide with Overlord, thus squeezing the Germans from both west and east. The Allies also promised to co-ordinate deception plans. In April, after weeks of negotiation, Moscow had approved Plan Bodyguard. Since then the D-Day deception planners had been sending fortnightly reports on progress. Surprise, both sides agreed, would best be achieved by fooling the Germans into thinking the real Allied offensives would come in July, later than actually planned. The Soviets also promised to liaise over deception aimed at Norway – although in the end they never did.

Just ten days before, at a meeting in the Kremlin, Stalin and his High Command had finished hammering out details of their summer offensive. Like Allied operations, it was densely guarded by complex deception stratagems. It would begin on 9 June with an attack in the north towards Finland. But this, along with an attack in the south on the Ukrainian front, was essentially a feint. The major attack would be launched against German Army Group Centre in Belorussia, deploying two and a half million troops, five thousand two hundred tanks and five thousand three hundred aircraft. Stalin, a 'hands-on' leader, personally checked the details. 'Zhukov and I,' recorded Alexander Vasilevsky, Chief of the Soviet General Staff, 'were several times summoned to Moscow. Time and again, Stalin spoke to us on various details by telephone as well.' He was referring to his colleague the Deputy Supreme Commander in charge of the first and second Belorussian fronts. Until late on the night of 30 May, Stalin, Zhukov, Vasilevsky and General Antonov worked together in the Kremlin to complete the final plan.

The next day the directives were issued to Red Army commanders. Stalin personally chose the code-name for this Soviet equivalent of Overlord – 'Bagration'. It was an artful choice. Prince Peter Bagration was commander of the Russian army who was mortally wounded at the Battle of Borodino against Napoleon in 1812, and a national hero. But his name evoked more than an historic campaign against invaders. Bagration was of Georgian and Armenian extraction, and the Bagratid dynasty had ruled Georgia for eight centuries before it was annexed to Russia in 1800. Georgia was Stalin's homeland. His choice of code-name was another shrewd reminder of who was in charge.

While each side had planned its campaign independently of the other, the two were intimately linked, ally in step with ally, the opening of their last and decisive assault on Nazi power in Europe. This was a lesson now preached almost daily by Churchill and Roosevelt. Only a few days before, the President's son Elliot had visited Widewing, and over a three-hour card game he and Eisenhower had discussed the Russian factor. Stalin was a stickler for keeping his word, said Elliot, and the great test for the Russians was 'whether Britain and the United States would keep their word with respect to the second front'. Soviet losses, he reminded Eisenhower, were running at sixteen million, both military and civilian. Eisenhower responded by saying he wasn't certain exactly what commitments had been made, but that he was confident 'there would be no welshing on the second front'.

The Supreme Commander, on whose shoulders Overlord now rested, knew that postponement, or a botched attempt, would have incalculable political and strategic consequences stretching far beyond the beaches of Normandy. That was why he felt strongly, even viscerally, that if at all possible D-Day should take place as scheduled. 'Only marked deterioration beyond that now expected would disarrange our plans,' he informed General George C. Marshall in an 'Eyes Only' top-secret Bigot message to Washington.

There was little more he could now do until the weather conference that evening, so he took the time to write home. His son John was due to graduate from West Point on 6 June, and Mamie would be there. 'There's nothing I would not have given to have been there with you and John,' he wrote, 'but c'est la guerre!' For most of the day, recorded his secretary Kay Summersby in her diary, he seemed very depressed.

While Ike agonised about the weather, a couple of miles away Churchill worked on his train until lunch. Ultra brought him more good news. The Germans were having to bring in special flak batteries to protect their ferries crossing the Seine now that all the bridges were down. An American submarine had sunk a Japanese light cruiser in the Pacific. An Allied raid on Wiener Neustadt had destroyed all remaining buildings in an aircraft factory. And from a diplomatic intercept he learned that the Japanese Minister in the Vatican was telling Tokyo that in the skies over Rome the German Air Force remained 'practically invisible'. Everyone was now waiting for the Germans to abandon the city, the 'blue jacket' revealed.

MI5's monthly report for May, however, introduced a cautionary note. It contained intriguing news about an influx of German spies into Iceland. All of them had been captured carrying instructions to send weather reports to Berlin. From this, MI5 concluded that the Germans were expecting an offensive operation of 'some magnitude' to be launched from the island in the near future. This was welcome confirmation that Allied deception about an attack on Norway was apparently working. But MI5 also told Churchill about the arrest in Spain of the Abwehr officer Jebsen and his forcible removal to Berlin. It meant, they pointed out, that the double-cross scheme was now passing through a critical phase. They also revealed that Garbo had been asked to find out the exact locations, including street numbers, of the Allied service headquarters concerned with D-Day. As German missions to assassinate Generals Harold Alexander and Mark Clark in Italy had recently been foiled, this could mean the Germans were contemplating similar attacks in Britain. The recent parachute-glider attack on Tito's headquarters in Yugoslavia was fresh in everyone's mind, and Churchill hardly needed reminding that his son Randolph had been lucky to escape with his life.

To add to his worries, MI5 revealed that there had also been some potentially serious security leaks. A man working in a factory making special tanks for D-Day had gossiped in a pub; a ship's fireman had written a letter revealing that his vessel would be used as a blockship in forthcoming operations and named other such ships, as well as their home port; an officer on a Dutch ship in Wales had explained that his vessel was loaded with petroleum and ammunition and would be off the French coast within the next two weeks; and a woman in southern England had written to relatives in Lancashire giving the whereabouts of General Montgomery's headquarters. This was just a sample of loose talk that might still jeopardise D-Day.

After lunch Churchill set off for Southampton with his Minister for Labour, Ernest Bevin, and General Smuts. Here he watched troops of the Tyneside Division embarking. Then, after boarding a motor launch, he reviewed a huge assembly of landing craft moored in the Solent. 'They are wonderful sights to see,' he wired enthusiastically to Roosevelt. He cruised in the launch down to Portsmouth and dropped into Southwick House for an impromptu chat with Eisenhower. 'The PM's caravan of cars and dashing cyclists swirled in . . . Filled their petrol tanks and diminished our supply of Scotch, there being some ten or more parched mouths to moisten . . .,' wrote Harry Butcher in his diary. Churchill told Eisenhower how the King had vetoed his boat ride to the invasion and asked if he could help change his mind. When Eisenhower refused, Churchill insisted that the Supreme Commander was also too valuable to go. Then he dashed off to his train for the evening.

For Glenn Dickin, waiting aboard the *Llangibby Castle* at Southampton docks, it was finally goodbye to Britain.

He'd been there for two years, a fresh-faced youth from the prairies who'd matured into a well-regarded officer and a worldly-wise young man. He still badly missed home, but no longer felt such a stranger in Britain. Like most Canadians of British origin, he still referred to 'the old country', and indeed Canada was still intimately tied to Britain in a myriad ways. King George VI was Canada's monarch too, a British Governor-General still resided in the federal capital, Ottawa, and Canadians were still British subjects. Indeed in parts of Canada pro-British patriotism ran so deep that on the outbreak of war thousands instantly volunteered for service. The very fact that, apart from his D-Day helmet, Glenn was wearing what was basically a British uniform, and that the 3rd Canadian Infantry Division was under ultimate British command, emphasised such ties. Yet their first direct encounter with 'the old country' often revealed to Canadians how North American they were, how different they were from the British, and this sharpened a growing sense of a distinct Canadian identity and nationalism.

This was Glenn's experience, made all the more acute because, like most English Canadians, his family had recent British links, although again, typically, he was the product of an ethnic mix. On his mother's side he could trace his ancestors back to Germany and the departure of the Guizdorfer family from Württemberg to North America after the failure of the German Revolution in 1848. Changing his family name to Christopher, the oldest son Charles Frederick had worked in Pennsylvania, then moved to Canada. In Ontario he married into a United Empire Loyalist family, refugees themselves from the American Revolution two generations before. Then he'd gone West, settling in Manor in 1893 to farm a hundred and sixty acres of prairie. His daughter Martha, Glenn's mother, was one of his twelve children. She was now sixty-five and herself the mother of ten children. Glenn was the youngest. Three of his brothers were also in the Canadian armed forces. One, Donald, had also served in the First World War. The others, Claude and Ferriday, were serving with the Royal Canadian Air Force in Britain. Occasionally Glenn would get together with them if he could.

Glenn's British roots came through his father. George Dodsworth Dickin was one of the thousands of young British settlers who emigrated to the Canadian prairies in the 1880s, attracted by the promise of cheap land and a new life. Even before Saskatchewan officially became a province, he'd arrived fresh from the family farm in Shropshire, close to the Welsh border, to build a new future. He'd done well enough to buy his own farm and other property in and around Manor, and had then become a government homestead inspector. He'd died in 1937, but his brother Frank was still running a smallholding outside the market town of Wellington, in Shropshire.

Glenn had gone to meet his English family as soon as he could. Since then he'd spent many of his leaves there, usually with his buddy Gordon Brown. Uncle Frank and his wife, Gertie, had five children and were doing well, reported Glenn to the family in Manor, milking some twenty-four cows, owning a lot of other animals and growing plenty of fruit. Uncle Frank, he wrote, 'gets quite a kick out of us and treats us swell'. This meant filling them with food – four eggs in one day, Glenn enthused, and, when summer arrived, plenty of pick-your-own strawberries and raspberries. The visit also gave the two young men time to sleep, relax and generally unwind from their rigorous training. Glenn also got to know his cousins. One, Isabel, had been a trophy-winning golfer before the war. Another had played tournament bridge for England. 'So you see,' he wrote home, 'some of our relatives are quite important people . . .'

By the time he embarked for Normandy, Wellington had become a home away from home and he'd discovered a new family. His latest stay had been in April, and he'd enjoyed himself like never before. 'I have a very nice time here going to the odd show and dances and playing ping-pong with the neighbours,' he wrote to his sister, Mona. 'There is quite a handsome wench lives down the road who has a car – she shows me around a bit, a good type you know – anxious to see that the Dominion troops are entertained . . .' He was being ironic. But the irony held genuine affection and warmth for the old country and its inhabitants.

Anyway, he'd be home soon.

Sonia d'Artois was beginning to fit in nicely at the SOE hideout. The first night the group spent in the grounds of the château, Hudson had given her a small tent of her own. What he didn't know was that she had a horror of snakes. In the middle of the night she woke up to feel something crawling underneath her. She screamed out loud but the others rushed in and dismissed her fears as groundless. 'Well then, pick up the sleeping bag,' she insisted. And there, writhing in the torchlight, was a snake. Since then she'd shared the same tent as the men.

She still had no idea of when or where D-Day would happen, and the waiting was now beginning to seem interminable. Hudson noticed her impatience, which was shared by 'Kiki' Glaesner. Both were young, on their first SOE mission, and eager for action. So Hudson devised a plan to give each of them a role. Kiki would take care of all Hudson's contacts south of Le Mans and some of the explosives would be moved to farms in his area. Hudson and Sonia would concentrate on the city of Le Mans itself, bringing in local businessmen who could supply clothes, shoes and other civilian necessities. One of the minor things bothering Sonia was her hair. Even if she could get to a tap, the water was always cold and she had to use ordinary soap, not shampoo, to wash it. It was beginning to look straggly. Ordinarily it wouldn't matter much, although in truth she always liked to be well groomed. But bad hair could wreck her cover, and was a security risk. She was supposed to be working for Louis Vuitton in Paris while recovering from bronchitis in the country. Looking like a scarecrow would raise suspicion.

Travelling to and from Le Mans took Hudson and Sonia about an hour each way by bicycle and always ran the risk of running into a roadblock, which would mean having their papers inspected. To cut down the journey time, Hudson managed to rent a small house on the city's rue Mangeard as a base for the two of them. Although Sonia had been sent as a courier for the whole circuit, they were already beginning to form something of a two-person team, and she also began to handle the circuit's finances. 'We just had a good working relationship,' Sonia said later, 'and a very good team, and he was an easy man to work with anyway.'

The SOE had provided Headmaster with plenty of French francs to ease its way, pay rent, buy civilian goods and purchase goodwill. When the money ran out, Sonia began borrowing from her contacts. The most useful proved to be the Abbé Chevalier, treasurer of the Diocese of Le Mans, and the uncle of Edmond Cohin, the owner of the château. Although Edmond's father was Jewish, his mother was Catholic, and the Abbé was her brother. Headmaster ran up such a huge bill that it was to be Sonia's job after the liberation of France to return with her husband and repay it. 'We got the money from London,' she recalled, 'and the briefcase was full of French bills. We stayed in the Archbishop's bedroom.'

In Le Mans Sonia and Hudson certainly needed plenty of money. Calculating that the Germans knew a female agent had landed and would suspect she was still lying low, they decided to fool the Gestapo by doing exactly the opposite. In town they would behave openly and normally, eating out in the many black-market restaurants that were flourishing in the town with its large German garrison. But this carried its risks, as Sonia explained: 'You had to take whatever seat was available, and if there was a free space at a table you had to make for it, otherwise you'd look suspicious.' Once she and Hudson found themselves seated next to a German officer, and they chatted amiably until she got up to leave. As she did, she dropped her handbag. The officer bent down to pick it up, but Sonia rapidly beat him to it. 'I knew damn well that if he picked it up, he'd find it rather heavy and wonder what I had in it,' she said. It was heavy because it contained her .32 Colt pistol, the model handed out to all SOE agents, both men and women, which she'd brought with her from London. It was a nice little gun, she thought. She'd hate to lose it, or have it betray her. Only later did they learn that the German officer had been none other than the head of the local Gestapo.

In Norway, Vidkun Quisling finally admitted that the campaign to recruit young men for labour service had failed dismally. Addressing an SS detachment of Norwegian Nazis, he complained bitterly that Norwegian youth 'hides and takes to the forests when we demand that it work for the people and the country'. Somehow, mobilisation would have to be enforced. 'You,' he promised the SS men, 'shall help enforce it.' In Oslo, the execution of five more Norwegians trained by the British for sabotage was announced. It brought to 264 the total number of such executions in Norway.

As usual, Peter Moen got up at 6.30 a.m., spent the day in his cell and by 8 p.m. was lying on his mattress with the blackout curtain in place. Long discussions with his cellmates, such as they'd had the day before, weren't always to his liking. He often preferred his own company. It wasn't just the diary he'd drop down the ventilator shaft page by page. Often he'd take the blackout pin to work out various mathematical or geometrical conundrums: prime numbers, fractions, circles or the volume of a cone. Once he covered several sheets with 'Notes about the Equator', full of calculations about the size of the globe. Other sheets consisted of nothing but translations of foreign words.

He'd had a traditional and narrowly sectarian upbringing in the small town of Drammen, about twenty-five miles south-west of Oslo, before entering the Idun Insurance Company. He was a quiet, hard-working man prone to bouts of melancholy and depression so serious that suicide often crossed his mind. Only fear of the unknown held him back. Like Veronica, Moen knew his Shakespeare, especially the famous lines from *Hamlet* where the Prince of Denmark meditates on death. 'What is it which binds us so to life but that dread of something after death . . . puzzles the will and makes us rather bear those ills we have than fly to others that we know not of,' he wrote in his diary, garbling the lines.

Life in the Resistance had offered Moen an escape from gloomy introversion, a welcome drug to treat his chronic depression. 'I grabbed eagerly at the excitement of underground life,' he confessed. He'd adapted well to the life, so much so that most of his comrades in the illegal press never dreamed that he'd been the prime mover in one of the defining moments of the Norwegian Resistance. He still kept the secret to himself. It wasn't even right for the diary.

Six months before, on a night in late November, fire had broken out in the Aula auditorium of the University of Oslo, a hall used for concerts and theatre performances. Alerted by a phone call, the fire brigade quickly extinguished the blaze and little damage was done. The episode might have been forgotten, except that it came after weeks of turmoil in Norway's only university still remaining open. Since the start of the occupation the Nazi authorities had been wary of it, and as early as the autumn of 1940 had broken up the students' association. A year later they arrested the Vice-Chancellor and replaced him with Professor Adolf Hoel, a supporter of Quisling's Nasjonal Sammlung Party (NS). Many of the students and teachers were involved in underground resistance of one kind or another, and were determined to defy any efforts to Nazify the university by making membership of the NS a condition of entry. So when new entrance rules were introduced in the autumn of 1943, they sparked angry protests that led the Nazis to fear a strike. To head it off, that October they arrested dozens of teachers and students, a measure that provoked a written protest by over two thousand students. It was amid this turmoil that the fire had broken out.

In an uncanny echo of the fierce controversy that had raged in Berlin over the burning of the Reichstag soon after Hitler came to power in early 1933, cries on one side went up that this was a deliberate Nazi provocation, while the German authorities pointed an accusing finger at the communists. Josef Terboven, the Nazi Reichskommissar, immediately met with Quisling to decide on a tough response. Word of their meeting leaked out to the leadership of Norway's civilian resistance movement, Sivorg, which sent an urgent warning to the students. Within hours Wehrmacht troops and armed police surrounded the campus, closed down the university and arrested more than a thousand students. But, six months on, who was responsible for the Aula fire remained a mystery.

Moen, however, knew the truth. It hadn't been set by the Nazis, nor had it been initiated by the communists. It was he and a small group of co-workers on the *London Nyatt* newspaper who were behind it, motivated by fears that official pressure would eventually lead to the university's successful Nazification. Rather than allow that, they decided deliberately to provoke the authorities into closing it down.

Moen had played no personal part in the practical details of starting the blaze. He'd simply been one of the brains who set the plan in motion. The arsonists had no intention of seriously damaging the building, and it was they who had telephoned the fire brigade. Of the one thousand students arrested, over six hundred were later deported to concentration camps in Germany. Only after the war would Moen's part in the episode emerge.

At its darkest, his diary was the journal of a man racked by guilt, remorse, self-doubt and lack of faith, the record of an intense and consuming inner turmoil. Years earlier he had read one of the most famous prison journals of the century, that of the Russian anarchist Alexander Berkman, an innocent man who spent twenty years in an American prison. Moen regarded it as 'the Bible of prison heroism', the keeping of which had given Berkman the strength and the will to survive, and an inspiration in his own personal battle against despair.

Yet, whatever personal demons he confronted, Moen never lost sight of the greater struggle of Norway itself. 'But of the deepest need, blue-eyed freedom is born for us.' Occasionally this line from his country's national anthem would burst upon him to remind him of his work with *London Nyatt* and the battles that still lay ahead. The landmarks of his life were now days in the calendar.

On 15 March, the Ides of March in the old Roman calendar, and the day in Shakespeare's *Julius Caesar* that the Roman emperor fell to his assassins, Moen recorded it as 'the tyrant's death day'. But in a world that was always producing new tyrants there were always prisoners who had resisted injustice and violence. Was their fight worthwhile? Moen asked himself. 'Yes, yes, and again yes,' he answered in a stirring declaration of faith. 'Without it and the sacrifice it demands all freedom would soon be crushed.' Three hundred prisoners were packed into the cells at 19 Mollergaten, but he regretted nothing he had done or written. 'There *should* be people in Nazi prisons,' he added. 'If I were not here, you would be – you who are free . . .'

That day, in the Great Hall at the Berghof, Hitler posed in front of a photographer for an official group portrait. Among the twenty or so people standing behind him was Heinrich Himmler, head of the SS, Martin Bormann, Hitler's powerful private secretary and presiding genius of the Obersalzberg, and Dr Theodor Morell, his private physician. Hitler, in the front row, wearing a white collar and tie, stared fixedly and unsmiling at the camera. To his left, her arm in his, stood a short, slight young woman, a ribbon in her hair. On his right was another young woman, also holding his arm, dressed in white, and likewise wearing a ribbon.

The two women were sisters. Gretl, on Hitler's right, had just got married at Salzburg town hall to SS Gruppenführer Hermann Fegelein – hence the presence of Heinrich Himmler, his boss – and they had arrived at the Berghof for an official celebration.

The bride's sister was named Eva Braun. She was thirty-two years old, and she was Hitler's mistress.

Hitler had no family and lacked any close personal friends. Magda Goebbels once said that he was 'simply not human – unreachable and untouchable'. In his bedroom at the Berghof hung pictures of his mother and his pre-war chauffeur, both dead. He often seemed closest to his dog, Blondi, an Alsatian who accompanied him everywhere. 'Animals are more loyal than people,' Hitler once stated, and he was fond of quoting Frederick the Great, who said, 'Since I have learned to know man, I love dogs.' Blondi, claimed Albert Speer, who knew Hitler better than almost anyone else, 'was more important [to Hitler] than even his closest associate'.

This may well have been true. But other Alsatians were being trained to kill by the Wehrmacht as part of its plan to repel the invasion. British commandos returning from pre-invasion raids along the French coast were reporting ferocious attacks by such dogs. As a result, some of them had taken to wearing their commando knives on their left leg so that valuable seconds weren't lost when they instinctively raised their right arm to fend off the 'Alsatian guard'.

Hitler's preference for Blondi didn't mean he was unappreciative of people around him at the Berghof. He was thankful, for example, that the wife of his aide Nicolaus von Below was part of his social circle. Usually she chatted with Hitler about their children or the running of their family estate, small talk that helped divert the Führer from his problems. Hitler could be gallant in an old-fashioned way with women, kissing their hands and bowing courteously when they entered or left the room. To Frau von Below he was especially grateful for one thing above all. She had become friends with Eva.

The Führer's mistress had followed him to the Berghof that winter, and been with him ever since. More than twenty years younger than him, she had met Hitler while working as an assistant in the studio of Hitler's favourite photographer, Heinrich Hoffmann. Some time in the early 1930s she became his mistress, although the precise nature of their sexual relationship has remained a mystery ever since. She was pretty, with an attractive figure, but dressed modestly and wore inexpensive jewellery. As well as liking sports, she was also a reasonably accomplished amateur photographer. Mostly she was interested in movies, fashion and gossip, and showed no interest in politics. Hitler liked this. 'A highly intelligent man,' he once told Speer, 'should take a primitive and stupid woman. Imagine if on top of everything else I had a woman who interfered with my work! In my leisure time, I want to

have peace.' Hitler would often ignore Eva, and early in their relationship she had taken an overdose. On another occasion she had
made a second feeble attempt at suicide with a revolver. Both were
classic cries for attention. Normally she was kept well out of public
view.

At the Berghof, however, and increasingly so now, Hitler was
allowing her to become more visible, and she regularly sat at the
dinner table with other guests and joined in the evening's events.
But it was all very forced. He forbade her to smoke, sunbathe or
dance, and she remained little more than a decorative piece of fur-
niture in his increasingly empty world. She lived, she once
complained, 'like a bird in a gilded cage'.

For Eva, the day's events tying her sister Margarete – Gretl was
the diminutive – to Hermann Fegelein, gave her a welcome status
in Berghof society that she had previously lacked. Officially,
Fegelein, a long-time protégé of Himmler and notorious careerist,
was the SS leader's liaison man with Hitler. An amusing raconteur
with an eye for women, he'd also put himself at the centre of the
Berghof's social life and ingratiated himself with Bormann. Since
his arrival in the spring, Eva had undoubtedly been attracted to
him. By this time Gretl had moved in with her at the Berghof. After
several failed attempts at marrying her off to other men in Hitler's
entourage, Eva had worked hard at pairing her off with Fegelein.
She planned the ceremonies and insisted on an elaborate wedding
to make up for the one she knew she would never have with Hitler.
Afterwards she felt triumphant. 'I want this marriage to be as
beautiful as if it were my own!' she declared. 'Now I am some-
body.' With Bormann's assistance, Hitler chose the bride's
expensive tiara.

Saturday was one of the three days each week that Albert Grunberg
met up with his wife, Marguerite, in his secret hideaway. Since he'd
gone into hiding she'd continued to run their hairdressing salon just
down the street. That beauty parlours remained open throughout
the Nazi occupation of Paris owed as much to Vichy efforts to support the fashion industry and boost male morale as it did to the

habits of French women. 'The more French women remain elegant,' declared the couturier Lucien Lelong, 'the more our country will show foreigners that it is not afraid of the future.' One women's magazine reminded its readers that 'Every Parisian Woman Is A Living Propaganda Poster', and others agreed. Such perfection wasn't easily achieved. Madame Grunberg's salon suffered, as did all coiffeurs, from numerous and sometimes lengthy power cuts. When hairdryers cut out, clients were seated outside in the sun, comb-outs on the pavements being common. One salon maestro was said to have hooked up his dryers to a furnace whose hot air was forced through stove pipes by a small army of boys furiously pedalling stationary bicycles. It was claimed that for every 320 kilometres cycled, 160 women emerged perfectly coiffed from his establishment. The Grunberg salon was not so lucky. To heat up the water for shaving her male clients in the morning, Marguerite had to rise at 7 a.m. to use the gas before it was switched off an hour later.

At eight o'clock that evening Churchill arrived back at his train after his visit to Ike and changed into the drill uniform of a colonel of the Hussars. He then sat down for dinner with Anthony Eden, General Smuts and Ernest Bevin. A 1926 champagne was served, and afterwards a grand old brandy out of balloon glasses. Churchill spent most of the time reminiscing with Smuts about the Boer War and South African politics at the beginning of the century. Bevin chatted amiably with the suave and elegant Eden. They were so evidently friendly that Churchill, who was in a convivial mood, joked that he was ready to give up the war leadership to either or both of them at any time.

By contrast, a sombre mood had descended on Southwick House, the 'nadir of strain and despondency', as Stagg wrote. While Churchill enjoyed his dinner, Eisenhower was chairing the second weather conference of the day in the library. Around him in a semicircle, seated on low chairs and couches, were his D-Day commanders. The atmosphere was palpably tense as Stagg brought dismaying news that the weather picture was now 'full of menace' for 5 June. The high-pressure system over the Azores that had recently been produ: ing benign weather was rapidly giving way to a series of depressions. From early Sunday morning – tomorrow – until late on Wednesday, he could only promise thick low cloud at five hundred feet, accompanied by high winds – between Force 4 and 6 – over the Normandy beaches.

Eisenhower sat grim-faced throughout the meeting. All his worst fears were coming true. When the soft-spoken Scot had finished, he asked him a simple question. 'Is there just a chance that you might be a bit more optimistic tomorrow?' But Stagg told him there was no chance of this now. Then he left the room.

The Supreme Commander took a poll. Leigh-Mallory feared that his aircrews would lack proper visibility; Ramsay thought the rough seas would make the Navy's job impossible. Only Montgomery remained optimistic. But then that was Monty, always eager to take on the Germans; after all, he'd mischievously named his two dogs Rommel and Hitler.

After an hour's discussion the sombre group agreed to put off a final decision yet again. The main body of the invasion troops was not due to set sail until just after dawn the following morning. So they would all reconvene in the library at 4.15 a.m. to hear Stagg's latest forecast. If it remained bad, they would have to postpone D-Day. In the meantime the forces already at sea should be allowed to proceed. They could still be recalled.

As the exhausted Eisenhower returned to his caravan for a few hours' sleep, one of his invasion commanders remained unhappy. In his diary entry that night Admiral Ramsay, the man in charge of Neptune, noted that the decision to postpone the decision was made only 'because Ike was over impressed with the frightful results of postponement'.

The Supreme Commander's burden was, indeed, the heaviest of all. But his commander of land forces remained confident. Tomorrow, Montgomery noted in his diary after the meeting, would be an interesting day, when the final decision would have to be taken, and, once taken, stuck to. 'Strong and resolute characters will be very necessary,' he wrote. 'Eisenhower is just the man for the job; he is a really "big" man and is in every way an Allied Commander – holding the balance between Allied contingents . . . I would trust him to the last gasp.'

In Churchill's train, the Prime Minister's military right-hand man, General Hastings Ismay, took a call from Southwick House about the bad weather. 'A sledge-hammer blow' was how he described it. At 2 a.m. he wrote a hurried letter to a trusted friend describing the day as 'bloody'. Arrangements on the train were hell, with no privacy, not a moment to himself, and three people with one telephone squeezed into a compartment four feet by three feet. There was no bath, and only a very poor shower. 'Master' – Churchill – had been busy all the time. 'Tonight,' Ismay ended, 'is the worst of the war from the "decision" point of view.'

Yet there was one small crumb of comfort. Since the alarming report by the Joint Intelligence Committee the previous Monday that Hitler might have correctly guessed that Normandy was the main Allied bridgehead, nothing detected since in the huge stream of intercepts being analysed by the Bletchley Park code-breakers backed this up. On the contrary, everything suggested that the Germans remained completely in the dark. Earlier in the day the Committee had met in London to make its final assessment of the Germans' expectations. 'There has been no intelligence during the last week,' it concluded, 'to suggest that the enemy has accurately assessed the area in which our main assault is to be made. He appears to expect several landings between the Pas de Calais and Cherbourg.'

At nine minutes past nine, as the evening weather conference began in the library at Southwick House, Garbo's radio operator tapped out the following message to Madrid from the house in Hendon: 'Harwich. Sign, not previously seen, of a yellow shield with three blue mountain peaks outlined in white. This newly arrived division from the USA.' In Berlin, the insignia was identified by German analysts as that of the American 80th Infantry Division, apparently a unit of the supposed First United States Army Group under

Patton. FUSAG's presence in the East Anglian port of Harwich was yet another pointer to an Allied build-up for an attack across the Channel towards the Pas de Calais.

That the Germans continued to be fooled owed much to their trust in the agent they knew as Arabel. It was a remarkable testimony to Allied deception. The deception plan itself had to be credible, and the skill of the planners could be thanked for that. But the Germans first had to trust the messenger. For that, Juan Pujol was the Allies' principal asset.

He had been from the start. 'We are now entering the most decisive phase of the war,' Karl Kühlenthal had told him back in February. 'Your first objective must be to discover as soon as possible *when* and *where* the first signs of preparation are noted.' The message had arrived in a letter addressed to a Mr Joseph Smith Jones, care of a Portuguese bank in Lisbon, and included glowing words of approval. 'I find everything so perfect,' enthused Kühlenthal, 'that there is practically nothing I can say with regard to the measures you have taken.'

Nothing since then had made him change his mind. He had, after all, been working with Pujol since 1941, and had personally taught him the tricks of the trade.

Although he was now Garbo, and operating under British control, much still depended on the personal talents of the real Juan Pujol himself. He communicated with Madrid by both radio and letter. The radio messages – well over a thousand – were composed by his British controllers, but it was up to Pujol to translate them into his own inimitable Spanish, with its flowery phrases and occasional eccentricities. As for the letters, some of them as many as eight thousand words long, they consisted of a 'cover' message, apparently innocuous, with the real message concealed between the lines in invisible ink. Pujol composed the cover messages, and wrote out all the secret ink messages in his own hand – always, however, in the presence of an MI5 officer.

He remained intensely engaged in developing his huge and fictional network of over twenty sub-agents, characters whose personalities and actions he relished elaborating. In short, the best person to convince the Abwehr that Arabel was a brilliant success was Pujol himself, a man who from the very start of this elaborate double game had sold himself to the Germans as a fanatical and energetic, if somewhat Quixotic, character.

Mercurial in real life he certainly was, as well as devious and manipulative. A short, brown-eyed man with slicked-back hair and a high forehead, Pujol was an enigma. Outwardly, he was simple and direct. Yet he had dexterously manoeuvred his way through the deadly maze of the Spanish Civil War, and on his own had fooled the Germans into accepting him as an agent. One British intelligence officer who came to know him well described him as 'a most capable liar with very few morals'. He later certainly proved adept at rewriting his personal history, completely airbrushing his wife, who helped him significantly during the war but whom he later divorced, from his memoirs.

Yet their stormy wartime marriage was inseparable from the Garbo story. Indeed, it had come close to wrecking the entire operation.

It had happened twelve months before. His wife, Aracelli González, whom he had married in 1940, spoke no English and had never before been out of Spain and Portugal. Marooned in London with two small children and racked by homesickness, she had begged to be allowed to go home for a brief visit to see her mother. This was judged far too risky by MI5. In the meantime she and her husband had befriended a Spanish couple, who invited them to the Spanish Club in London, where they would be certain to meet members of the Spanish Embassy. Garbo also vetoed this as far too dangerous. But the refusal proved the last straw for his lonely and desperate wife, and precipitated an enormous row. Later that day, beside herself with fury, she telephoned Tomas Harris and threatened to walk into the Spanish Embassy and reveal the secrets of Garbo's double-cross game unless she got her travel papers.

There had been marital spats before. Yet nothing so critical or threatening as this had ever erupted. Harris immediately alerted MI5 and arranged to have her picked up if she approached the embassy. Then he sat down with Pujol, and the two of them concocted a chillingly calculated plan.

Garbo disappeared for a few hours. Then two CID police officers went to his house and solemnly informed his wife that he had been arrested. She immediately burst into tears and swore that her husband had always been loyal to Britain. The next day, sobbing and blaming herself for the arrest, she put her head in the gas oven with all the taps turned on – although not before telephoning Garbo's radio operator and begging him to come round. When she recovered, she promised that if her husband was released she would never again misbehave or ask to return to Spain.

This was not the end of the drama. Blindfolded, she was taken to a detention camp, where her husband was brought in unshaven and wearing prison clothes. Again she cried, promising not to misbehave, and signed a statement to that effect. Only the next day, after being escorted to an intimidating office block in Whitehall, was she told that, after much careful deliberation, her husband would be allowed, after all, to continue his work. After that, operations had returned to normal and had run smoothly ever since.

As Harris remarked, this remarkable episode was 'not without interest in assessing the qualities of Garbo and his wife'. She had only threatened to go to the Spanish Embassy in order to get her papers, and would probably never have revealed the secrets of his work. As for Garbo, he had shown implicit confidence in his British controllers by allowing them to deal with the crisis in the way they did – one, of course, mapped out by himself. 'Had it failed,' noted Harris, 'it would have ruined forever his matrimonial life.'

To put it more brutally, Pujol, not to mention Harris, was quite prepared to risk his wife's life for the sake of Garbo. As he admitted at the time, while he was used to his wife's emotional outbreaks and was fairly sure the stratagem would work, there still remained a 10 per cent chance that she really would commit suicide.

At SHAEF headquarters, plans were hatched to bolster Garbo's deception about a second landing.

Over the previous few months several SOE agents in the Pas de Calais region and elsewhere in France had been picked up by the Germans. The Abwehr had then 'played back' their radio sets to Britain, hoping to fool the Allies into sending in more agents and revealing the secrets of D-Day. But Allied intelligence knew about this radio game because they had broken Abwehr codes, and they outplayed the Germans by continuing to send messages as if nothing had happened. One day, they reckoned, the channels could be used for deception. That moment had now arrived. Ten days after D-Day they would send warning messages over the BBC about the supposed second landing, along with other bogus material. Today special forces liaison officers at Ike's headquarters issued orders to book the necessary air time for the nights of 15 and 16 June.

'Michel has shaved off his moustache,' read the BBC announcer from the regular list of personal messages. It meant that the night before, Gustave Bertrand, the Frenchman with the Enigma secret, had successfully made his rendezvous with the RAF Lysander and was safely back in Britain. SIS now urgently needed to know if he had betrayed the secret to the Germans.

For this, Secret Intelligence Service chief Sir Stewart Menzies turned to Paul Paillole, the head of French counter-intelligence in London, and a pre-war colleague of Bertrand's in the Deuxième Bureau, France's Secret Service. At 5.30 p.m. Paillole sat down and read through the report that Bertrand had produced earlier in the day. Then he interrogated him. It was obvious that Bertrand had sailed dangerously close to the wind in agreeing to collaborate with the Germans, even if it was just a ruse to escape. Paillole found some details of the story hard to believe. Could the Germans really have been so naive as to let Bertrand deceive them into giving him the freedom to escape? Yet Bertrand spoke so frankly and openly about everything that Paillole concluded that he couldn't be a traitor and hadn't revealed the Ultra secret. Only one thing really bothered Paillole – Bertrand's efforts to squeeze out of him the actual timing of D-Day so that his contacts in France could be told by radio. Did he naively trust they were secure? Or was this a way of warning the Germans?

To be on the safe side, SIS placed Bertrand under house arrest until after the landings.

In Algiers, after an anxious morning for Duff Cooper, General de Gaulle finally agreed to fly to London. The British Ambassador spent most of the day scrambling to make arrangements. Finally, at 4.30 p.m., the Free French leader, accompanied by Cooper, took off in the aircraft provided by Churchill. Their first stop was Rabat, in Morocco, where they had dinner. De Gaulle, anxious about the continuing need for secrecy, decided not to leave the airfield and to eat on board. Dinner, noted Cooper, was 'a sticky affair', although whether he was referring to the heat, the food or de Gaulle's volatile mood, was unclear. At any rate, the two men then walked up and down the runway talking of everything except what was uppermost in their minds: the coming invasion and the impasse over Allied recognition of de Gaulle as the head of a French provisional government. The aircraft finally took off at 10.30 p.m. and after a trouble-free flight landed in England at exactly 6 a.m. the next day.

As the two men were pacing the runway at Rabat, the regular Free French evening broadcast on the BBC, *Les Français parlent aux Français*, insisted that the coming liberation of France must be a double one: liberation from the enemy and liberation from Vichy. For that, it pronounced, it was time the Allies recognised the governmental authority of de Gaulle and his movement. As always, the broadcast opened with a reminder of how long the struggle for national liberation had already lasted. Today was the one thousand four hundred and forty-first day of shame since May 1940, when Pétain had signed the armistice with Hitler.

That morning at La Roche-Guyon, Rommel busied himself at the château with anti-invasion preparations, pressing his staff for more coastal defences, demanding more multiple rocket launchers, requesting Luftwaffe co-operation in dropping mines in the navigation lanes around the Isle of Wight, and ordering a crash programme to extend beach defences down to the low-tide mark. The deadline for this last task, he instructed, was 20 June.

He also had an interesting visitor, Major General Hans Kramer, his successor as the last commander of the Afrika Korps, who had been captured by the British after the fall of Tunisia and held ever since in a prisoner-of-war camp in Britain. Sick, he had recently been released in a POW exchange arranged by the Swedish Red Cross. Being driven under escort on his way to repatriation via Sweden, he had noticed a large build-up of forces in south-east England. It seemed obvious from this, he told Rommel, that the Allies were planning to invade somewhere in the region of the Pas de Calais. As this coincided with Rommel's own belief, the Desert Fox readily concurred.

Neither man realised that this, too, was part of British deception, and that Kramer had been deliberately deceived. He'd been driven from his POW camp in Wales through the real Neptune assembly areas so that he could witness the massive build-up. But he had been told that he was in south-east England, and had even been introduced to General George C. Patton, with the American being described as the Commander-in-Chief of FUSAG, the mythical army group.

After Kramer's departure and his usual spartan lunch, Rommel stepped into his Horch and motored up the Seine to see von Rundstedt at his headquarters at St-Germain-en-Laye. He could see for himself the devastating damage inflicted by Allied bombers. In the words of a top-secret report produced that day in Berlin by the German Air Force Operations Staff, as a result of Allied attacks 'Paris has been systematically cut off from long distance traffic, and the most important bridges over the lower Seine have been destroyed one after another'.

Rommel told the Commander-in-Chief West that he wanted to leave early next morning for his home in Herrlingen, where he planned to celebrate his wife's fiftieth birthday. Then he would go and visit Hitler at the Berghof to urge him to release two more panzer divisions for use in Normandy, as well as an anti-aircraft corps and a mortar brigade. He would be back at La Roche-Guyon on the 8th. Von Rundstedt saw no reason why he shouldn't go home, since there was still no sign of an imminent invasion.

Walter Schwender's army unit was not the only German force stationed at Nantes, where the Navy had over a dozen patrol boats and minesweepers. But nowhere did Navy Group West, commanded by Admiral Theodor Krancke, have surface warships near the Channel ports on the French side. Instead, Hitler's first line of defence against the invasion fleet was to be his U-boats. But the 'wolf packs' were no more. Allied sub killers and aircraft, with the help of Ultra, had seen to that.

Operational flotillas of submarines were based in Bordeaux, Brest, La Pallice, Lorient and St Nazaire, this last downstream on the Loire from Walter. Although its huge dry dock had been destroyed by British commandos earlier in the war, St Nazaire still sheltered the U-boats in their pens, as did the French Atlantic ports. Here, under fifteen feet of concrete, they could be repaired and outfitted while their crews slept in specially constructed barracks. Masses of anti-aircraft guns guarded the pens, which were immune to bombing, although many French civilians had been killed as raids attacked supporting installations. But when the U-boats put out to sea they were vulnerable.

Writing in his operational journal just two days before, Grand Admiral Dönitz, the Commander-in-Chief of the German Navy, had secretly confided that it was becoming increasingly difficult for his submarines to locate ships and aircaft responsible for protecting convoys. Successes up to then had been largely the product of the tenacity and self-sacrifice of his crews. 'Now, however,' he wrote, 'the chances of success are greatly reduced. Indeed the odds are great that a submarine will not return from a mission. In these past few months, only 70 per cent of our U-boats have returned safely to base.'

But Admiral Ramsay and the D-Day planners had to prepare for the worst. On this same date, they estimated that the Germans would have 120 combat-ready submarines, with ninety in the invasion area. It would be the job of the anti-submarine forces to keep the U-boats away from the invasion lanes and ensure that none of the Norwegian-based subs made it to the Channel.

Germany's navy was no better than the army or air force in guessing where or when the invasion would come. A few naval officers, noting that the Bay of the Seine was not being heavily mined, wondered if this pointed to Normandy as the spot. But Hitler's own convictions and Allied deception plans meant that Dönitz had drawn up plans for a three-part anti-invasion U-boat force. One was based mostly in Trondheim and Narvik, in northern Norway; another around Bergen, in southern Norway; and the third in the French ports. All were ready to put to sea in six hours.

In France, forty-nine U-boats were waiting, but only thirty-five were actually ready to sail: fifteen in Brest, two in Lorient, four in La Pallice, and fourteen in St Nazaire – only half the Allies' prediction. And only a few, contrary to Churchill's fears, were actually fitted with *Schnorchels*.

Walter Schwender waited, unaware, behind Hitler's first line of defence, the U-boats, the second line, the mines, and the third line, the beach defences. He and his comrades were the fourth line.

In Berlin, SS intelligence passed on Oskar Reile's information about the SOE warning messages on the BBC over to Dönitz, observing that invasion was possible within the next two weeks. No one on his staff took it seriously. Perhaps, they suggested, it was no more than an exercise.

Across the Atlantic, at 4.39 Eastern time that afternoon, an Associated Press report announced that the invasion had begun, electric news that was immediately picked up and broadcast by over five hundred wireless stations owned by the big four American networks, as well as stations in Cuba, Chile and Moscow. In New York, a baseball game was halted while players and spectators stood in silence for a minute of prayer. The Cathedral of St John the Divine hurriedly prepared for a special service. At a racecourse on Long Island officials prepared to cancel the last two races of the day, and the New York telephone exchange was swamped with enquiries.

Five minutes after the report was transmitted, Associated Press issued an urgent correction. But by then the mistaken news had been heard by millions of people in both North and South America. It took several hours for telephone systems to return to normal. All through the evening radio commentators were kept busy denying the news and explaining how the error had occurred.

The explanation was simple. A teletype operator in the news agency's office had been engaged in a practice run of the release, prepared by SHAEF a couple of days before. Accidentally, the machine had been left switched on for the transatlantic link-up, and she'd hit the keys too hard.

Eisenhower, however, was too exhausted or preoccupied to care. When Harry Butcher told him the news next morning, he simply grunted.

That evening, at 3rd Canadian Infantry Division's headquarters in Cowes, war correspondents were provided with details of the Juno Beach landings. It was nearly dark when their briefing was finished. As he walked down the stairs into the night air, one of them suddenly had a strange foreboding. It had been in this very same building that he'd been briefed on the Dieppe raid two years before, and heard all the plans, full of similar detail and bursting with confidence. Pensively, he returned to the jetty and the launch taking him back to his ship. The sea was rougher than ever, and the boat tossed wildly in the foam-specked waves.

8

ONE HELL OF A MESS
Sunday 4 June

Shortly before dawn, Eisenhower dragged himself from his caravan to hear what Stagg had to say about the weather. As he drove the short distance through the park to Southwick House, stars lit the sky and the wind was calm.

But the meteorologist delivered bad news. Overnight he'd been studying the latest reports coming in from the Atlantic and checking them against the historical record. Fate was now dealing them a rotten hand. 'In all the charts for the forty or fifty years I had examined,' he recorded, 'I could not recall one which at this time of year resembled this chart in the number of depressions it portrayed at one time.' The outlook was more like winter than summer.

'Do you foresee any change?' asked Eisenhower. 'No,' replied Stagg. It was Ramsay's turn. 'When do you expect the cloud cover to arrive?' queried the Neptune commander. 'In four or five hours time,' answered the RAF man. Then he withdrew while the D-Day commanders deliberated. Montgomery was still for going. Ramsay was neutral. But Leigh-Mallory warned that with low cloud cover the air forces could carry out only a fraction of their tasks. This factor, above all, decided Eisenhower. Effective air cover was vital for the troops on the ground. With no one round the table dissenting, he ordered a twenty-four-hour postponement. They would take a second look at the situation that evening.

Orders were immediately issued to all commands, and ships already steaming towards the Channel turned back. Some missed the order, and over a hundred ships carrying US infantry to Utah Beach continued on their way until a British Coastal Command plane dropped warning flares when the convoy was almost thirty miles south of the Isle of Wight.

OSS European intelligence boss David Bruce heard the news at 6.30 a.m. on board the *Tuscaloosa* off Falmouth, and the heavy cruiser spent most of the rest of the day ploughing a huge circle off the Bristol Channel. The postponement strengthened his concerns about D-Day, reflecting Donovan's view that it was all a tremendous gamble. 'The fickle British climate,' noted Bruce, 'is the true mistress of these seas.' Previous Allied amphibious landings such as those in Sicily had been directed against far weaker defences and in reasonable weather. But for the Normandy landings to penetrate Hitler's Atlantic Wall required proper cloud conditions for the bombers and calmer seas for the assault troops. The success of D-Day, thought Bruce, appeared to hinge largely on a series of optimistic assumptions.

What was more noteworthy was his pessimism about the intelligence aspects. Too much, he feared, was riding on the element of surprise. 'We have selected for the attack the most obviously favourable points of attack,' recorded Bruce, who was briefed on the deception plans. 'In spite of the projected diversions, it might be assumed that the enemy, seldom notorious for deficiency in staff work, has reached a generally correct estimate as to its direction,' he wrote, adding, 'nor does it seem possible for a huge armada, some slow elements of which must begin this journey twenty-four hours or more ahead of H-Hour, to escape unfriendly observation long before its arrival at its destination.' And although he was confident that British intelligence had fully mastered German spies in Britain, other vagaries of fortune, he concluded

gloomily, might be more unfavourable to the Allies than to the
land-based Germans.

Before the ships had struggled back to port, Stagg's dismal forecast
came true. The wind rose and angry clouds massed overhead. At
11 a.m. a gale warning was issued for the Channel. For thousands
of seasick troops now trapped in their landing craft and unable to
disembark, it was to be a miserable day.

Bedell Smith, Ike's chief of staff, phoned Churchill's train to tell
him the news. An unshowered and uncomfortably cramped
Hastings Ismay took the call at 4.45 a.m. 'The worst – or almost
the worst – has happened,' wrote the Prime Minister's military
chief of staff to his confidante. 'Anyway, we're in a hell of a mess.
But we'll get out all serene if we keep our heads and our tempers.'
He was still working hard on getting Churchill back to London as
soon as possible, because he felt they were hopelessly out of touch
parked in their railway track at Droxford. 'How I've hated the last
forty-eight hours,' he added. When Bedell Smith's call came
through, Churchill was asleep, so Ismay didn't disturb him and
went to bed himself. Half an hour later, Churchill awoke. When
Ismay told him the news, the Prime Minister seemed dumbstruck.
Untypically, he said nothing in reply.

Worse was to come. While this drama was unfolding, General de
Gaulle arrived in England. His York aircraft touched down at
Heston airfield, just outside London, at 6 a.m. to a guard of honour
and an air force band playing the Marseillaise. He was then driven
into London, where he checked into the Connaught Hotel and
headed for the Free French headquarters in Carlton Gardens. Here
he found a welcoming letter from Churchill. 'My dear General,' it
began effusively, 'Welcome to these shores.' Churchill proposed
that de Gaulle drive down to Portsmouth and visit him for lunch,
after which they'd call together on Eisenhower for a full briefing on
D-Day.

De Gaulle arrived at Droxford, bemused by the sight of the
train parked outside the small rural station. Churchill – fresh and

pink from his morning's ablutions – walked down the track with his arms outstretched, as though they were long-lost pals. And at first all was bonhomie, the only small cloud on the horizon being the presence of General Smuts, who not long before had publicly and incautiously declared that since France was no longer a Great Power she might as well join the Commonwealth. But for the moment de Gaulle was genuinely moved by the occasion. Seated at the centre of a large green table, Churchill dramatically revealed the D-Day plan and the need for a postponement of twenty-four hours. 'In all sincerity,' recorded de Gaulle later, 'I expressed my admiration to the Prime Minister for the result of his endeavours . . . [it] was striking justification of the courageous policy which he himself had personified since the war's darkest days. At this moment a similar flood of esteem carried away everyone present, Frenchman and Englishman alike.'

Over dessert, however, things turned sour. 'We should talk about political matters,' said Churchill abruptly. As de Gaulle had made it clear before leaving Algiers that he was visiting England only to talk over military matters, he immediately bridled. If Roosevelt refused to join in on political matters, he asked, what was the point? In any case, why should he seek Roosevelt's or anyone else's consent to govern France? The familiar row resumed, and the General's voice rose angrily as he talked. Soon, Churchill was shouting back. The horrified diplomats round the table shrank back, and the scene descended into a shambles. 'We are going to liberate Europe,' barked Churchill, 'but it is because the Americans are with us.' This incensed de Gaulle. If the Americans were so desperate to make an arrangement with him, he replied, why had they gone ahead without his consent and printed so-called French currency that they intended to issue as soon as they'd landed in France? Scathingly, he denounced it as 'false money'.

That sent the temperature even higher. Earlier in the day Churchill had sent Roosevelt a heartfelt message. 'Our friendship is my greatest stand-by amid the ever-increasing complications of this exacting war,' he told the President, adding that in the post-war world, when Germany would have to be held down for twenty years, he was not sure that Britain could ever depend on a Gaullist France. Now, furious, he told de Gaulle to his face that no quarrel would ever rise between Britain and the United States. 'Every time I have to choose between you and Roosevelt,' he promised, 'I will choose Roosevelt.'

This Laurel and Hardy scene was not improved by Churchill's execrable French. An inept intervention by Ernest Bevin didn't help. The Labour Party would be hurt, said the Minister of Labour, if the General refused political talks. 'Hurt?' shot back an infuriated de Gaulle, '*You'll* be hurt? Don't you think France is wounded? Don't you have any thought for *her*?' Delivered in French, this tirade left the uncomprehending Bevin looking blank. It wasn't just the Channel that separated France and Britain.

Somehow, things calmed down enough for Churchill to accompany de Gaulle while he visited Eisenhower. Ike, as always, was gracious and diplomatic, patiently explaining the technicalities of the D-Day operation to the fascinated General. He also flattered de Gaulle by seeking his opinion of his decision to postpone. 'What would you do?' he tactfully asked. De Gaulle had little doubt. 'If I were in your place,' he replied, 'bearing in mind the disadvantages of a delay of many weeks, which would prolong the psychological tension of the attacking forces and endanger secrecy, I should not put it off.'

But even this congenial amity between generals hit a landmine. Ike warmly offered to show de Gaulle the text of his liberation declaration, to be issued on D-Day. The General immediately saw that it didn't mention him or his Committee of National Liberation and instead asked the French population to obey Eisenhower's orders. The climate immediately turned cold. After a few frigid exchanges, Eisenhower agreed to see if he could change the text. De Gaulle had agreed to stay for dinner with Churchill. Instead, he haughtily clambered into his car and left on his own for London.

It was a bad end to a difficult day, and far more serious than a mere surface ruffle on diplomatic waters. The Allies were counting on the French Resistance to create havoc behind enemy lines on D-Day. Yet on the very eve of the invasion, the row with de Gaulle drew a question mark over the complex plans agreed between SHAEF and General Marie-Pierre Koenig, de Gaulle's military delegate and liaison with the Free French Forces of the Interior.

In Caen, André Heinz was all keyed up. Since receiving the alert message, he'd been expecting the invasion at any moment. Sunday might be the day, he thought. But as the hours passed and nothing happened, he grew discouraged. Friends had invited him to a dance that night but he'd refused in case he had more urgent things to do. One of his recent missions for Courtois had been to find and recruit people from his own age for 'combat', bands of armed fighters who would attack the Germans as soon as the Allies landed. He'd got some of his friends involved, and secretly envied their prospects. Maybe when D-Day came there would be a chance for him, too, to take up arms.

Restlessly, he hung around at home, wandering down into the cellar to tune into his crystal set to pick up any news from the BBC. Allied planes continued to fly overhead, and there were several air-raid alerts.

When nothing had happened by early evening, he decided to go to the dance after all. But try though he did, he couldn't stop thinking about the epic events he knew were almost upon them. Catching breath on the edge of the dance floor, he suddenly had a strange sensation. 'I felt like a little God because I knew the future – I knew what was going to happen. It was strange to feel so different from the others. Then all of a sudden I was sad again because I couldn't warn them to hide, take shelter, and so on. I wondered how many would survive? I couldn't help protect them.'

'Ten Miles to Go to the Gates of Rome' cried the headline in the *Sunday Times*, which reported that Allied troops had finally smashed their way through the Alban Hills, were racing for the Italian capital and had taken fourteen thousand prisoners. News was also good from the Russian front, where the Red Army was striking back against last-ditch German resistance at Jassy, in Romania. In

South-East Asia, where American forces were closing in on Biak airfield, in New Guinea, Tokyo was now describing the island as its inner defence line. The air offensive continued over France, with Marauder and Havoc aircraft, escorted by Mustangs and Thunderbolts, hitting targets for the seventeenth successive day. Bridges, railway yards and tracks all came under attack without the loss of a single Allied bomber.

Yet the really big news in Britain was what had *not* yet happened. Writing her regular letter from London for the *New Yorker*, correspondent Mollie Panter-Downes noted a mood of expectation hanging over the capital. 'In the curious hush of the moment – a hush that is not merely figurative, since Londoners haven't been awakened by sirens for a month – it seems as though everyone is existing merely from one ordinary day to the next, waiting for the great, extraordinary one.' Hints and premonitions about the invasion continued to be plentiful. Picturing a telephone with a train loaded with camouflaged tanks passing through its dial, an official notice in the *Sunday Times* urged people to think twice before making long-distance calls. 'You doubt whether there is any careless, unnecessary use of trunk calls in your office or works?' it asked. 'Try this test. At the end of any day ask to see the trunk call records, and check whether any of today's calls could have been yesterday's letters. Do this for your own satisfaction – but as an extra service for the war as well.'

If security remained vital as the nation stood poised on the edge of history, so did faith and courage. The Bishop of Southwark reminded readers that today was Trinity Sunday. Exactly four years before, amid the catastrophe of Dunkirk, Churchill had rallied the nation with his stirring broadcasts. Now, wrote the Bishop, 'Trinity Sunday falls again this year at a turning point in the history of nations, as we stand on the threshold of events by which – under God – will be decided for good or ill the course of future centuries.'

The newspaper also published a short poem by Edward Shanks entitled 'The Article'. It was prefaced with a famous quote by the Duke of Wellington before the Battle of Waterloo, on the subject of the British soldier: 'It all depends upon that article, whether we do the business or not. Give me enough of it, and I am sure.' The poem read:

> What, if we dared, should we say now to you,
> You, soldier, idling down the dusty way,
> Parades, fatigues forgotten for the day,
> Only this empty afternoon in view?
> The half-closed eyes are lazy in the sun,
> Burnt skin makes fine an ordinary face,
> Heavy shod feet move somehow with a grace
> We shall remember after they have gone.
>
> This is the article four years a-making,
> The same that stood, that other time, unbreaking
> While Ney's grim troopers charged the stubborn squares,
> Of this we think, but which of us shall say
> All that we think upon this sunfilled day?
> Why, no one, soldier, for there's no one dares.

In the Solent, there was a Sunday hush on board the *Hilary*, headquarters ship of the 3rd Canadian Infantry Division. Officers quietly went over their plans and checked last-minute details. Every now and again one of the war correspondents went up on deck to look at the sea and check on the wind. Rumours about the postponement had started to spread. A gale was sweeping in from the Atlantic . . . Ships in the Channel were being swamped . . . All was calm off the French coast . . . The Germans had found out about Normandy . . .

Waiting on board the passenger liner *Llangibby Castle*, Glenn Dickin was luckier than the thousands of infantrymen who'd embarked in small landing craft but were now stranded on board for an extra twenty-four hours. As the sea grew rougher by the hour, and the wind rose, these smaller vessels tossed and heaved in the waves until the decks were awash with vomit.

The last time Glenn had been seasick was in early May. He and Gordon were at Hiltingbury when the last big invasion exercise took place along the south coast. Code-named 'Fabius III', it involved four assault divisions and associated naval forces. It, too, had encountered heavy seas. The two of them had served as umpires with the De La Chaudière Regiment. It had been so rough that they'd both had to resort to their vomit bags.

For Garbo, 'vomit bags' featured in many of his messages, as a convenient shorthand for invasion. Unwittingly, Glenn and Fabius III had played an important part in his elaborate double-cross game.

'All the 3rd Infantry Division are concentrated here ready to embark,' Garbo's fictional Agent Four, based at Hiltingbury Camp, had informed him on 30 April. 'There are other camps full of troops ready for attack . . . it is extremely difficult to leave the camp. They are preparing cold rations for two days, also vomit bags, lifebelts for troops' sea voyage . . .' Garbo had passed this intelligence on to Kühlenthal in Madrid, adding that his sub-agent at Hiltingbury was convinced that the invasion was imminent. The following day Agent Four also told Garbo that the 3rd Division had just left Southampton with embarkation orders. 'My opinion,' he proffered, 'is that, assuming they have not landed on the Channel coast, the troops which must embark must at this moment be moving towards their far-off objective . . .' Here he was hinting at an attack on Norway.

Kühlenthal took the bait and passed this intelligence on to Berlin, and soon the message was being scrutinised by Hitler himself at the Berghof. Then, a few days later, Four backtracked with the revelation that the Canadian troops had returned to Hiltingbury. Obviously, reported an angry Garbo, the whole thing had been just an exercise and his agent had been a 'simpleton'.

But why use the Canadians and Fabius III as part of the deception campaign, when it would obviously have to be revealed as nothing but an exercise? Would the ploy not discredit, rather than enhance, the credibility of Garbo?

The ingenious Tomas Harris and the Double-Cross Committee thought not, and through Juan Pujol had constructed Garbo's deception so skilfully that by now, on the very eve of D-Day, the agent's credibility in Berlin was riding higher than ever. Harris and Pujol were now an inseparable duet, working in almost perfect harmony, with the Catalan spending a lot of his time at the art dealer's home in Mayfair and the Jermyn Street office. It was in Jermyn Street that Pujol would meet with SHAEF personnel and others running the double-cross campaign. He had fully entered into the spirit of the game, and his devious mind found a perfect foil in the brilliant inventiveness of the erstwhile art dealer. 'Tomas Harris had endeared himself to me right from the start,' he recorded, 'not just from the firm way he had shaken my hand but because he had also put his arm round my shoulders in a gesture of protection and friendship.' Together, they tried to make Garbo human. For that, they calculated, he also had to appear fallible.

German intelligence believed that Garbo had a network of sub-agents in Britain, all of whom in reality were invented by Pujol and Harris. Besides Four there was also 'J(5)', a woman supposedly employed in the War Office. When Four at Hiltingbury had predicted invasion, Garbo had also reported to Madrid that J(5) had pooh-poohed the idea by saying the Canadian troops were only out on manoeuvres. Between them, Garbo had supported Four, concluding that J(5) was telling 'lies'. Then, when the truth had come out and the troop movements were revealed as nothing but an exercise, Garbo had wired Madrid that his comment about her should be ignored. 'I see that her information was true and that the fault is partially mine through being impressed by the agent [Four]. I see that I could get more accurate information through my Ministerial friends.' Kühlenthal responded by telling Garbo not to worry; Four had obviously made an honest mistake, and he shouldn't be discouraged in his task because the next time it might really be the invasion.

With this convoluted story, Harris had brilliantly achieved two objectives. First, he had shown Garbo to be capable of mistakes, and therefore human and more credible. And he had implanted firmly in the Germans' minds the idea that Garbo's source in the War Office was likely to be more reliable about Allied intentions and plans than an agent making observations at a military camp. When the time came, Harris planned, it would be a similar source at a ministry in London that would play the key role in the final D-Day deception. For that, Garbo's Whitehall contacts would be key.

But, for today, Garbo contented himself with an item building up the threat of an attack on Norway. Another of his army of fictional sub-agents was '3(3)', a Greek man based near Glasgow. At 7.56 that evening, Garbo told Madrid that 3(3) had received news of the landing of a large troop contingent from Ireland that was now encamped near Lockerbie, in south-west Scotland. From the troops' insignia, Garbo concluded, it was Britain's 55th Division. Agent 3(3) had also observed another large assembly of men and vehicles at Motherwell. As part of the credibility campaign, Garbo expressed doubt about all this. 'I recommend that you pass on this information to Berlin with all reserve,' he told Madrid, 'as in spite of the fact that the agent speculated these troops were en route to embark in the Clyde he has not convinced me and therefore I reserve all advice until I am better acquainted with the facts.'

This was further nice work by Harris and Pujol. By depicting Garbo as ultra-cautious about the intelligence being passed on by his sub-agents, they were adding yet a further layer to the trust Berlin already had in him, as well as maintaining the illusionary threat to Norway.

Today was the one thousand seven hundred and thirty-sixth day of the war, and Peter Moen's one hundred and twenty-second day of incarceration at 19 Mollergaten. Since his capture in February he'd been obsessed by death. Suicide was never far from his thoughts. If he'd given in to the temptation he would have been far from alone. Over the course of the Nazi occupation, at least forty captives of

the Gestapo at the prison took their own lives. In Moen's case, suicide offered a tempting escape from the agonising shame of having
talked under torture.

On the day of his arrest he'd been driven straight to Gestapo
headquarters at Viktoria Terrasse, or 'V.T.' as it was known in
shorthand, for interrogation and torture. There he'd been 'broken'
and told the Gestapo the names of two of his Resistance contacts.
Six weeks later, cold and half-starved in solitary confinement, he'd
finally been able to record in his secret diary what had happened.
He could well imagine, he began, his friends now describing him as
'cracked'.

'Well, well, that's how it is. When one has stood a whole night
in the ice-cold cellar at Viktoria Terrasse with the sweat of fear on
one's brow – with one's back flogged by rubber whips and rope as
thick as a clenched fist, with one's clothes and body filthy with
blood and dirt from the floor and the kicks of heavy boots – then
one becomes cracked. I have done it and become so weak in the
knees that I bowed then and prayed, "Lord, save me – I perish." I
was horribly near suicide then. A broken electric bulb and a cut
over the wrist would have done it. I was alone . . . no, I was not
alone. Something invisible held back my hand.'

Since then, self-reproach and the search for God had haunted his
days in prison. 'I am not brave. I am no hero,' he wrote. God
eluded him, and he'd been unable to find any foothold 'for faith or
conviction that anything divine spoke to me or within me'. Sharing
a cell with the other men had forced him to think about different
things, but melancholic introversion always lingered beneath the
surface. There were days when he wanted nothing but peace and
quiet, and sometimes he even missed his solitary confinement.

Today was one of them. 'It is impossible,' he wrote, 'to find
peace of any kind either of religious or worldly kind.'

By the time Veronica Owen had finished breakfast at her friend's
home, the weather had worsened and she had to bicycle the ten
miles back to her quarters at Heathfield head-on into a roaring gale.
On watch at Fort Southwick for the rest of the day, she learned that

all stand-offs had been cancelled. 'Ominous?!' she scribbled in her little pocket diary. Before going early to bed, she also had time to record the big event of the day: 'Rome fell.'

Such laconic entries were typical. Only in her letters home would the excitement she felt about her work with the Wrens really surface. She loved practically everything about her wartime work. She would have liked to have been a Petty Officer, and twice so far had been recommended for a commission. But officers had to be over twenty and a half years old, and she was still too young. Secretly she was rather relieved, because promotion would have elevated her to the more rarefied atmosphere of the cipher office. As it was, she enjoyed the social mix of people she was working with. She also suspected that an officer's uniform would restrict her freedom when she went out with friends to cafés or the cinema.

Besides, she felt proud to be a rating. Although traditional in her values, she lacked social pretension. And, as had happened to many of her contemporaries, some of her views had been radicalised by service in the armed forces. She was firm in her belief in equal pay for equal work, and hoped strongly that a new and better world would emerge from the war. She keenly supported the idea of the United Nations, began a university correspondence course in History, Economics and Logic, and thought that 'more discussion groups, politics, and listening to the better BBC talks etc. necessary for the future women of Great Britain'.

Her father frequently teased her about what he called her 'Lower Deck Complex'. But he understood. As a submariner, he'd had to get used himself to the cramped quarters and the forced close companionship among all serving ranks at sea.

A submarine featured heavily that day in fears about D-Day security. Task Group 22.3, a 'hunter-killer' force of one aircraft carrier and five destroyers, captured the US Navy's first enemy warship taken on the high seas since the war of 1812 against the British. And they couldn't tell anyone. This time the prize wasn't a British man-of-war, but a German submarine, the U-505, operating out of Lorient. Some of its crew thought the U-boat jinxed. Since 1942 at least twelve of its missions had been cut short, including the trip on which the captain committed suicide during a depth-charge attack by an American warship. With a new captain, U-505 had been patrolling the West African coast off Sierra Leone and Liberia, hoping to sink Allied shipping. All prey had eluded them for two weeks, leading one crewman to complain that 'the hex is still with us'. Indeed it was, although not by witches, but by Ultra. Using intelligence provided by Bletchley Park, the Americans had been tracking the U-boat and making sure that Allied shipping gave it a wide berth.

Running low on fuel, the captain finally decided to make for home using a shorter route skirting the Cape Verde islands. The American carrier *Guadalcanal* and its destroyer escort knew U-505's general route, but couldn't find the submarine. Also now low on fuel, they headed for Casablanca.

Then, on this very morning, the destroyer *Chatelain* picked up the U-boat on its sonar and dropped depth charges. While they caused flooding, the submarine was not seriously damaged and the captain ordered a depth dive. Instead, U-505 went into an uncontrolled descent and the order was frantically reversed. 'Take us up, take us up before it's too late,' shouted the captain, and the sub, its rudder out of action, popped out of the water like a cork. On the surface, his opposite number radioed to the other ships of the American force: 'I'd like to capture that bastard if possible.'

A three-man boarding party found no booby traps or armed resistance – just an open scuttle valve flooding the U-boat and the jammed rudder, which sent her round and round in a circle. After capping the open valve, the boarding party quickly offloaded nine mail bags holding more than a thousand pounds of signal books, Enigma machines and their enciphering keys. Lashing their prize to the carrier, but fearing they would run out of fuel before reaching Morocco, the force set off triumphantly for Dakar, in Senegal, which was under the control of the Free French.

But Washington and London were horrified. From the Admiralty in London the British First Sea Lord cabled Admiral King, head of the US Navy: 'In view of the importance at this time of preventing the Germans suspecting a compromise of their ciphers, I am sure you will agree that all concerned should be ordered to maintain complete secrecy regarding the capture of U-505.' King himself threatened to court-martial the force commander. Whatever the cost, Churchill's 'golden eggs' of Ultra mustn't be cracked on the eve of D-Day.

Dakar was teeming with Nazi spies. If the capture of U-505 led the Germans to change their Enigma security, then the Allied invasion might be launched without the help of one of its most important tools. So the *Guadalcanal* and her now dangerous prize were ordered to change course and head for Bermuda, the British outpost off America's Atlantic coast some two thousand miles to the west. All three thousand men of the task force were ordered to maintain complete security ('keep your bowels open and your mouth shut,' they were told), the U-boat's surviving crew were kept carefully segregated from other German POWs in a US Army camp in Louisiana, and news of their capture was not released to the International Red Cross. There were to be no 'loose lips' to sink Operation Overlord.

As usual, Albert Grunberg spent much of the day with his ears glued to the wireless, listening to the BBC and Radio Paris. It was a daily ritual interrupted only by power cuts, which were becoming more frequent. 'No *Ondes Joyeuses* [joyous airwaves],' he'd lamented recently during a day-long cut.

He was not alone in this devotion to his radio set. On the eve of D-Day some 5.3 million French households had radios, and an unknown number had sets not notified to the authorities. Early in the occupation Vichy created Radiodiffusion Nationale (RDF) to lure listeners away from the BBC's French-language broadcasts. Later, operations had been consolidated in Paris and the sale of radios was banned. Every day RDF pumped out some fifteen hours of sport, popular and classical music and variety shows. Serialisations of Georges Simenon's crime novels were popular. There were initially seven, and later ten, newscasts each day, the star presenter being a bilingual Swiss national. Under the direction of the former head of Radio Stuttgart, the station was firmly German-controlled.

Radio Paris, the other local station, was regularly denounced by the BBC as German and therefore 'given to broadcasting nothing but lies'. Grunberg tuned in frequently and then would scribble furiously in his diary to denounce the rubbish he'd just heard. As for listening to the BBC, it was a seriously punishable offence, although thousands risked it every day. Among weighty items and up-to-date war news, there was always the chance of getting a wry smile from hearing Churchill's mangled efforts to speak French. Nonetheless, Grunberg listened to both legal and illegal broadcasts as he sought to pass the hours in his self-imposed captivity.

Over the last week, in addition to the Allied advance on Rome, BBC news bulletins about the war in Europe had been full of news about the Red Army. Along the Soviet-German front, stretching two thousand miles from north to south, 1944 was to become known as 'The Year of the Ten Victories'. By June, at the cost of over a million German casualties, the Red Army had delivered three of them. After two and a half years they had finally broken the siege of Leningrad and sent German forces reeling back to the Estonian border. Under Marshal Ivan Konev they had liberated Ukraine and crossed the border into Romania. And in May they had stormed the great fortress of Sevastopol – 'City of Glory', in Nazi hands for almost two years – and recaptured the whole of the Crimea. A comparative lull had then fallen across the front. But then on 30 May, the Germans had suddenly struck out with a desperate counter-offensive from their enclave at Jassy. Hitler was not going to yield ground without a fight. For the last few days newspaper headlines and BBC bulletins had been reporting bitter fighting.

Two powerful reasons drew Grunberg's special attention to Jassy. The first was that the city – site of an historic peace treaty in 1774 between Russia and Turkey during one of their unceasing battles for control of the Balkans – lay in Romania, just a hundred miles north of his home town, Galatz. The pro-German Romanian government, urged on by the fanatically fascist and anti-semitic

Iron Guard, had sided with Hitler and joined in the attack on Russia, and Grunberg now derived a fierce satisfaction at watching them receive their comeuppance. The pleasure was multiplied by the second reason that kept him glued to the news: those delivering the punishment were the forces of the Red Army and the Soviet Union.

Grunberg was a communist and a fervent supporter of the Parti Communiste Français, and by extension the Soviet Union, the motherland of communism. He was by no means an uncritical supporter of the Party, blaming it fiercely for its refusal to join the pre-war Popular Government of Léon Blum, criticising its delay in joining de Gaulle's Committee of National Liberation and exulting when it finally did, in April. 'The Communist Party has proven to the world that its followers know how to die for the independence of their country!' he wrote. Grunberg was a patriotic fan of the Free French. He rarely missed an opportunity to cheer when the forces of de Gaulle scored a victory on the battlefield. Recently he'd proudly noted the outstanding part played by Free French forces in the battle of Monte Cassino, in Italy. 'French troops can beat the Boche when they're not betrayed,' he scribbled proudly. Like de Gaulle too, he was always ready to spot any slight on the honour of France, or to complain when France, a Great Power, was left out of inter-Allied conferences. 'The lights of France are eternal,' he wrote, 'and sooner or later she will be needed.'

Yet it was the Red Army that truly mesmerised him, its heroic forces carrying his hopes for the future of a brave new world. Noting the lull that had fallen on the Eastern Front after the great victories in Ukraine, he'd told himself – correctly – that it was because of the vast Soviet preparations to deliver the final assault against the 'monster' Hitler to coincide with the landings in the West. Grunberg rarely mentioned Hitler's name without adding such an epithet. These days he usually mentioned the Red Army in his daily chats with Madame Oudard. Eventually she became faintly sick of it. 'Whenever you pass on the news,' she complained, 'you always talk about the Russians.'

For the next few days, however, his eyes and ears would be fixed firmly on news in the west.

Hidden in a forest outside Smolensk lay the headquarters of the Red Army's 3rd Belorussian Front. A command post had already been established, linked by radio and telegraph to Stalin in the Kremlin and other commanders along the front of the coming great offensive. A carefully devised campaign of deception to fool the Germans about its place and timing was already paying off. In command was General I.D. Chernyakhovsky; it was the task of his armies to advance through Minsk and Vilnius towards East Prussia. At 4 p.m. that afternoon Chief of the Soviet General Staff Vasilevsky flew in from Moscow as Stalin's eyes and ears on this crucial front. For the remainder of the day he listened carefully as Chernyakhovsky laid out his plans.

Slowly, Sydney Hudson was asserting control of his SOE network. George Jones was the most vulnerable to capture because of German detector vans, and he was close to nervous exhaustion with his perilous daily wireless transmissions. But he believed that Hudson was 'a true leader', and felt secure under his command. Some of Hudson's leadership qualities undoubtedly sprang from his own personality: self-confidence, the ability to control and even conceal his emotions, keep a distance, however slight or large, from those he was leading, view situations 'from above', and, Jones added, 'the ability to get a good night's sleep in the most adverse circumstances!'.

Added to these innate qualities were those that he quickly learned: a belief in the value of his objectives; a sense of mission and the ability to communicate it to others; the ability to formulate his ideas clearly both in writing and verbally; and the power to arouse emotions in his agents and give them a sense of direction.

Hudson had fairly quickly realised that his recruiting problems in the Sarthe owed much to the German penetrations of SOE networks the year before. He gave top priority, therefore, to security. The 'cell' structure was basic; members of the network should be connected with one another only through him. Even for Hudson, it would be best not to know where others were living. 'Use the smallest possible group possible to achieve your objective,' he stressed, 'assure your line of retreat, never put anything in writing unless absolutely necessary and then afterwards destroy it, have a good cover story and if captured hold out for twenty-four hours; and if you want to conceal something, don't swear everybody to silence. Tell as many other stories as possible!' It was particularly important that the network leader should avoid capture. Then, whatever happened to the others, the organisation could be re-formed.

This was why Hudson separated himself physically from the others to move into Le Mans. Sonia d'Artois embodied another lesson he'd learned through observation: 'Women may be better agents than men and certainly less liable to arouse suspicion. A man together with a woman will also attract less notice than a man.'

Hudson carried his own false ID card produced by the SOE forgers. Ostensibly issued by the Paris Prefecture of Police the previous December, it identified him as Jacques Étienne Laroche, born in Paris on 1 August 1910 and living at 74 rue de la Faisanderie, Paris 15. A supplementary note recorded a recent temporary change of domicile to the Château des Bordeaux. His alleged profession was that of a travelling salesman in cosmetics, which was nicely tailored to fit in with Sonia's cover working for Louis Vuitton. The document was the usual careful blend of truth and fiction. The photograph, the fingerprints and Hudson's height and physical features, noted as 'blue eyes, oval face, and pale complexion', were accurate. Everything else was false, including his marital status – '*célibataire*' ('bachelor'). Jacques Laroche might not be married, but Hudson was – although, by now, uncertainly so. He'd married in Switzerland, and his wife and their two-year-old daughter were living with her parents in England. Since joining the Army and the SOE, he'd seen very little of them. Over the next few days and weeks, as danger threw him and Sonia intimately together, with neither knowing whether they would survive from one day to the next, they began an affair that would make the gulf with his family back home unbridgeable.

Sonia was perfect cover for him, too. With her familiarity with France, she was acutely aware of the dangers around them. The risk came not just from the Gestapo, but from French collaborators. Once she was heading for a safe house owned by a university professor and his Scottish-born wife, who was being kept under house arrest. As she turned the corner into their street, some gut feeling told her not to keep the rendezvous but to wait until an agreed back-up meeting three hours later at another spot. She made the right decision. The Germans had been tipped off by an informer and were waiting for her. 'I just had that sixth sense not to go,' she recalled, 'and my guardian angel was watching over me and I went to the other meeting afterwards . . .'

Sending her to France had been a gamble that had paid off. She'd received some poor reports from her instructors complaining she wasn't suitable for the rigours and discipline of the secret life of an agent behind enemy lines. She'd been impetuous, wild and unpredictable, a reflection of her tomboy personality and a rebellious childhood that was scarred by divorced parents and a constant shuffling from place to place and school to school. Fortunately, it wasn't the instructors who had the last word, but the avuncular Maurice Buckmaster, the man who headed the SOE's French section. He'd read the reports and then taken her aside. 'Look, Toni,' he told her, 'what you've got to do is not behave like a teenager. Convince people you're older than you are.' She'd taken his advice to heart. In a way it also helped to know she was almost the youngest female agent ever sent to France. It gave her courage, and made her determined to prove her instructors wrong.

As Eisenhower was waking up for his early-morning weather briefing, and General de Gaulle was landing in London, one of the two British midget submarines designated as navigational markers for the invasion was arriving in position about a mile off the Normandy coast near the mouth of the River Orne. Through the periscope its commander could see a cow on the beach and planes landing in the

distance in Caen. Later he observed a typical seaside Sunday afternoon, with lorry loads of German soldiers playing beach ball and
swimming. A couple of them, he thought, were good enough to be
Olympic champions. 'That amused us,' he recalled, 'because they
obviously hadn't any idea we were there or what was soon to
happen.'

Outside Nantes, Walter Schwender might have been one of those
carefree soldiers seen by the British submarine commander, as he
continued eating fresh strawberries, going to the beach to swim
and sunbathe. He was still working in the army repair shop. Fixing
bicycles took up much of his time, which was hardly surprising
given their importance for the mobility of the German army in
France.

For all its apparent strength on paper, Hitler's forces in France
were badly prepared to resist an invasion, and Walter Schwender's
continuing faith in Nazi Party promises that the Allies would be
hurled back into the sea was badly misplaced. His unit was part of
the 7th Army under Rommel's Army Group B, positioned north of
the Loire and west of the Orne. Here, in an area directly threatened by invasion, there were only six panzer divisions. Elsewhere,
along the 1250 miles of the Atlantic front, the army consisted
mainly of some twenty-three 'static' divisions, described by
Rommel's chief of staff, Hans Speidel, as mostly 'personnel from
old-age classes, frequently without combat experience . . . mate-
rially quite inadequately equipped . . . almost immobile and poorly
horse-drawn'. Max Pemsel, the 7th Army's chief of staff, was even
more critical. Because of a constant combing out of men to send to
the Eastern Front, he remarked, few of those left behind in France
were combat-fit.

As for equipment, the 7th Army was largely a make-do outfit. Its
artillery consisted of a mish-mash of different makes, varying cali-
bres and a wide variety of extremely limited ammunition. Anti-tank
guns and self-propelled assault guns were thin on the ground.
Worse was the scarcity of fuel even for the few motorised vehicles
available. The situation was so bad that regimental commanders

were permitted to use their cars only once a week. Otherwise they had to straddle a horse or mount a bike. By the summer of 1944, in anticipation of the invasion, strenuous efforts were being made to make all units in the 7th Army command more mobile. But this meant little more than providing more bicycles and rounding up French vehicles with French drivers, another makeshift solution given the propensity of the Frenchmen to disappear during air raids. In spite of repeated requests, no German drivers were made available.

The position in the air was even worse and Rommel was right to despair. The Allies had eleven thousand aircraft for D-Day but in the whole of the West the Luftwaffe possessed only three hundred planes. Few German soldiers in France had the slightest inkling that the situation was so bad. 'We often discussed the Allied landing, and where it might be' was the typical comment of one of them, no doubt shared by Walter Schwender. 'We thought, let them get here, we'll throw them out again. We genuinely believed – and we were always being told – that we were so strong we would throw them out in no time. But then we also thought there were several thousand German aircraft ready to come and give us support. We firmly believed that.'

At sea, matters were little better. Admiral Theodor Krancke, commander of Navy Group West, possessed only a few minesweepers, a handful of destroyers and some torpedo boats and speedboats. In addition, forty or so of Dönitz's U-boats were assigned to counter the invasion, although in practice fewer than half actually set sail, and then they proved incapable of countering Admiral Ramsay's vast armada. On the eve of D-Day, Hitler's entire naval force in the West, admitted Dönitz himself, could inflict 'only fleabites'. It was little wonder that Rommel was constantly frantic with worry.

At 7 a.m. the Desert Fox climbed into the front seat of his chauffeur-driven Horch outside the château at La Roche-Guyon and left for Germany. With him were his operations officer, Colonel von Tempelhof, and his aide, Hellmuth Lang. Beside him on the seat lay a box containing the pair of handmade grey suede shoes he had bought in Paris the day before for his wife's birthday.

Over breakfast he'd been briefed by his staff on the weather conditions and concluded that unfavourable tides and the apparent lack of Allied air reconnaissance made invasion extremely unlikely. This was no thanks to Luftwaffe defences, which had been conspicuously absent for most of the last few months. Time and time again Rommel had pleaded for more air support, but Goering was simply unable to deliver.

Still, just in case, Rommel had gone over the alert procedures with Speidel. He knew that the anti-invasion measures he'd been calling for over the previous five months were far from complete. In fact, the building of low-tide beach obstacles had only just begun, mining was still going on and the panzer divisions were still stationed much too far away from the beaches for his liking. That, however, was an issue he hoped to sort out face to face with Hitler during his visit to the Berghof after his wife's birthday.

On the Obersalzberg, celebration of Gretl Braun's marriage the day before continued up at the Eagle's Nest, as well as at Bormann's house, while the locals gossiped about the consumption of incredible amounts of French champagne, liqueurs and delicacies.

Amid the festivities, however, there was a more sombre encounter: a meeting between Hitler and Albert Speer. The fiasco over the ME-262 plane – fighter or bomber? – had crystallised a long-running feud over aircraft production between Speer as armaments minister and Hermann Goering as head of the Luftwaffe. So far, Goering had kept control. But now, two days before D-Day, things finally changed.

By now Air Marshal Goering, Hitler's chosen successor, was a spent force. The former First World War air ace had risen to giddy heights as Prime Minister of Prussia, head of the Four Year Economic Plan, Chairman of the Reich Defence Council and Scientific Research Council, Reichsmarschall and head of the Luftwaffe. He was also lazy, corrupt, addicted to drugs and weakly resistant to the increasingly unrealistic demands of Hitler. Above all, the steady eclipse of the Luftwaffe during the year-long succession of German defeats since Stalingrad had eroded all credibility in his capacity to save the day. 'Politically,' noted one of Goebbels's aides scathingly in 1943, 'Goering might as well be dead.'

By the eve of D-Day, none of Hitler's generals took his designated heir seriously. Only the Führer's continuing loyalty to his old street-fighting Nazi comrade kept him in place. But even that was stretched to the limit. Goering spent most of his time at his famous lodge, Carinhall – a memorial named after his dead first wife – just north of Berlin, or at Schloss Vildenstein, a baroque monstrosity outside Nuremberg, where he'd grown up. But like all the members of Hitler's inner circle, he also owned a villa on the Obersalzberg, flying in frequently for *tête-à-tête* meetings with Hitler. He was there now. Only the day before, Hitler had come striding down the hill to wish Goering's six-year-old daughter, Edda, a happy birthday, and had gallantly kissed the hand of Goering's wife, addressing her as 'Frau Reichsmarschall'.

Speer was circling the Berghof too, staying in his own Obersalzberg villa, equipped with its specially designed architect's studio and tucked away remotely behind the pines. He'd come to argue his case, once again, for taking over aircraft production from Goering. After a brief period of eclipse he was now back in Hitler's favour. Speer was the only man who really understood the infrastructure of armaments production, Hitler had recently admitted to his aide Nicolaus von Below. Goering continued to bluster about the Luftwaffe's capacities. But the hard-working Speer realised that recent attacks on the Romanian oilfields and fuel plants in central Germany were now critically threatening Germany's capacity to go on fighting.

Briefly facing harsh truths, today Hitler finally abandoned Goering. 'Air armaments must be incorporated into your Ministry,' he told Speer, 'that is beyond discussion.' He broke the news personally to his old friend, and soon afterwards Speer arrived at Goering's villa to discuss details of the transfer. The Luftwaffe boss complained bitterly about Hitler's change of mind, but conceded that if that was what he wanted, of course he'd obey. 'But it was all very baffling,' Speer reported him as saying, 'since only a short while ago Hitler had thought that I [Speer] had too many jobs on my hands as it was.'

Still, it all seemed a relatively minor matter given the chaos now being inflicted daily on Germany by Allied bombers.

Bill Tucker woke up at Cottesmore airfield to heavy rain and strong winds. Then word came down that operations had been postponed for twenty-four hours. But it was too late to cancel the special pre-planned meal laid on for the paratroopers that night and jokes about the condemned men eating a hearty last meal could be heard all over the airfield. For many of the 82nd Division's paratroopers it was the best meal they could remember eating since leaving the States.

As the others sweated it out, Tucker felt less worried about the big day than he had done about some of his practice drops. After the previous day's briefing they'd been given a pep talk by Gavin, who told the paratroopers that in their drop zone they'd out-number the Germans. 'He had a very quiet voice,' Tucker said. 'There was neither dramatic inflection nor gestures such as waving his arms or the like. He simply stated what was to be done and assumed everything would happen the way he laid out . . . it did inspire confidence in his leadership.' Traditionally, armies were trained to de-emphasise the individual, who had to become part of a larger unit, a cog in a machine constantly drilled to move in squads and platoons. But the creation of parachute infantry revolutionised things. Dropped behind the lines into the midst of the enemy, the paratrooper had to be trained how to operate far more independently. Gavin's gift lay in knowing how to instil a new sense of individual pride and skill in his men. Significantly, as a parachutist Tucker wore an individual name-plate, a novelty for the US Army. It made him feel part of a true elite, an institution, he said, part 'of immortality, like Rommel's Afrika Korps, or the elite wagon units of Napoleon's Grand Army'.

After Gavin had spoken, Major 'Cannonball' Krause followed with his usual bombastic performance, which Tucker found both fascinating and repellant. Holding up an American flag, the battalion commander told them it had been the first to fly over Gela, in Sicily, on their first combat drop, and was the first American flag also to fly over Naples. 'Tomorrow morning,' he added, 'I will be sitting in the mayor's office in Sainte-Mère-Église, and this flag will be flying over that office.'

At 9 p.m. Eisenhower and his commanders-in-chief met again to discuss the weather. Outside, the wind was still howling and rattling the windows, the pine trees tossing around wildly. Earlier, the weathermen had held a fraught two-hour meeting arguing among themselves about the outlook.

But when Stagg gave his forecast that evening he held out a glimmer of hope. 'Mercifully, almost miraculously,' he recorded, 'the almost unbelievable happened at about midday.' The experts had suddenly spotted a lull between two depressions that would offer a thirty-six-hour window of opportunity, beginning late on the Monday. By the morning of Tuesday 6 June the wind would slacken, the sea would get calmer and the cloud cover might lift. Conditions would not be ideal, but neither would they be disastrous.

Among the exhausted and worried men slumped in their chairs and settees around the library of Southwick House, a cheer went up. Kenneth Strong, Eisenhower's intelligence chief, declared that he'd never heard a group of middle-aged men cheer so loudly. Tonight, contrary to usual practice, Stagg stayed to hear the discussion in case more weather questions came up. The atmosphere, he recorded, was 'tense and grave'.

The air chiefs, worried about visibility for the bombers and airborne troops, thought it still sounded chancy. But Admiral Ramsay said that the conditions for naval bombardment seemed acceptable. More importantly, he warned that any further delay would mean postponement for a full two weeks. His ships would have to refuel, and could not do so in time for another go on the 7th. After that, tide and moon conditions ruled out another attempt until the middle of the month. And, he added, time was rapidly running out. If the armada was to set sail for D-Day on the 6th, he would have to issue the orders very soon.

Finally, Eisenhower turned to Montgomery. 'Do you see any reason why we should not go on Tuesday?' he asked. 'No,' replied Montgomery emphatically. 'I would say, "*Go*."' 'It's a helluva gamble,' remarked Bedell Smith, 'but it's the best possible gamble.' Stagg and his team of meteorologists withdrew.

For an agonising two minutes the Supreme Commander, hands clasped behind his back, his shoulders hunched and head sunk on his chest, walked slowly up and down the room. Finally he stopped and looked up. 'The question is,' he asked, 'how long can you allow a thing like this to just kind of hang out there on a limb?' Another long minute followed. Finally, he said, 'I'm quite positive we must give the order. I don't like it, but there it is. Let's go.'

Outside, Stagg met him in the hall. The phones were already working overtime to send out orders to the invasion forces. 'Well, Stagg, we're putting it on again,' said Ike, smiling. 'For heaven's sake hold the weather to what you told us and don't bring any more bad news.' Stagg went back to work. There would be one last look at the weather at 4.15 next morning, just in case things had changed. As midnight approached he was still poring over weather charts and telephoning meteorological stations around the country to get the latest updates. When he finally retreated to his tent to snatch a few hours' sleep, through the trees he could see that the sky was overcast with low cloud. It was raining heavily and the wind was tossing around the branches. What a paradox, he thought. That morning, when the weather had been good, D-Day had been postponed. Now, in a thrashing storm, it had got the go-ahead. It must all seem a little mad, he thought.

By now Churchill had returned to London on his train, gone straight away to his underground bunker and reviewed the progress of the war in the Map Room. Then he summoned his secretaries and worked until well after midnight, almost falling asleep over his papers. Among them was his daily diet of Ultra. Again, it consisted mostly of military reports from Italy, one of which revealed that at ten o'clock that morning Allied troops were literally at the gates of Rome. Another carried German instructions for the destruction of the city's airfields on the Adriatic coast so that none should fall into Allied hands. There was also a diplomatic intercept reporting on a conversation that the Japanese Ambassador had had with the deposed Italian dictator Benito Mussolini, now ruling over a Fascist republic in northern Italy. The Germans remained confident about the second front in Europe, Mussolini told the Ambassador, and he hoped that 'it would be opened quickly as they [the Germans] would be able to avail themselves of an excellent opportunity to strike the enemy a decisive blow'.

While Churchill was sitting in the Map Room, the BBC was broadcasting Pablo Casals playing a cello concerto on the radio and American forces reached the centre of Rome, abandoned by the departing Germans. One of the city's inhabitants watched as they entered the Piazza di Spagna, at the foot of the historic Spanish Steps. After a few tanks, she recorded, 'the soldiers came march-ing in the moonlight. They were silent, very tired, marching almost like robots. The people came out of the houses to cheer them but they only smiled, waved, and kept on going.' Nearby, a script girl making a movie ran into the Italian film director Roberto Rossellini, who was smoking a Camel cigarette. 'We have to make a movie,' he said. 'Right now. All we have to do is look around us and we'll find all the stories we need.'

News of Rome's fall was flashed to Churchill. 'How magnifi-cently your troops have fought!' he telegraphed Roosevelt. 'I hear that relations are admirable between our armies in every rank there, and here certainly it is an absolute brotherhood.' Spending the weekend at the Charlottesville, Virginia, home of his chief of staff, 'Pa' Watson, Roosevelt downed a mint julep on hearing the news.

Late that night Admiral Krancke reported from his headquarters in France to Berlin: 'It is doubtful if the enemy has yet assembled his invasion fleet in the required strength.' But the signals were mixed.

At 15th Army headquarters, an agent reported that the invasion would take place the next day and a full-scale alert was issued. During that night also, all the French-speaking drivers from Alsace-Lorraine in the elite German 6th Parachute Regiment stationed near Sainte-Mère-Église deserted except for one, who was found shot in the morning. Presumably, it was later concluded, they had heard whispers about the invasion from the French Resistance. But at his family home in Herrlingen, several hundred miles from the French coast, Erwin Rommel lay sound asleep next to his wife. It was his deepest sleep in weeks.

9

O.K., WE'LL GO

Monday 5 June

The rain was almost horizontal and the wind was buffeting his caravan when Eisenhower got up at 3.30 a.m. and made his way to Southwick House. Stagg had already been working the scrambler phones to get the latest weather reports. After a welcome mug of hot coffee, Eisenhower and his commanders settled down in their comfortable chairs and got down to business. All were in battle-dress except Montgomery, who opted for corduroy trousers and a high-necked fawn pullover. No one was smiling. This was the decisive moment. Either they would go ahead with the invasion, or they would have to fix a new date, a move fraught with incalculable consequences.

Quickly, Stagg put them out of their misery. 'Gentlemen,' he began, 'no substantial change has taken place since last time but as I see it the little that has changed is in the direction of optimism.' Next to him, Eisenhower had been sitting taut and tense. Now, as the Allied commander-in-chief listened to the details, his face broke into a smile. 'Well, Stagg,' he said, 'if this forecast comes off, I promise you we'll have a celebration when the time comes.' There were only a few questions. Then he uttered the historic words: 'O.K., we'll go.' It was five o'clock. The irrevocable decision had been made. Tomorrow, 6 June 1944, would be D-Day.

As the group dispersed, Bedell Smith came up and gripped the weatherman by the arm. 'You've given us a helluva break, Stagg,' he said. 'Hold on to it and then you can go off on a week's leave and get rid of those hollows under your eyes.' Dawn was breaking and the sky had miraculously cleared. As he settled in his tent to catch a well-earned nap, Stagg could hear the birds singing, and knew he had done all he could for the invasion. The only thing to do now was hope that the weather would match his forecast.

For Admiral Ramsay, too, the worst was over. 'What are you going to do now?' asked Montgomery as they left Southwick House together. For Neptune's commander, the answer was simple. 'The operation has begun and it is too late now to stop it. There is wireless silence and we can expect no signals. I am going to bed.'

Along the Channel coast the sea was rough and the wind was still blowing strong. On board one of the landing craft a young British captain caught the opening scenes of the great drama in his diary. 'Soon after breakfast we weighed anchor and sailed. The chalk cliffs lit up in the sun like white curtains along the shallow green coastline. The white fleet of tank landing and supporting craft with their large silver barrage balloons and the motor boats throwing up white plumes of spray make a lovely picture of blue and white and silver. Part of Britain's armada: it looks more like a regatta . . .'

At 7 a.m. officers finally opened their sealed orders and learned the names of their objectives the next day. Two hours later the vast collection of vessels that had been gathering in the Solent cast off their moorings and made for Area Z, the huge assembly area south of the Isle of Wight. Force S was to land on Sword Beach, Force G on Gold Beach and Force J on Juno Beach. From points further west the armada carrying the Americans joined them: Force U for Utah Beach, Force O for Omaha Beach. Behind them, the English coastline disappeared into the mist. Six-foot-high waves meant it took most of the day for the two thousand vessels to manoeuvre into position. Darkness was falling when the leading ships passed the buoys marking the carefully mineswept channels leading to the

Normandy beaches. So far, not a single German plane had spotted them.

Waiting aboard an American landing craft in an English port, a war correspondent observed the countless ships around him. 'These tight-packed ships,' 'he wrote, 'represent only one of the rivers of men and machines that all along the coast are pouring out into the sea. Four years ago, almost to the day, the tide of war had flooded from the east into the French Channel ports before swirling back on Paris and far beyond. Now the tide has turned, and in this suspended moment of history the first mighty wave is gathering before it crashes down on the enemy's beaches. And the near observer gets no more than the fleeting, awesome glimpse of it that a solitary swimmer would have of a great breaker in an angry sea.'

On board the *Llangibby Castle*, Glenn Dickin now learned the real names of his D-Day targets. He and Gordon Brown had said goodbye and wished each other good luck two days before, and gone their separate ways. Gordon was the regiment's transport officer, in charge of overseeing the safe landing of over fifty vehicles, including mortar carriers, jeeps, three-ton supply trucks, motorcycles, gun-towing carriers and a water truck. He'd already led his 'serial' out of Hiltingbury to an intermediate staging post with numbered parking places hidden under tall trees. 'I was astonished at the efficiency and the careful planning that had taken place in assigning dozens of serials like mine and ensuring that enemy aircraft would not be able to see such activity,' he remembered. Now he was aboard a landing craft with twenty of his vehicles. Confined in cramped quarters, he found he couldn't sleep. The apprehension and tension were almost unbearable.

The Canadian D-Day beach was Juno, a four-and-a-half-mile stretch of coast sandwiched between the two British beaches of Gold, to the right, and Sword, to the left. Each of these beaches was further subdivided. Nan Beach, two and a half miles long, was bounded to the east by the small resort of Bernières-sur-Mer and to the west by La Rivière, with its lighthouse and wireless mast. Nan Beach was itself divided into sectors. Glenn and the Regina Rifles would land on Green sector in front of the small port of Courseulles-sur-Mer, at the mouth of the River Seulles, a town renowned for its oysters. A couple of wooden breakwaters in a bad state of repair protected the entrance to the river. First to land would be Companies A and B. A Company would hit the beach right by this entrance. Glenn and B Company would take care of an eight-hundred-yard stretch to their left.

By now Glenn knew every feature of Courseulles as well as he knew his home town of Manor: the water tower, the church steeple, the school, the town hall, the railway station. Intensive Allied reconnaissance had seen to that. Pre-war maps, the patient work of the code-breakers, tips from local resistance, interviews with refugees and even pre-war tourists, but above all continuous overflights by planes equipped with high-resolution cameras had built up a detailed and up-to-date picture of the beach, the town and the landscape beyond it. With almost pinpoint accuracy, Glenn could see what would greet him on D-Day.

He knew that the beach was flat and sandy, easy for landing, with just a few scattered and isolated outcrops of rock at low tide, and hardly any cross-current to worry about. At the top of the beach was a ten-foot-high stone seawall at a sixty-five-degree gradient that shouldn't cause too much of a problem with the help of scaling equipment. Once he reached the top he had to cross a twenty-four-foot wide promenade with a low wall on the other side. Then he'd be in the maze of narrow streets and stone buildings radiating out from the Place de la Mairie, with just a narrow road bridge across the river, leading to Bayeux. Before the war the town's population had been a thousand, but Allied intelligence thought that up to 80 per cent of its people might have been forcibly evacuated by the Germans.

Glenn knew he couldn't assume that all the locals would be friendly. When the Germans withdrew, they would leave agents behind. 'All civilians will be treated with suspicion until their

status as patriots has been established,' read his intelligence briefing. Many of the houses, none of them more than two or three
storeys high, had allotments, and there were orchards scattered
throughout the town. Normandy, after all, was apple and calvados
country. The town boasted a single-track narrow-gauge railway,
running parallel to the beach, linking it with Bernières and La
Rivière, but Allied planes had picked up no signs of locomotives,
and the line was probably disused.

Beyond Courseulles lay open cultivated fields dotted with
numerous tiny villages surrounded by more orchards. The regiment's topographical intelligence summary, issued four days
before, informed Glenn that the landscape 'offered little cover
except for occasional hedges and the brush growing along the val-
leys of the Seulles, Mue and small tributary streams'. The Canadian
target for midnight on D-Day was the main east–west railway line
running a few miles inland and linking Bayeux with Caen.

Glenn also knew exactly how the Germans would try to stop
him.

Courseulles was an established strongpoint in Rommel's Atlantic
Wall, manned by a single regiment of the 716th Infantry Division,
the same division whose headquarters in Caen was being spied on
by André Heintz. Allied intelligence evaluated the division as being
of 'low category', with just two infantry and one artillery regiment, and a high proportion of Ostroops and over-age conscripts.
Still, it could inflict lethal damage. On the jetty at Courseulles
stood a pillbox with a machine gun capable of raking the beach with
its fire, and immediately behind it were two gun casemates with
light infantry guns. Two more pillboxes stood atop the seawall,
with probably another half dozen machine guns.

Glenn knew that his landing craft, when approaching the beach
under heavy fire, would also face the gallery of underwater
obstacles planted at Rommel's orders: six-foot-high iron-built
tetrahedrons; steel obstacles of eight feet by seven feet known
simply as 'Element C', constructed to be linked together but here,
luckily for B Company, spaced out at regular intervals. There were
wooden posts sticking up five feet above the sand that might or

might not be topped by mines. If he landed safely and got across the beach, then he'd run into the barbed wire, coiled up in six-foot-high entanglements for hundreds of feet along the seafront. All the while he'd remain in the machine gunners' sights as they attempted to kill him before he got off the beach. If he made it that far, on the other side of the promenade he'd find German infantry concealed in slit trenches and strong houses scattered all through the town. Beyond Courseulles lay the open and unprotected Norman country-side.

He also learned his D-Day password. If he was suspicious about someone's identity, all he had to do was call out the letter 'V'. The correct response was, 'For Victory'. On D+1, the day after the invasion, the challenge was the word 'Handle'. The answer: 'With Care'.

As the *Llangibby Castle* took its place in the vast armada setting sail from the Solent, a Divine Service was conducted on board, and Glenn listened to a reading of the famous prayer proffered by Admiral Nelson before the Battle of Trafalgar, Britain's great maritime victory over Napoleon:

'May the great God Whom I worship grant to my country and for the benefit of Europe in general, a great and glorious victory: and may no misconduct in anyone tarnish it; and may humanity after victory be the predominant feature of the British fleet. For myself, individually, I commit my life to Him Who made me, and may His blessing light upon my endeavours for serving my country faithfully. To Him I resign myself and the just cause which is entrusted to me to defend. Amen. Amen. Amen.'

André Heintz awoke to a clear sky in Caen. All day he heard planes overhead and the sound of bombing in the distance, although once he heard a bomb explode close by on the city's Carpiquet airfield. The fall of Rome was the big news of the day. Around the city the Germans had just stuck up posters, depicting the Allies in the shape of a snail crawling up Italy, ironically asking, 'When Will They Reach Rome?' He'd gone around surreptitiously tearing them down. So the news was great for his morale.

Again, the morning train from Paris failed to get through. André kept going down to the cellar to listen to the BBC through his earphones. 'You'll get us all shot with that set,' scolded his mother. But he took no notice.

It was raining at La Roche-Guyon when Rommel's naval adviser left after breakfast to chivvy Admiral Krancke's staff in Paris about speeding up mine-laying in the Channel. The programme had been badly delayed when a flotilla of minesweepers heading to Le Havre had been decimated by Allied bombing while at sea. Nothing indicated to Rommel's staff that anything was untoward, and they worked quietly at their tasks as though it were any other day. Rommel himself was now at home in Herrlingen, resting. The only piece of business he undertook was to phone the Berghof and fix an appointment to see Hitler on Thursday the 8th.

In Paris, Albert Grunberg woke early as usual, ate his breakfast, lit his first cigarette of the day and stared out of the window. Today, for the first time since he'd gone into hiding, he'd treated himself to a special scalp treatment he'd saved from before the war. Outside it was gloomy and raining, wafts of cold air from the open skylight occasionally buffeting his face. The window was low enough for him to see out, but he was careful not to be observed, and he peered carefully through the slits of the wicker basket used by his wife to bring him groceries. On the roof of the house next door, a man soaked to the skin was attempting to sweep the chimney. Grunberg watched for a long time, but the chimney sweep wasn't making much of an effort. A bit of a shirker, thought Grunberg. He could also see one of his neighbours across the courtyard. But he was careful not to be seen by him, too, and peeped cautiously from behind the curtain.

When he got bored with gazing out of the skylight he turned to his latest book, a biography of the nineteenth-century poet Charles Baudelaire. Like most other Parisians, even the non-captive, he often retreated into an inner world through his reading. While some books had been banned early in the occupation, a huge number of new ones had been published over the past four years. They sold out rapidly as people sought relief from the politics of everyday life, violence on the streets or enforced indoor activity during curfews. Public libraries were swamped, and the book-sellers in their stalls along the Seine were besieged by customers eager for something, anything, to read. Grunberg, under perma-nent curfew, read voraciously from the selections brought by his wife.

There was also a flourishing underground press, such as the famous Éditions de Minuit in Paris, publishing books by pseudon-ymous authors that were passed secretly from hand to hand and read by as many as twenty people apiece. Its best-selling book was *Le Silence de la Mer*, by Vercors, but its most recent product was a sixty-page pamphlet entitled *L'Angleterre*, written under the *nom de plume* 'Argonne'. Its theme, as D-Day approached, was Anglo-French friendship. With the Vichy government constantly evoking the martyred Joan of Arc as an historic and anti-English patriotic icon, the author suggested that more important values now lay at stake. 'Two realms, maybe, but almost a single people,' he argued. 'Our heart can beat for England in all tranquillity, without fearing any contradictions from the past. There are bonds no sword-cut can harm: bonds of the spirit. The history of thought and civilisa-tion is more important than that of battles: it is they which make nations.'

Today, though, Grunberg found it difficult to concentrate. Somehow, the gloomy weather made him nostalgic, and he found himself thinking about his pre-war life and especially Marguerite, his wife. 'How beautiful she is,' he wrote in his diary. Then, of course, there was the big news of the day also to distract him: the liberation of Rome and the steady Allied advance northwards up the spine of Italy. In bold capital letters he made this heartening news the final entry in his diary for the day.

Early that morning Hitler's High Command issued a communiqué reacting defiantly to the fall of Rome. The struggle in Italy would be continued with unshakeable determination, it promised. 'The necessary measures for an eventual German victory are being taken in close collaboration with Fascist Italy and other Allied powers. The year of the invasion will bring Germany's enemies an annihilating defeat at the most decisive moment.' Later Hitler attended a conference to discuss tungsten imports from Portugal, and then went to the regular noon meeting of the OKW, the Oberkommando der Wehrmacht, or Wehrmacht High Command, which was almost totally taken up with events on the Italian front.

Whatever outward confidence he was showing, Hitler was also preparing for a darker scenario. A few days before, Albert Speer had suddenly been struck by a vision of the Allies destroying all the Rhine bridges and landing in Germany itself. Given the lack of any Home Army, imagined Hitler's erstwhile architect, they could even capture Berlin and other major cities, while German forces in the West struggled in vain to return across the Rhine. Hitler had been so struck by Speer's idea that today he decided to create skeletal divisions into which, in an emergency, the three hundred thousand troops always on home leave in Germany could be slotted. Speer would assist with a crash programme of weapons production and a plan to smokescreen the Rhine bridges to protect them against Allied attack.

Churchill spent most of the morning in bed, reading his supply of Ultra material and catching up with his correspondence. The box from Menzies consisted mostly of routine intercepts from the Italian front, and nothing at all from Normandy. Churchill's main concern now was to bring Stalin into the D-Day picture. 'Tonight we go,' he informed the Soviet leader by telegram, after having explained the reasons for the day's delay. 'We are using 5000 ships and 11,000 fully mounted aircraft.' Now that Rome had fallen, he added, the Allies would have to decide how best to use their forces in Italy to support 'the main adventure'.

On this issue, Churchill had a very decided view. Instead of shifting forces from Italy for a secondary landing in the south of France after D-Day, as had been agreed with the Americans, why not strike further north between Bordeaux and St Nazaire on the

Atlantic coast, thus gaining additional ports and joining forces with
Eisenhower's forces in Normandy? he asked in a telegram he dictated for Roosevelt.

While he was busy at work, his wife sent him a brief, handwritten note. 'My darling,' Clementine wrote, 'I feel so much for you
at this agonising moment – so full of suspense which prevents one
from rejoicing over Rome. I look forward to seeing you at dinner.
Tender Love from Clemmie . . .' As usual, next to her name, she
sketched a small cat.

It was four months since Peter Moen had had any contact with the
outside world. For a man so deeply involved in underground political tasks this was difficult enough. But really bothering him today
was the fate of his wife, Bella.

When the Gestapo had come for him, they had arrested her as
well and flung her into the notorious Grini prison camp on the outskirts of Oslo, although whether this was as a Resistance associate
of her husband, or as just the hapless and innocent wife of one, was
obscure. She was thirty-six, and described in her identity papers as
a 'housewife'. Her full name was given as Bergliot Svanhilde Fjeld
Gundersen. Like her husband, she had been given a prison number:
9720.

In shock immediately after his arrest and torture, Moen agonised
about her fate, and blamed himself. 'This evening I am thinking of
Bella,' he wrote in the very first entry he made in his secret diary,
a week after his capture. 'Wept because I have done Bella so much
harm. If I live Bella and I must have a child.' He spoke to her frequently through his diary. 'Bella, darling, good night,' and 'Bella,
my dear . . . good night. If I live I will serve you. For mother's sake
you will forgive my terrible weakness,' he had written in these
early days. Thoughts of his mother were also a powerful source of
comfort. His tenth day in prison had coincided with the anniversary of her burial, and was also her birthday. 'Blessings on her
eternally. I will take refuge in her memory today,' he wrote. 'If only
I had such a brave heart as she.' He envied the strong religious
faith she had enjoyed.

Moen's knowledge that Bella was still in Grini was a source of constant pain and guilt. Today he made himself a promise: 'to be especially good and loving in *everything* concerning her when at last the prison doors are opened.' But such thinking only worsened his sense of inadequacy and made him fear the future. Sometimes the dread was so strong that he thought he'd be better off staying in prison. Then, as always, there remained the alternative. 'In the background stands *Death* beckoning: "Come to me. In my house is peace,"' he wrote. He also left behind a poem to his wife, discovered with his diary after the war:

> It should have been stars
> Which gilded your brow
> Like a glittering frame,
> And a golden diadem in your hair
> Where strands of pale silver
> And glimmering gold
> Flicker and shine
> Like the Northern Lights' rays
> In the evening air.

Eisenhower was showing no doubts about D-Day, whatever he privately felt. While the Prime Minister was reading his Ultra intercepts and drafting his message to Stalin, the Supreme Commander was exhibiting utmost public confidence. That morning he went down to South Parade Pier in Portsmouth and watched the loading of British troops on to landing craft, smiling cheerfully and chatting casually with the men. When he returned to his caravan he played a game of checkers with Harry Butcher. 'Just as I had him cornered with my two kings and his one remaining king,' recorded Butcher, 'damned if he didn't jump one of my kings and get a draw.'

The newspapers also displayed a quiet confidence in the future. *The Times* featured an advertisement placed by Harvey Nichols of Knightsbridge for sunglasses with frames in assorted colours, a want ad sought a white cricket sweater and summer shirts to fit a boy of nine, and a company promoted 'The All Electric Home of the Future' with an illustration of a modern-day lounge equipped with power points for a vacuum cleaner, polisher, radiogram, electric heating and air-conditioning, and electric switches controlling windows and shutters. An item from Washington DC speculated on the likely turnout for the coming November presidential election, the New York stock exchange remained firm, and from Malta came news that trial by jury, suspended since 1940, was now being resumed. In Leicester Square the film *None Shall Escape* invited its audience to imagine that the war was over and they were acting as jury in a war-crimes trial.

The only real hint of the momentous events to come appeared with the announcement that the National Fire Boat Service had released all its sea-going boats to play their part in 'forthcoming operations' and a note that the crews had received special training. And a hint of caution about Britain's longer-term future appeared in a report of a speech at Plymouth made by Lord Chatfield, Admiral of the Fleet. The war had revealed the British Empire to be vulnerable, he warned, and if there was another world war Britain could not defend it alone. 'Armed strength must be in the hands of peace-loving nations,' he declared. 'We cannot afford to shrink back again comfortably into our island home. We must be strong enough for our responsibility, and to make our voice respected in the world.'

In Rome, the Pope appeared on his balcony before a crowd of thousands to give thanks that the Eternal City had been spared the horrors of war. In Ottawa, the Canadian Prime Minister, Mackenzie King, declared that the liberation of Rome was a milestone in the freeing of Europe, and it was announced that the Canadian Navy had sunk yet another U-boat in the Atlantic. In South Africa, the *Johannesburg Star* asked how, if Hitler had failed to save Rome, he could possibly pretend to save the Balkan capitals. 'How,' it added, 'in the assigned hour of doom, can he hope to save Berlin?' In Washington, President Roosevelt greeted the Australian Prime Minister, John Curtin, prepared for a tricky meeting with

Poland's Prime Minister, Stanislas Mikolajczyk, and addressed the nation in one of his avuncular evening 'fireside chats'. He welcomed the fall of Rome with the words: 'One up and two to go.' But he warned sternly against complacency. To guarantee that Germany did not again, within a single generation, recommence its drive for world conquest would prove tough and costly. 'The United Nations,' he declared, 'are determined that in future no one race will be able to control the whole of the world.' On the island of Biak, American troops continued to encounter desperate opposition from last-ditch Japanese defenders.

Over lunch Churchill met with his Chiefs of Staff in the underground war rooms in London, only to discover that they disapproved of his idea about more landings in France. General Alexander, they insisted, should not be robbed of troops that would give him 'the full fruits of victory' in Italy. But the chiefs also had their own agenda, which was to use any surplus troops in Italy for a thrust to the north east at the head of the Adriatic. As this, too, would eventually involve an argument with Roosevelt and the Americans, they wanted for the time being to keep their powder dry. As a result, Churchill's telegram to Roosevelt was never sent.

The lunch also highlighted disputes on another front. Churchill had returned from Portsmouth in an excitable mood, and both Admiral Cunningham, First Sea Lord and Chief of the Naval Staff, and Field Marshal Sir Alan Brooke thought he was now far too optimistic about D-Day. Brooke, who had spent most of the weekend at his home in the country peacefully bird watching, was deeply uneasy about the whole enterprise. 'At best it will fall so very short of the expectation of the bulk of the people, namely all those who know nothing of its difficulties,' confided the Chief of the Imperial General Staff to his diary. 'At worst it may well be the most ghastly disaster of the whole war. I wish to God it were safely over.'

Eisenhower's lunch was more informal, eaten privately with Harry Butcher in Southwick Park, where the two of them swapped political yarns. Afterwards Eisenhower went off to his special tent to brief the press and broadcasting agencies, including the BBC, Reuters, NBC and Associated Press, about the invasion. 'As usual,' recorded Butcher, 'he held them on the edge of their chairs. The nonchalance with which he announced that we were attacking in the morning and the feigned nonchalance with which the reporters absorbed it was a study in suppressed emotion that would interest any psychologist.'

After the reporters left, Eisenhower sat down at his portable table and hastily scrawled on a small pad of paper a press release that he hoped he would never have to use. 'Our landings in the Cherbourg-Havre area have failed to gain a satisfactory foothold,' he wrote, 'and I have withdrawn the troops. My decision to attack at this time and place was based on the best information available. The troops, the air and the Navy did all that Bravery and devotion to duty could do. If any blame or fault attaches to the attempt it is mine alone.' Then he put it in his wallet and forgot about it.

What he could not ignore, however, was the worsening furore over de Gaulle and the part the Free French leader would play in D-Day.

When he woke up at the Connaught Hotel in London that morning, the General was still smarting over the wording of Eisenhower's declaration, so he sent him a revised proposal. But the amendments were rejected. It was simply too late in the day for Washington to consider changes. Besides, some eight million copies had already been printed for distribution to the troops and to the people of occupied France.

To make de Gaulle's mood even worse, a Foreign Office official arrived to tell him about arrangements for his BBC broadcast to the French people the next day. First would come the exiled heads of state: the King of Norway, the Queen of the Netherlands and the Grand Duchess of Luxemburg; then the Prime Minister of Belgium, followed by General Eisenhower and, after him, de Gaulle.

Again, de Gaulle took offence, instantly perceiving in the order of broadcasts an invidious attempt to distinguish his status from that of the other Europeans, and also to imply approval for Eisenhower's statement. He replied angrily he would broadcast, but only when he wanted to, and not when he was told. And if the Allies didn't like it, that was just too bad. Their plans suggested to de Gaulle that France was being occupied, like the ex-enemy Italy, rather than liberated.

By noon, David Bruce, on board USS *Tuscaloosa*, was off Plymouth with the flotilla of battleships and cruisers whose guns would bombard German defences the next morning. Everyone on board was wearing a helmet and either carrying or wearing a lifebelt. The cabins had been stripped of glass, and anything on deck that could move had been tightly lashed down. The fire power of the fleet of three thousand two hundred warships that would take part in Neptune was impressive. The *Tuscaloosa* alone had nine eight-inch and eight 5¼-inch guns, and she was merely one of twenty-seven cruisers taking part. In addition there were six battleships, 124 destroyers, 143 minesweepers and countless other auxiliary ships – quite apart from the hundreds of landing craft of various types. Flanked by destroyers, the flotilla passed through two large convoys of transports packed with troops, one of them flying over sixty barrage balloons and then, not long after, a convoy of landing craft carrying tanks that was five and a half miles long and four rows wide. 'Included in our firepower,' noted Bruce, 'will be 5,000 rockets, to be fired from five rocket ships in clusters of one thousand each.' Altogether, he thought, the prospect of giving and receiving punishment was formidable.

Word of de Gaulle's position on the D-Day broadcast reached Churchill after lunch. Arriving slightly garbled, it sounded as though the General was refusing to broadcast at all. Churchill, now thoroughly fed up, fell into a fury and denounced his awkward French ally as 'an obstructionist saboteur'.

At teatime, Hitler walked leisurely to the Tea House accompanied by Goebbels, who had flown in from Berlin on one of his periodic visits, including a chat with Dr Morell on some health problems of his own. The Nazi propaganda minister found the Führer looking calm and relaxed. 'From a distance people think that they would find him a severely tested man, bent double under the strain, his shoulders threatening to collapse under the burden of responsibility,' noted Goebbels in his diary, 'in reality they are confronted by an active and determined character who does not betray the slightest sign at all of depression or psychological distress.'

Hitler appeared completely unaffected by the news from Rome. In fact, he told Goebbels, it was all the Italian Fascists' fault anyway, and with the city's fall Fascism had lost its political and intellectual centre. As for the decisive battle in the West, Rommel still had his trust, and he was certain that when the invasion came his forces would throw the Allies back into the sea. He also planned to retaliate with a massive attack on London by three to four hundred flying bombs, which were almost ready for action. He would never, he told Goebbels, do a deal with Britain. That country and its ruling plutocracy – people like Churchill, Eden and Sir Robert Vansittart, the former head of the Foreign Office – had plotted war against him since 1936, and was now half finished. He would be happy to administer its death blow, and then would make it pay for the war. Hitler's plans for the future, including the development of the war itself were, confessed Goebbels, with perhaps unconscious irony, 'conceived on a grand scale and bear witness to an extraordinarily profound power of imagination'.

Privately, Goebbels queried Hitler's judgement, not on the war itself but on some of his coterie, such as Joachim von Ribbentrop, the Foreign Minister, and Alfred Rosenberg, erstwhile Nazi ideologist and Minister of the Eastern Occupied Territories, both of whom he thought incompetent. On their stroll back to the Berghof, Hitler confided that he was thinking of replacing von Ribbentrop with Rosenberg. Goebbels was appalled – 'out of the frying pan into the fire,' he thought. The two Nazi leaders did, however, agree on one point. Goering was entirely to blame for the Luftwaffe fiasco, and Speer was the man to improve production. But they also agreed that politically Goering's ouster was impossible. He remained too widely popular, and his removal would do irreparable damage to the authority of the Nazi Party and the Reich.

At almost exactly the same time, Air Marshal Leigh-Mallory, commander of the D-Day air forces, briefed the information staff at his headquarters at RAF Bentley Priory on the outskirts of London. Outside the tall, spacious room with its French windows and RAF carpet of blue and pink, the rhododendrons were in full bloom. Inside, on the mantelpiece behind him, were ranged photographs of the Allied commanders as well as General Sperrle, commander of the Luftwaffe.

After explaining the strategy and listing the results of the sustained attacks on roads, railways, coastal batteries and radar stations, the normally cautious Leigh-Mallory exuded a more positive note. 'The enemy do not seem to know where we are going,' he said, 'and possibly not when . . . When the battle is joined, from an air point of view, if the German Air Force are really thrown into it they will be beaten. I am quite sure of that.' For a man who had so recently told Eisenhower that he feared a 70 per cent casualty rate among the D-Day paratroopers, he revealed a remarkable sense of optimism.

At his headquarters in Caen, down the street from André Heintz's family home, General Richter held his weekly late-afternoon conference with his regimental commanders. There was plenty to discuss. The heavy seas were threatening to wash away some of the underwater anti-invasion obstacles the men had been laying along the Normandy beaches, and there was still plenty of training to be organised for the under-experienced troops. Almost as an afterthought, he remarked that he'd just heard from Paris that the invasion might come any time between 3 and 5 June. 'I should perhaps add, gentleman,' he said sardonically, 'that we have received similar warnings every full-moon period, and every no moon period, since April.'

At 6.30 p.m., in the underground war rooms, Churchill presided over the last meeting of the War Cabinet to be held before D-Day. There were plenty of peacetime items to be considered, such as the composition of the British delegation to the Bretton Woods meeting setting up the International Monetary Fund, and membership of the United Nations, where Stalin was making a transparent bid for more than one Soviet seat by appointing Foreign Commissars to the constituent republics of the Soviet Union.

But it was D-Day, and the absent de Gaulle still stewing at the Connaught Hotel, that dominated proceedings. After revealing that the Allies would land in France the next morning, a still furious Churchill announced that if de Gaulle didn't broadcast that was fine by him and that he'd be happy to see him fly back to Algiers as soon as Allied troops were ashore. Even as he was speaking, a messenger came in with a note for Anthony Eden reporting that de Gaulle was now also refusing to let his French liaison officers accompany the invasion forces because of the lack of any agreement over civil affairs. It was now just a few hours before D-Day. This latest news tipped the wrought-up Prime Minister over the edge into a furious tirade. 'On this subject, we get away from diplomacy and even common sense,' noted Sir Alexander Cadogan, the Permanent Under-Secretary at the Foreign Office, who witnessed the scene around the Cabinet table 'It's a girls' school. Roosevelt, PM and – it must be admitted – de Gaulle, all behave like girls approaching the age of puberty. Nothing to be done.'

Churchill closed the proceedings by saying that maybe they should just bundle de Gaulle on an aircraft and send him back to North Africa straight away. As the War Cabinet broke up, what de Gaulle would do, and what to do about de Gaulle, remained dangerously unresolved.

Meanwhile, at La Roche-Guyon, Hans Speidel was hosting a dinner party. With Rommel at home in Germany, Army Group B's chief of staff had seized the opportunity to invite some of his closest friends from Paris. Among them was the distinguished writer Ernst Jünger, author of *Storm of Steel*, one of the most famous German accounts of slaughter on the Western Front during the First World War. Jünger was also involved in plans to overthrow Hitler – as was Speidel himself. Convinced that Hitler was leading

Germany to disaster, both men had linked up with the rapidly forming army plot to assassinate him. Jünger had even brought along a peace manifesto he'd drafted that was to be published immediately Hitler was dead. After the dinner was over and the handful of guests had finished their brandies and taken a stroll around the château's grounds, Speidel and Jünger disappeared into a secluded part of the building to talk the document over.

At 9.15 p.m. European time (8.15 p.m. British time) the BBC began broadcasting the open-code action messages telling the French Resistance to be ready for the invasion within forty-eight hours. Since the broadcast on the night of 1 June of the first part of the Verlaine stanza, German intercept services had been on high alert. At 11.37 p.m. a junior officer from the intelligence staff of General Alfred Jodl, chief of operations at the OKW, received an urgent message from Oskar Reile in Paris telling him that the BBC messages included the second part of the stanza: 'Bercent mon coeur d' une langueur monotone.' It meant that D-Day was imminent. Reile also sent the message to Rommel's and von Rundstedt's headquarters at La Roche-Guyon and Paris, as well as to Zossen and 15th Army headquarters.

No one took it seriously, and it was either filed or dismissed. There had been too many false alarms before, and in any case it gave no clue at all to *where* the invasion was taking place. Besides, one only had to look out of the window to see that the weather was far too bad for a Channel crossing. At Jodl's headquarters the report was simply filed. In Paris, the crucial message was taken by Colonel Bodo Zimmerman, von Rundstedt's operations officer. He was willing to accept that the message might herald a new and intensified phase of sabotage, but he was reluctant to go further. 'We cannot expect that the invasion itself will be announced in advance by radio,' he declared in a signal sent to all stations. Although the 15th Army was placed on alert, no one really thought it meant very much.

At La Roche-Guyon, the phone rang and Colonel Staubwasser, Rommel's intelligence officer, took the call. It was 15th Army headquarters reporting the Verlaine poem and the state of alert now in force throughout the Pas de Calais. Staubwasser put down the phone and went in search of Speidel. 'Phone von Rundstedt's headquarters in Paris,' came the chief of staff's response, 'and get their advice.' But all that Staubwasser received was Zimmerman's sceptical response, and an order *not* to alert the 7th Army along the Normandy coast. As this fitted in with Staubwasser's firm belief, echoing that of Rommel, that the invasion would be in the 15th Army's sector further east, which included the Pas de Calais, he didn't question the order. He too knew about the BBC code messages. But he argued that since they were being broadcast all the time, it didn't mean the invasion was about to start. 'The increased transmission of alarm phrases by enemy radio since 1 June for the French underground cells,' he reported, 'is not, on previous experience, to be interpreted as an indication that the beginning of the invasion is imminent.'

Nor did Speidel feel alarmed. Around midnight his guests began to leave the château for the now dangerous and difficult drive back to Paris, and by 1 a.m. he was in bed. That night Admiral Krancke, commander of Naval Group West, also received reports about the BBC messages. Accustomed to false alerts, he too dismissed their significance. Besides, the weather in the Channel was vile, with winds of Force 5–6, thick cloud and a rough sea. It was an unlikely night for an invasion.

So, too, thought General Friedrich Dollman, whose 7th Army was occupying Normandy. He'd ordered all his divisional commanders, along with selected regimental commanders, to take part in a war-game exercise at Rennes, in Brittany, beginning at 10 a.m. the next morning. But although they'd been ordered to wait until after dawn before travelling, by midnight at least half of them were already in their hotel room at Rennes or still on the road and away from their headquarters. Another participant, General Edgar Feuchtinger, commander of the 21st Panzer Division, was in Paris, spending the night with his girlfriend.

At the usual time, André Heintz tuned in to hear the evening code poems and heard the fateful message he'd been waiting for ever since his meeting with Madame Bourjeot: 'The Dice are on the table.' Now he knew that the invasion would take place within the next forty-eight hours. But exactly where? He still had no idea.

I mustn't go to bed, was his first thought, remembering also that he had to meet Courtois the next morning. He stayed up as long as he could, and kept his clothes on when he finally turned in for the night.

'Everything is absolutely fine with me,' wrote Walter Schwender that day to his parents, 'and I hope the same goes for you. The cherries and the strawberries are still very good. And after all, that's the main thing. They won't be as far advanced with you, of course.' Other than yet another delayed delivery of mail, now a normal fact of life for German troops in France, there was nothing to bother the twenty-year-old's peace of mind.

At the Château des Bordeaux, SOE wireless operator George Jones picked up the action messages for Sydney Hudson's Headmaster: 'Les couventines sont désespérées ('those in the convent are desperate)', for attacks on railroads; 'On ne les aime pas, on les supporte' ('we don't like them, we help them') for attacks on roads; and 'La valse fait tourner la tête ('the waltz makes the head whirl'), for the sabotage of telephone and cable networks.

But Hudson himself was hiding out with Sonia d'Artois at the safe house in Le Mans. As it was now past curfew, it was impossible to get the news to him. In any case Jones and Hudson had agreed to meet up at eleven next morning at the château. He would pass on the news then.

At 9 p.m. the *Tuscaloosa*, making for Utah Beach, was encountering heavy seas in the Channel and sailing under strict wireless silence. Overhead, cloud banks were towering ominously. The only signals being received were those of the BBC radio, where David Bruce was listening to on-the-spot reports on the liberation of Rome. He could hear sounds of cheering crowds and rumbling tanks in the background.

Breakfast of bacon and eggs had been ordered for 9.30 p.m., a clear warning that action was imminent. From now on, food would appear at irregular and unpredictable times. The men of the American cruiser were on the alert, many of them smoking pipes or cigarettes and looking happy at the prospect of action. Admiral Deyo had exercised with his punchbag, taken a bath and sat down with Donovan and Bruce to a dinner of mock-turtle soup, steak and vegetables, and vanilla ice cream with chocolate sauce. Donovan himself was spruce, shaved and ready for action. He'd buttoned his trousers above his ankles, put on rubber-soled shoes, taken out his olive wool cap and was calmly eating an apple – a sure sign, noted Bruce, that he was prepared for trouble.

At a quarter to midnight Bruce heard anti-aircraft fire from land on the starboard side. It lasted about fifteen minutes. Unknown ships making about twenty-five knots eleven miles away appeared on the radar screen. They were finally identified as friendly. At midnight, again on the starboard side in the direction of the French coast, four star shells suddenly shot high into the air.

After catching up with his sleep, late that day Admiral Ramsay recorded the morning's momentous events at Southwick House in his diary. 'Thus,' he wrote, 'has been made the vital and crucial decision to stage and start this great enterprise which will, I hope, be the immediate means of bringing about the downfall of Germany's fighting power and Nazi oppression.' He was well aware that, although the weather was improving, the day was a rough one for all those on board his armada. Everything depended now on the first few moments of the meticulously planned landings. Success at that critical moment, he knew, would be in the balance. To tip it in Allied favour, he wrote, 'We must trust in our invisible assets.' By this he meant their excellent intelligence and the strategic and tactical surprise so carefully prepared by Allied deception.

Today was one of the most important in the life of Juan Pujol.

At the heart of the D-Day deception campaign lay the aim of convincing the Germans that the Normandy landings were merely a diversionary prelude to the 'real' invasion to take place later in the Pas de Calais. This stratagem was devised to keep Rommel's troops in the 15th Army sector pinned down, and not rushed in as reinforcements for German troops trying to throw back the actual invasion. For this to succeed, however, deception would have to continue after the real D-Day. Garbo would be the key, and for that his credibility had to be unimpeachable. To guarantee that this remained so after D-Day, most of the information about Allied units that he'd sent to Madrid had been accurate – except for the location of certain fictional formations. When the Germans encountered the real units in Normandy, therefore, they would have no reason to doubt Garbo.

Yet this was not in itself enough. So great were the stakes, and such importance did Eisenhower attach to the post-D-Day deception, that something much bolder had to be tried. It was Tomas Harris who had the brainwave. How about having Garbo provide information *in advance* about the real D-Day itself? Then, when it proved accurate, Garbo's credibility would be riding so high the Germans would go on to swallow the bait about the second, fictional landing. The key, of course, would be to alert the Germans in advance, yet do so too late for the intelligence to be acted upon. Pujol had enthusiastically embraced the idea, and he and Harris had had to fight hard for it, but in the end they prevailed. Today they put the final pieces of the risky plan in place.

After intense discussions with Eisenhower's staff, the double-cross team arranged to have Garbo send his warning of imminent invasion to Madrid three and a half hours before the first Allied troops hit the beaches on 6 June. From their knowledge of Abwehr communications, Harris and Pujol knew that the intelligence would only reach Berlin at H-Hour – that is, when the landings were just beginning.

There was a small problem. Garbo transmitted his messages to Madrid according to a strictly agreed transmission schedule that guaranteed his Abwehr controller would be waiting for them. But 3 a.m. British Summer Time (BST) was not one of them, as Madrid went off the air half an hour before midnight and did not tune in again until 7 a.m. So the two men had to concoct a trick to ensure that Madrid would be listening at the right time.

For this they turned to Garbo's fictional sub-agent, the Greek in Glasgow known as 3(3). The day before, when Garbo had passed on the Greek's information about troops massing near Glasgow, he had also complained that the non-existent sub-agent had foolishly travelled down to London to report to him in person; foolish, Garbo pointed out to Madrid, because he might be missing some important developments. So he'd sent the man straight back to Glasgow with firm instructions to telephone Garbo using a special code word if anything important had happened in his absence. In case he phoned in the middle of the night, Garbo warned, it would be important for Madrid to be there so that they could receive the news immediately.

Thus, on the very eve of D-Day, at 7 p.m., Garbo's radio operator tapped out a crucial message to Madrid from the house in Hendon. With him were both Harris and Pujol, as well as the chief deception officer of SHAEF and 'Tar' Robertson, the MI5 officer in charge of the double-cross agents, who had driven out to Hendon specially for the occasion. The operator's name was Charles Haines, an NCO from Field Security and peacetime clerk at Lloyds Bank, who'd been with Pujol from the start of his double-cross life in Britain. His code-name was 'Almura'. Harris and Pujol told Madrid that he was a wireless mechanic and left-wing conscientious objector who had supported the Republicans during the Spanish Civil War. Almura, the Germans were told, had been fooled into believing that Garbo was also a Republican, anxious to keep in touch with the communist underground in Spain. He would never know the truth, Garbo assured Madrid, because he was always given the messages he had to transmit fully enciphered. The transmitter Almura used was a portable 100-watt set that had been seized from a real captured German agent in South America.

'Still without news from 3(3),' began the message. 'I have arranged with Almura that he should be available to receive another message therefore you should listen according to the plan of 2 May [an emergency transmission plan]. Almura communicates that your transmitter has a very bad sound and that it might spoil the contact and suggests that you adjust the apparatus.'

Then, at 9.47 p.m., Garbo followed up with a second message: 'I have just received a telegram from 3(3) to say that he will be arriving in London tonight at eleven. Something must have happened which cannot be explained in the code which had been agreed between us for announcing the sailing of the Clyde fleet. Therefore you should be listening tonight at 1GMT [3 a.m. BST].'

If the plan worked, and the Madrid station was open to receive Garbo's message, what should he tell them to hammer home his credibility? It would have to be something the Germans would experience in reality next morning. Here, once again, the Canadians and Hiltingbury Camp, so familiar to Glenn Dickin, were assigned a crucial role.

Garbo's fictional agent Four was still in place at Hiltingbury, having supposedly been sealed in along with Glenn Dickin late in May. Harris and Pujol now 'arranged' for him to break out of the camp that night, along with two deserters from the US Army Signal Corps, and report that the 3rd Canadian Infantry Division had departed for D-Day armed with iron rations and the all-important vomit bags. The information should reach Berlin at almost the same moment Glenn was wading ashore on Juno Beach. And with that, Garbo, one of Ramsay's crucial invisible assets, would be established beyond any scintilla of doubt as an A1-reliable source on the invasion.

Veronica Owen was on watch that night at Fort Southwick. At 9 p.m. Captain Sinker, the Senior Signals Officer, visited each of the Wren sections individually and broke the news. 'We're off,' he told Veronica and her fellow Wrens, 'and before you go off watch our troops will be in France. Tomorrow is D-Day.' Admiral Andrew Cunningham appeared soon after in a show of support. Veronica could barely contain her excitement. Paradoxically, because radio silence was in full force on this 'night of nights', she had no signals to decode before about 6 a.m., so she took advantage of the calm to write a lengthy letter home. 'Let's hope it's as quiet as this all night,' she told her parents. 'The less work the better the crossing.'

Since April the tight security clampdown had meant she couldn't get up to London. Now, perhaps, she'd be able to see her parents again. They were finally leaving their cramped London hotel for a flat of their own and were busy furnishing it. Perhaps she could now go up and help them. But after bringing them up to date on her personal news, she returned to the war. 'The fall of Rome is a bit of marvellous news, isn't it?' she wrote. 'And I suppose soon the Russians will start cracking and the Germans will soon find themselves so hemmed in that it will be impossible for them to dig themselves out.'

She was right about the Russians. Even as Veronica wrote her letter Stalin was in his special suite in the Kremlin poring over plans for the coming Soviet offensive. On one side of the room was a long, rectangular table where his military staff could roll out their maps. At the end of the table, standing on the floor, was a large globe. On the walls hung historic portraits of Suvorov and Kutuzov, famous generals in Russian military victories. Pacing up and down along the table, occasionally pausing to stuff his pipe with tobacco, Stalin followed progress on the battlefront.

At about midnight Moscow time he took two phone calls, one from Marshal Vasilevsky, Chief of the Soviet General Staff, the other from Marshal Zhukov. They were bringing Stalin up to date on preparations for the coming attack. The Soviet leader had already received the day's message from Churchill breaking the news that D-Day in the West was scheduled for the next day. Preparations for the Soviet offensive, Zhukov now confirmed, were pressing relentlessly ahead.

While Hans Speidel was hosting his dinner party at Rommel's château, Hitler was hosting Goebbels to dinner at the Berghof. The Minister of Propaganda was in an expansive mood, offering his opinions on a number of issues. Also at the table was General Kurt Zeitzler, the army chief of staff responsible for operations on the

Eastern Front, with plenty of news to impart about the bitter battles being fought against the Red Army.

Afterwards they watched a newsreel and talked about movies
and the theatre in general. Eva Braun, now more confident of her
position on the Obersalzberg since her sister's marriage to
Fegelein, joined in. Goebbels was impressed. She was developing,
he wrote, 'an extraordinary ability to discern and make apposite
critical comment in this field'. They sat around the fire reminiscing and chatting until two o'clock in the morning, when Hitler
finally went to bed. 'All in all,' wrote Goebbels in his diary, 'the
mood is like the good old times.'

Throughout the evening a frantic shuttle between Whitehall and
the Connaught Hotel went on in a desperate effort to get de Gaulle
on board in time for D-Day. At 10.30 p.m. his ambassador in
London, Pierre Vienot, was summoned to the Foreign Office,
where he denied that the Free French leader was refusing to broadcast but reaffirmed his decision not to send his liaison officers with
the invasion fleet. Back at the Connaught, he found de Gaulle still
fuming and refusing to back down. Churchill was nothing but a
gangster, shouted the General, and the Allies had deliberately set
out to trick him. 'I will not be tricked,' he insisted. 'I deny their
right to know whether I shall speak to France!'

Returning with this message to Whitehall, the hapless ambassador was taken to see the Prime Minister. It was now almost
midnight.

Churchill had dined alone with his wife in the underground
war rooms, a rare occurrence that revealed how deeply he needed
her emotional support on this momentous night. Afterwards he
went to the Map Room, where he took one last look at the invasion plans. As he was gazing at the huge diagram, Clementine
briefly joined him. 'Do you realise,' he said, 'that by the time you
wake up in the morning twenty thousand men may have been
killed?'

But for whom were they dying? What Churchill saw as de
Gaulle's apparent indifference to Allied efforts, and what might

be huge casualties, enraged him. Over the course of the evening he told various people that Eisenhower should send the Frenchman back to Algiers, in chains if necessary, and at one point he even dictated a letter ordering de Gaulle to leave Britain immediately. When the General's ambassador arrived, Churchill subjected him to another passionate tirade. 'It was an explosion of rage,' recorded the Frenchman, 'an explosion of hatred for de Gaulle, who was accused of "treason at the height of the battle". Ten times he told me that this was a monstrous failure to understand the sacrifice of the young Englishmen and Americans who were about to die for France. "It is blood that has no value for you."' At one point Churchill even said that, knowing de Gaulle, he thought the misfortunes of France were both understandable and deserved.

When the interview ended, Churchill refused either to stand or hold out his hand to the Frenchman. Nonetheless, the emissary retained his dignity. 'You have been unjust,' he told Churchill, 'you have said untrue and violent things that you will regret. What I wish to you on this historic night is that in spite of everything France thanks you.' Churchill looked at him astonished, and appeared suddenly deeply chastened and moved.

While this political tempest was roiling in London, Eisenhower had left his headquarters. He was driven north for two hours, accompanied by press correspondents and photographers, to an airfield outside Newbury, in Berkshire, to watch the departure of paratroopers from the US 101st Airborne Division and the British 50th Infantry Division. Hundreds of paratroopers, many with their faces blackened, were milling around the runways packing their gear, checking their guns and getting ready for the drop. Ike waded in with cheery banter to put them at their ease. 'Hell, we ain't worried, General, it's the Krauts that ought to be worrying now,' said one. Another, a Texan, jokingly offered him after the war a job on his ranch, where at least the food was good. Eisenhower stayed as the men were loaded and then watched them take off, one C-47 at a time, until the airfield was silent. As he walked back slowly to his car his driver, Kay Summersby, saw tears in his eyes. 'Well,' Ike said, 'it's on.'

Simultaneously, a war correspondent was witnessing the departure of a British parachute unit of the 6th Airborne Division. 'Each of the black-faced men appeared nearly as broad and as thick as he was tall by reason of the colossal amount of equipment the parachutist carried with him,' he recorded. 'The brigadier and the lieutenant-colonel made brief speeches. "We are history," said the latter: there were three cheers, a short prayer, and in the gathering darkness they drove off to the aerodrome with the men in the first lorry singing, incredible as it seems, the notes of the Horst Wessel song [the Nazi marching song] at the tops of their voices.'

Back in his caravan at Southwick House, Eisenhower sat around and chatted idly with Harry Butcher before finally going to bed. By the time his head hit the pillow, Private First Class Bill Tucker had already landed in France.

It had been a long day at Cottesmore airfield. He'd heard the news that the invasion was on again at reveille, and dozens of C-47s, their wings now daubed with the three white stripes of the airborne invasion fleet, were parked around the airfield. All in all, some thirteen thousand American and British parachutists would jump in the first drop, and over eight hundred planes scattered around airfields in Britain were ready for action.

Tucker had also received his final loading instructions. He would be one of a 'jump stick' of eighteen men under the direction of a jumpmaster. After a final briefing on the latest jump conditions and his target, for the umpteenth time he checked his equipment and went over everything again with his buddy Larry Leonard. As ordered, he'd had his hair cut to half an inch in case he got a head wound. He'd been checked to see he had his two metal identity tags around his neck. He'd also blackened his face – awful stuff that also got in his hair – and learned the password he'd need when he landed in the dark in France to distinguish friend from foe. It was 'Flash', to be answered by 'Thunder', accompanied by the clicking noise of the little metal toy 'cricket' that each man had now been issued with.

In the Midlands, unlike further south and over the Channel, it was a beautiful day. As the hours passed, anticipation among Tucker and the men of the 82nd Airborne slowly built up. 'A hush filled the air,' he recalled, 'like when birds and monkeys in the jungle all stop making noises because a tornado is on the way.' Many of the paratroopers were playing cards or frantically gambling, but he preferred to keep quietly to himself, occasionally doing callisthenics just to make sure he was loose and fit. He read a bit more from *A Tree Grows in Brooklyn*, but then put it down because he found it hard to concentrate.

At 10 p.m., as the light was fading into a glorious sunset, he heard the order ''Chute up!' Equipment bundles had already been loaded on to racks in the plane, and he stepped forward to pick up his main and reserve parachute from the carefully laid out packs on the runway, and adjusted his harness. He was now carrying about 150 pounds of equipment and, like all his mates, was burdened, as one observer has put it, 'like some medieval knight'. Then he heard the words 'Load Up', and he joined the others in his jump stick in following the time-honoured ritual of heading for the tail of the plane to relieve himself for one last time before take-off, not an easy task with the layers of clothes he was wearing. He clambered heavily up the short ladder and into the aircraft. Down each side of the fuselage was a long metal bench, and he carefully manoeuvred himself into place next to Larry. Like everyone else, he was wondering if he'd make it. As he boarded, Chaplain Woods and his fellow Catholic padre, both of whom would be jumping with the men, had been reciting the Lord's Prayer.

The engines coughed a few times, then caught and roared into the high-pitched whine of full throttle as the pilot tested them for a couple of minutes. Then he eased off, released the brake and the heavily laden C-47 took its place in the queue taxiing for take-off.

Tucker looked out of the window. There were hundreds of people lining the runway, standing two or three deep; US Air Force and RAF ground crew, British Army girls, cooks and bakers.

They weren't moving or cheering, just staring at the long and impressive lines of planes. Jesus, this is something, thought Tucker. It feels like I'm on the winning team.

Finally it was his turn to take off, and as the C-47 gathered speed the waiting lines of people faded rapidly into the darkness. He felt the aircraft suddenly lighten as it left the ground, on its way to France and the target of Sainte-Mère-Église. It was 11.30 p.m. He was on his way at last.

10

IT MUST BE THE LANDINGS

D-Day

It was pitch-black outside as the C-47 carrying Tucker crossed the English coastline and headed towards the Channel Islands. Turning sharply to the east, it headed for the Cotentin Peninsula and Sainte-Mère-Église. The plane flew low and bounced around so much that at least one of his fellow paratroopers immediately lost his breakfast. Tucker kept twisting, trying to catch sight of land. But as soon as he thought he saw the coast, the plane entered heavy cloud and began to jerk violently. Suddenly gun flashes lit up the cloud and the plane started swerving and bucking. The jumpmaster shouted, 'Stand up and hook up.' The light flashed red, then green. Tucker was number five. Right behind him was Larry. He could see lines of tracers coming straight at them. 'Jesus Christ, Tucker,' he heard Larry shout, 'we don't get paid enough for this.' Then came the command 'Go!' and first out of the plane was the jumpmaster. The next thing Tucker knew, he was in the air with his parachute open. The tracers were still hurtling towards him. Behind him he heard a buddy who'd been hit before by a bullet while jumping into Sicily, yell, 'Son of a bitch, I've been hit again.'

At 1 a.m. David Bruce heard American planes returning as he watched from the deck of the *Tuscaloosa*. 'Feel sorry for the paratroopers tonight,' he scribbled in his diary. 'There is a high wind and they will probably be badly scattered in landing.' The cruiser was following a lane lined with buoys dropped by minesweepers, and to port he could see an endless row of landing craft. At 1.55 a.m. he noted that the wind was blowing at thirty-two knots and the sea looked rough. Everyone was muffled in sweaters and heavy jackets. At 2.35 a.m. the *Tuscaloosa* dropped anchor to wait awhile.

Tucker hit the ground with a terrible jolt. He picked himself up and checked that his gear hadn't been ripped away by the force of the air as he jumped. It was just after 1 a.m. All around he could hear the metallic click-click of the crickets as the paratroopers tried to identify one another in the dark. He saw someone running towards him and shouted out the password, getting ready to fire. But it was only a man from his own company. Three or four soldiers from his plane quickly found each other, and with a sergeant leading the way, they began to link up with others. Tucker was happy to find Larry safe and sound. Quickly they assembled their machine gun.

So far, no opposition. The only gunfire they heard was directed at the seemingly endless stream of planes roaring past a few hundred feet above them. Many of the American paratroopers that night dropped widely dispersed because of poor navigation or cloud cover that hindered visibility. But Tucker's company landed close to their designated drop zone near the church of Sainte-Mère-Église. He had no way of knowing that it had already proved fatal for some of his comrades.

Just before midnight the mayor of the town, Alexandre Renaud, had been wakened by a loud and persistent knocking at his front door. The curfew was in force, so he opened it cautiously. Outside stood the fire chief, gesturing towards the square. 'There's a fire,' he said urgently. Behind him, Renaud could see, silhouetting the chestnut trees round the church, a bright red glow. Running to German headquarters, he got permission to call out the volunteers. Within minutes two lines of half-dressed men and women were frantically passing buckets of water from hand to hand, fighting to save the small villa belonging to Madame Pommier on the edge of the park opposite the church. Soldiers from the only Wehrmacht unit in the town, an anti-aircraft battery manned mostly by over-age Austrians from the Tyrol, stood guard as they fought the flames. As the fire spread to a woodshed stocked with dry timber, the church bell rang out urgently, appealing for more help.

Suddenly a huge plane appeared directly overhead. Flying only about four hundred feet above the houses, and with all its lights ablaze, it was followed by another, then another. The exhausted civilians stopped and looked up into the moonlit sky. To Renaud it seemed as though pieces of huge confetti were floating to the ground. Then he realised what they were.

Paratroopers! The soldiers started firing wildly at the white-canopied ghosts descending on the square. The civilians scattered for shelter and Renaud watched as one of the parachutists, wildly but hopelessly manipulating the cords of his harness in an effort to avoid the flames, plunged through the burning roof timbers into the furnace, sending up a shower of sparks. Another followed, mortars strapped to his waist, and set off a massive explosion. The mayor saw the legs of a third jerk sharply in the air as he was hit by a bullet. One landed on the roof of the church. Horrified, Renaud saw his chute catch on the steeple, leaving him hanging there, a ready target for the Germans and a helpless spectator of the panic and chaos below. One American landed in a chestnut tree. To Renaud, he looked like a snake as he wound his way carefully down through the branches until he was spotted by a German machine gunner and his hands abruptly stopped moving and his body fell limp in its harness, slowly turning in the moonlight. 'He hung there with his eyes open,' said Renaud, 'as though looking at his own bullet holes.'

Amidst this chaos a paratrooper suddenly walked out of the gloom into the melee of the civilians frantically working the water pump and asked a few questions in English. But as none of them understood a word, he quickly disappeared down a sidestreet. By this time the Wehrmacht unit had gathered its wits and ordered Renaud and the townspeople to get back inside their homes. As he crossed the square and headed for his house, the mayor ran into one of the soldiers. 'Tommy parachutists, all *kaput*,' said the man, and insisted on showing him a dead American lying near his parachute.

By this time Tucker and a handful of others had moved away from the town while they regrouped into a larger body to attack in force. It was still pitch-dark as they slowly groped their way through the huge Norman hedgerows, six-foot-high mounds of earth topped by jungles of bushes and thorn that haphazardly criss-crossed the fields and blocked their progress at every turn. They reminded Tucker of the stone walls of his native New England; only they were bigger and meaner. He certainly hadn't been warned about them in his briefings.

Exhausted, he almost fell asleep while sheltering behind a hedgerow; later, famished, he frantically tore open his rations. By this time the few Germans in the town were fighting back. A machine gun suddenly started firing from close by on their left. Eager for action, Tucker whispered to Larry, 'Let's knock it off,' and they started up over the hedgerow before a stream of tracer bullets stripped off the leaves over their heads. They quickly changed their minds.

Soon it began to get light. Tucker now saw they were on a narrow sunken track that was almost covered by foliage. Ahead of them, through the gloom, they spotted a French farmer who'd stumbled into the middle of the gun battle. Remembering that Tucker had high-school French, the sergeant asked him to find out if they were headed in the right direction. 'Où est le centre de la cité?' managed Tucker. The farmer pointed, and on they went. By now one of the company's medics, William Barrow, otherwise known as 'Red the Medic', was being kept busy tagging corpses for collection.

They got close to the square and Tucker began to recognise buildings from the briefing photographs. By now the firing had died down and civilians were scurrying around trying to find shelter from the commotion. Tucker thought he'd give them some encouragement. 'Vive la France,' he shouted, but they kept their heads down, running for cover. He and Larry reached the German truck park close to the centre of the town. They set up their machine gun and began firing; they weren't sure at what. When their fire wasn't returned they crept into the park beside the church. They saw a large tree and a stone wall about five feet high.

It seemed very quiet, too quiet. Tucker felt something move beside him and swung the machine gun around. He saw nothing until he looked up. Hanging from the branches a dead parachutist slowly swung back and forth. His helmet covered his face. Tucker noticed he had big hands.

As it got lighter, he spotted another dead American lying in the grass about ten yards away, near the gate to the park. Tucker noticed that his boots had gone. As he looked around he saw the bodies of half a dozen more paratroopers hanging from the trees. Then Tucker spotted his first dead German, lying face up outside one of the church doors. His skin was a little blue and a trickle of blood had run out of the corner of his mouth. His uniform was immaculate, and beside him lay his rifle with its bayonet fixed. He'd have survived, thought Tucker, if he'd fired instead of trying to nail his opponent with the bayonet.

Tucker kept on moving. He noticed several empty parachutes hanging from roofs and chimneys before he reached the other side of the town, and the company began to reassemble. By now it was about 5 a.m. The Germans had left. The Americans were in control of Sainte-Mère-Église. In front of the town hall 'Cannonball' Krause, the battalion commander, just as the day before at Cottesmore he'd boasted he would, proudly raised the American flag, the first to fly in liberated France. But not before he'd found the communications cable linking Cherbourg to Berlin and sliced through it. That done, he sent a runner to his regimental commander saying the town was theirs.

Meanwhile Mayor Alexandre Renaud had returned home, as ordered by the Germans. At about 2 a.m. he heard engines on the road outside and guessed that the anti-aircraft unit was pulling out. Peering through the shutters, he saw motorcycles speeding past and a few cars, their lights out, heading south. An hour or so after that he saw the flash of lighted matches and the glow of a torch in the church square. He could see men lying around under the trees. Germans or British? he wondered, confused by the whole business. Like everyone else, he'd been sure the Allies would land in the Pas de Calais, where the English Channel was the narrowest and the road to Berlin the shortest. Back in April the Germans had ordered special teams to plant tree trunks in the surrounding fields strung together with barbed wire. 'It's in your interest to work quickly,' an officer told Renaud. 'Once the work is done English planes and gliders won't be able to land and you'll be safe from invasion.' The townspeople had enjoyed a good laugh at the notion that the Allies would land in Normandy. The fields of trees, 'Rommel's candles', as the French called them, had never been finished.

Slowly the night dissolved and Renaud realised that the men under the chestnut trees were not 'Tommies' but Americans. He'd seen their rounded helmets in pictures in German magazines. Some of them were lying on the ground, others were standing behind the wall of the small park. By comparison with the impeccably dressed Germans he'd got used to during the four years of occupation, the GIs' uniforms seemed shabby and neglected. 'Machine gun cartridge belts were slung over their shoulders, then draped about their waists,' he remembered. 'They cut a really inelegant figure in their loose fatigues . . . of an indefinable colour somewhere between gray, green and khaki, and open in front. The tunic had a huge pocket stuffed with ammunition and food, and another one for bandages; there were pockets in the pants, too, even along the legs, on the sides and in the back. Besides all this, a dagger in a sheath was strapped to their right leg.' To Renaud, their wild, neglected look and blackened faces reminded him of Hollywood gangsters and comic-book heroes rather than real-life liberators.

By the time the sun came up, many of the inhabitants of Sainte-Mère-Église had crowded into the square. Everything was quiet. Giant parachutes, white, red and blue, waved gently in the air from trees or rooftops, or lay oddly deflated on the ground.

Already groups of small children were eyeing them enviously. A few bodies lay scattered around, and in a nearby field was a glider with its wings torn off, but no sign of the troops it had carried. Madame Pommier's villa and the woodshed next door were still gently smouldering. One of her neighbours was helping a wounded paratrooper lying in a ditch drink from a large bowl of milk.

American soldiers were patrolling the streets, chewing gum or smoking cigarettes clamped between their teeth. By now Tucker and I Company had been sent into reserve and were resting in a small apple orchard on the south-west side of the town, away from Utah Beach. It began to get hot. Tucker suddenly realised he was exhausted. He didn't feel like talking. So he just lay there quietly, happy to have survived, waiting for orders.

On the rain-lashed deck of the *Hilary* the wind howled through the radio masts and the vessel creaked and groaned as it pitched and rolled in the heavy waves. It was 1 a.m., and completely dark in the English Channel. In the wardroom, a war correspondent set out his one-man news desk on a mess table. Beside him, the ship's doctor carefully laid out a dressing table. The sick bay was already prepared, but casualties might be far higher than estimated and the wardroom would act as overflow space if needed.

At 5 a.m. a green light began flashing from one of the two midget submarines off the coast of Normandy. For the previous two days it had been lying submerged to guide the Canadians of the invasion flotilla in to Juno Beach.

Clutching his rifle and wearing his Mae West life jacket, Glenn Dickin clambered down the grappling net strung over the side of the *Llangibby Castle* and jumped carefully into one of the eighteen landing craft carrying three companies from the Regina Rifles that had been lowered from the davits into the choppy sea below. Packed in with thirty other men, he was in the first assault wave. The regiment's chaplain, Captain Graham Jamieson, was with them. As the Royal Marine crew and its Royal Navy stoker started up the motor, Glenn was still seven miles from the beach at

Courseulles. It was just getting light. Ahead, landing craft carrying amphibious tanks and other armoured vehicles bobbed around wildly in the heavy sea. They would land first and clear the way for the infantry.

Soon afterwards the big guns of the accompanying battleships, cruisers and destroyers, assisted by artillery from some of the landing craft, opened up with a huge barrage aimed at softening up the gun emplacements and beach defences. The noise was deafening. On board the *Tuscaloosa*, off Utah Beach to the west, David Bruce's teeth rattled in his head, the deck trembled under his feet, and the very joints of the ship appeared to creak and stretch as it fired its salvoes. Bilious yellow smoke curled up from the guns, the air was acrid with powder and dust fell on the deck like lava from a volcanic eruption. Off Gold Beach, the cruiser *Ajax* opened fire on the German battery at Longues-sur-Mer, whose co-ordinates had earlier been sent to London by André Heintz's friend in the Resistance. One hundred and fourteen six-inch shells later, at about 6.20 a.m., the battery fell silent.

From his landing craft Glenn could see shells bursting on the beach, huge flashes lighting up the sky, and plumes of smoke. When the ships finally stopped firing after an hour, the silence that descended lasted only a few moments. Glenn suddenly heard the roar of engines, and successive waves of planes hidden by the heavy cloud dropped their bombs on the beach defences in front of the town.

To the Canadian riflemen, cold, wet and fearful, tossed around in their landing craft for three hours and swallowing handfuls of seasickness pills, it was a heartening sight. Everyone knew what had happened two years before at Dieppe. There a lack of air support and pre-landing bombardments led to the troops being caught in murderous fire that killed or maimed most of them the moment they hit the beach. This time it would be different. By the time the naval guns and air force bombs had pummelled the coastal defences, they would wade ashore against little or demoralised opposition. Endlessly, the 'Johns' had discussed or mulled over their chances of surviving the landings. Glenn's buddy Gordon was pretty hopeful. Since Dieppe, he argued, the Nazis had taken a pounding in Russia and Italy and would be overwhelmed by Allied naval and air power. He thought the few remaining Germans would surrender immediately.

This optimism proved sadly wrong. The heavy cloud, which had so worried Stagg and the air commanders, forced the bombers to use aerial radar instead of identifying targets by sight. Afraid of hitting the men in the landing craft, aircrews delayed dropping their loads for several seconds. As a result, most of the beach defences at Courseulles remained largely intact.

Glenn soon found this out. By the time the bombers had finished, his landing craft was a couple of miles offshore. Suddenly it turned and began circling. The sea ahead was so congested that a delay had been ordered in his landing time. After ten minutes of tossing around in the waves, the craft resumed its journey to the beach. He could clearly see the shoreline, and began to pick out the landmarks he'd memorised: the church spires of Bernières and Courseulles; the grass-covered dunes; the pristine white beaches. Once again he checked his equipment and ammunition, made sure he had his water bottles and rations and adjusted his Mae West. Half a mile offshore German machine-gun bullets and small-arms fire began to ping off the sides of the landing craft and whiz overhead.

At 8.15 a.m. the ramp went down. Holding his rifle high to keep it out of the water, Glenn ran forward into the waist-high surf as fast as he could with his eighty pounds of equipment, making for the beach. It wasn't a time to be afraid, just to focus on surviving. To his right he could hear heavy machine-gun fire. A Company, landing at the same time, was pinned down by fire from the big casemate by the pier, which had been left untouched by the bombers. Men were toppling in the water and falling on the beach. He could see that some of the tanks just ahead were already disabled, neither moving nor firing.

Now he was on dry sand. Keeping low, he sprinted across the fifty yards of beach, clawed his way up and over the sea wall and scrambled through the barbed wire without getting hit.

Ahead of him lay Courseulles. As B Company edged its way forward from the beach into the maze of streets, German troops hiding in fortified houses began filtering back behind them along carefully constructed slit trenches and tunnels. But, right now, Glenn's job was to help his company move forward and gain control of his targets. The riflemen following on behind would have to take care of the Germans.

On his D-Day maps, the planners had carefully divided the town into blocks numbered one to twelve, and B Company knew exactly which ones to head for. From blown-up aerial photographs, Glenn knew exactly where the Germans had put their strongpoints. He could recognise the terrain almost as though he were moving through the streets of Manor. He'd also been trained for street-fighting.

They made steady progress. They had attacked at block two, completed the job on time, and while A Company was still struggling on the beach they also cleared blocks four and five. Off the market square a large old building housed the local German military headquarters. Behind it, in an orchard, stood heavily reinforced air-raid shelters. The Rifles had little trouble in storming and entering the building. Once they did, its surviving German officers quickly surrendered or fled. By this time reserve waves of infantry and dozens of tanks had successfully come ashore to help. The regimental commander, Colonel Foster Matheson, and battalion headquarters were also ashore. And so was Gordon Brown.

Glenn's buddy had only just survived a tricky landing with his vehicles. His landing craft had hit two mines which badly damaged the ramp, preventing it from being lowered. He had to leap out of his Bren-gun carrier and into the waist-high water to help manually push it down. After that he had to wait for a bulldozer to make a ramp before his vehicles could get over the sea wall. While he was supervising the unloading, a sniper took a potshot at him, but missed. He found his cousin Doug, who'd landed with A Company, lying wounded on the sand, one of the eighty-five men killed or injured out of its complement of 120. He could see plenty of other bodies sprawled on the beach.

By 11 a.m. the Regina Rifles were in control of Courseulles. Civilians began to emerge from the houses to greet them with flowers. Bottles of wine, long hidden from the Germans, were dug up from gardens or taken down from attics and offered to the tired and thirsty liberators. Most of the Germans were either dead or had fled. A few taken prisoner, some eighty or so, had been marched to the beach and were removing bodies from the surf and piling them up by the sea wall. Stretcher bearers were already moving the badly wounded on to emptied landing craft operating a shuttle service to the larger ships offshore. Before day's end they would be safely in hospitals in Southampton or Portsmouth. Nearly all the casualties had been on the beach. There was little street-fighting in the town. The main problem had been a few snipers.

After resting for an hour or so and gulping down their rations, Glenn and B Company moved off in the direction of Reviers, a small town just a little way inland. By now it was 1.30 in the afternoon. So far, so good.

Shortly after midnight André Heintz heard planes overhead. The answering heavy anti-aircraft fire went on for much longer than usual. About 2.30 a.m., now wide awake, he suddenly realised that Normandy, not the Pas de Calais, must be the D-Day target. Hearing his mother leave her bedroom, he went out on to the landing to meet her. 'It must be the landings,' she said, but even then he didn't like to confess that he knew. 'Why haven't you undressed?' she said, suddenly noticing his clothes. He shrugged and went back to his bedroom.

Staring out of the window, he could see that nothing was happening at the German military headquarters across the street. Then, at 3.45, he heard a dispatch rider roar up on his motorbike, shouting. After that everything briefly fell quiet. About forty-five minutes later he saw several vehicles leaving. Again his mother, disturbed by the noise of revving engines, came out on to the landing, and once more André pretended he didn't know what was happening.

At almost the same moment the sky to the north began to light up. The huge Allied naval guns were opening their bombardment of the coastal defences. A deep-red glow suffused the horizon. 'It might be a good idea to fill the bath up with water,' he said finally. 'Who knows what'll happen now.' She ran down to the cellar and buried her jewellery, then checked the gas. It was still connected, so she quickly cooked a huge pot of potatoes. It was just as well. By 8 a.m. all the gas, electricity and water supplies were switched off. Normal service wasn't resumed for several weeks. André felt sorry for the people in towns along the coast who were being shelled.

He kept his secret morning rendezvous at the Gare St Pierre. He passed plenty of people going about their normal business, for the citizens of Caen had got used to bombings and planes overhead. Even those who'd caught the BBC's announcement of the landings, as André's father had, assumed they were really taking place further north. Some were stocking up on food. When the Ouistreham train didn't arrive, and Courtois failed to turn up, it was a bitter blow. Suddenly André felt completely cut off from the Resistance, stranded with nothing to do. He didn't even know how to put his hands on a gun; only Courtois could have told him where the weapons were hidden. After months of waiting it was all a terrible and demoralising anti-climax.

In the end, action was forced upon him. That afternoon Caen came under heavy attack from Allied bombers. Ancient timbered buildings in the city centre were set ablaze, the fire service was overwhelmed and hundreds of casualties poured into hastily improvised ambulance stations and first-aid posts. 'I'd be more use if I helped the Red Cross,' André thought, and then suddenly he knew exactly what he should do. His sister Danielle was a nurse, and she quickly found him work with the ambulance corps. Hurrying to staff one of its outposts, he was caught in an air raid and took shelter in a doorway. As he ran he watched the bombs dropping and felt as though he were trapped between two railway lines with trains rushing madly towards him. Suddenly there was a terrific explosion and a huge cloud of dust rose as the house behind him took a direct hit. Dazed, he helped as best he could while ambulances ferried the wounded away, three to six at a time. He was astonished when a couple of girls stumbled unharmed from a cupboard where they'd taken shelter.

Later the Bon Sauveur hospital, a former lunatic asylum where Danielle worked, was bombed by an Allied plane, wounding several patients and sending the handful of former inmates who remained behind screaming in panic around the wards. 'You must do something, André,' insisted Danielle. The obvious solution was to paint a red cross on the roof of the building. But how was he to find red paint with most of the shops now closed and city transport in chaos? He thought of trying one of the local churches, which put out red carpets during weddings, but it was locked and no one could find a key. Finally, in desperation, he and Danielle took four large white sheets from the hospital's linen supply, soaked them in pails of blood they found in the operating room and laid them out in the form of a cross in the hospital's vegetable garden. As they were hard at work, a plane came out of the clouds and headed straight for them. They were about to run for cover when the pilot waggled the wings. He'd recognised the red cross and banked sharply away, disappearing into the cloud. Eventually the hospital's nuns found some old red curtains and put them on the roof.

By the end of the day André was punch-drunk with fatigue. But at last he had found the action he'd craved, and was there for his country on D-Day, helping.

That morning, Alexis Lelièvre, André's former Resistance contact, the man he'd met regularly in the local church, was shot in Caen prison by the Gestapo. He was one of seventy or so prisoners executed in a murderous D-Day killing spree by the Nazis.

The Gestapo's orders were clear. No political prisoners should fall into Allied hands: they were to be deported to Germany. Plans to evacuate those in Caen were well in place when the Allies appeared. At 4 a.m., when the alert first sounded, preparations

began to move them to Caen's main railway station for the morning train to Belfort, near the French-German border. The
prisoners were ordered to pack their possessions. But, an hour
later, the station at Caen was knocked out of action by Allied
bombs. Army commanders told Harald Heyns, the city's
Gestapo chief, that they needed all their trucks and couldn't
supply him with ground transport. From his office on the rue des
Jacobins, Heyns telephoned the Gestapo office in Rouen asking
for instructions.

At eight o'clock, just as Glenn Dickin was struggling ashore on
Juno Beach, Heyns's assistant, Kurt Geissler, arrived at the prison
with three other Gestapo men. 'We're here to shoot our prisoners,' he announced, 'it's got to be done here, and straight away.' He
took a list of names from his pocket.

In a small courtyard off a walkway outside, graves were hastily
dug among the flower beds. Then, along the corridors of the
prison's third floor, where the 'politicals' were kept, the cry went
up, 'Out! Out! Hands on head. Don't bother with your packages.'
Half a dozen at a time, the prisoners were escorted downstairs and
out of the small door leading to the walkway. A machine gun rattled, a few pistol shots rang out, and then the next victims were
taken down.

At 10.30 a.m. the killing stopped and the Gestapo team
returned to the rue des Jacobins. Four hours later they came back
with another list. The shootings resumed. By the time they had finished, late in the afternoon, all the political prisoners, both men
and women, had been shot. As André was frantically making a red
cross from bloody sheets to protect his sister's hospital, German
soldiers swabbed down the scene of the massacre in Caen prison
with buckets of water.

Sonia d'Artois was fast asleep in the safe house on rue Mangeard in
Le Mans when she was woken early in the morning by the sound of
heavy explosions as Allied bombers put the railway station out of
action. Downstairs Sydney Hudson was sleeping on a sofa in the
living room. Hearing the bombardment, he rushed upstairs to see

if she was all right. But he needn't have bothered. She was just lying there calmly, not scared at all.

After breakfast Hudson got on his bike and cycled the ten miles to the château at Amné for his eleven o'clock rendezvous with George Jones. When he got there his radio operator told him about the coded messages of the night before, and that the Allies had landed that morning.

Hudson was almost disappointed by the news of D-Day. The radio instructions to him and his circuit followed the general SOE pattern: to launch immediate attacks on German communications such as telephone lines, cables, roads and railways. Telephone cables were his main objective, and eventually they were attacked over and over again. To prevent French postal workers repairing the cables, Hudson's men spread the rumour that booby traps had been planted at the points where they'd been cut. After that the Germans themselves had to do the work. Headmaster also successfully blew up the military telephone exchange in Le Mans.

But on the morning of D-Day Hudson felt he wasn't yet fully ready for action. The Sarthe had already proved stony recruiting ground. Paradoxically, news of the invasion made his task even harder. In a report to the SOE in London, Hudson later described the impact of the landings. '[They] appeared to have an adverse effect on the morale of the population,' he wrote. 'A considerable number of people, seeing the possibility of action approaching, began to get cold feet and to think of their responsibilities to their families.'

After Hudson left on his bike, Sonia went out and took her usual break in a local café. The radio was on, and she was surprised by the news of the Allied landings. She hadn't expected them so soon. When they got together later in the day she and Hudson sat down to figure out what they were going to do. Their first thought was to abandon the château. German reinforcements would undoubtedly soon be passing through Le Mans and their safe house was likely to be requisitioned. They also assumed that the Allied advance would be rapid, and so decided to recruit as quickly as possible bands of young men for three Maquis groups. Hiding in nearby forests, they would provide bases for small groups to carry out sabotage and harass the Wehrmacht at every turn.

In his Paris hideout, Albert Grunberg was woken at 4 a.m by his brother's heavy snoring. He lay there for a while trying to get back to sleep, but finally gave up and moved to the kitchen, where he tried the radio. He found an American station and the BBC, both talking about the liberation of Rome, but not much else. By 8 a.m., when he tried to tune in to Radio Paris, the electricity had been switched off. He washed and made himself a coffee. Three quarters of an hour later Lulu knocked quietly on the door, bringing food from his wife.

At 10 a.m. Sami finally vacated the bed and Albert fell into a deep sleep, punctuated by some wild dreams, until he was abruptly awakened an hour and a half later by Professor Chabanaud, his downstairs neighbour, with news of the Allied landings. Excitedly, Albert knocked on the partition wall between his room and the kitchen to alert Sami. But his brother took no notice, and in the end Albert had to get dressed and go next door to tell him the news.

At that moment the air-raid sirens went off. As the electricity was always briefly reconnected during alarms, Grunberg seized the chance to tune into London, and now heard for himself official confirmation of the invasion. Radio Paris, however, was still off the air. Nothing would have given him more pleasure than to hear it, with 'rage in its heart', announce the news of the landings it had so long dismissed as a fantasy.

Oddly, he noticed he wasn't overjoyed. Outside, everything remained silent. None of the neighbours who sometimes chatted with him came to see him, and neither did his wife nor Madame Oudard. He and Sami chewed half-heartedly through their solitary meal. Food was getting even scarcer in Paris, and he found it difficult to enthuse about undercooked carrots, dry bread and desiccated cheese. Only the next day, when the news had really sunk in and Marguerite and Madame Oudard finally came to see him, did he feel any exhilaration. Happily confident that his own captivity, and that of France, would soon be over, he and the two women embraced one another warmly. As they listened together to the news on the BBC, his wife clapped her hands like a child.

'Sh-sh-h-h!' warned the Ministry of Information in a large advertisement placed in *The Times* on the morning of D-Day. 'The Germans are desperately anxious for any scrap of information about our invasion plans. An odd word, unwarily spoken, may give to listening ears the clue to a whole operation. Now, more than ever, careless talk is dangerous. It may cost thousands of lives and delay victory for months. What do I do? I remember that what seems common knowledge to me may be valuable news to the enemy. I never discuss troop movements or ship's sailings or convoys I have seen on the road. I never talk about my war work, or the position of factories or deliveries of war material. I keep a special guard on my tongue in public places – in parks, pubs, buses, restaurants, railway stations and trains, and when talking on the phone. Whatever I see, learn, or happen to know – I keep to myself.'

The newspaper had rolled off the presses hours before news of the Normandy landings broke. Its headlines still trumpeted the news from Rome, and letter writers were still hotly debating the issue of Pocohontas's English descendants. Not a hint appeared about the momentousness of the day. All over Britain people went to work as usual.

News about the landings officially broke at 9.30 a.m. through a SHAEF press release. It prompted little jubilation, and Albert Grunberg's reaction to the news proved typical. A sense of relief that the waiting was over competed with a sombre realisation that many more lives would be lost before victory was achieved. Above all, thoughts turned to the men fighting on the beaches and to the sailors and airmen lending their support.

In London a special service of prayer was rapidly organised at St Paul's Cathedral. The congregation sang 'Oh God Our Help in Ages Past 'and 'Soldiers of Christ, Arise'. Young women who heard the news while at work in their City offices, lacking their Sunday hats, used handkerchiefs as impromptu head cover. At Westminster Abbey people prayed beside the tomb of the Unknown Warrior. Flag sellers for the Red Cross did well, and people queued up quietly at newsstands for vans to turn up with the latest editions. The mood was subdued and serious. Shops had a bad day, as did taxis, while cinemas, theatres and even pubs were half empty, as though people wanted to be alone or at home with their thoughts. 'In the queer hush,' wrote journalist Mollie Panter-Downes, 'one could sense the strain of a city trying to project itself across the intervening orchards and cornfields, across the strip of water, to the men already beginning to die in the French orchards and cornfields . . .'

In New York the stock exchange closed for two minutes of prayer; the city's *Daily News* scrapped its leading articles to print the Lord's Prayer. In Madison Square Park, at the Eternal Light memorial to the dead of the First World War, an afternoon prayer meeting was held. At his regular 4 p.m. White House press conference, President Roosevelt warned against overconfidence. 'You don't just walk to Berlin,' he said, 'and the sooner this country realises that, the better.' That night he spoke to the nation by radio and offered up prayers, addressing God – as one correspondent put it – 'in familiar, conversational, and explanatory tones, as if it were a fireside chat beamed at heaven'.

In Canada churches across the country held services that had long been planned, and in the House of Commons in Ottawa Members of Parliament sang the Marseillaise, followed by 'God Save the King'. Later Prime Minister Mackenzie King spoke to the nation on the radio. The fighting was certain to be heavy, bitter and costly, he warned. They should not expect early results, but be ready for local reverses as well as successes. Then he echoed the sentiments expressed by the Canadian Army commander, General Crerar, in his final message to his assault troops. He had total confidence in his men, and the Germans would have even more to fear from the Canadians now than they'd had in the First World War. King ended by urging everyone to pray for the success of the Allies and the early liberation of the peoples of Europe. In South Africa, which was lending thousands of fighting men to the struggle, sober enthusiasm was the order of the day. The Governor-General attended a midday service at St George's Cathedral in Johannesburg, and across the Dominion people flooded the churches with prayer.

Only in Moscow, where the official Soviet radio station released the news early in the afternoon, did people gather excitedly in the streets. As loudspeakers revealed the gigantic scale of the great D-Day armada, heads appeared at windows, passengers jumped off trams, Britons and Americans had their hands shaken in the street, crowds gathered to discuss the news and smiling strangers talked to one another, relating the details. One British war correspondent quickly found himself taken off to the Moskva Hotel for endless toasts of vodka with some British and Soviet officers. In the hotel lounge his secretary was embraced by a total stranger when he learned she was working for an Englishman. That evening the streets, washed pale blue by the moon, 'were crowded with people up to curfew time [and] the air was vibrant with hope and gaiety so long suppressed in expectation of this day'. The Soviet journalist Ilya Ehrenburg, in a rush of international proletarian sympathy, waxed enthusiastic about the day's events in Normandy. 'The heroes of Stalingrad and the Dnieper are proud of their allies,' he rhapsodised. 'The seasoned soldiers of Russia with all their soul greet their comrades in arms, the weavers of Manchester, the students of Oxford, the metal workers of Detroit, the clerks from New York, the farmers of Manitoba, and the trappers of Canada, come from afar to put an end to Nazi tyranny.'

Early on D-Day Chief of the Soviet General Staff Alexander Vasilevsky visited the headquarters of the Red Army's 5th Army, now poised to strike on the northern flank of the coming Soviet offensive. After carefully examining the plans to co-ordinate infantry, tanks, artillery and aviation, he left, fully confident the army was in 'firm, bold, and reliable hands'. That same morning, at 5 a.m., from the Poltava base in the Ukraine, American heavy bombers carried out yet another raid. This time their target was Albert Grunberg's Romanian home town of Galatz.

It was noon before Churchill appeared in person in the House of Commons. The expectant chamber was packed, the atmosphere subdued. Business began as normal, with questions to ministers. Then the Speaker announced a ten-minute interval. The white-haired David Lloyd George, Britain's Prime Minister during the First World War, made a carefully staged entry into the chamber to take his seat. Churchill's wife, Clementine, accompanied by her eldest daughter, Diana, took her place in the Speakers' Gallery. Finally Churchill himself entered to loud cheers. After apologising for being late, he spent several minutes celebrating the liberation of Rome and General Alexander's leadership of Allied forces in Italy. Then he paused, ratcheting up the tension, before making the announcement that everyone was waiting for. 'During the night and early hours of the morning,' he said, 'the first of the series of landings in force upon the European continent has taken place. In this case the liberating assault took place upon the coast of France.' As he spoke, he continued, the landings were going well, and tactical surprise had been achieved. The speech was greeted with more cheers. But the Communist MP Willie Gallacher also struck a resonant chord by saying that everyone's hearts and thoughts must be with 'those lads and their mothers who are at home'.

Later in the day Churchill returned to bring the House up to date on the day's further events in Normandy, and to praise Eisenhower for his courage in taking some difficult decisions, especially about the weather. The outstanding feature of the invasion, declared the Prime Minister, had been the landing of the airborne troops, 'on a scale far larger than anything that has been seen so far in the world'.

Churchill's highly public reference to D-Day as being the first in a series of landings caused consternation to Tomas Harris and the Garbo double-cross team.

At 3 a.m. that morning Harris, Pujol and MI5's 'Tar' Robertson had waited, taut with expectation, as radio operator Charles Haines tapped out his call sign to Madrid, ready to 'reveal' the impending invasion to the Germans, and thus put in place the ultimate proof of Garbo's credibility. But no answer came back. Haines tried again and again. Soon they had to face the dismaying truth that, despite Garbo's request the day before, Madrid was not going to come on air.

At first this appeared a terrible setback. But as Harris wrestled with the implications, it dawned on him that it could offer a new opportunity. If the Germans were not going to come on air until 8 a.m. – their regular transmission hour – then he and Pujol could include even more accurate information about the invasion, because by then the landings would be well under way and the risks to Eisenhower's forces almost nil. It would then become apparent to the Germans, argued Harris, 'that these facts would have been available to them before H-Hour had they been less negligent and inefficient'. That way Garbo would gain the upper hand, psychologically, over the Abwehr. He and Pujol spent the rest of the night rewriting their texts.

At 8 a.m., right on schedule, Haines received a reply to his call sign and began sending the amended messages. Thus, by an extraordinary coincidence, Madrid received Garbo's report about vomit bags and the departure of the Canadians from Hiltingbury Camp just as Glenn Dickin and his buddies, unknowing players in the Garbo deception, were fighting their way ashore at Juno Beach.

Then Churchill threw his spanner in the deception works with his remarks in the Commons. And so did Eisenhower, who was busy urging the French not to rise prematurely but await 'the proper time'. Did this imply there would be further landings later on?

As part of Garbo's cover, Harris and Pujol had portrayed him as being privy to the Political Warfare Executive's secret directives about the press coverage of D-Day. In forwarding one of these entirely fictional documents to Madrid, Garbo urged that the Abwehr read it 'in reverse', in order to uncover its 'real' meaning, and thus outwit Allied deception. The Directive urged that 'care must be taken to avoid any reference to further attacks and diversions'. If the Germans did what Garbo told them, they would conclude that 'further attacks and diversions' were exactly what the Allies had in mind.

But Churchill's speech and Eisenhower's comments ran counter to the fictional PWE Directive, by *publicly* speculating about more landings. Harris immediately feared that the Abwehr would ask awkward questions. Even worse, they might conclude that Garbo had made up the Directive, and was thus a fraud, a double agent controlled by the British.

Thus, on D-Day itself, the entire future of Fortitude South, with its crucial plan to persuade Hitler that the Normandy landings were merely a feint, appeared threatened. Paradoxically, the crisis was caused by statements which, on the face of it, appeared to support the deception. And, ironically, this happened because both Churchill and Eisenhower thought they could help the deception plan. Their speeches had been submitted to SHAEF in advance for clearance, and been approved. Someone at Eisenhower's headquarters had made a potentially catastrophic mistake.

But now was no time for recriminations. For the second time in twenty-four hours, Harris was faced with the unexpected. During the rest of D-Day, as Allied troops battled their way ashore, he scrambled to repair the damage. He decided to prepare an evening message to Madrid that would plausibly explain everything.

At 8 p.m. Garbo went on air and boldly told his German masters that Churchill and Eisenhower had both breached the PWE Directive. This had caused dismay inside the office, claimed Garbo, and he'd felt obliged to raise the issue himself with the agency's director, who had acknowledged the problem. But, argued Garbo, the Prime Minister and the Supreme Commander had really had no choice. Eisenhower *had* to discourage premature uprisings, and in any case his words were not very specific. Churchill had felt obliged, as the man in charge, to avoid distorting the facts. Or, as Harris, pulling Garbo's strings behind the scenes, put it, 'great men and leaders of countries are bound to tell the truth to their people even if the truth is against the interests of Security'. Harris and the deception planners hoped this breathtakingly open confession would still keep Garbo in play.

But the deception team had not finished their D-Day tasks. Towards midnight Garbo closed his transmissions on a congratulatory note, saying he was delighted to have given the Germans advanced warning of the invasion. Then, almost immediately, he changed his tune. In an angry message half an hour later, he reported that he had just learned that his radio operator, Almura, had failed to get through with the crucial message the night before. It was obviously all Madrid's fault – they had failed to come on air. Harris and Pujol went to town with words of feigned outrage that perfectly fitted the melodramatic and hot-headed Catalan whose character they had so carefully constructed over the previous two years. 'I am very disgusted in this struggle for life and death,' Garbo told Madrid. 'I cannot accept excuses or negligence. I cannot swallow the idea of endangering the service without any benefit. Were it not for my ideals and faith I would abandon this work as having proved myself a failure. I write these messages to send this very night though my tiredness and exhaustion, due to the excessive work I have had, has completely broken me.'

And on this reproachful and self-pitying note, double-cross agent Garbo ended D-Day.

Not a whisper of the day's events penetrated Peter Moen's cell. The prison guards carried out the first of their twice-daily inspections, calling out his name and number and then flinging open the door to search the cell. One of them the prisoners had nicknamed 'Grandpa'. He always came in, snooped in every corner, made a fuss about any untidiness or trivial infraction of the rules and made himself thoroughly unpleasant. 'A typical prison rat,' thought Moen.

Ignorant of the landings on which he pinned his hopes of personal liberation, Moen passed the day chatting idly with his cellmates but longed to be left alone. 'In spite of everything,' he wrote in his diary, 'there was an *excitement* in solitary confinement which no amount of company can make up for.' He'd lost his faith in God, but his stern Lutheran upbringing, with its stress on individual responsibility, kept coming to the fore. Sharing misfortunes with his cellmates helped, but nothing would remove his own culpability.

He also worried about his wife and friends. Ironically, the knowledge that his wife was also a prisoner brought him closer to her than he'd felt during their peacetime years together. Back in February, when he was in isolation, he'd woken up one clear winter morning to realise it was her birthday. 'One summer day when Norway is once again a free country,' he wrote, 'Bella and I will walk in the woods and sing: "What is the country where you live called?" Happiness!! Oh God, I beg for this. Bella! A new bond goes between us from 19 Mollergaten to Grini. We suffer for our cause and are comrades in what is for us a new sense of the word. Comrade Bella. We will live and love.'

D-Day took the Germans completely by surprise.

Unlike the rest of Hitler's acolytes, Goebbels did not have his own house on the Obersalzberg, preferring like Dr Morell to stay at a hotel in Berchtesgaden. On his way back there after his late evening with Hitler, he dropped in for an hour or so to discuss politics with Martin Bormann at his villa, and to share in the continuing celebrations of the marriage of Hermann Fegelein and Greta Braun. When he finally left, a tremendous thunderstorm was rumbling over the mountains. It was 4 a.m.

An hour earlier the telephone had rung at OKW headquarters in Berchtesgaden reporting paratroops and gliders on the Cotentin Peninsula. At 6.45 a.m. 7th Army headquarters telephoned 15th Army headquarters reporting the naval bombardment, but noted that so far no landings had taken place and they were confident they could take care of the situation themselves. 'So,' remarked the 15th Army's commander, General von Salmuth, 'the enemy invasion has failed already,' and he went to bed. Naval Headquarters in Paris took another couple of hours to conclude that the landings marked the opening rounds of a real invasion.

Even then, neither von Rundstedt nor the OKW was convinced. 'Are you so sure that this is the invasion?' asked chief of operations Jodl. 'According to my reports it could be a diversionary attack.' Only a further telephone call to Berchtesgaden at 8.15 a.m., full of details about the vast armada of ships off the Normandy coast, finally convinced the High Command that indeed the Allies had opened their long-awaited second front in Europe. An hour later they received official confirmation by way of Eisenhower's broadcast over the BBC.

'Has the Führer been woken up?' asked Albert Speer when he arrived at the Berghof for a meeting at 10 a.m. 'No,' replied a military aide, 'he receives the news after he's had his breakfast.' Hitler, fooled by Garbo and Allied deception, had been predicting for days that the initial landings would be only a feint. No one now dared wake him just to tell him about a ruse.

When he did finally get up, put on his dressing gown and hear the news, he was positively jaunty, as though a sudden weight had fallen from his shoulders. 'The news couldn't be better,' he said exuberantly to Keitel. 'As long as they were in Britain we couldn't get at them. Now we have them where we can get at them.' OKW headquarters were spread around various buildings in Berchtesgaden. All morning, telephones rang frantically across the town as its scattered staff tried to draw a coherent picture of what was happening on the Normandy beaches.

Hitler's regular military conference at noon today took place at Schloss Klessheim, an hour's drive away, where a Hungarian state visit was taking place with a special lunch for General Sztojay, the Hungarian Prime Minister. When the Führer arrived, members of his High Command were solemnly gathered in a side room clustered round maps and charts. Hitler chuckled as he looked at them. 'So, we're off,' he said in his broad Austrian accent, before repeating his view that now they had the chance to settle scores with the enemy. No one challenged him. Goering exuded his usual optimism, von Ribbentrop offered no dissent and Jodl sounded confident.

Yet Hitler also remained cautious. 'Do you recall?' he asked rhetorically, conveniently forgetting his own earlier prediction that

Normandy would be the true invasion site, 'that we recently received a report exactly predicting the time and place? That just proves that this is not yet the real invasion.' After increasingly desperate pleas from Paris for most of the morning, it was only at 2.30 p.m. that he finally agreed to release the two reserve panzer divisions near Paris for action. He also ordered the long-planned flying-bomb offensive on London to begin.

As the party left Schloss Klessheim Hitler was buoyant, predicting a quick expulsion of Allied troops and the destruction of the Allied airborne forces. 'The Führer is very moved as we take our leave,' recorded a more sceptical Goebbels in his diary. 'He expresses his unshakeable conviction that we shall succeed in expelling the enemy from European soil within a relatively short time. The degree of certainty with which the Führer believes in his mission is very impressive.' The rain was coming down in streams, and across the Salzburg valley hung a thick fog. It would be good, thought Goebbels, if the weather were like this all over France; it would knock the plans of Churchill and Roosevelt on the head. That night, partying on the Obersalzberg, the propaganda minister got drunk, sounded off about culture and disappeared behind a piano to play a duet with a countess.

Back at the Berghof, Hitler met with a delegation of Nazi Party dignitaries and their wives, and seized the opportunity to lecture them on the merits of vegetarianism. 'The elephant is the strongest animal,' he told them, deploying his own personalised brand of logic. 'He also cannot stand meat.' He took his usual walk to the Tea House, had a nap and then confidently reiterated his conviction that the landings were nothing more than a feint.

At the Schloss Klessheim lunch, Goebbels sat next to the Hungarian Prime Minister's chief of staff, who told him that Hungary's Regent, Admiral Horthy, was in the clutches of a Jewish clique. This proved, said Goebbels' informant, that 'anti-Semitic measures in the country [are] not succeeding'.

Even as he spoke, another consignment of Hungarian Jews arrived by train at Auschwitz and were sent to the gas chambers;

two sets of twin sisters were kept aside for medical experiments; one hundred Hungarian Jews already at Auschwitz I were transferred to Monowitz, Auschwitz III, for labour at the camp's Buna factory complex; and a further two thousand deemed still fit for work were sent to Mauthausen concentration camp in Austria, to be worked to death.

Hitler's confidence that Nazi forces would quickly drive the Allies back into the sea was shared by young Walter Schwender. D-Day found him on telephone duty at his post in Nantes. With time on his hands and access to an office typewriter, he wrote another letter to his parents at their home near Auschwitz. 'It's now really a problem with the post, isn't it?' he remarked, having heard nothing from them for several days. 'Things don't arrive any more.' He wondered whether the flowers were yet in bloom in their garden. He told them that he'd recently written to his father's brother, Hans, who'd been promoted to the rank of lance-corporal, and that his uncle had replied that he'd rather have had a different sort of promotion – the sort, Walter guessed, 'that sends you back home', adding, 'Everyone would like that best of all.' Hans had also told him that they'd had 'a lot of visits from the English', meaning RAF bombers. Otherwise, he was happy to report, everything was fine with his uncle.

In fact, typed Walter, everything was just fine in Nantes as well. He was still occasionally eating in the best hotel in town. He'd heard that the English had landed during the night up on the Channel coast, and he would certainly be hearing a lot more about that over the next few days. 'But they will be beaten back straight away,' he promised. 'They certainly won't have anything to smile about.'

Walter's happy-go-lucky reaction to D-Day was not necessarily shared by his fellow soldiers on the front line in Normandy. One German artillery officer, on watch overlooking Sword Beach, picked up his binoculars, peered through the grey light of dawn and saw the horizon literally filling with hundreds of ships. 'It was an unforgettable sight. I had never seen anything so well organised and disciplined,' he recalled. 'We watched, absolutely petrified, as the armada steadily and relentlessly approached.'

Rommel was still in his dressing gown, arranging his wife's birthday presents in the flower-decked family living room, when the telephone rang. It was Speidel reporting landings on the Normandy coast. After a second call from his chief of staff at 10.30 a.m. confirming that this was indeed the invasion, Rommel hastily abandoned the celebrations and drove back to La Roche-Guyon. The journey took him most of the day, and he constantly urged his driver to go faster, impatiently punching one gloved fist into the other, and swearing loudly that it all just proved he should have had control over the panzers close to the beachhead.

It was 9.15 p.m. before he finally arrived. His aide, Lang, jumped out of the Horch and ran hurriedly ahead up the steps of the château. From Speidel's office along the hall he could hear the strains of an opera. 'General, the invasion's begun and you're able to listen to Wagner,' he remarked in surprise. 'My dear Lang,' replied Speidel, 'do you honestly believe that my listening to Wagner will make any difference whatsoever to the course of the invasion?'

German intelligence was bad, its generals in disarray and its leader now more than ever encased in a world of his own. Now the Wehrmacht's response to the landings revealed gaping cracks in its outwardly impressive military machine. The troops on the ground offered only sporadically successful resistance – most notably at Omaha Beach – and the Luftwaffe launched only a single bombing mission, consisting of four twin-engined Junkers, against the beaches. Otherwise they surrendered total air supremacy to the Allies for the crucial first forty-eight hours of the invasion. This was undoubtedly, as the journalist Chester Wilmot wrote of D-Day more than fifty years ago in his classic account *The Struggle for Europe*, 'the most important single factor in the success of the invasion'.

As for the Navy, even Hitler's single-minded obsession with U-boats failed to pay off. When the size of the D-Day armada became clear, Admiral Dönitz, himself a former submariner and the father of two sons killed during the war, made a desperate plea to his submarine commanders in Brest, Lorient and St Nazaire. His exhortation summed up well what he believed was at stake:

'The enemy has started his invasion of Europe. The war has thus entered its decisive phase. If the Anglo-American landing succeeds, it would mean for us the loss of large territories vital to our war economy and an immediate threat to our most important industrial regions without which the war cannot be continued. The enemy is at his weakest at the very moment of landing. Everything must be done to hit him at this moment and to inflict such losses on him that he will have no desire ever to try any landing again. Only then, furthermore, can the forces lacking on the Eastern Front be sent there. Men of the U-boat arm! On you too the future of our German people depends, now more than at any other time. I therefore require of you the most unstinting action and no consideration for otherwise valid precautionary measures. Each enemy vessel useful to him for landing is to be subjected to all-out attack, even where there is danger of losing your own U-boat. Every enemy man and enemy weapon destroyed before landing diminishes the enemy's prospect for success. In this crisis I know that you men of the U-boat arm – who have been tried in the toughest battles – are men on whom I can rely.'

Nine 'snort boats' were to attack the invasion force off the Isle of Wight; a smaller force of seven subs, not yet outfitted with *Schnorchels*, was to be stationed at the Channel entrance. To prevent an Allied landing further south, the last nineteen U-boats were to stretch out across the Bay of Biscay. Yet in the end, not one German submarine, Hitler's first line of defence against Operation Neptune, sank a single ship of the Allied invasion fleet on D-Day.

That afternoon Glenn Dickin's company's route to Reviers, two miles to the south of Courseulles, had already been cleared by C Company. The road had been barred by a tangle of barbed wire and death's-head notices warning of mines. These proved only for show, however, and the advance to Reviers, the first inland target of the Regina Rifles – code-named 'ADEN' in the top-secret Bigot briefing Glenn had received at Hiltingbury – proved relatively easy. The few enemy troops they encountered, mostly Ostroops, offered little resistance and quickly surrendered.

As Glenn entered open country on the edge of the town, he ran into Gordon Brown. His buddy was roaring back from Reviers on his Norton motorbike after delivering a convoy of Bren-gun carriers and anti-tank guns to the front line. Gordon was going about ninety miles an hour with a message for the Regiment's commanding officer, Foster Matheson, who was still in Courseulles, when he suddenly spotted Glenn on the road. Skidding to a halt, he leaped off the bike and gave him a bear hug, relieved to see him after their separation at Hiltingbury. Since he had been scheduled to land with the first assault wave, Glenn's chances of getting off the beach intact had been only fifty-fifty. After excitedly catching up with their news, the two friends went their separate ways.

Glenn's path now took him along the narrow country road that skirted the River Mue, a tree-lined ribbon of water barely ten feet wide winding its way through the Normandy pastures. It offered few serious obstacles. By three o'clock he'd reached Reviers and, soon after, Battalion Headquarters. Again his company rested. Three hours later he moved off in the direction of Fontaine-Henry, the next village to the south. It was code-named 'BOLIVIA'.

Back in England, Eisenhower spent the day with little to do but wait and hope that the great crusade was off to a successful start. At 7 a.m. Admiral Ramsay telephoned to report that, so far, all was going well. When Harry Butcher entered the caravan a few minutes later, he found the Supreme Commander sitting up in bed smoking a cigarette and reading a Western. Then Ike dictated a message to General Marshall in Washington repeating Ramsay's encouraging news and reporting on his previous night's visit to witness the departure of the airborne troops. The men, he told Marshall, had had 'the light of battle in their eyes'. The message was dispatched just as Bill Tucker and the men of the 82nd Airborne were resting after taking Sainte-Mère-Église.

For the rest of D-Day, Eisenhower stayed mostly at Southwick Park, pacing endlessly, chain-smoking and poring over the patchy and sometimes contradictory reports as they flooded in from France. He talked again to Ramsay, briefly visited Montgomery, ate dinner early and then went to bed. Earlier in the day his son John graduated from West Point, and the school commandant read out a message to the graduating class from his proud father, the Allied Supreme Commander.

Churchill's day was hectic. It began in the early hours. Still furious at de Gaulle, he ordered Desmond Morton, his personal intelligence adviser and right-hand man on French affairs, to have the General deported to Algiers as soon as possible, and in chains if necessary. After a brief nap, at 3 a.m. he picked up the phone linking him directly to the code-breakers at Bletchley Park. It rang in the office of its head, Edward Travis. Here Travis's twenty-five-year-old assistant, Harry Hinsley, was on duty, waiting to pass on to the Allied commanders news of the first intercepted German reactions to the invasion. 'Has the enemy heard we are coming yet?' asked Churchill brusquely. Hinsley replied that the first German naval signal was already on its way by teleprinter to London and that the Prime Minister would receive it shortly. An hour and a half later Churchill rang again. 'How's it going?' he queried. 'Has anything gone wrong yet?' This time Hinsley was able to tell him that shortly before 4 a.m. the German 5th Torpedo Boat Flotilla had been ordered to attack landing boats off the Normandy coast. The decoded message was already on its way to Allied commanders. Churchill grunted and hung up.

By now fully awake, and with the troops about to land on French soil, Churchill had second thoughts about de Gaulle and rescinded his deportation order. For the rest of the morning until he delivered his statement in the Commons, he followed progress on the beaches in the Map Room. Then he took lunch with the King at Buckingham Palace. In the afternoon, after telegraphing Stalin to tell him that all had started well, he visited Allied air force head-quarters in St James's Square with the King and General Smuts. Afterwards he made his second statement to the Commons, and returned to the underground war rooms to study the Bletchley Park intercepts now relentlessly flooding in.

Mostly they provided graphic detail about the frenzied German response to the invasion: the parachute drops, the glider landings and the first assaults on the beaches, all giving him gratifying evi-dence of the chaos and confusion that was running throughout the German command. They also revealed positive news from Italy. Resistance partisans were seriously harassing the retreating Germans, as well as encouraging Italians still fighting with them to desert. So unnerved was Kesselring, indeed, that he had informed the SS he was expecting an imminent Allied landing to link up with the guerrillas.

Pleased but exhausted, Churchill took to his bed, ate dinner there and caught up with another batch of intercepts.

But the de Gaulle issue still rankled. At midnight he had a ter-rible row with Eden on the telephone. De Gaulle had earlier risen magnificently to the day's events and delivered a stirring broadcast to the French people. A huge attack, he told them, had been launched from the shores of 'old England'. The supreme battle *for* France, and *of* France, was now joined. They should be sure that action behind enemy lines was co-ordinated with the advance of Allied and French troops. 'Behind the heavy cloud of our blood and our tears,' he concluded, 'the sun of our greatness is shining again.'

Churchill had listened to the talk. On hearing the reference to 'old England' he burst into tears. Noticing that Ismay was staring at him, he snorted, 'You great tub of lard, have you no sentiment?' Nonetheless, he was angry at a reference to 'the Government of France', and he still wanted to see the back of de Gaulle. On the phone at midnight, despite Eden's insistence on some agreement with the man to whom the French so clearly looked for leadership, he remained adamant. On this issue, he flatly told his Foreign Secretary, 'FDR and he would fight the world'.

Glenn Dickin reached the outskirts of Fontaine-Henry at about 7 p.m. Cautiously, keeping close to the low houses and using every bit of cover they could, his company advanced slowly along the main street. This was what Glenn had been trained for. He'd graduated second from Officers' School in Canada, and at battle school in England he'd performed well, with confidential reports grading him 'A' for Reliability, Leadership, Sense of Responsibility and Group Value. The houses were shuttered, the streets deserted. Behind them they could hear the distant boom of heavy naval guns on the coast, but here the only sounds were the crunch of their boots on the gravel, the occasional barking of a dog and the clucking of hens. They'd spotted no sign of any Germans by the time they rounded a corner at the end of the village. Ahead of them, topping the brow of a gentle rise, lay the church, with its stubby grey spire outlined against the evening sky.

Villagers had reported there were German soldiers hiding in the tower. It was late spring and the trees were in full leaf, and by now the sky had cleared. Glenn loved the countryside. Just three weeks before, on a Sunday evening at Hiltingbury, he'd gone for a walk and waxed lyrical to his mother about the ditches and hedgerows bursting with flowers. He'd even arranged for flowers to be delivered to her on Mother's Day, and sent her a special letter. 'I hope you realise,' he wrote, 'that I think you are the best that a man could have. Don't you be worrying too hard Mom and don't worry about me. I am a pretty capable person.' Spring was always a special time on the prairie. The snows finally melted and it was time to get outside, repair damage from the winter storms and plant the crops. He knew how much his mother relied on his help. It was too late for this year, though. Next year, he promised, he'd try to be back for the spring cleaning.

To his right now lay the village square, a gently undulating patch of grass dotted with chestnut trees. The memorial for those who died during the First World War lay beyond. The road ahead

curved sharply up, vanishing behind the church in the direction of
Le Fresnay-Camilly, another of the honey-stoned small towns dot-
ting the rolling countryside. It was code-named 'AMAZON', and
was the battalion's designated headquarters for the night of D-Day.

Glenn passed the huge wrought-iron gates of the Château de
Fontaine-Henry. Its steeply sloped slate roof topped an intricate
tracery of stonework, friezes and balustrades. Beneath the massive
building a maze of medieval cellars doubled as air-raid shelters for
the villagers. Hugging the railings, the company crept along the
low stone wall of the cemetery and, fifty yards on, reached the
church gate.

They could turn either way. To the right stood the main body of
the churchyard with its maze of old gravestones. A wall of trees
beyond was rapidly being enveloped by shadows. To the left were
an ancient yew tree and the rear wall of the château's grounds.

They turned left on to the flagstones beneath the church tower.

It was then that a mortar shell struck, hurling its deadly fragments of shrapnel against the stonework, gouging the yew's trunk
and killing Glenn instantly, along with Frank Peters and Alan
Kennedy. They died huddled next to the wall by the front door of
the church.

A deep silence fell. The evening gently faded into dusk. Nothing
moved and the houses on the green remained shuttered. Then, as
darkness fell, shadows flitted between the trees and climbed up the
steps of the church. The French villagers, great bundles of roses in
their arms, gently and lovingly covered the bodies of Glenn and his
friends with blossoms.

The three comrades lay there all night. The next morning the
villagers made wooden coffins, dug a triple grave and brought
white linen sheets as shrouds. After a short funeral they covered
each of the graves with a sheaf of flowers tied with a French tricolour ribbon.

'It is now Tuesday evening and what a day,' wrote Veronica Owen
to her parents, throwing punctuation to the winds in her excitement. 'I still cant believe we have actually landed in France that

what we've all been waiting and waiting for such ages should at last have happened and so far apparently successfully.' The last two hours of her overnight watch, when the invasion armada finally broke radio silence, had been crazy as messages began flooding into Neptune's underground nerve centre. After she came off duty she went into Fareham to do some shopping, caught the official announcement of the landings on the BBC, then fell deeply asleep until four o'clock in the afternoon. Then she wrote her long letter home, mended some clothes and got on her bike and went to Titchfield. Here she helped the Spurways pick and arrange roses from the vicarage garden. After dinner the three of them sat alone around the wireless set and listened to the King's broadcast at nine o'clock. 'Very good indeed,' Veronica noted in her diary. Then she bicycled back to Heathfield to catch a good night's sleep before her afternoon watch the next day. The day's events were to herald weeks of relentless work and little sleep for anyone. 'But good fun!' Veronica noted happily.

In Paris, von Rundstedt's headquarters was trying to make sense of it all. So far it seemed as though only a small portion of the troops available in southern Britain had been deployed in the assault. According to a recent reliable Abwehr report, said von Rundstedt's analysts in a situation report on the day's events, they were divided into two army groups: the British 21st Army Group, under Montgomery, and the First United States Army Group, under Patton. Oddly, not a single unit of Patton's group had been spotted. There was only one conclusion to be drawn. The enemy was planning a further large-scale landing on the Channel coast. And the obvious place for that would be in the Pas de Calais.

Allied deception, and the great effort and ingenuity put by Tomas Harris and Juan Pujol into creating a credible Garbo, were clearly working their magic.

Bill Tucker, resting in an apple orchard at Sainte-Mère-Église, was lucky even to make it to lunch.

Creeping along a hedgerow, a German soldier suddenly opened fire on the exhausted men of I Company, pinning them down under the trees, unable to grab their weapons. Luckily, one of the paratroopers had gone off to a nearby well for water, taking his grenade launcher with him. On his way back he spotted the German firing into the orchard and blew him up with a single shot.

By this time the Germans had begun to shell and mortar the town from dug-in positions to the north and south. At 10 a.m., knowing that the fate of the entire Utah bridgehead depended on holding his position, 'Cannonball' Krause ordered I Company to attack the Germans firing from the tiny hamlet of Fauville, about a mile south, straddling the N13, the main north–south road. Skirting the western edge of the town, Tucker quickly found himself lost in the maze of hedgerows. Not even manoeuvres had trained him for the feeling that he was vainly going round in circles as he and Larry dragged the pieces of their machine gun through thickets. They finally emerged hot and weary on the N13 just south of the town.

Less than a mile ahead, along the arrow-straight road, they could see the scattered houses and farm buildings of Fauville at the top of a small rise. Ditches along each side of the road offered minimal cover, and they took it. As they struggled to reassemble the machine gun they came under heavy fire. Only twenty yards away, Germans lobbed grenades at them from the other side of the road. Then the company came under fire from a field to the left, and decided to withdraw. Tucker began crawling backwards along the ditch, only to tumble into a hole dug by French civilians as protection against Allied bombing. The man behind him yelled at him to keep going. As Tucker desperately dragged himself out, he was forced to leave the barrel of the machine gun behind.

By this time his pack of provisions was riddled with bullet holes, his cigarettes had been shredded into loose tobacco and one leg of his trousers had been ripped off. He was glad to find shelter with Larry in a small sunken orchard. Hardly had he caught his breath than a machine gun opened up and he dived for cover over the nearest hedgerow, right into a pig slop. Covered with stinking black slime, he finally made it back into the centre of town just after midday.

Krause now sent I Company into reserve. Tucker and Larry spent most of the afternoon digging a trench in the backyard of a house in Sainte-Mère-Église while shells whizzed overhead.

Throughout the town civilians were still frantically seeking cover. None of their houses possessed deep shelters because of the high water table, so most inhabitants returned to trenches they'd already dug as protection against Allied bombing. Mayor Renaud and his family made for a ditch near a fountain close to their house, lining it against the damp with parachutes collected from a nearby field. As night fell, the mayor could hear squadrons of planes over-head, shells falling close by and machine guns firing in the distance. In the shadows he watched two German soldiers run past his hide-out pursued by silent figures.

'Dig in deep,' ordered the sergeant, and for the rest of the day all Tucker could think about were the Germans he'd encountered outside Fauville, who would attack that night. He'd been told to recover the machine gun's barrel, but this was obviously a fatuous order and he simply ignored it. As darkness fell, more heavy shelling began. G Company, sheltering close by, was badly hit. Tucker kept his head down and hoped for the best.

Suddenly there was firing in the street just a few yards away. Tucker cautiously peered out of his trench. On his left was a small outhouse, and he could dimly make out a man crawling around the side of it. It was a German soldier, and after rounding the corner he was coming straight for Tucker. The paratrooper raised his carbine and pulled the trigger. The bolt moved forward, then stopped halfway. Tucker's desperate crawling through the dirt and ditches had clogged the magazine. Terrified, he frantically worked the bolt. Then the fear passed as suddenly as it had arrived. The German, hearing the sound of the bolt, had taken off into the darkness.

When midnight came and the 'longest day' had ended, the stars and stripes still flew over Sainte-Mère-Église and the Utah bridge-head had linked up with the paratroopers of the 82nd and 101st

Airborne Divisions. All along the fifty-mile Normandy front, exhausted men of the British, Canadian and American armies were digging in for the night. Nowhere had they penetrated more than about ten miles inland, and at Omaha Beach they were only just hanging on. With the exception of Gold and Juno, none of the individual bridgeheads had yet linked up, and few of the ambitious targets for the day had actually been achieved. But one hundred and thirty-two thousand men were safely ashore, along with countless tanks, vehicles and artillery pieces. When dawn broke a few hours later, another huge and irresistible wave of the invading forces would come ashore. And although in some places casualties had been very high, overall they were far lower than expected. Meanwhile, thanks mainly to Garbo's skilful game of deception, Hitler refused to throw his 15th Army into the battle while he waited for the 'real' invasion to take place further north. Resisters were mobilised and already creating turmoil behind German lines.

On the one thousand seven hundred and thirty-ninth day of the Second World War, liberation now beckoned for Western Europe. The long road to Berlin lay open ahead.

EPILOGUE

What Became of Them?

During the six weeks after D-Day, SONIA D'ARTOIS, SYDNEY HUDSON and other members of the SOE's Headmaster circuit carried out numerous sabotage missions, especially against German telephone lines and cables. They also suffered a serious setback when a Maquis group they established in the forest of Charnie was broken up by the Germans and a number of their supporters killed. But they soon recovered, and following the Allied breakout from Normandy the Germans evacuated Le Mans on 8 August. The two SOE agents then linked up with the American forces of Patton's 3rd Army and, disguised as married collaborators, carried out several reconnaissance missions behind German lines for US Army intelligence. On one of these missions they were briefly held as hostages, and Sonia d'Artois was raped at gunpoint by two German soldiers.

After completing their work with Patton's army, they met up in Paris with other members of the SOE's French section, including Guy d'Artois, Sonia's husband, who had led a Maquis group in Burgundy. Soon afterwards Sonia sailed to Canada to begin her married life with Guy, with whom she had six children. He died in 1998, and she now lives in Hudson, Quebec. On returning to London, his marriage now over, Sydney Hudson was determined to find some new purpose in life and volunteered for SOE in the

Far East, known as Force 136. He spent the rest of the war behind Japanese lines, first in Thailand, then in Vietnam. For his SOE work he was awarded the Distinguished Service Order. After the war he worked on re-education programmes in Germany for the British Control Authority, and later as a personnel manager for the Shell Petroleum Company and the Bank of Scotland. He now lives near Edinburgh with his second wife, Ruth. In 2001 he was reunited with Sonia d'Artois for the first time since the war, to make a television documentary about SOE.

In his Oslo prison cell, PETER MOEN heard about D-Day eleven days after the Normandy landings. 'Don't know how it's going. Will it finish this year? And – shall I be alive then? I get dizzy at the thought,' he wrote in his diary on Saturday 17 June 1944. Tragically, it was not to be, and Moen was never reunited with his beloved wife, Bella. On 6 September, after Paris and Brussels had been liberated, he was put on board the ship *Westfalen*, along with fifty fellow countrymen, for transfer to a concentration camp in Germany. The ship was sunk by a torpedo attack in the Skagerrak, and Moen, along with most of the prisoners, was drowned. But he'd had time to tell a survivor the secret of his diary and after the war it was retrieved from the air duct in his former cell and published. His wife was liberated from the Grini camp at the end of the war. They had no children.

On leaving the Wrens at the end of the war, VERONICA OWEN took a history degree at the University of London, captained the women's cricket team, where she specialised as a slow bowler, taught history in independent and state grammar schools, and from 1960 to 1968 was headmistress of Limuru Girls' School in Kenya, whence she once led an expedition of girls up Mount Kilimanjaro. She returned to Britain to become headmistress of Malvern Girls' College, before retiring in 1983. The author of a book of prayers, *Fire of Love*, she was an active member of the Anglican Church and in her retirement loved walking the Malvern Hills. She never married, and died in July 1999.

The octagonal font in St Peter's Church, Titchfield, where Frank Spurway was the vicar and Veronica frequently worshipped during the war, was built as a memorial to the troops who passed through the town on their way to the D-Day landings.

ANDRÉ HEINTZ still lives in Caen. After working for the Red Cross, and then, following the liberation of Caen on 9 July 1944, assisting Allied occupation forces, he spent the first two years of peace at the University of Edinburgh as an instructor in French. For the following thirty-six years he taught French as a foreign language to students from abroad at the University of Caen's Institute of Technology. He married his wife, Marie-Françoise, in 1948 and they have five children. Now an active supporter of the Mémorial de Caen, he acts as guide and interpreter for tours of the Normandy battlefields.

For André, D-Day meant liberation and hope for the future. 'We were in a position to know what freedom meant,' he told the author. 'The day of the liberation of Caen was the most beautiful of my whole life. There are memories of lack of freedom and Nazi crimes that I cannot forget: like the shooting of the members of the Resistance in Caen on the morning of D-Day, among them my leader, Alexis Lelièvre. But, as de Gaulle said several years after the war, "It is high time for reconciliation with Germany". I did my best so that my children would not keep the same feelings as I have.'

ALBERT GRUNBERG remained in hiding until the liberation of Paris, returning to his own apartment on Wednesday 23 August 1944 and joining the Free Forces of the Interior on the barricades outside the Prefecture of Police two days later for the final hours of fighting against his hated Boche. He then returned to running his hairdressing business. The last entry of his diary appeared in October 1944, in which he wrote of his support for the Communist Party and his hopes for the creation of a French Soviet Republic that would bring justice for the people of France. 'But my joy would be complete,' he wrote, 'if I had news of my children in Chambéry.' Grunberg died in Paris in 1976, aged seventy-eight. His diary was deposited by his son, Roger, in the National Archives in Paris in 1998. Grunberg's brother Sami died soon after the war, partly as a result of his maltreatment in the Drancy prison camp. Madame Hélène Oudard, the concierge who sheltered him and to whom he owed his life, died in Paris in June 1999, aged ninety-eight.

WALTER SCHWENDER did not survive the war. American troops liberated Nantes on 11 August 1944, and the following month, still posted in France, Walter was shot through the right arm and shoulder, probably by an Allied plane. Taken to a military hospital at Menge in Germany, close to the French border, he died after the amputation of his arm and was buried there. After the war he was reinterred in the family grave in Altstadt in the Saar. His name is engraved on the great gate that leads to the graveyard, along with those of his brother Karl and all the other young men of the village who were killed in Hitler's war.

After thirty-eight days of combat in Normandy, BILL TUCKER, along with the remainder of his regiment, returned to the base at Quorn, in Leicestershire. Of the just over two thousand men who had parachuted into France, only half made it back: 186 were killed, 60 were missing, 656 were wounded and 51 were captured. Of the 144 men in Tucker's I Company, only 45 returned to England. 'When the men got off the boats in England,' recorded 'Chappie' Woods, the chaplain, 'they knelt down and kissed the ground. This, to them, was hallowed ground.' To Tucker, Britain now felt even more like home than America. On the journey back to Quorn, he noted, 'the oddest thing happened'. Somewhere on a train or at a railway station he found another copy of *A Tree Grows in Brooklyn*, 'so I got to finish it after all'. Tucker went on to fight with the 82nd Airborne Division throughout the remainder of the European campaign and took part in the Arnhem attack and the Battle of the Bulge, where he was wounded.

After the war he returned to Boston and became a lawyer. He has since been Chairman of the United States Interstate Commerce Commission, Vice President of the Penn Central Railroad, and a special consultant to Eastern Airlines. Married, he lives in Massachusetts and has two daughters.

'Anyone who served with the 82nd from Africa to Berlin,' he has written, 'never really left the 82nd in spirit. No other education or maturing processes ever equalled the impact of being an 82nd trooper. We always remembered the words: "Never retreat. Never accept defeat." My 82nd Airborne education has been invaluable to me in terms of taking on any tough job – and getting it done.'

The deception pair of JUAN PUJOL and TOMAS HARRIS survived the war and remained friends. 'Garbo' was awarded the MBE in December 1944 (having previously been awarded the Iron Cross by the Germans for his supposedly reliable intelligence reports as 'Arabel') and in 1945 he settled in Caracas, in Venezuela, where for many years he worked as a language teacher for Shell Oil. To protect him, MI5 spread a rumour that he had emigrated to Angola and died there of malaria. Only in 1984 was his cover broken, when he returned to Britain to receive the personal thanks for his war work from the Duke of Edinburgh. He died in Caracas in 1988.

Harris resumed his profession as an art dealer, moved to Majorca with his wife, Hilda, and was killed in a car crash in 1964. Post-war speculation about his possible connections with Soviet intelligence through his friendship with Philby and Blunt has never been confirmed.

ERWIN ROMMEL did his best with the forces available to him in Normandy, but lost the campaign, and his life. Indirectly implicated in the failed bomb plot against Hitler in July 1944, he was given the choice between a trial involving the disgrace of his wife and child, and an honourable suicide that would permit him to be buried with full military honours. He chose the latter and swallowed poison in October 1944. He is buried in Herrlingen, near Ulm. His son, Manfred, later served as a post-war Mayor of Stuttgart.

ADOLF HITLER led his country to destruction and killed himself and his mistress Eva Braun, whom he married on the eve of their suicide, in the ruins of the Chancery in Berlin on 30 April 1945 as Red Army troops occupied the city. His body was burned and its remains were later discovered, removed and then hidden or dispersed by the Soviets.

After presiding over Allied victory in Europe, WINSTON CHURCHILL was defeated in the British general election of July 1945. As leader of the opposition and a revered world statesman, he warned eloquently of the Soviet threat, urged a strong Anglo-American alliance and lent powerful support to the campaign for European unity. He was elected Prime Minister in 1951, a position from which he finally stepped down in 1955. He remained a Member of Parliament until 1964 and died the following year, aged ninety. He is buried in the churchyard at Bladon, in Oxfordshire, close to his birthplace at Blenheim Palace.

DWIGHT D. EISENHOWER remained Allied Supreme Commander until the defeat of Germany, became Supreme Commander of Allied Forces in Europe under NATO (1950–2), and was elected thirty-fourth President of the United States as a Republican, serving for two successive terms (1953–61). He lived with his wife, Mamie, at Gettysburg, Pennsylvania, and died in the Walter Reed Army Hospital in Washington DC in March 1969, after speaking his last words: 'I've always loved my wife. I've always loved my children. I've always loved my grandchildren. I've always loved my country.' He was buried after a military funeral in Abilene, Kansas, his childhood home.

After the war, DAVID BRUCE, described by his biographer as 'the last American aristocrat', followed a distinguished diplomatic career, becoming US Ambassador to France (1949–52), to the Federal Republic of Germany (1957–8) and to Great Britain (1961–9). He was the chief negotiator at the Paris peace talks over Vietnam in 1970, served as chief US representative in the People's Republic of China in 1973–4 and was US Permanent Representative to Nato in 1974–6. He died in 1977.

The Free French leader CHARLES DE GAULLE landed on French soil at Courseulles-sur-Mer, liberated on D-Day by Glenn Dickin and the Regina Rifles, on 14 June 1944, entered Paris in triumph on 25 August – the day Albert Grunberg joined the barricades – and was elected head of the provisional government of France in October 1945. After abruptly resigning a few months later, he spent several years in retreat until emerging to save his country from the crisis over the Algerian war. In 1958 he was overwhelmingly elected President of the new Fifth Republic, which he dominated until his resignation in 1969. He died a year later at his home in Colombey-les-Deux-Églises.

After masterminding Operation Neptune, Admiral SIR BERTRAM RAMSAY remained Allied naval commander-in-chief and by the end of 1944 was headquartered at St Germain-en-Laye, outside Paris. On 2 January 1945 he took off in his RAF Hudson from the airfield at Toussy-le-Noble for a meeting with General Montgomery in Brussels, but the plane crashed on take-off and he was immediately killed. He lies buried in St-Germain-en-Laye.

GLENN DICKIN's body remained buried in the churchyard in Fontaine-Henry until after the war, when his remains, along with those of Frank Peters and Alan Kennedy, were reinterred at the Canadian war cemetery in Bretteville-sur-Laize in Calvados, France. The cemetery contains 2957 Second World War burials, most of them Canadian. A memorial service to Glenn was held in Manor, at St Margaret's Anglican Church, on Friday 17 June 1944. The first boys born to his brothers following his death were all named Glenn. Dickin Island, in Saskatchewan, is named in his memory.

APPENDICES

1. General Eisenhower's Order of the Day, distributed by SHAEF to all Allied troops on D-Day

Soldiers, Sailors and Airmen of the Allied Expeditionary Forces!: You are about to embark upon the Great Crusade, towards which we have striven these many months. The eyes of the world are upon you. The hopes and prayers of liberty-loving people everywhere march with you. In company with our brave Allies and brothers-in-arms on other Fronts you will bring about the destruction of the German war machine, the elimination of Nazi tyranny over oppressed peoples of Europe, and security for ourselves in a free world.

Your task will not be an easy one. Your enemy is well trained, well equipped and battle-hardened. He will fight savagely.

But this is the year 1944! Much has happened since the Nazi triumphs of 1940–41. The United Nations have inflicted upon the Germans great defeats, in open battle, man-to-man. Our air offensive has seriously reduced their strength in the air and their capacity to wage war on the ground. Our Home Fronts have given us an overwhelming superiority in weapons and munitions of war, and placed at our disposal great reserves of trained fighting men. The tide has turned! The free men of the world are marching together to Victory!

I have full confidence in your courage, devotion to duty and skill in battle. We will accept nothing less than full victory!

Good Luck! And let us all beseech the blessing of Almighty God upon this great and noble undertaking.

2. General Eisenhower's Message on the Conduct of Troops in Liberated Countries, distributed with his Order of the Day on D-Day

You are soon to be engaged in a great undertaking – the invasion of Europe. Our purpose is to bring about, in company with our Allies, and our comrades on other fronts, the total defeat of Germany. Only by such a complete victory can we free ourselves and our homelands from the fear and threat of the Nazi tyranny.

A further element of our mission is the liberation of those people of Western Europe now suffering under German oppression.

Before embarking on this operation, I have a personal message for you as to your own individual responsibility, in relation to the inhabitants of our Allied countries.

As a representative of this country, you will be welcomed with deep gratitude by the liberated peoples, who for years have longed for this deliverance. It is of the utmost importance that this feeling of friendliness and goodwill be in no way impaired by careless or indifferent behavior on your part. By a courteous and considerate demeanor, you can on the other hand do much to strengthen that feeling.

The inhabitants of Nazi-occupied Europe have suffered great privations, and you will find that many of them lack even the barest necessities. You, on the other hand, have been, and will continue to be, provided adequate food, clothing and other necessities. You must not deplete the already meagre local stocks of food and other supplies by indiscriminate buying, thereby fostering the 'Black Market', which can only increase the hardship of the inhabitants.

The rights of individuals, as to their persons and property, must be scrupulously respected, as though in your own country. You must remember, always, that these people are our friends and Allies.

I urge each of you to bear constantly in mind that by your actions not only you as an individual, but your country as well, will be judged. By establishing a relationship with the liberated peoples, based on mutual understanding and respect, we shall enlist their wholehearted assistance in the defeat of our common enemy. Thus shall we lay the foundations for a lasting peace, without which our great effort will have been in vain.

ACKNOWLEDGEMENTS AND SOURCES

My greatest debt of gratitude is to those whose personal stories populate the pages of this book, and to their families and relatives. Wherever possible I have tried to reconstruct the narratives from original diaries, letters or other contemporary documents. But where this has not been feasible, I have relied on sources produced as close in time to D-Day as possible, to oral memories that can be checked against contemporary documentation and to interviews with those involved.

At the Special Forces Club in London in June 2002 Sonia d'Artois and Sydney Hudson of the SOE 'Headmaster' circuit helped me reconstruct their movements and activities day by day over this period, accounts that I have cross-checked with their post-operational debriefing reports in recently released SOE files in the Public Record Office (HS 6/566, 'Blanche's [D'Artois'] Report', and HS 6/572, 'Albin's [Hudson's] Report'). Sydney Hudson also kindly let me read the manuscript of his SOE memoirs *Undercover Operator*, subsequently published by Pen and Sword Books in April 2003, while Sonia d'Artois readily gave me permission to read the transcript of her interview for the BBC TV programme on SOE's female agents, *The Real Charlotte Grays*, made by Darlow Smithson Productions, in which she appeared in 2001.

Both have also expanded on many points in person or by telephone, and have patiently done their best to answer my many questions about events now far distant in their lives. Any errors are mine. Sonia d'Artois kindly provided me with the wedding photograph of her and her late husband, Guy, that appears in the picture section.

For material on Glenn Dickin, I am profoundly grateful to members of the Dickin family in Canada who responded enthusiastically to my request for help with letters, photographs and reminiscences; to Terry Dickin, and most especially to his niece, Dolores Hatch, of London, Ontario, for most generously letting me read copies of Glenn's letters home, providing me with a great deal of information about the Dickin family, sending photographs and providing Glenn's official service record. Glenn's wartime buddy Gordon Brown, now of Red Deer, Alberta, shared his memories of him with me, as did his old schoolmate and friend 'Dutchy' Doerr, also of London, Ontario. To both of them I am deeply indebted, especially as their fond memories of Glenn inevitably resurrect some pain and grief. None of my account of Glenn, however, would have been possible without the extraordinarily generous help of my friend Professor Terry Copp, of Wilfrid Laurier University, in Waterloo, Ontario, who opened doors and provided an enormous amount of valuable background material on the wartime experience of the Regina Rifles, such as extracts from war diaries and D-Day briefing documents. I have also drawn heavily on the invaluable book co-authored by Gordon Brown and Terry Copp, *Look To Your Front . . . Regina Rifles: A Regiment at War, 1944–45*.

One of the more memorable moments of my research was a meeting at Fontaine-Henry, in France, with Guy Chrétien, who has made it his life's work to tell the story of the Canadians in Normandy to his fellow countrymen and the world, and who walked me round the scene of the action on the evening of D-Day where Glenn met his death. I am also deeply grateful to Madame La Comtesse d'Ouilliamson, of Château Fontaine-Henry, who very kindly responded to my impromptu request for assistance during a visit to her home. The journalist on whose memoirs I occasionally draw for background was the Canadian press war correspondent Ross Munro, whose book is listed in the bibliography; that by the Australian journalist Alan Moorehead, also listed, proved helpful too.

Peter Moen's sadly forgotten diary was originally published in English in 1951, and further helpful recent information about his role in the Norwegian Resistance has been given to me by Dr Ivar Kraglund and Dr Arnfinn Moland of the Norges Hjemmer-frontenmuseum, Norway's Resistance Museum, in Oslo. I am especially grateful to Ivar Kraglund and the Museum for permitting me to use the photographs of Peter Moen held by the Museum, and to Ian Herrington for answering many of my questions about the Norwegian Resistance and, in particular, events surrounding the Aula fire.

Albert Grunberg's diary was deposited in the National Archives in Paris in 1998 and an abbreviated version was published in French in 2001. For drawing my attention to this diary I am particularly grateful to Professor Renée Poznanzki of Ben-Gurion University, in Israel, and to my friend and former colleague Michael Marrus, Professor of Holocaust Studies at the University of Toronto, both of whom have also written extensively about the Jewish experience in wartime France and on whose published work I have drawn for background material.

For Bill Tucker, I have drawn on the original copy of the chronology of his wartime experiences with the 82nd Airborne Division, written in 1946, which can be found in the archives of the Mémorial de Caen, another version of which appeared in Deryk Wills's privately published account *Put on Your Boots and Parachutes!* Tucker subsequently produced a further, more polished and complete version, *Parachute Soldier* (1994), and during the writing of this book he helped me with further questions that arose from my reading of these accounts, as well as generously providing photographs. Deryk Wills is also owed a word of thanks here for answering questions, putting me in touch with Bill Tucker in Massachusetts and keeping the 82nd Airborne's torch of memory alight in Britain.

The letters of Walter Schwender can be found in the Feldpost Archiv, in Berlin, to which I am indebted for permission to quote from them. Dr Clemens Schwender and the Schwender family provided me with further background material, and I am deeply grateful to Clemens for answering my many questions about his uncle and his family so readily and frankly. He, too, provided photographs that I have used in the book. Here, also, I wish to thank my indefatigable friend in Berlin, Willie Durie, for making all this possible in the first place.

In Caen, André Heintz was an extremely generous host, spending considerable time with me in going over his pre-D-Day activities in the French Resistance, and providing me with much valuable background material, including photographs. Memorably, he also kindly introduced me to two of his friends involved with the legendary Maquis of Saint Clair, Philippe Durel and André Héricy, whom it was a privilege to meet. *En route*, he drove me to the Canadian cemetery at Bretteville-sur-Laize, where Glenn Dickin and his comrades are buried. For putting me in touch with André, I am grateful to Duncan Stuart, CMG, former SOE Adviser at the Foreign and Commonwealth Office.

The letters of Veronica Owen to her parents are to be found in the Imperial War Museum, London, and I thank the Trustees for allowing me access to them. Veronica's brother, Captain Hugh Owen RN, also kindly let me read her diary, which is in his possession, generously filled in further details about the Owen family, provided me with a photograph of her and answered some important naval questions. For all his help, and for that of Sam Hesketh of Malvern Girls' College, I am profoundly grateful.

The 'Garbo' files on Juan Pujol have recently been released in the Public Record Office: see especially KV 2/39, 2/40, 2/41 and then 2/63–71. The official summary of the Garbo case written by Tomas Harris was published by the Public Record Office, with an introduction by Mark Seaman, in 2000 under the title *Garbo: The Spy Who Saved D-Day*. This provides a useful corrective to the helpful but sometimes misleading memory of Juan Pujol himself, as reflected in his autobiographical account, *Garbo*, written in collaboration with Nigel West. For the episode of the escaped NCO, Western Command and the D-Day security panic related in Chapters 5 and 6, I have drawn on the memoir of Major H.R.V. Jordan, of Military Security Intelligence, Western Command, which is deposited at the Imperial War Museum archives in London.

For the major historical characters I have found the following sources most useful: for Churchill, Martin Gilbert's official biography is indispensable, as are the many volumes of the official history of British Intelligence in the Second World War edited by F.H. Hinsley and, of course, Churchill's own history of the Second World War. I have supplemented these with documents mostly from the PREM, HS, HW, KV, WO and CAB series in the Public Record Office, Kew: the wartime MI5 reports to Churchill may be found in KV 4/83, and Lord Selborne's correspondence with Churchill about SOE rests in the HS8 files.

Eisenhower has been well covered in biographies by the late Stephen Ambrose, Carlo d'Este and David S. Eisenhower. The published diaries of his naval aide, Harry S. Butcher, have been useful, despite having been heavily censored after the war to protect the deception secret. Ike's wartime papers, edited by Alfred D. Chandler, are invaluable. For David Bruce and the Office of Strategic Services (OSS), I have drawn on the published diary edited by Nelson D. Lankford, as well as on the Francis P. Miller papers held at the George C. Marshall Foundation in Lexington, Virginia, which provide some interesting insights into the OSS 'Sussex' missions.

Of the many studies of Hitler, Ian Kershaw's recent two-part biography proved helpful, while Albert Speer's memoirs and the diaries of Josef Goebbels assisted in pinning down his day-to-day activities at the Berghof. Rommel has also been well served by biographers, especially David Irving in *The Trail of the Fox* and David Fraser in *Knight's Cross*. For Charles de Gaulle, I have drawn mostly on the studies by François Kersaudy, Charles Williams and Jacques Lacouture, as well as on his own war memoirs. For material on Auschwitz, I found Danuta Czech's *Auschwitz Chronicle 1939–1945* especially helpful, and I am grateful to Sir Martin Gilbert for drawing it to my attention.

There are too many books on the general background, including D-Day itself, to mention individually here, and I have included the most useful in the bibliography. Of particular help in recapturing the perspectives of the day were newspapers, and I have frequently drawn on the London press, especially *The Times*, the *Sunday Times* and the *Daily Telegraph*.

In order not to distract the reader's attention with a bevy of footnotes or endnotes, I have refrained from providing references to particular documents, quotations, etc, but I shall be happy to provide these on request.

I have also leaned heavily in many different ways on the help of friends and colleagues around the world. With apologies to any I may have inadvertently omitted, my sincerest thanks to all of you: Dr Paul Addison, Dr Sarah Colvin, Dr Jeremy Crang, Marianne Czisnik, the Reverend Bill Day, Vicar of St Peter's, Titchfield, Dr Hilary Footit, Professor Jürgen Förster, Professor Arthur Layton Funk, Sir Martin Gilbert, Professor Jack Granatstein, Fanny Hugill, Madeleine Haag, Colonel Dr Winfried Heinemann of the Militärgeschichtliches Forschungsamt, Berlin, Professor Dr Gerhard Hirschfeld, Oliver Hoare, Bob Hunt, Professor Roderick Kedward, Robert McCormick, Professor Jim McMillan, Russell Miller, Esther Poznansky, David Ramsay, Dr Olav Riste, Bob Steers and Dominic Sutherland.

No scholar can operate without the assistance of the regiments of dedicated professionals who run libraries and archives, and I wish in particular to thank the staffs of the following institutions, whose expert knowledge of their manuscript and other collections made my own task so much easier: the Imperial War Museum, London; the National Library of Scotland; the Public Record Office, Kew; Portsmouth City Museums and Records Service, where Andrew Whitmarsh guided me through its D-Day collection; Ms Dawn Bowen, at the Hampshire Record Office; Dorothy Sheridan and the Mass Observation Archive at the University of Sussex; Irina Renz at the Bibliothek für Zeitgeschichte in Stuttgart, Germany; Mike

Timonin, of the Marshall Research Archives in Lexington, Virginia; Alan Edwards OBE, who helped me with records from the Intelligence Corps Museum Archives kept at the Defence Intelligence and Security Centre at Chicksands; Stéphane Simonnet, Franck Marie and Marie-Claude Berthelot of the Services Archives et Documentation at the Mémorial de Caen (Caen Memorial), Normandy. As always, I am grateful to Anthea Taylor and the staff at the Institute for Advanced Studies at the University of Edinburgh for making my work much easier, and to Professor John Frew, Director of the Institute, I am grateful for providing me with an office where I was able to complete the bulk of my early research. Thanks, too, go to David Darlow, Sam Organ and Nion Hazell of Darlow Smithson Productions for facilitating access to the transcripts of interviews made with Lise de Baissac and Sonia d'Artois for their TV programme *The Real Charlotte Grays*.

I owe the idea of writing this book to my agent, Andrew Lownie, and although as it grew the book inevitably changed shape, I am deeply grateful to him for this and all his other patient assistance. At Time Warner, my editor, Alan Samson, was always ready with a sympathetic ear and provocative mind, and the fact that this book landed safely on its own D-Day mission on schedule owes much to his unerring guidance. Thanks, too, to Linda Silverman for patient and creative picture research, to Stephen Guise for many valuable suggestions and for guiding the book through its various stages of production, and to Richard Dawes for eagle-eyed copy-editing and his help with some of the translations from French.

Finally, I wish to place on record my gratitude to Walter and Bettye Cannizzo, my parents-in-law, whose customary generosity and support helped make possible my stay in the United States to write this book; to the staff at the Collier County Library in Naples, Florida, whose helpfulness and first-rate collection of books give a heartwarming lie to the notion that Florida is an intellectual desert and that the United States is a country without a vibrant public culture; to Barry Weisler and the staff at Computer Connection of Naples, Florida, who patiently guided me through some tricky word-processing problems and printed out the first draft of the manuscript; to Darlene Plog, who helped with accommodation; to my sister, Margaret Crowe, for helping with bibliographical research; and to Michael Conroy, and to my cousin, Elizabeth Wilde McCormick, for hospitality in London during some of my researches. And, as always, to my wife, Jeanne: intrepid researcher, creative editor of first resort, thoughtful critic, and supportive companion on yet another writing venture.

Edinburgh, Scotland, April 2003

SELECT BIBLIOGRAPHY

Alanbrooke, Field Marshal Lord, *War Diaries 1939–1945* (eds. Alex Danchev and Daniel Todman), London, Weidenfeld and Nicolson, 2001

Ambrose, Stephen, *Citizen Soldiers*, New York, Simon and Schuster, 1997

—— *D-Day*, New York, Touchstone, 1994

—— *Eisenhower, Soldier and President*, New York, Simon and Schuster, 1990

—— *Ike's Spies: Eisenhower and the Espionage Establishment*, New York, Doubleday, 1981

—— *The Supreme Commander*, London, Cassell, 1971

Astley, Joan Bright, *The Inner Circle*, London, Quality Book Club, 1972

Barnouw, David, and Van Der Stroom, Gerrold (eds.), *The Diary of Anne Frank: The Critical Edition*, New York, Doubleday, 1989

Baudot, Marcel, *Libération de la Normandie*, Paris, Hachette, 1974

Below, Nicolaus von, *At Hitler's Side*, London, Greenhill Press, 2001

Bennett, Ralph, *Behind the Battle: Intelligence in the War against Germany*, London, Sinclair-Stevenson, 1994

—— *Ultra in the West: The Normandy Campaign of 1944–45*, New York, Scribner's, 1979

Berthon, Simon, *Allies at War*, London, HarperCollins, 2001

Bialer, Seweryn (ed.), *Stalin and His Generals*, London, Westview, 1984

Blair, Clay, *Hitler's U-Boat War: The Hunters 1939–1942*, New York, Random House, 1996

—— *Ridgway's Paratroopers: The American Airborne Forces in World War II*, New York, The Dial Press, 1985

Blandford, Edmund, *Two Sides of the Beach*, Shrewsbury, Airlife, 1999

Bleicher, Hugo, *Colonel Henri's Story*, London, Kimber, 1954

Botting, Douglas, *The U-Boats*, Alexandria, VA, Time-Life Books, 1979

Bradley, Omar, *A Soldier's Story*, New York, Henry Holt, 1951

Breuer, William, *Hoodwinking Hitler: The Normandy Deception*, Westport, CT, Praeger, 1993

—— *The Secret War with Germany*, Shrewsbury, Airlife, 1988

Bristow, Desmond, *A Game of Moles*, London, Warner, 1994

Broadfoot, Barry, *Six War Years 1939–1945: Memories of Canadians at Home and Abroad*, Don Mills, Ontario, Paper Jacks, 1976

Brown, Anthony Cave, *Wild Bill Donovan: The Last Hero*, New York, Times Books, 1981

Brown, Gordon, and Copp, Terry, *Look To Your Front . . . Regina Rifles: A Regiment at War, 1944–45*, Waterloo, Ontario, Laurier Centre for Military, Strategic, and Disarmament Studies, Wilfrid Laurier University, 2001

Brusselmans, Anne, *Rendez-Vous 127*, London, Edward Benn, 1954

Buchheim, Lothar-Günther, *U-Boat War*, New York, Alfred Knopf, 1978

Buffetaut, Yves, *The Allied Invasion Fleet, June 1944*, Annapolis, MD, Naval Institute Press, 1994

Butcher, Harry, *Three Years with Eisenhower*, London, Heinemann, 1946

Carell, Paul, *Invasion, They're Coming!*, London, Corgi, 1962

Carter, Miranda, *Anthony Blunt: His Lives*, London, Macmillan, 2001

Casey, William J., *The Secret War Against Hitler*, Washington DC, Regnery Gateway, 1988

Chalmers, W.S., *Full Cycle: The Biography of Admiral Sir Bertram Home Ramsay KCB, KBE, MVO*, London, Hodder and Stoughton, 1959

Chandler, Alfred D., *The Papers of Dwight D. Eisenhower*, vol. 3, *The War Years*, Baltimore, MD, Johns Hopkins Press, 1970

Churchill, Winston S., *The Second World War*, 6 vols. New York, Bantam Books, 1948–1953

—— *Memories and Adventures*, New York, Weidenfeld and Nicolson, 1989

Collier, Richard, *D-Day*, London, Cassell, 1992

—— *Ten Thousand Eyes*, London, Collins, 1958

Cooper, Lady Diana, *Autobiography*, London, Michael Russell, 1979

Cooper, Duff, *Old Men Forget*, London, Rupert Hart-Davis, 1953

Cowley, Robert (ed.), *What If? The World's Foremost Military Historians Imagine What Might Have Been*, London, Macmillan, 2000

Czech, Danuta, *Auschwitz Chronicle 1939–1945*, New York, Henry Holt, 1990

Dahla, H.F., and others, *Norsk Krigsleksikon 1940–1945*, Oslo, J.W. Cappelens Forlag, 1995

Deane, John R., *The Strange Alliance*, London, John Murray, 1947

Dear, I.C.B. (ed.), *The Oxford Companion to World War II*, New York, Oxford University Press, 1995

D'Este, Carlo, *Fatal Decision: Anzio and the Battle for Rome*, London, HarperCollins, 1991

—— *Decision in Normandy*, London, HarperCollins, 1994

—— *Eisenhower: A Soldier's Life*, New York, Henry Holt, 2002

De Gaulle, Charles, *War Memoirs: Unity 1942–1944*, London, Weidenfeld and Nicolson, 1959

De Guingand, Francis, *Operation Victory*, London, Hodder and Stoughton, 1947

Dixon, Piers, *Double Diploma*, London, Hutchinson, 1968

Doughty, Martin (ed.), *Hampshire and D-Day*, Crediton, Hampshire Books, 1994

Eden, Sir Anthony, *Memoirs*, vol. 2, *The Reckoning*, London, Cassell, 1965

Eisenhower, David, *Eisenhower: At War 1943–1945*, London, Collins, 1986

Eisenhower, Dwight D., *Crusade in Europe*, London, Heinemann, 1948

—— *The Eisenhower Diaries* (ed. Robert E. Ferrell), New York, Norton, 1981

Ellis, Major L.F., *Victory in the West*, vol. 1, *The Battle of Normandy*, London, HMSO, 1962

Erickson, John, *The Road to Berlin*, London, Weidenfeld and Nicolson, 1983

Farago, Ladislas, *The Game of the Foxes*, London, Hodder and Stoughton, 1971

Fest, Joachim, *Hitler*, New York, Harcourt Brace Jovanovich, 1974

Fischer, Klaus P., *Nazi Germany: A New History*, New York, Continuum, 1995

Fletcher, M.H., *The WRNS: A History of the Women's Royal Naval Service*, London, Batsford, 1989

Fourcade, Marie, *Noah's Ark*, London, George Allen and Unwin, 1973

Frank, Wolfgang, *The Sea Wolves*, New York, Rinehart, 1956

Fraser, David, *Knight's Cross*, New York, Harper, 1995

Fritz, Stephen G., *Frontsoldaten: The German Soldier in World War Two*, Lexington, KY, University of Kentucky Press, 1995

Gallagher, Tag, *The Adventures of Roberto Rossellini*, New York, Da Capo Press, 1998

Gavin, James M., *On To Berlin*, New York, Viking, 1978

Gilbert, Martin, *The Second World War*, London, Phoenix, 1995

—— *Winston S. Churchill*, vol. 7, *Road to Victory*, Boston, MA, Houghton Mifflin, 1986

Glantz, David, *Soviet Military Deception in the Second World War*, London, Cass, 1989

Granatstein, J.L., *The Generals*, Toronto, Stoddart, 1993

Granatstein, J.L., and Morton, Desmond, *Bloody Victory: Canadians and the D-Day Campaign*, Toronto, Lester and Orpen Dennys, 1984

Grunberg, Albert, *Journal d'un coiffeur juif à Paris, sous l'Occupation*, Paris, Les Éditions de l'Atelier, 2001

Gutman, Yisrael, and Berenbaum, Michael, *Anatomy of the Auschwitz Death Camp*, Bloomington, IN, Indiana University Press, 1994

Hamilton, Nigel, *Monty: Master of the Battlefield 1942–1944*, London, Hamish Hamilton, 1983

Harriman, A., and Abel, E., *Special Envoy to Churchill and Stalin 1941–46*, New York, Random House, 1975

Harris, Brayton, *Submarines*, New York, Berkley Books, 1997

Harrison, Gordon A., *Cross-Channel Attack*, Washington DC, Department of the Army, 1951

Harvey, John (ed.), *The War Dairies of Oliver Harvey*, London, Collins, 1978

Hastings, Max, *Overlord: D-Day and the Battle for Normandy*, London, Michael Joseph, 1984

Haswell, Jock, *The Intelligence and Deception of the D-Day Landings*, London, Batsford, 1979

Hinsley, F.H. (ed.), *British Intelligence in the Second World War*, vol. 3, part II, London, HMSO, 1988

Höhne, Heinz, *The Order of the Death's Head*, London, Penguin, 2000

Howard, Michael, *British Intelligence in the Second World War*, vol. 5, *Strategic Deception*, (ed. F.H. Hinsley), New York, Cambridge University Press, 1990

Howarth, David, *Dawn of D-Day*, London, Collins, 1959

Hudson, Sydney, *Undercover Operator*, Barnsley, Pen and Sword, 2003

Irving, David, *Goering: A Biography*, New York, William Morrow, 1989

—— *Hitler's War 1942–5*, London, Macmillan, 1983

—— *The Secret Diaries of Hitler's Doctor*, New York, Macmillan, 1983

—— *The Trail of the Fox*, London, Macmillan, 1985

Jacob, Alaric, *A Window in Moscow, 1944–1945*, London, Collins, 1946

James, M.E. Clifton, *I Was Monty's Double*, London, Rider, 1954

Joachimstaler, Anton, *The Last Days of Hitler*, London, Arms and Armour, 1998

Jutras, Philippe, *Sainte-Mère-Église*, Bayeux, Éditions Heimdal, 1994

Kahn, David, *Hitler's Spies*, London, Hodder and Stoughton, 1978

Kardorff, Ursula von, *Diary of a Nightmare*, London, Rupert Hart-Davis, 1965

Keegan, John, *Six Armies in Normandy*, Harmondsworth, Penguin, 1982

Kersaudy, François, *Churchill and De Gaulle*, London, Collins, 1981

Kershaw, Ian, *Hitler*, vol. 2, *1936–1945: Nemesis*, London, Allen Lane, The Penguin Press, 2000

Kershaw, Robert J., *D-Day: Piercing the Atlantic Wall*, London, Ian Allan, 1993

Kharlamov, N.M., *Difficult Mission*, Moscow, Progress Publishers, 1986

Kimball, Warren (ed.), *Churchill and Roosevelt: The Complete Correspondence*, vol. 3, *Alliance Declining: February 1944–April 1945*, Princeton, Princeton University Press, 1984

Lacouture, Jean, *De Gaulle*, vol. 1, *The Rebel*, New York, W.W. Norton, 1990

Lang, Jochen von, *The Secretary: Martin Bormann*, New York, Random House, 1979

Lankford, Nelson D., *The Last American Aristocrat*, Boston, MA, Little, Brown, 1996

—— (ed.), *OSS Against the Reich*, Kent, OH, Kent State University Press, 1991

Latimer, Jon, *Deception in War*, London, John Murray, 2001

Levi, Primo, *If This Is A Man: Remembering Auschwitz*, New York, Summit Books, 1986

Lewis, Adrian R., *Omaha Beach: A Flawed Victory*, Chapel Hill, NC, University of North Carolina Press, 2001

Longmate, Norman, *The GIs in Britain*, London, Hutchinson, 1975

Manvell, Roger, and Fraenkel, Heinrich, *Goering*, New York, Simon and Schuster, 1962

Marrus, Michael, and Paxton, Robert, *Vichy France and the Jews*, New York, Basic Books, 1981

Mason, Ursula, *Britannia's Daughters: The Story of the WRNS*, London, Leo Cooper, 1992

Masterman, J.C., *The Double-Cross System*, New Haven, CT, Yale University Press, 1972

Mein, Stewart A.G., *Up The Johns! The Story of the Royal Regina Rifles*, North Battleford, Saskatchewan, Turner-Warwick, 1992

Miller, Francis Pickens, *Man From The Valley*, Chapel Hill, NC, University of North Carolina Press, 1971

Miller, Russell, *Nothing Less Than Victory*, London, Penguin, 1994

Moen, Peter, *Peter Moen's Diary*, London, Faber and Faber, 1951

Moorehead, Alan, *Eclipse*, London, Hamish Hamilton, 1945

Morgan, Lieutenant-General Sir Frederick, *Overture to Overlord*, London, Hodder and Stoughton, 1950

Morison, Samuel Eliot, *The Invasion of France and Germany 1944–1945*, Boston, MA, Little, Brown, 1984

Müller, Melissa, *Anne Frank: The Biography*, London, Bloomsbury, 1998

Müller, Rolf Dieter, and Volkmann, Hans-Erich (eds.), *Die Wehrmacht: Mythos und Realität*, Munich, Oldenbourg, 1999

Munro, Ross, *Gauntlet to Overlord*, Toronto, Macmillan, 1945

Murphy, Robert M., *Le Meilleur Endroit Pour Mourir*, South Dennis, MA, Robert Murphy, 1998

Nansen, Odd, *Day After Day*, London, Putnam, 1949

Neillands, Robin, and De Normann, Roderick, *D-Day 1944*, London, Cassell, 2001

Neufeld, Michael J., and Berenbaum, Michael, *The Bombing of Auschwitz*, New York, St Martin's Press, 2000

Newton, Verne E., *FDR and the Holocaust*, New York, St Martin's Press, 1996

—— *The New Yorker Book of War Pieces: London, 1939 to Hiroshima, 1945*, New York, Schocken Books, 1947

Noli, Jean, *The Admiral's Wolf Pack*, New York, Doubleday, 1974

O'Connell, Geoffrey, *Southwick: The D-Day Village That Went to War*, Ashford, Buchan and Enright, 1994

Origo, Iris, *War in Val d'Orcia*, London, Jonathan Cape, 1951

Ose, Dieter, *Entscheidung in Westen 1944; Der Oberbefehlshaber West und die Abwehr der alliierten Invasion*, Stuttgart, Deutsche Verlags-Anstalt, 1982

O'Toole, G.J.A., *Honorable Treachery*, New York, Atlantic Monthly Press, 1991

Padfield, Peter, *Himmler*, New York, Henry Holt, 1990

'Passy' (André Dewaurin), *Mémoires du Chef des Services Secrètes de la France Libre*, Paris, Odile Jacob, 2000

Pawle, Gerald, *The War and Colonel Warden*, London, Harrap, 1963

Perrault, Gilles, *The Secrets of D-Day*, London, Arthur Barker, 1965

Petrow, Richard, *The Bitter Years: The Invasion and Occupation of Denmark and Norway – April 1940–May 1945*, New York, William Morrow, 1974

Philby, Kim, *My Silent War*, London, MacGibbon and Kee, 1968

Pogue, Forrest Carlisle, *The Supreme Command*, Washington DC, Department of the Army, 1954

Polmar, Norman, and Allen, Thomas B., *World War II*, New York, Random House, 1996

Poznanzki, Renée, *Être Juif en France pendant la Seconde Guerre Mondiale*, Paris, Hachette, 1994

Pujol, Juan, with Nigel West, *Garbo*, London, Weidenfeld and Nicolson, 1985

Quellien, Jean, and Vico, Jacques, *Massacres Nazi en Normandie*, Condé-sur-Noireau, Éditions Charles Corlet, 1994

Ramsay, Admiral Sir Bertram, *The Year of D-Day*, Hull, University of Hull Press, 1994

Raczynski, Count Edward, *In Allied London*, London, Weidenfeld and Nicolson, 1962

Reile, Oskar, *Der Deutsche Geheimdienst im II Weltkrieg Westfront*, Augsburg, Weltbild Verlag, 1990

Reit, Seymour, *Masquerade: The Amazing Camouflage Deceptions of World War Two*, London, Robert Hale, 1979

Renaud, Alexandre, *Sainte Mère-Église*, Paris, Juilliard, 1986

Reuth, Ralf Georg (ed.), *Joseph Goebbels Tagebücher 1924–1945*, Band 5, *1943–1945*, Munich, Piper, 1999

Reynolds, David, *Rich Relations: The American Occupation of Britain 1942–1945*, London, HarperCollins, 1996

Richards, Sir Francis Brooks, *Secret Flotillas*, London, HMSO, 1996

Ruffin, Raymond, *Résistance Normande et Jour 'J'*, Paris, Presses de la Cité, 1994

Ruge, Friedrich, *Rommel in Normandy*, London, Macdonald and Jane's, 1979

Ryan, Cornelius, *The Longest Day*, Sevenoaks, New English Library, 1982

Scheid, Michel, *Nantes 1940–1944*, Éditions Ouest-France, Caen, 1994

Schoenbrunn, David, *Soldiers of the Night*, New York, E.P. Dutton, 1980

Seaman, Mark (introduction) *Garbo: The Spy Who Saved D-Day*, London, Public Record Office, 2000

Seaton, *The Russo-German War 1941–45*, London, Arthur Barker, 1971

Sebag-Montefiore, Hugh, *Enigma: The Battle for the Code*, London, Phoenix, 2000

Smith, Bradley, *Sharing Secrets with Stalin*, Lawrence, KS, University Press of Kansas, 1996

Smith, Sally Bedell, *In All His Glory: The Life of William S. Paley*, New York, Simon and Schuster, 1990

Soames, Mary, *Clementine Churchill*, London, Cassell, 1979

Speer, Albert, *Inside The Third Reich*, London, Weidenfeld and Nicolson, 1970

Speidel, Hans, *Invasion 1944: Rommel and the Normandy Campaign*, Chicago, Henry Regnery, 1950

Stacey, C.P., and Wilson, Barbara M., *The Half-Million: The Canadians in Britain, 1939–1946*, Toronto, University of Toronto Press, 1987

Stafford, David, *Churchill and Secret Service*, London, John Murray, 1997

—— *Camp 'X': Canada's School for Secret Agents*, Toronto, Lester and Orpen Dennys, 1986

—— *Roosevelt and Churchill: Men of Secrets*, London, Little, Brown, 1999

—— *Secret Agent*, London, BBC Worldwide, 2000

Stagg, James, *Forecast for Overlord*, London, Ian Allen, 1971

Steen, S. (ed.), *Norges krig 1940–1945*, vol. 3, Oslo, Gyldendal Norsk Forlag, 1950

Strong, Kenneth, *Intelligence at the Top*, London, Cassell, 1968

Tedder, Arthur William, *With Prejudice*, London, Cassell, 1966

Thompson, Julian, *The Imperial War Museum Book of Victory in Europe*, London, 1995

Thompson, Kate (ed.), *Fareham: D-Day. Fifty Years On*, Fareham, Fareham Borough Council, 1994

Toland, John, *Adolf Hitler*, New York, Doubleday, 1976

Tucker, William H., *Parachute Soldier*, Harwichport, MA, International Airborne Books, 1994

USSR Departments of State and Public Institutions, *Stalin's Correspondence with Churchill, Attlee, Roosevelt and Truman 1941–45*, London, Lawrence and Wishart, 1958

Vasilevsky, A., *A Lifelong Cause*, Moscow, Progress Publishers, 1981

Wadge, D. Collett, *Women in Uniform*, London, Sampson Low, Marston, 1946

Wallace, Robert, *The Italian Campaign*, Alexandria, VA, Time-Life Books, 1981

Warlimont, Walter, *Inside Hitler's Headquarters 1939–45*, London, Weidenfeld and Nicolson 1964

Weitz, Margaret, *Sisters in the Resistance*, New York, John Wiley and Sons, 1995

Werner, Herbert, *Iron Coffins*, New York, Holt, Rinehart and Winston, 1969

Werth, Alexander, *Russia at War*, London, Pan, 1964

Williams, Charles, *The Last Great Frenchman*, London, Little, Brown, 1993

Wills, Deryk, *Put On Your Boots and Parachutes!*, Oadby, Deryk Wills, 1992

Wilmot, Chester, *The Struggle for Europe*, London, Collins, 1952

Wilson, Theodore (ed.), *D-Day 1944*, Lawrence, KS, University Press of Kansas, 1994

—— *The World At Arms*, New York, Reader's Digest, 1989

Young, Martin and Stamp, Robbie, *Trojan Horses: Deception Operations of the Second World War*, London, Mandarin, 1991

Ziegler, Philip, *London at War*, New York, Alfred Knopf, 1995

Zucotti, Susan, *The Holocaust, the French, and the Jews*, New York, Basic Books, 1993

INDEX